Supplier Relationship Management

Supplier Relationship Management
Unlocking the hidden value in your supply base

Jonathan O'Brien

KoganPage

LONDON PHILADELPHIA NEW DELHI

First published in Great Britain and the United States in 2014 by Kogan Page Limited
Reprinted 2015 (twice)

2nd Floor, 45 Gee Street	1518 Walnut Street, Suite 1100	4737/23 Ansari Road
London EC1V 3RS	Philadelphia PA 19102	Daryaganj
United Kingdom	USA	New Delhi 110002
www.koganpage.com		India

© Jonathan O'Brien, 2014

The right of Jonathan O'Brien to be identified as the author of this work has been asserted by him in accordance with the Copyright, Designs and Patents Act 1988.

ISBN   978 0 7494 6806 4
E-ISBN   978 0 7494 6807 1

British Library Cataloguing-in-Publication Data

A CIP record for this book is available from the British Library.

Library of Congress Cataloging-in-Publication Data

O'Brien, Jonathan, 1967-
    Supplier relationship management : unlocking the hidden value in your supply base / Jonathan O'Brien.
      pages cm
    ISBN 978-0-7494-6806-4 (paperback) – ISBN 978-0-7494-6807-1 (ebk)   1. Purchasing.
2. Industrial procurement.   3. Customer relations.   4. Business logistics.   I. Title.
    HF5437.O263 2014
    658.7'2–dc23
                                                                                        2014027009

Typeset by Graphicraft Limited, Hong Kong
Print production managed by Jellyfish
Printed and bound by Ashford Colour Press Ltd, Gosport, Hampshire

For Elaine, Emily and Hugh

CONTENTS

ABOUT THE AUTHOR

Jonathan O'Brien is the CEO of the international purchasing consultancy and training provider, Positive Purchasing Ltd (**www.positivepurchasing.com**). Jonathan has over 25 years' experience working in Purchasing. He has worked all over the world to help global organizations increase their purchasing capability through training, education and working directly with practitioners and executive teams to drive in the adoption of category management, supplier relationship management, negotiation, and other strategic purchasing methodologies.

Jonathan is an electronics engineer who ended up in Purchasing. His career in engineering soon moved into supplier quality assurance, and it was the hundreds of supplier audits undertaken involving detailed examination of business practice and process that provided a sound understanding of how organizations work, and thus began the process of working with companies to help them improve. A move to senior buying role in a large utility company shifted the focus to the commercial aspects of purchasing and this career path culminated in a global category director role for an airline business. Jonathan moved to an internal consultant role and helped lead a series of major organizational change programmes. A subsequent move into consultancy, initially with a large global strategic purchasing consultancy and later with his own business, provided Jonathan with the opportunity to work with some of the biggest and most well-known companies in the world to help improve purchasing capability and gaining a rich experience along the way.

Jonathan holds an MBA from Plymouth University Business School, a Diploma in Marketing and an HNC in electronics, is a Member of the Chartered Institute of Purchasing (MCIPS), and NLP Master Practitioner and a former registered Lead Assessor of quality management systems.

Jonathan and his team at Positive Purchasing Ltd have developed and created the 5i® Category Management process, the 5A™ SRM process and the Red Sheet® negotiation tool that has become the way many individuals and corporations approach negotiation.

Jonathan has published three books. He is also an accomplished broadcaster and artist and lives with his family in Plymouth, UK.

You can e-mail Jonathan at **jonathan@jonathanobrien.co.uk**

PREFACE

A supply base represents a wealth of possibilities and opportunities for any organization, however, few ever get past interfacing with suppliers at anything other than a transactional or contracting level. Yet amongst the multitude of suppliers most organizations carry: value, innovation, efficiency, reduced cost and increased security of supply area available to those that can find it and unlock it. There may even be a handful of suppliers who hold the potential to help grow a brand or business, or improve competitive advantage. The secret is identifying who these are and figuring out how to engage with them in a way so as to enable this to happen. This is a practical book that helps do just that.

Not all suppliers are the same; despite the aspirations many hold to have a closer relationship with you only a small number actually warrant this in terms of the potential value a relationship can bring. Supplier relationship management (SRM) is an umbrella term that is about deciding the level of intervention and the extent and nature of any relationship needed with suppliers. For the vast majority this should be minimal with our precious resources being directed only at working with those suppliers with whom we can realize significant and worthwhile value.

The term 'SRM' holds different meanings to different people and this book seeks to bring clarity here. SRM is a strategic, organization-wide philosophy, that brings together a series of discrete supplier and supply chain approaches including supplier performance measurement (SPM), supplier improvement & development (SI&D), supply chain management (SCM) and strategic collaborative relationships (SCR). SRM provides the means to select and integrate these different components according to how an individual supplier or a supply chain can add value to a business. SRM is therefore an ensemble of complementary supply base interventions, determined and coordinated strategically according to corporate aims and objectives. This book explores each of these components and how, when combined, they form the 'orchestra of SRM'.

If you seek competitive advantage for the future in an ever-changing world, if you need more from your suppliers or if you struggle to get the performance or response you need, if you are concerned about risk in your supply chains or if you believe that your supply base can make a much greater contribution to your future business aims and aspirations then you need to read this book.

I am interested to learn of your experiences of SRM and using the approaches outlined in this book. Please feel free to connect with me on LinkedIn or e-mail me at **jonathan@jonathanobrien.co.uk** and share.

ACKNOWLEDGEMENTS

This is my third book and concludes my ambition to create a suite of books that provide purchasing practitioners with the tools and techniques they need to be highly effective and make significant contributions in the organizations they work for.

I cannot take any credit for inventing SRM – it is out there, interpreted and applied in a multitude of ways. I have sought to provide clarity of definition; to codify it and provide suite of tools and concepts that can make it an effective reality that adds great value. Much of what I have learnt over the years has come from working as a practitioner, coach and trainer in many large organizations and has found its way into this book in some form. It has also come from some bright and brilliant people who have shared wisdom along the way and have helped me shape ideas and concepts to create what you will read in this book. You all know who you are and if that is you, then thank you.

Thank you to all those I worked with in my early career when I was a Supplier Quality Assurance Engineer. I've finally found a way to connect the wisdom that I accumulated in that role around quality management and supplier quality assurance, with effective supplier management for the purchasing community.

Thanks to Dr Alan Ebbens for his passionate and determined help and research support to figure out what really needs to happen to collaborate with a supplier and make joint working a reality. Thanks to Dave Smith for once again helping to illuminate my thinking, and especially helping figure out how social interaction can transform collaborative supplier relationships, a concept that has become a key thread throughout this book. Thanks to Andrew Northmore for help on how measurement in organizations really works and how it can really be transformed.

Thanks to pilot Pete Olsen for the Kennedy Example, to Lisa Barton for sharing examples of how ego gets in the way of consistency in managing suppliers and thanks also to Julia at Kogan Page for being patient so I could finish the book and make sure it was the right book.

The biggest thank you is once more to my family. Thanks to my wife Elaine for relentlessly proofreading the entire book and even remarking with a touch too much surprise, 'It's actually quite interesting and I now have some idea what you do.' But I have to thank my entire family for putting up with me writing another book without complaining. I've now promised not to write another for a while.

Finally, thank you to you for buying this book. I hope it equips you with something worthwhile.

Most of the models and concepts in this book are new and original work; many are groundbreaking. I have made every effort to properly research, reference and duly credit all work of others, however I apologise in advance for any omissions.

Introduction

Using this book

This is a book about 'supplier relationship management' or SRM. Say 'SRM' and some will think of measuring or managing suppliers, others will think of it as something more strategic where we have a special relationship with suppliers who are particularly important. Does SRM apply to all or just some suppliers, and do we mean suppliers or the entire supply chain? In fact there is, it seems, no common understanding of what 'SRM' is; it holds multiple meanings depending upon whom we are talking to.

As we move through this book I will provide clarity here and describe SRM with its various component parts in detail and I will attempt to explain how these fit together. This is a practical book for anyone who interfaces with, or manages, suppliers in any way. It will provide purchasing practitioners with the framework and tools to understand, segment and drive in systematic approaches to manage an entire supply base effectively so as to secure the optimum value possible with the resources available. Equally it will help anyone who needs to engage with or have some sort of relationship with suppliers to ensure those engagements are effective.

SRM is somewhat unique as it is not a single linear process or series of steps that leads to an outcome. Rather, it is philosophy that frames a collection of individual actions, interventions, approaches and mindsets. This is fundamental to grasping SRM and why much of what is published in this space seems to fail to articulate the concept as SRM is not something that can follow a single process. Instead SRM is like an orchestra, with different sections that play when needed to create a complete piece of music unique to an individual supplier. This *orchestra of SRM* concept is the basis for this book and so the chapters are organized to explore how each section can work in concert to create something magnificent.

A strategic purchasing trilogy

This is my third book on key strategic purchasing methodologies and is designed to enhance, complement and integrate with the frameworks and approaches of category management and negotiation planning. Indeed, SRM uses many of the strategic tools found within these methodologies.

Therefore this book has been written so as to be used together with *Category Management in Purchasing* and *Negotiation for Purchasing Professionals* (also published by Kogan Page). Where a tool has already been expanded in one of these previous works it is not repeated again in this book but referenced at a high level. It is recommended that all three publications are used together to provide the complete strategic purchasing approach.

20 SRM pathway questions

This book is organized so as to explore each component or section of an overall SRM approach and show how these fit together. It seeks to provide answers and practical steps for 20 key or 'pathway' questions. If you can answer all of these questions with confidence then you're in great shape. However, for many organizations these are difficult questions that represent the gap between aspiration and reality. They also help reveal the pathway to move towards making effective SRM a reality. This book will help to not only form answers to these questions but will help to develop real actions that enable the firm to progress and realize great value from the supply base.

SRM pathway questions

1 What is the contribution we need from our supply base and why?

2 Which suppliers are important to us and why?

3 How much resource do we need and if we have only so much resource, which suppliers should we direct this at and why?

4 How are our suppliers performing?

5 Are we getting the most from our suppliers and how can we be sure?

6 What supplier improvements would make a difference to us and how can we drive these?

7 Do we know everything we should know about our suppliers?

8 Are suppliers meeting their contractual obligations?

9 What contracts are due to expire or need to be reviewed in the near term and how are we planning for this?

10 What are the risks with suppliers or back up our supply chains and how is this risk being managed?

11 Do we have the right relationships with the right suppliers and are we in control of these?

12 Do we understand and are we in control of all other relationships and interfaces people have with suppliers across our business?

13 Do we understand our supply chains? Are we maximizing any opportunities to make them more effective?

14 What innovation do we need from our supply base and how are we going to get it?

15 Which of our important suppliers hold the potential to make a dramatic difference to our business and why?

16 Are we working collaboratively with those critical suppliers towards jointly agreed goals that will make a dramatic difference?

17 Are all our efforts with suppliers coordinated and aligned with our corporate goals?

18 Is corporate strategy informed by supply chain possibilities?

19 Across our organization does everyone know what is expected of them when working with suppliers?

20 Do we have capability, structure and processes we need here?

What we need from our suppliers is...

01

This chapter explores our changing environment and the implications for organizations and their supply base. It considers how this is driving organizations to place new demands on their suppliers and how the supply base is responding. Finally it concludes with a definition of what organizations now need from suppliers and the modern role organizations require important suppliers to fulfill.

PATHWAY QUESTION ADDRESSED IN THIS CHAPTER

1 What is the contribution we need from our supply base and why?

Our changing world

The world is a fast changing place. Organizations are changing and adapting like never before as they try to figure out how to compete, survive and succeed on an ever-evolving planet. Those who didn't manage to keep up have failed. New organizations with new ideas, innovative ways to do business and an insatiable hunger to succeed continue to emerge the world over ready to satisfy our changing needs and expectations (Figure 1.1). The supply base, the role of the supply base and the way organizations are engaging with suppliers is changing. Many factors are driving this and if we are to determine how purchasing and the supply base can add value for the future we first need to understand the landscape around us that is creating new and exciting challenges, imperatives and opportunities for us all.

FIGURE 1.1   The changing landscape

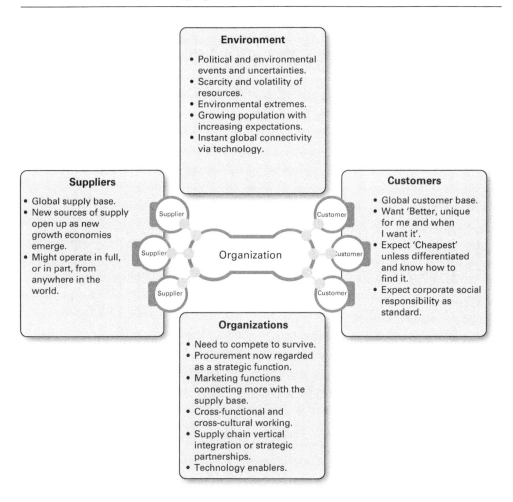

A redefined global marketplace

The biggest recession since the Great Depression of the 1930s has changed economic landscapes around the world and redefined the global marketplace, leaving significant casualties along the way. Security of supply has become an increasing worry. Organizations that once flexed their corporate leverage in a buoyant and competitive marketplace found themselves working to make sure they could get the goods in the first place. Add to this political uncertainties, unprecedented environmental events, exceptional peaks in demand for certain raw materials by developing nations and the picture is one that suggests we can no longer take for granted the availability of what we need, when and where we need it from our suppliers.

Resources are getting scarce (Hieber, 2002). The world and those on it with an eye to future generations now demand that the actions of industry are sustainable. Where raw materials are not yet scarce they could well become volatile, perhaps switching the leverage and balance of power to those in the supply chain (Gradinger, 2009).

The world continues to become smaller with a global marketplace that has long since been open for business, but the nations that supply the world are changing. China now equals the United States in terms of manufacturing output (Markillie, 2103), but as China's workforce expect their pay to rise, other developing countries are waiting in the wings to take on the world's manufacturing at lower cost. India is pushing Japan aside to become one of the biggest purchasing nations on the planet. Libya's economy shows great promise, so too does Mongolia's with its mining boom from the advent of copper production in the Gobi desert fuelling an 18 per cent growth in GDP in 2013, and economies such as Macau may take us by surprise.

Banking institutions are suddenly more accountable and corporate financial affairs can no longer be secret – instead transparency in everything is a pre-requisite for success (Barnes *et al*, 2009).

Our planet now has more people on it and many more on the way, living in more densely populated regions, who move around more and interact more. Global communication is just a tweet away and global commerce requires just a click or two. Suppliers, or at least some of their operations, can now operate from anywhere on the planet, wherever there is a willing, capable and organized workforce with sufficient infrastructure to make it viable. The suppliers of tomorrow may not reside in the countries they are in today and may not even exist in any single building or location but rather could be sprawled across the globe, connecting and interacting though technology. The world is no longer a collection of different groups of people isolated by geography and culture, but is now a giant network, connected in real time.

More confidence in our supply chains please

Once upon a time supply chains were a fairly linear collection of individual entities, each operating independently and the entire chain little more than the consequence of a series of separate needs, interactions and relationships; collectively forming a chain. Companies needed only concern themselves with their immediate supplier and customer with whom a contractual relation-ship existed. This is how many supply chains still exist today, but things are changing as organizations figure out that this traditional approach is no longer adequate to manage risk or gain competitive advantage. Today being a retailer alone is not enough; to make it work retailers are now also becoming transport companies and farming consultants (Wooldridge, 2013) or even farmers and processors so they can manage the entire supply chain and minimize risk.

Once companies outsourced, divested and focused on their core competencies; now vertical integration is once again an attractive proposition for many. Haven't we been here before? Rewind the clock 50 years and you'll find organizations did everything. Didn't someone then tell us not to do this but to stick to the things we know and are good at and outsource everything else? Sure, but things have changed! Whilst risk and volatility may be driving vertical integration in some parts of the Western world, elsewhere the big conglomerate organizations are returning. Wooldridge (2013) reminds us that in the 60s and 70s we witnessed the birth of corporate giants such as ITT (amassing 350 acquisitions or mergers in 80 countries during its time) only to watch many, but not all, of these business giants become dinosaurs over the next three decades, possibly because any core competency long since became diluted by size and diversification. These conglomerates are now remerging with the rise of emerging markets. Highly diversified companies are appearing, driven by opportunism, ease of communication and global commerce, but also as a result of government incompetence: in a third world country where social investment is lacking, industry still needs a fit and educated workforce so companies quickly start building, owning and operating schools, hospitals and our necessary amenities. These companies also acquire other facilities, processes and resources as needed. For example, Tata steel now has over 100 companies and makes cars, is a chemical company, has its own consulting business, owns its own hotels, is a significant player in power generation and produces tea.

Outsourcing is not dead, nor is the concept of focusing on core competencies but it seems that vertical integration or even wholesale acquisition now have their place too. So too do new forms of collaborative partnership with key providers. It seems organizations are taking different approaches out there. The common factor, however, is that organizations are realizing the need to have more confidence and control over supply chains *and* realize greater value from them. In essence, it doesn't seem to matter whether or not we own our key suppliers, it matters that we are able to work closely with them and that they are more loyal and responsive to us than other customers.

How the 2013 horsemeat scandal allowed Morrisons to publically demonstrate the confidence it had in its supply chains

In mid-January 2013 Irish food inspectors announced they had found horsemeat in some beef burgers stocked by UK supermarket chains. The story was headline news, retailers cleared shelves and consumers emptied freezers. Weeks later the international frozen food producer Findus were forced to announce that one of their beef lasagne products had been found to contain up to 100 per cent horsemeat. Consumers felt betrayed and checked their freezers once more and the entire UK food industry started to check their supply chains. The government ordered DNA testing across all beef products on sale and the concern soon spread across Europe and beyond. Up to 100 per cent horsemeat was subsequently found in several ranges of frozen food in the United Kingdom, France, Switzerland, Germany, Sweden, Austria and Norway. Then, new concerns that a drug used to treat horses, which is harmful to humans, could have entered the food chain emerged. Meat was traced from France, through Cyprus and the Netherlands to Romanian abattoirs. Investigations suggested that the use of horsemeat was no accident but part of a criminal conspiracy some way back up the supply chain to take advantage of the fact that horsemeat typically costs one fifth of that of beef. As many retailers were forced to issue very public apologies, others used the scandal to create a competitive advantage by showing how vertical integration of their supply chains meant their products were safe. The UK retailer Morrisons was one of these and was quick to allow TV cameras to film their own meat processing and packaging plants using meat supplied by their own abattoirs.

Social responsibility is not an optional extra; it is expected!

What happens many contractual steps removed up a supply chain can no longer be ignored when engaging the immediate supplier. Today most consumers now expect companies to be socially responsible (Penn *et al*, 2010) and some even manage to factor this into their buying decisions although there remains a significant gap between good intention and action

(Pelsmacker *et al*, 2005). Whilst this gap will most likely close, there seems to be a growing expectation on the companies we buy from, that they have their entire house in order. Perhaps sustainable, fair trade, responsible, ethical can no longer be a unique differentiator that attracts premium pricing, but a basic feature for everything a company does. Perhaps the person who picks the coffee beans is as much part of the product as the experience of the outlet itself. If our societies didn't hold this expectation then there wouldn't be so many investigative journalists trying to find cracks in the reputation of big corporates for what lies in their supply chains and organizations wouldn't be so worried in case something unexpected gets uncovered. It seems customers and consumers are also now paying more attention to stories of how household names operate and are ready to question any suggestion that things are not in good shape.

Purchasing is a strategic function

The way we view what contribution their supply base can offer is changing as companies try to keep up and find new ways to create wealth from the ever-changing customer demands. The role of purchasing to help make this happen is changing too. Increasingly suppliers are being engaged to made greater contributions, and will need to continue to do so.

The role of purchasing as a strategic contributor to the bottom line and future success of the business rather than a cost centre is being recognized in the way organizations structure themselves. Twenty years ago purchasing was rarely considered a strategic function; today the need for a chief purchasing officer or chief procurement officer with executive remit is regarded by most global businesses as essential.

Organizations are recognizing the need to view the contribution purchasing can make with new eyes, shifting away from the established view of purchasing's role as the function that buys things but instead the function must place itself at the centre of the business, align itself with all the other strategic contributors and become an integral enabler to the way the organization pursues its goals and aspirations using the supply base to support this. It must also engage with the suppliers in a new way. Changing how purchasing contributes to overall business success requires a rethink and organizations with many years of tactical purchasing, predicated by an organizational structure, capability and mindset built around this tend to find the challenge of making the change to become a strategic enabler extremely difficult, but not impossible.

Better, faster and just for you right now

Finally what we want as consumers is changing too. 'Better, faster, cheaper' still stands, forcing organizations to compete or die. Securing lowest cost in the market for non-differentiated and commonly available goods and services is no longer a specialist activity. Globalization means the marketplaces have wider or no boundaries opening up huge choice and alternatives. Somewhere in the world there is a willing, cheap and sophisticated capability, and waiting in the wings is the next emerging market ready to do even better, even faster and more cheaply. The internet has created a new form of competitive tension allowing us access to all markets and real-time comparative pricing data. e-Auctions create a competitive environment for a specific requirement at organizational level and consumers can now find the lowest price in seconds online.

We expect 'cheap' but we don't need it. As consumers become more affluent with more choice than ever before we seem to know where to find the best deal but yet consumers are prepared to pay for something unique. Once standardization helped make corporates efficient, presenting the customer with a limited set of choices. Now the ability to create something personalized and unique for every customer is opening up a new differentiation opportunity enabled through module production and using new technologies such as 3D printing. Time is of the essence too. Consumers have become impatient and often happy to go elsewhere. 'Better, faster and just for you right now' might well be the winning formula for the future.

Supplier – friend or foe?

Machiavelli is quoted as saying 'Keep your friends close and your enemies closer'. What he was suggesting here is we always want to have good relationships and keep our friends close as those are the people we can trust and rely upon but that we should always keep an eye on what our enemies are doing in case they try to hurt us. So is a supplier a friend or an enemy? It is easy to find examples of organizations that treat suppliers as both or as neither. Considering suppliers as enemies could be viewed as unproductive and confrontational. However, that is just how many firms treat their suppliers; using clever leverage tactics to gain an advantage, and why not in many cases as they are playing the same game on us? Similarly it can also be disadvantageous to view suppliers as friends; an approach that can give them power over us and work against us, yet this could also be the approach that creates winning collaboration.

The different types of supplier relationship

There are many different types of relationship we can choose or wind up in with a supplier. The challenge is ensuring we have the right one and we are as in control of the process as we can be. There is also much terminology out there with a variety of different labels that seem to mean different things according to who is using them; one person's *strategic supplier* is another's *preferred supplier* and so on. The point is, amongst these labels is a recognition that there are different types of supplier relationship. It doesn't matter what label is used, it matters that within this we adopt the right relationship with the right supplier and for the right reasons and we all understand what we mean. Table 1.1 lists those commonly found and these are mapped according to the importance to the business and the intensity of relationship in Figure 1.2.

TABLE 1.1   Common types of supplier relationship

Relationship type	Explanation	Typical nature of relationship
Arm's length supplier	A simple and commonly found buyer/seller transactional arrangement for named goods or services.	• Contractual fulfilment only, perhaps no or little interaction beyond communicating the requirement (eg via an order) and fulfilment.
Subcontractor	A supplier, usually of services, engaged to complete a specific task or supply a package of work, perhaps as part of a bigger project or to deliver the entire project. Examples might include construction trades on a building site, software contractors.	• Typically involves communication of detailed requirements and interaction regarding technical or specification matters. • May be working alongside our people and other subcontractors. • Can gain know-how of our needs that can afford them an advantage.
Preferred supplier	Supplier who has a formally or informally recognized status as one who is mandated or selected in preference of other suppliers.	• Potentially defined within a framework or master agreement where the terms of engagement, and perhaps even commercial terms have been agreed in advance. • Preferred status might be defined within a list or instruction to those with buying authority. • Assumes and requires a degree of centralized control over the companies procurement.

TABLE 1.1 *continued*

Relationship type	Explanation	Typical nature of relationship
Outsourced provider	A supplier who has taken on responsibility to fulfil a core activity and requirement or function of a company, perhaps one previously fulfilled in-house. Examples include outsourced call centre, cleaning, data management, IT support.	• Close, day-to-day interaction at an operational level. • Relationship and contract built around performance and operational management.
Critical supplier	A supplier who fulfils a requirement that we cannot do without, and where we cannot easily switch suppliers or source elsewhere.	• Should be one where we work to develop a good relationship with the supplier, however many companies fail to identify critical suppliers and place themselves at risk.
Strategic supplier	A supplier who is of strategic importance and has something that can help enable our business to realize our goals and aspirations, eg innovation, complementary offerings, capacity, know-how, coverage.	• Needs to be very close and collaborative in order to realize the potential but this often falls short.
Partner	Perhaps called an *Alliance Partner*, *Technology Partner* or *Creative Partner*. Parties have agreed to work together, perhaps with some sort of excusive arrangement. The arrangement could be informal or a formal contract and even incentives might exist.	• Needs to be very close and collaborative in order to realize the potential but this often falls short. • Close day-to-day interaction in the area concerned (eg at a technical level).
Group company	A supplier who we own or is owned within the group.	• Relationship should be 'as if one of us' however if the company is separated by distance, culture or organizational structure or has recently been incorporated into the group the relationship can be no different to that of a preferred supplier

FIGURE 1.2 Intensity and importance for different types of supplier relationship

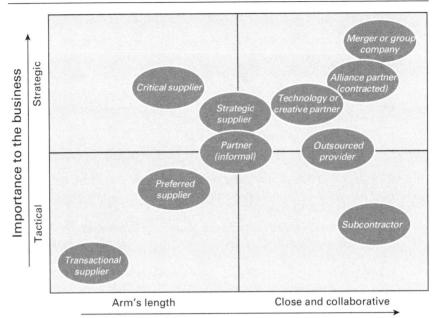

Rethinking the 'arm's length' mindset

> In my opinion [Ford] seems to send its people to 'hate school' so that they learn how to hate suppliers. The company is extremely confrontational. After dealing with Ford, I decided not to buy its cars. (Senior executive, supplier to Ford, October 2002 (quoted by Liker and Choi, 2004)).

An organization that views its supply base simply as the collection of suppliers who provide the goods or services requested of them is missing the point. For many global corporations the role the supply base is expected to perform is now one that is much more enabling, integral and even pivotal to success and future value.

The traditional, and highly tactical, view of suppliers is that they are there to supply what we require when we say so and we, as the customer, are the one in control and of course the customer is always right!

This 'one size fits all' view of suppliers as subordinates is one that seems to arise from the way we as buyers have learnt our profession. Principles of 'arm's length' relationship, transparency and keeping suppliers 'in their place', finding leverage and assuming the controlling role seem to underpin most standard purchasing theory. Furthermore buyers are taught to watch out for suppliers trying to find ways to grow an account by creating added value extras and to be weary of upselling of new products. Such approaches may be entirely appropriate for the majority of situations, but not all. There are typically a small number of suppliers with whom a more collaborative and mutually benefiting form of intervention and interaction is appropriate and beneficial. To realize this we need to rethink some of the basic principles we as buyers learn but with the maturity to know when to leverage and when to collaborate. To illustrate this think about the way people learn to drive. In the United Kingdom people are initially taught to place their hands on the steering wheel at ten to two (as per a clock face) and to feed the steering wheel through the hands; never crossing them. However, this technique is generally unsuitable for advanced situations such as where police and other services might need to respond to an incident at speed and who need a high degree of maneuverability in cornering. Advanced driving tuition for experienced drivers therefore teaches people to move away from this in favour of larger sweeps. The point is a driver needs to unlearn the basics in order to progress to a more advanced form of control and know what to use and when. The same is true for supplier relationships and, for a small number of suppliers, buyers actually need to unlearn the standard mindset in favour of a new paradigm that recognizes different, more collaborative and integrative relationships are more appropriate for certain suppliers; perhaps even going against the basic 'arm's length' principles. By doing this great things are possible and suppliers can bring significant added value and make a dramatic contribution to business success. Failure to change our mindset for these few suppliers can halt opportunity, introduce unnecessary conflict and act as a disincentive for suppliers in terms of bringing additional value over and above what they are contracted to provide.

What we need from our suppliers

So organizations need to be able to have *confidence* in their suppliers and supply chains and need to get *close* to those suppliers who are important, which means we need *clarity* regarding who is important and who we should spend time with. However, there is more, there are in fact five 'Cs' that summarize what organizations need from the supply base (Figure 1.3).

Organizations are also demanding greater *contribution* – the supplier base is a key enabler of competitive advantage for organizations attempting to find new opportunities in our ever-changing world. However, new approaches and a rethink regarding how to engage with suppliers and who to engage with are needed in order to realize this potential. Ultimately organizations need value and if it is possible to unlock more value from the supply base, in line with what the organization needs, then the supplier base is beginning to contribute more strongly to organizational success.

In highly competitive markets, the simple pursuit of market share is no longer sufficient to ensure probability, and thus, companies focus on redefining

FIGURE 1.3 The '5 Cs' definition of what organizations need from the supply base

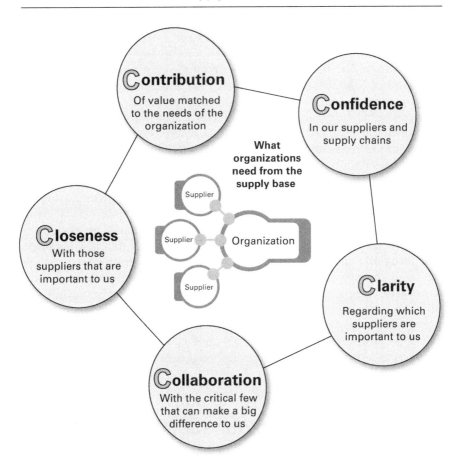

their competitive space or profit zone (Bovet and Sheffi, 1998). Companies now buy more components and services from suppliers than they used to and business are increasingly relying on their suppliers to reduce costs, improve quality and develop new processes and products faster than their rivals can (Liker and Choi, 2004). Organizational survival and prosperity now demand innovation and differentiation and so organizations are turning to their suppliers also to help find breakthroughs: *how* the goods are manufactured is now equally a part of the breakthrough as the breakthrough idea itself (Markillie, 2013). It seems organizations need more from their suppliers and organizational success is linked to the contribution some suppliers can make. Organizations that are looking beyond their traditional company boundaries and finding new ways to involve key suppliers who can help them gain the competitive edge they need; Apple perhaps being a notable example in the way it approached the development of many of its flagship products. So, for the critical few suppliers who possess the ability to really help build our business we need *contribution* but we also need *collaboration* as true innovation and breakthrough cannot happen in isolation, but rather happens by working together with key suppliers.

Therefore the 5 Cs (Figure 1.3) defining what organizations need from the supply base in today's ever-changing world are as follows and as the chapters unfold I will explore how SRM can help organizations realize these:

- *Clarity* – regarding who are suppliers are, how our supply chains are organized and which suppliers are important and so who to spend time with and then what exactly should be done with these suppliers to unlock value.

- *Confidence* – like never before and not just to ensure assurance of supply but also supplier and supply chain capacity, the right controls are in place and assurance that any appropriate corporate social responsibility (CSR) principles are in place.

- *Closeness* – with those suppliers is important; close relationships, coordination between parties and, where worthwhile, collaboration for mutual benefit.

- *Contribution* – the value that suppliers can bring to the business in line with our goals. This ranges from fulfillment of orders to suppliers who can be agents for change and contribute to organizational success, bring creativity and clever thinking to support the process of innovation, new product development and helping finding ways to differentiate.

- *Collaboration* – with the critical few suppliers who can make a difference to our business.

Five good reasons to get close to our suppliers

02

This chapter explores the potential and different types of value available from the supply base to an organization when the right type of intervention or supplier relationship is effected. The types of value are defined in a hierarchy that represents the different reasons for pursing interventions and relationships with suppliers and each level is explored in detail.

PATHWAY QUESTION ADDRESSED IN THIS CHAPTER

1 What is the contribution we need from our supply base and why?

Setting the direction for SRM

Organizations need *contribution*, *clarity*, *confidence*, *closeness* and *collaboration* from their suppliers and so therefore we need the right relationships with the right suppliers in order to achieve this and unlock benefits. Where do we start and how can this translate into a series of specific actions with individual suppliers? Reaching the point where there is full confidence in our supply base and supply chains means we need to understand them fully and get close to the bits that matter. It is easy to say 'let's collaborate more with suppliers' or 'we need innovation from the supply base', but why and for what purpose? Unless we can be clear about this then these are just directionless aims. Worse still if our suppliers were to suddenly start bombarding us with new and innovative ideas because they have been asked to then the effort is wasted unless we are ready and equipped to do something with them.

Here is where our journey towards SRM begins and the starting place is to determine the direction for our SRM initiative, which starts with what the organization needs. We must identify the specific reasons why we need or want a relationship with certain suppliers, ie the problem we are trying to solve or the corporate goal we are trying to reach and therefore what additional value we are attempting to secure. Only then we can begin to determine what the required relationship and intervention should look like and with whom.

SRM requires a selective approach. We cannot have a relationship with every supplier; for many suppliers we simply need them to provide what we want, on time, in full, to agreed budget or price. For others some form of intervention may be necessary to keep things on track and yet, for perhaps a small number of other suppliers, it is possible to secure much greater value; value that can, in some cases, make a dramatic and game changing contribution to our business. Our supplier base therefore harbours huge potential; ranging from the potential to prevent damage to our business through to the potential to add great value to our bottom line and help us grow. All we need to do is decide what we need and then go and get it and here we use the VIPER model: five headings that define what is possible from the supply base and therefore five good reasons to get close to suppliers, five good reasons for intervention or to build supplier relationships and five headings that allow us to define our requirements for the relationship.

VIPER: defining the value we need from suppliers

VIPER is a model used to determine the value the organization needs and wants to realize from the supply base (Figure 2.1). VIPER stands for *Value, Innovation, Performance improvements, Effectiveness (of business and operations)* and *Risk*. VIPER defines our different requirements and the reasons for instigating some sort of relationship or intervention with a supplier. It also summarizes the different levels of value possible. VIPER is a hierarchy that ranges from intervention that is essential, to additional value that could be realized should both parties put the energy into realizing it. VIPER also begins to provide the framework to connect the goals of the organization to specific supplier interventions. VIPER therefore operates at two levels within an SRM approach:

FIGURE 2.1 The VIPER model

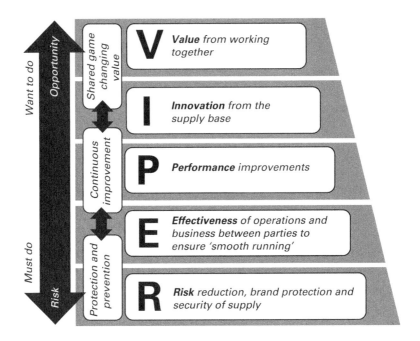

- *Macro or organization-wide level* – to define the high-level requirements of the organization and specific types of value the organization needs, eg 'to secure a new technological capability' or 'to find key partners to outsource current business activities'.
- *Individual supplier level* – to define the specific relationship requirements and the nature of intervention needed with individual suppliers. At this level VIPER is used in response to supplier segmentation (covered in Chapter 4).

Once we are clear *why* we might need or want a certain type of intervention with a specific supplier, ie what value we wish to secure, then we can set about *how* we achieve this and *what* type and nature of relationship is needed.

It is notable that *price* or *cost* are not called out as individual themes within VIPER. This is because there can be a conflict between the sole pursuit of reduced price and cost and that of developing a close relationship with a supplier. In a sourcing scenario where there is little risk, we have plenty of alternatives, where we can easily switch suppliers and we hold leverage then, there is unlikely to be much need for a relationship with the supplier or indeed any sort of special intervention beyond the transaction. Instead we simply need to use our leverage in the marketplace to secure the best value for the lowest price. Yet there are other supply situations where only collaboration will deliver benefit, perhaps even including that of reduced price and cost, perhaps because reaching the goal is only possible if parties work together. Price and cost alone are therefore not normally reasons to pursue a supplier relationship unless some sort of relationship is necessary in order to achieve price and cost goals. Nevertheless price and cost can be consequential and beneficial outcomes across the entire VIPER framework.

The value required is typically not considered, instead organizations go straight to implementing a relationship that seems about right. Where a firm needs innovation it seeks a technology partner. Ask a site foreman of a construction company why he is managing subcontractors in a particular way and he is unlikely to describe a definition of value needed using the VIPER model, instead he just knows what he needs and does it. There is a natural correlation between the nature of relationship organizations establish with suppliers (as covered in Chapter 1) and the nature of value that is important in each case (Figure 2.2). This correlation reflects what organizations tend to do, rather than what necessarily should happen. The point here is determining the nature of relationship according to the value required is a crucial step, and one that is often missed. The VIPER framework therefore forms an integral backbone to SRM and one that we will come back to throughout this book. However, first I will expand on each component of VIPER starting with risk.

FIGURE 2.2   Correlation of VIPER to types of supplier relationship

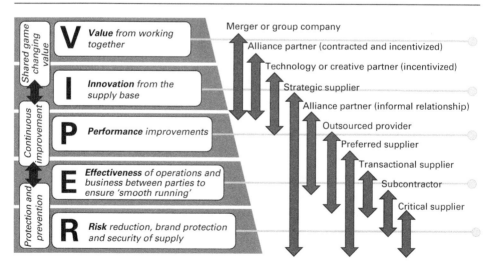

'R': managing supply base risk

The most critical reason for supply base intervention is the effective management of supplier and supply chain risk. Taking steps to prevent crisis or catastrophe, or at least be prepared for it, is arguably the greatest source of value an organization can secure from the supply base. 'Risk' therefore forms the foundation of the VIPER hierarchy.

There are certain areas of spend where a failure in the supply chain can present significant risk to an organization. The severity of this risk can vary significantly. Goods that turn up wrong or a service that underperforms can be an inconvenience; however, if a production line is stopped because one component is not available the cost of lost time can be immense. Worse, if it is the end customer who discovers a problem caused by a supplier, then it can damage sales, goodwill and perhaps even damage a brand.

If a business does not understand and make plans around supply chain risk there may be a time bomb ticking away ready to cause havoc at any moment. Yet many organizations simply fail to consider this risk and assume that supply chains never fail. They do. When things go wrong within a business action can be taken to remedy the situation. When they go wrong outside the business the ability to influence outcomes or recover the situation may, at best, be limited and companies can find themselves impotent in the face of a crisis.

Land Rover's catastrophic supply failure

In 2001 Land Rover, then owned by Ford, encountered a major supply problem for chassis. The specialist process of chassis manufacture had been outsourced to UPF Thompson; the sole source manufacturer. On 4 December 2001 Land Rover's management team were shocked to hear that UPF Thompson had been placed into receivership meaning that, with no alternative supply, Land Rover production would soon stop. KPMG was appointed as the receiver for UPF Thompson and initially kept production running to allow chassis deliveries to continue but signalled plans to cease deliveries. As a result Land Rover sought a court injunction to prevent this but had to inject £1 million into UPF Thomson to shore up supplies short term. In order for Land Rover to properly recover the situation and secure the future supply of chassis they had to agree to KPMG's demands, which involved Land Rover taking on the debts of UPF Thompson so the business could continue as a going concern. The extent of these debts was never revealed but various analyses suggested this figure could be as high as £75 million.

By considering the likelihood and potential impact of risks around supply failures, delays, quality problems or price hikes it is possible to develop responses that either prevent or prepare for these risks being realized. However, there are other potential risks out there in the supply base where the consequences can go far beyond that of a short-term crisis but can prove catastrophic or even terminal for an organization. Typically these are the risks that take away a company's competitive edge or differentiator, or that cause irreparable brand damage. It is a common misconception that big global companies are prepared for such occurrences but often they are not. The Marsh Report (2008) suggests that supply chain disruptions and brand reputation risks are growing in frequency and impact, with 71 per cent of respondents from across industry reporting an increase in financial impact damaging bottom lines, customer retention and brand equity, yet not a single respondent said their company was highly effective at supply chain risk.

One possible reason behind this is that it is very difficult to anticipate every possible risk. The risks that seem to do the most damage are the ones that appear *out of left field*; when two often unrelated sets of circumstances collide or when a new event suddenly forces us to question what was to be good practice. For example, during the Fukushima nuclear power plant disaster in 2011, systems deemed 'fail safe', failed. Equipment designed to shut reactors down in the event of an earthquake worked, but this set of circumstances, combined with complete loss of power in the region, and flooding of emergency generator rooms as a result of the tsunami meant there was no power to critical cooling pumps and meltdown followed, leaving the world to learn new lessons for future generations.

Similarly, in the supply base, it is the unexpected that can cause the most damage; the horsemeat scandal described earlier being a case in point. Findus was one of many brands who were caught up in this but one that seemed to attract much attention. Up until that point Findus had been a household name for more than 50 years with sales exceeding £1 billion. As the company carefully managed its way out of the situation the executive team grappled with the question of exactly how much the brand damage had been sustained and whether or not it was recoverable. Brand damage and reputational risk can cause huge loss of market share overnight. Millions and billions can be wiped off the value of a business as share prices plummet. This can mark the end for many organizations, yet some companies recover and share prices bounce back, sometimes higher than before where investors view the company's ability to manage itself out of trouble positively. Managing supply chain risk is therefore not just about prevention but is also about the ability to prepare for, and effectively manage through, catastrophe.

Effective management of supply chain risk requires a thorough and regularly revised understanding of the potential risk areas in the supply base, the likelihood of these risks being realized and the severity of impact. It also requires targeted intervention with some suppliers, and upstream in some supply chains, to either prevent, minimize risk or accept, and be prepared for, certain risks being realized. This means we need to identify those suppliers that present risk to us so we can do something, and the process of supply base segmentation in Chapter 4 tackles this. However, before that, as part of the macro level VIPER determination, the organization must first decide on the degree of risk it needs under control. Many organizations never even consider supplier or supply chain risk until things go wrong. VIPER prompts us to think about this and macro requirements such as 'must have contingency plans for all single sourced scenarios' help focus effort where needed whilst supplier-specific requirements such as 'ensure no trade with the Ivory Coast for any goods sourced' can set clear boundaries for a specific relationship.

'E': effectiveness of operations

The second reason for intervention with specific suppliers and therefore source of supply chain value is that of ensuring the 'smooth and effective running' of the business and applies where operations necessitate ongoing communication with, or the involvement of, certain suppliers. In such cases a close working relationship regarding these operational matters becomes essential.

There are certain situations where suppliers need to be much more involved than others. For example, a construction project where subcontractors fulfil large parts of the project requires robust project management to manage and coordinate these suppliers. Contractors will need to interact on a daily basis and work together with other staff on site to accomplish the task. An outsourced call centre needs to function 'as if they were part of the business' with supplier's staff having access to company systems and the ability to directly interact with, influence and determine the activities of other parts of the company's operations. Relationships in support of effectiveness of operations tend to be more prevalent with service providers but can also be required in some cases for suppliers of product. For example, a software company providing a customized system is unlikely to deliver exactly what is needed without regular interaction and review throughout the design process. The developmental process necessitates a relationship. In all these situations successful outcomes are entirely dependent upon a deliberate and well-structured close working relationship for operational matters. Key identifying characteristics for such relationships here include:

- Achievement of the required outcome is only possible with good interaction between parties.
- Suppliers are typically providing some sort of capability or capacity that the organization doesn't have or chooses not to have; they may well be specialists in their area.
- Suppliers might work as if part of, or an extension of the business as opposed to a supply scenario where goods are handed over, or a simple service executed.

- Suppliers tend to gain know-how about the work that, over time, can give them a unique advantage making it difficult to switch suppliers creating a situation of dependency.

Relationships with suppliers for the purposes of ensuring effectiveness of operations are not without risk. If a supplier is critical to achieving business outcomes or if the dependency upon a supplier becomes too great then the risk of failure or exploitation needs to be considered. These risks are heightened if the supplier is less interested in the relationship. Therefore the relationship dynamics and degree of mutual interest and dependency must be understood. Where effectiveness of operations is identified as a need for certain suppliers, it follows that they will require certain provision as part of ongoing supplier management, typically including:

- qualification, eg security, health and safety, capability etc;
- setting clear requirements, deliverables or outcomes;
- defined ways of working, interacting and lines of communication;
- provision to retain essential knowledge; and
- contract provision for exit.

'P': performance

The third reason for intervention with suppliers and source of value in the VIPER hierarchy is that of performance and performance improvement. Supplier performance and driving improvements with suppliers are both entire subjects all of their own and indeed four full chapters are given to these topics later.

Supplier performance could encompass many areas: quality, timeliness, correctness, price, performance, risk management and so on; so there are many areas that could be considered – more on these later. It is easy to chase performance improvements with suppliers but it is not always worthwhile. For example, I would really like it if the software package I use to create presentations didn't always seem to crash at the point when I haven't saved my work for some time. I could even pursue the large global company that created it but my actions here are unlikely to provoke a response. If the guy who cleans my windows keeps failing to do a good job then I can simply find another window cleaner, writing off what I have already paid. In both these cases putting energy into pursuing performance improvements with the current supplier is simply not worthwhile. But if my bank keeps applying incorrect charges to my account I will want to seek both performance improvements and reimbursement or even compensation for my losses as the effort to switch banks is unpalatable.

The value in performance improvement therefore comes by developing supplier relationships or interventions for the specific supply situations where it is both possible to pursue improvement and where the effort required will deliver worthwhile results. This may not be limited to first tier suppliers (those suppliers with whom we have a direct contractual relationship) but could even be appropriate with second or third tier suppliers or indeed suppliers way back in the supply chain many contractual steps removed. Here it becomes more difficult (but not impossible) to pursue improvements as we don't own the direct contractual relationship.

Supplier performance improvements can potentially add value when:

- performance is not what was agreed or expected;
- we can secure greater value if performance can be improved above that agreed or expected; and
- there are unacceptable supply chain risks that must be addressed.

For each of these, effort to drive improvement is worthwhile if and when:

- we stand to gain or lose significantly;
- our intervention is likely to yield a result;
- we have few alternatives so we need to make it work (eg because we have progressed too far with the supplier, because we cannot easily switch to another supplier or because the market is difficult); or
- the supplier is unable to improve without help.

Performance improvements can be either directive (telling the supplier to improve) or collaborative (working with the supplier to deliver improvements) and both approaches have their place depending upon the type of relationship we want in place.

Performance improvement is not easy. The reality is securing improvements can be much harder than often realized. For example, a specialist manufacturing company making precision components might be struggling to achieve good accuracy resulting in high wastage and therefore increased costs for every good unit supplied. If the company could reduce waste it would. Driving performance improvements here may not simply be a case of telling the supplier to get on with it but rather might need some support, perhaps investing in having one of our technical experts to help them or even consider if we can help them fund new equipment to become more accurate. Either way improvements may require our help to realize them.

VIPER helps the organization define the broad areas where performance improvements might be required, for example the need for general supply base improvement might be identified in response to corporate objectives to reduce defects or customer companies regarding service failures. VIPER also helps us identify performance improvements for specific suppliers where we know there is an issue, for example: 'bring working conditions at factories in India in line with our Corporate Responsibility policy'.

'I': an endless source of innovation

Innovation can deliver game changing value to an organization. When it does happen it can establish and build a brand, create differentiators, create and grow market share and drive business growth. Innovation alone has the potential to transform a business and unlocking it requires some unique approaches. Therefore the fourth reason for a relationship and source of value is that of innovation.

It is easy to assume that supplier innovation means the supplier brings innovation to us. However, there are in fact four levels of supplier innovation, each providing different potential value (Figure 2.3). In its simplest form supplier innovation can mean taking advantage of new offerings or new technologies that a supplier provides into the marketplace, available to all. For example, the Apple iPad and successive tablets allowed organizations to use this new tool to become more effective: estate agents/realtors no longer need to carry files, school classrooms don't need books and designers can sketch out a concept and transmit it immediately. If we can agree exclusive rights to a supplier innovation, whether proposed by them or specifically commissioned by us, then the potential value is greater as we are securing the resultant competitive edge solely for our benefit. However, the ultimate value from supplier innovation comes through collaboration with the supplier throughout the entire innovation process, creating innovations that will either help the supplier and be made available to all or will be exclusive to us.

When Apple launched the world's first iPod back in 2001 it achieved this through supplier collaboration and managed to create new global demand in an entirely new and uncontested global marketplace; it created something people needed but hadn't realized so until they saw it. Kim and Mauborgne (2005) call this 'Blue Ocean' strategy and one that can create dramatic wealth and value for an organization. Many contributors helped create Apple's Blue Ocean product including key suppliers. The first iPod brought together many new supplier-led component innovations necessary to combine functionality with miniaturization including – ultra miniature hard drives, new flat lithium iron battery technology and new touch wheel technology. This, together with collaborations with content suppliers to create iTunes, and the innovation was realized. The rest is history, and the succession of different innovative world leading products since the iPod all feature significant supplier contributions within the innovation process. In November 1998 Steve Jobs told *Fortune Magazine*: 'Innovation has nothing to do with how many R&D dollars you have.' Indeed Apple's innovation appears to be more about the approach used which seeks to involve rather than instruct. Apple innovate *with* their suppliers rather than have their suppliers innovate for them. These suppliers didn't happen to turn up at the right time with precisely what Apple needed, instead it required a coordinated effort and that is precisely what is needed if we want innovation from our suppliers.

FIGURE 2.3 Degrees of supplier innovation

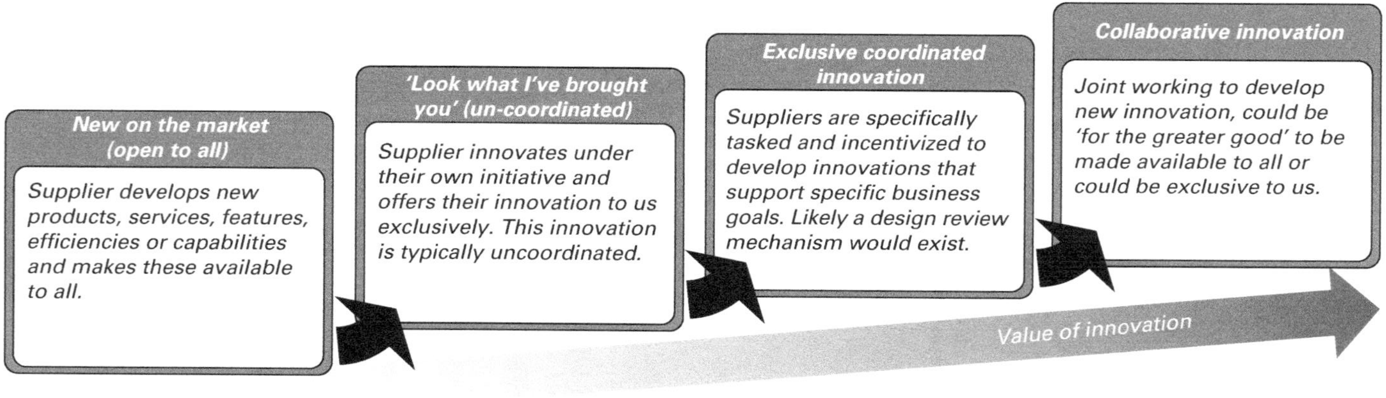

New on the market (open to all)

Supplier develops new products, services, features, efficiencies or capabilities and makes these available to all.

'Look what I've brought you' (un-coordinated)

Supplier innovates under their own initiative and offers their innovation to us exclusively. This innovation is typically uncoordinated.

Exclusive coordinated innovation

Suppliers are specifically tasked and incentivized to develop innovations that support specific business goals. Likely a design review mechanism would exist.

Collaborative innovation

Joint working to develop new innovation, could be 'for the greater good' to be made available to all or could be exclusive to us.

Value of innovation

A further example is that of the Indian car manufacturer Tata who launched the Nano in 2009 – the *cheapest car in the world*, with a price tag of around $2,500. The Nano is made and sold in India and quickly became not only the lowest-cost four-wheeled passenger vehicle in the country but also one that rapidly appealed to the many Indians who drove motorcycles as, prior to the Nano, a car would have been unaffordable. In essence the Nano also opened up an entirely new marketplace. Achieving the Nano necessitated a complete innovative approach to car manufacturing. At the heart of the Nano was extensive *Frugal Engineering*, a phrase previously coined by Renault Chief Executive Carlos Ghosen in 2006 (Sehgal *et al*, 2010). However, this doesn't really do justice to the innovation behind the Nano, which is much more than just doing the same thing cheaper: instead it demanded a completely new approach called *Low Cost Disruptive Innovation* (Lim, Seokhee and Hiroshi, 2009). This disruptive innovation was achieved by putting the right suppliers on the design team but first Tata needed to select the suppliers they were going to work with. Although the Nano is an Indian car, Tata selected a handful of suppliers; each global players and leaders in their respective fields. Tata decided to engage with those companies who had the knowledge and expertise that could be applied to create a disruptive innovation product. Fuel and engine management systems by Bosch, tail lights by US company Lumax, driveshafts by GKN, hollow steering shafts from Germany by Sona Koyo, Software by French company Dassault and exhausts by Emcon (Lim, Seokhee and Hiroshi, 2009). In the end Tata limited the number of direct suppliers to 100 who had the right capacity and capability to help Tata achieve its goals. 85 per cent of the Nano's components were outsourced to 60 per cent fewer suppliers than normal thus increasing leverage, economies of scale and reducing transaction costs (Johnson *et al*, 2008). This ground-breaking innovation was possible because the right suppliers were part of the design team.

'V': Together we are better; together we create value

The ultimate reason for a supplier relationship within the VIPER hierarchy is the additional value that is possible from suppliers, especially through working together with certain, specific suppliers who possess the capability to help us achieve our corporate goals. *Value* sits at the top of the VIPER hierarchy and represents, perhaps immense, benefit that we can choose to pursue if we want to. *Value* could include many things: price and cost reduction, innovation, outsourcing benefits and many others; however, the point with value here at the top of the hierarchy is the ability to unlock the next level of value, beyond the traditional list of standard benefits, that can really make a difference.

Outsourcing certain activities to suppliers who are experts at what they do to look after specific, bounded parts of our operation and, in theory, do it better and more effectively than we can, makes us more effective. For example, a finance company using an outsourced call centre provider might be able to improve effectiveness and reduce operating costs. It doesn't always follow that improved effectiveness and reducing costs go together; often this is true but there are scenarios where tapping into supplier capabilities will increase costs but will deliver much more than would otherwise be possible. A marketing function may have the capability to devise an adequate advertising campaign but outsourcing this to a creative agency could deliver a winning campaign.

With the right model of engagement and relationship, certain suppliers can contribute significant value to an organization that in turn will help create and grow brand equity. Brand equity is the value that a specific brand can hold when consumers believe the brand's offerings are better then others and choose it in preference. Neumeier (2006) suggests that brand equity can be one of the most valuable assets a company can have and a good brand can help a business grow market share, increase profit margin and establish long-term revenues through customer loyalty. It is no surprise then that companies invest billions in building and protecting their brands. Arguably *just being a supplier* helps build brand to some extent by fulfilling requirements, but given the right conditions some suppliers can contribute much more and in some cases can be instrumental in the development of a competitive edge or even an entire brand identity. There are, therefore, different levels at which suppliers can contribute to brand equity development beyond fulfilment (Figure 2.4).

Traditionally the role to develop brand equity has been viewed as that of the marketing function. However, today, as businesses choose to outsource more non-core activities to carefully chosen suppliers, these suppliers hold the potential to make a solid contribution to the brand equity of a business and as such redefining the role of the purchasing function to help make this happen. Brand equity is created where suppliers can help us create a differentiator or something that gives us a competitive edge. This could take many forms, for example:

- working with a supplier to reduce cost through the entire supply chain helps grow margin or even establish price leadership;

- where our brand can be enhanced by association with the supplier's brand; and

- if a supplier has a unique capability, feature or offering that can enhance our offering we can use this to help create a differentiator, especially if we can secure exclusivity.

Unlocking the next level of value requires a new form of supplier collaboration. If buyer and supplier choose to work together the value of what can be achieved is sometimes greater than the sum of each parties' achievement if we act independently. However, it is easy to assume that all suppliers would naturally want to collaborate with us if we so desired. This may not be the case, despite what they might say. For value to be unlocked through a

FIGURE 2.4 How the supply base contributes to brand equity

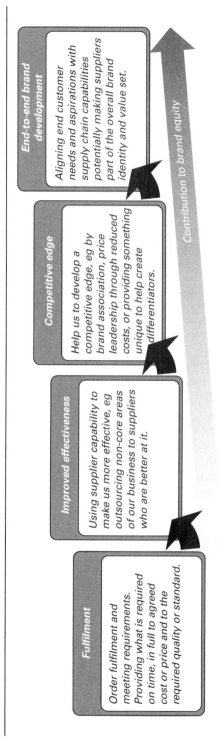

Fulfilment

Order fulfilment and meeting requirements. Providing what is required on time, in full to agreed cost or price and to the required quality or standard.

Improved effectiveness

Using supplier capability to make us more effective, eg outsourcing non-core areas of our business to suppliers who are better at it.

Competitive edge

Help us to develop a competitive edge, eg by brand association, price leadership through reduced costs, or providing something unique to help create differentiators.

End-to-end brand development

Aligning end customer needs and aspirations with supply chain capabilities potentially making suppliers part of the overall brand identity and value set.

Contribution to brand equity

collaborative relationship then both parties need to be truly interested and want to put additional effort into making it work and actually follow through to make it work. The game of 'Stag Hunt' from the world of game theory helps us understand this. This is illustrated by Skyrms (2004) who explains the concept as one where each party makes a rational choice as to their course of action. He likens it to two women rowing a boat: The outcome is the best for both women if they make headway. If both choose not to row neither has lost anything as both stay in the same place; however, if the one in front rows and the one at the back does not, it is the worst outcome for the one rowing as she expends all her energy but the boat makes little headway. The same is true for those supplier relationships that hold potential for us; we both must want to row the boat and make headway if we are to unlock value. For example, a small supplier providing something unique and of interest to us would benefit by surety of future revenues and we will benefit if we can secure future supply. This could develop further and by providing the supplier with a contracted volume commitment and guaranteed growth, we would enable the supplier to invest in business development whilst we benefit from greater security of supply and the opportunity to secure and lock in preferential terms. We could take this a step further and get more involved with the supplier so as to align their offer and development with our future plans and needs. We could even choose to acquire a stake in their business or simply buy them. Value therefore has degrees depending upon the degree of mutual collaboration (Figure 2.5).

Everyday suppliers might jump at the chance of a close relationship that affords them the chance to grow their business but there may be little benefit to us, especially if we have choice and the ability to switch in the marketplace. Similarly some suppliers will be uninterested in us beyond convincing us to buy from them. Others might speak of collaboration but not mean it. If neither rows the boat, we have lost nothing, we are merely transacting for the supply of goods or services but the worst outcome is if one party believes the relationship is collaborative while the other pretends, as this will not enable value creation. The key to this type of value lies in the will of both parties to want to collaborate, and therefore the potential pay-off by doing so. One test of how serious a supplier is to row the boat with us is the degree of investment the company puts into achieving outcomes. If the 'joint working' extends only as far at the Key Account Manager then the commitment on their part may be superficial. However, if the collaboration extends further into their business then it is usually real.

Collaboration for mutual value development doesn't just happen but needs to be structured, with a joint team, jointly agreed mutually beneficial goals and both investing time and resources to do so. Here, using the Strategic Collaborative Relationships (SCR) process can provide the process and framework to do this and we'll cover this in Chapter 13.

FIGURE 2.5 Degrees of collaboration

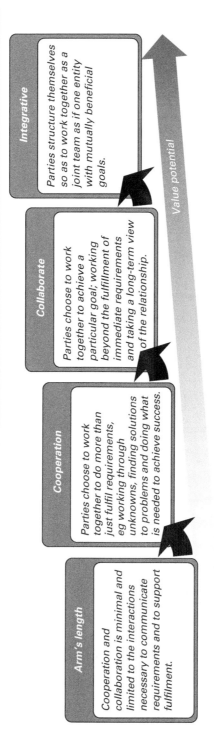

Arm's length

Cooperation and collaboration is minimal and limited to the interactions necessary to communicate requirements and to support fulfilment.

Cooperation

Parties choose to work together to do more than just fulfil requirements, eg working through unknowns, finding solutions to problems and doing what is needed to achieve success.

Collaborate

Parties choose to work together to achieve a particular goal; working beyond the fulfillment of immediate requirements and taking a long-term view of the relationship.

Integrative

Parties structure themselves so as to work together as a joint team as if one entity with mutually beneficial goals.

Value potential

Relationship requirements

Within category management, the entire process is underpinned by the *Business Requirements*; a comprehensive definition of exactly what the organization needs and wants for a specific category of spend or group of products/services. Business requirements are developed cross-functionally with key stakeholder engagement and must translate corporate objectives into specific requirements that determine what the organization buys. The process of developing business requirements challenges what has gone before and, if done well, can be the source of great breakthrough. There are different frameworks for business requirements. I favour the RAQSCI model in Figure 2.6 which, like VIPER, is also hierarchical.

VIPER works in a similar way and underpins the entire SRM process as the means to define the *Relationship Requirements*. It provides the framework to define what we need from the supply base at a macro level or indeed specific requirements for individual suppliers. At a macro level we can use the framework to modulate the wider corporate aims or objectives of the organization together with any specific needs the business has from the supply base in general. At a supplier-specific level it helps us convert a problem or opportunity into a target that will be achieved with a specific piece of supplier intervention.

FIGURE 2.6 The business requirements framework, as used with category management

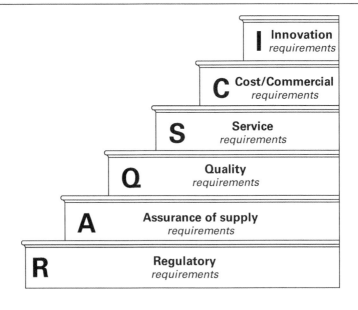

Within SRM, business requirements are relevant also, as what we need or want for *what* we buy, influence the relationship requirements for *whom* we buy from. This is one of the key linkages between category management and SRM and Figure 2.7 shows how business and relationship requirements integrate. It could be argued that both requirement frameworks are doing the same thing or that business requirements can define what is needed from the supply base. Indeed many of the inputs are common, for example the requirements 'must comply with company CSR policy' could apply to both goods sourced and suppliers. Any overlap is not important, instead by using VIPER relationship requirements alongside RAQSCI business requirements means we are effectively considering what is needed from a supplier through two separate lenses, which helps us see broader opportunities. Where an organization is using both category management and SRM, both definitions of requirements should work in concert across both initiatives for the good of the firm.

VIPER therefore seeks to answer the pathway question *what contribution do we need from our suppliers and why?* This contribution is defined in our relationship requirements, at a macro level initially and then at individual supplier level. Figure 2.8 provides an example of macro relationship requirements using VIPER. Here note how this collection of requirements resembles an overarching purchasing strategy and that is simply because at a macro level VIPER is effectively a framework for defining a key component of a firm's purchasing strategy. This initial and often neglected step is crucial as it forms the basis for how we will identify those suppliers who are important to us and therefore require some form of intervention.

FIGURE 2.7 Using business requirements and relationship requirements together

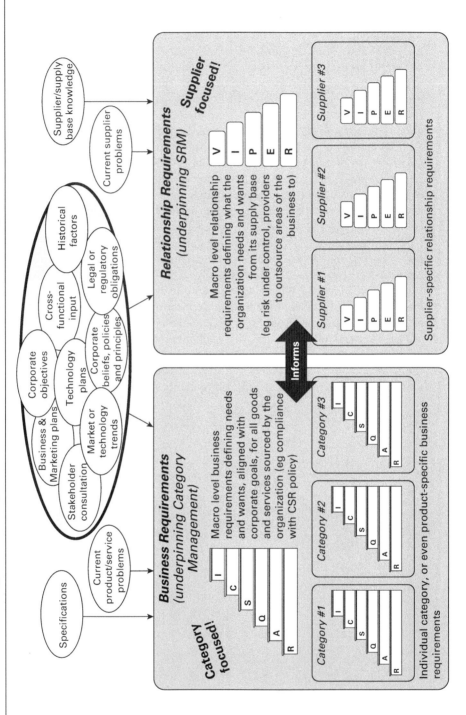

FIGURE 2.8 Example of macro level relationship requirements

Requirement	Need?	Want?
Macro level or overarching VIPER Relationship Requirements *What the organization needs from its entire supply base*		
Value • Partnerships with key providers to enable outsource of billing, call centres and facilities management.	✓ ✓	
Innovation • New technology innovations to develop the next generation online solutions for our products. • Five new ideas in next year that will strengthen our brand.	✓	✓
Performance Improvement • Total cost of ownership programmes across key spend areas. • Performance measurement and supplier improvement programme for key important suppliers. • 7% reduction in cost across supply base within two years. • Continuous Improvement plans for top 50 suppliers by spend.	✓ ✓ ✓	✓
Effectiveness of operations • Supplier 'expectations and code of conduct' for all suppliers who attend site. • Regular supplier management and review meetings for all top 50 suppliers by spend.	✓ ✓	
Risk • Rolling programme of supply base risk assessment and management in place. • Contingency plans must be in place for all single sourced, critical suppliers. • Compliance with CSR policy for all suppliers and supply chains. • Audit of all strategic suppliers every two years.	✓ ✓ ✓ ✓	

Introducing the orchestra of SRM

This chapter defines supplier relationship management. It considers the evolution of different supplier focused approaches and developing purchasing maturity that makes SRM the overarching strategic philosophy and framework for intervention for certain suppliers. It describes how SRM must fit and exist within a business and the different components that must come together to be effective.

PATHWAY QUESTIONS ADDRESSED IN THIS CHAPTER

1 What is the contribution we need from our supply base and why?
2 Which suppliers are important to us and why?
3 How much resource do we need and if we have only so much resource, which suppliers should we direct this at and why?
17 Are all our efforts with suppliers coordinated and aligned with our corporate goals?
18 Is corporate strategy informed by supply chain possibilities?

Defining SRM

A well-executed SRM approach can provide competitive advantage, fuel growth and brand development, reduce cost, improve efficiency and effectiveness and reduce supply side risk or at least help understand it so it can be mitigated. However, SRM is not something that can simply be 'bolted on', it is an organization-wide philosophy that needs to be embraced by all if it is to deliver these benefits and so we start by understanding what SRM is and how it works in practice.

The story so far

The way organizations look after, interact and manage their suppliers is not a single subject, but forms part of the literature on purchasing, logistics, operations management and also marketing. It is perhaps no surprise that there is some confusion regarding the various different approaches and terminology that seem to exist. To make sense of this we need to look at how these approaches have evolved.

Rewind the clock to the 1960s and the intervention with suppliers was decentralized to the extent of focusing on warehouse management, transportation and operations management (Hieber, 2002). In the 70s and 80s 'centralization' drove new ways for supplier management and as the 'quality movement' arrived organizations embraced Deming, Kiazan, Total Quality Management, Total Cost Management and Continuous Improvement. The way organizations viewed suppliers began to change and objectives to optimize cost, quality and customer service came to the fore (Hieber, 2002). The Japanese showed the world how partnerships with suppliers could add great value to an organization. Companies slashed the number of suppliers, awarding contracts to survivors and empowered the winners to manage lower tier suppliers. The rest of the world tried to copy the model but something got lost in cultural translation. Amongst these were American companies who made some superficial changes to supply chains but the fundamental nature of the relationship with suppliers changed little and relationships remained largely adversarial. Today some automobile giants continue to have adversarial relationship with their suppliers whilst others including Toyota and Honda can boast effective partnering models (Liker and Choi, 2004).

The concept of 'supply chain management' gained momentum in the 1990s where, for the first time, the supply base was seen as an important enabler to help organizations achieve their aspirations and targets. Companies started to develop strategies for their entire supply chains with visions, objectives and goals being set; a new type of relationship with certain important suppliers was emerging.

The philosophy of supplier relationship management (SRM) emerged around the millennium as a single, overarching strategic approach to bring some order to the different types of supplier intervention that enabled the firm to reach its goals. The concepts of 'supplier management', 'supplier performance measurement' and 'supply chain management' naturally fell under the SRM umbrella as approaches relevant for certain groups of suppliers. Furthermore, organizations began to recognize that by focusing on developing better relationships with the critical few most important suppliers they could create huge value from the supply base. Again this became part of the SRM approach for many organizations.

In 2010 the world's first formal standard for supplier collaborative relationships was launched, initially as a British Standard (BS11000) and then an international standard (ISO11000) defining, for the first time, a framework for establishing and improving collaborative relationships between organizations enabling firms to achieve internationally recognized accreditation for putting such arrangements in place.

Today the picture is less than clear with many different forms of supplier intervention and the various labels used interchangeably. This perhaps accounts for a general level of confusion regarding what SRM is and how it adds value.

An organization-wide philosophy

SRM programmes in organizations tend to be championed from within the purchasing function and therefore can get viewed by others as purchasing-led initiatives. It follows that if purchasing looks after, and is the main interface with the external parties from which it sources, then it is logical that SRM would live here. However, for SRM to have a purpose and to contribute effectively to organizational success it requires wider terms of reference and cross-functional participation. In fact, if an SRM initiative is to have any significant impact then it must be an integral component in the way the organization connects its *sourcing* with the way it *satisfies* its end customers and the overarching *strategy* of the firm (Figure 3.1). The relationship between these three is fundamental if an organization wishes to gain competitive advantage by capitalizing on the potential that resides in the supply base. The purpose of SRM to enable this is to drive a convergence of *Sourcing* and *Satisfying* customers and *Strategy*. Without this the initiative may well be little more than a handful of great ideas by well-meaning buyers that never gain traction, pursue the wrong goals or make little significant difference. The key to understanding how to achieve this convergence in practice lies with the way value flows into and through an organization and on to the end customer.

The flow of value

Organizations need to source materials, goods, services or people in some way. It's hard to picture an organization that doesn't. Purchasing (and indeed any dedicated supply chain management function) therefore has one of the organization's primary externally facing roles to *source* on behalf of the organization. At the other end, the other primary externally facing role is that of *satisfying* what customers need and might want; a role usually fulfilled

FIGURE 3.1 The 3 S model

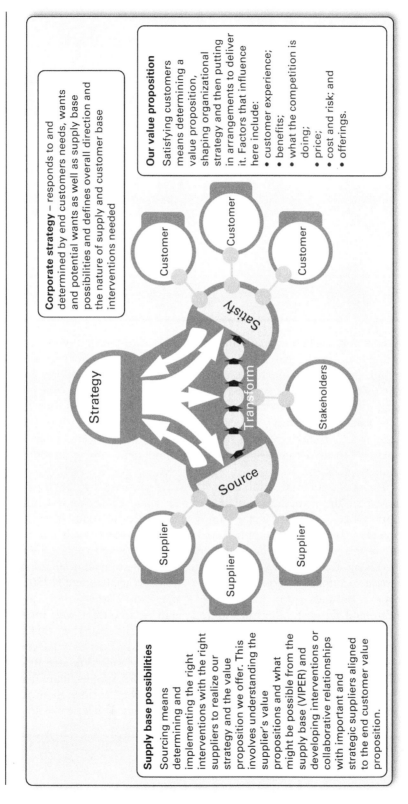

Corporate strategy – responds to and determined by end customers needs, wants and potential wants as well as supply base possibilities and defines overall direction and the nature of supply and customer base interventions needed

Our value proposition

Satisfying customers means determining a value proposition, shaping organizational strategy and then putting in arrangements to deliver it. Factors that influence here include:

- customer experience;
- benefits;
- what the competition is doing;
- price;
- cost and risk; and
- offerings.

Supply base possibilities

Sourcing means determining and implementing the right interventions with the right suppliers to realize our strategy and the value proposition we offer. This involves understanding the supplier's value propositions and what might be possible from the supply base (VIPER) and developing interventions or collaborative relationships with important and strategic suppliers aligned to the end customer value proposition.

FIGURE 3.2   The 'source, transform and satisfy' value chain

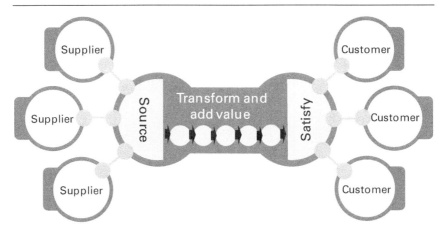

by sales and marketing teams amongst others who interface with customers in some way or are part of the process of fulfilment. In between these two are all the different functions, departments, processes, handoffs and steps that transform what is sourced into something that satisfies the customer (Figure 3.2) so they buy and keep buying. Ideally this transformation adds some value in some way. Porter (1985) describes the concept of the 'value chain' with products passing through an organization and each business function directly or indirectly adding value in some way to create the final product or service.

Whilst the internal value chain between *sourcing* and *satisfy* adds the value that the firm then exploits, similar value chains exist within each supplier back upstream in the supply chain extending back to the original growers, raw material suppliers or service providers. Each entity in the supply chain therefore adds value in some way by enhancing, combining, processing, building, mixing, packaging, coordinating, shipping and so on to create products or services that our customers buy. Lanning (1980) defines this in a business as 'a value delivery system' and Porter (1985) called this end-to-end flow of value the 'value system' – a concept well founded in economic theory. If our customers are not the end user then this value is further built upon by the next organization and the flow of value continues onwards through each of our customers in the chain, ultimately providing value to the final end customer (Figure 3.3). In fact supply chains are rarely this linear – a more modern concept is to recognize this chain more as a network rather than a linear sequential system. I will return to that in Chapter 12.

FIGURE 3.3 The value system

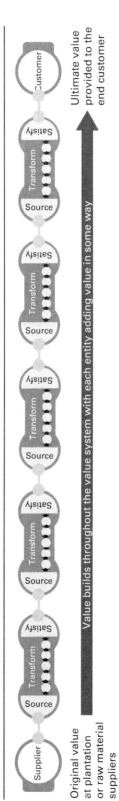

Original value at plantation or raw material suppliers

Value builds throughout the value system with each entity adding value in some way

Ultimate value provided to the end customer

Satisfying *customers*

Many SRM programmes are purchasing led, perhaps driven by a desire for purchasing to manage its suppliers better or improve effectiveness etc. This is good and in turn benefits our end customer. However, this inward focus limits possibilities. If an SRM programme can be driven more by how the entire business can better *satisfy* its end customers then this change in perspective can change our entire view of the value we need from the supply base in order to create the value customers want or need.

The value that *satisfies* the end customers is called the *value proposition* (Lanning, 1980), which is the reason they buy; because a need or want will be fulfilled in some way; it is a promise of value to be delivered together with a belief held by the customer that the value will be secured or experienced. Barnes *et al* (2009) define the value proposition as:

$$Value = benefits - cost$$

This is an equation that is possibly not in the minds of a customer when choosing supplier or product A over B yet this is something we all do whether we realize it or not. *Value* is subjective and a perception of value is unique to the individual and situation. The benefits that represent value can be tangible such as a cold drink on a hot day or intangible such as how we feel about showing off the latest designer sunglasses on the same hot day. These are benefits that respond to a need or want but customers may also experience, or come to realize benefit, from something they hadn't contemplated. This of course is the ultimate goal for any marketing function and why billions gets spent on advertising and educating the customer. As I write, the technical press are carrying reviews for the next generation of ultra high definition or '4k' TV panels boasting four times the resolution of current HD sets. Prior to reading the article I hadn't contemplated such a thing but I can feel a 'want' emerging, which holds the potential to head towards 'need' status subject to the usual domestic approval and sign off, which could be tricky and may cost me dear.

The cost of realizing benefits from a purchase could of course be money and could also be other factors that impact us such as risk, inconvenience, effort or other factors that could affect us in the future. In any purchase scenario we therefore weigh up what we will get against the cost of getting it.

The value proposition is the way a supplier defines what it will do and offer and how it organizes itself so as to provide value to the customer experience. Barnes *et al* (2009) state that 'by building a value proposition you will provide profitable and superior customer value, more profitable and more superior than if you hadn't built on'. Therefore if a firm can build customer value and *satisfy* its customers this in turn creates sustainable value for the organization (Kaplan and Norton, 2004). So the more you can satisfy customers the more value you create. Obvious perhaps but consider for a moment if organizations are organized or structured around a value proposition or have a value centred strategic intent? Barnes *et al* (2009) suggests traditionally the vast majority of businesses have not been because they are focused either on pushing an offering to customers from the inside out (persuade the client to buy what we do) or an outside-in approach (respond to, and provide whatever the customer wants). Arguably both of these approaches are sufficient and organizations have done just fine for many years working in this way. Giving the customer what they ask for is a great business model, so long as they know what they want or can see how something could be of value to them but this is not always the case. As Steve Jobs said, 'It's really hard to design products by focus groups. A lot of times, people don't know that they want until you show it to them' (*Business Week*, 2008).

Convincing the customer to buy is the first challenge and one marketing departments work very hard at. However, there is a second challenge and one we explored back in Chapter 1. Remember in our changing landscape customers are becoming better informed, more discerning and can access an entire global marketplace. Companies are therefore having to work harder to stay in the game and find new differentiators in order to satisfy customers.

Satisfying customers therefore requires companies to be clear about the value proposition that will resonate with customers and will therefore drive demand. This means the firm must get close to customers, develop a deep understanding of what would they would value (especially the value they haven't realized they need or cannot articulate) and develop a differentiated offering. This is much more than any initiative from a marketing function but requires a corporate strategy based around satisfying customers with the right value proposition and requires the entire organization to be structured, aligned and organized behind this. The traditional drivers that enable this are:

- the brilliant minds of those innovating and creating new ideas or ways of doing things;
- unique or highly effective internal processes that help make 'better, faster, cheaper' a reality;
- location, distribution channels or routes to market; and
- brand building that creates a certain perception in the minds of a customer.

All these continue to hold great potential to deliver competitive advantage, however there is a further vast and often untapped source of value and innovation if an organization can figure out how to capture it – the supply base.

Sourcing *value*

Linking end customer value with value we source drives a change in mindset in the role of our supply base and the way we need to interact with it. If we view our suppliers as there only to fulfil orders, and assume they present no risk or opportunity then their role is purely tactical and the supply base has little or no bearing on the way the organization satisfies its customers beyond fulfilment of current need; sourcing is merely a responsive activity. Indeed this is the traditional model of purchasing, commonplace for many years. Yet, as we have seen, organizations now need more from the supply base because customers want more from them. Add to this increased scarcity and security of supply issues and a supply base can no longer be managed tactically.

The idea that the supply base is host to new and future sources of value is not a new concept. Indeed organizations have in fact been taking ideas, concepts and innovations from willing suppliers for years, crucially though this has tended to be at an individual level rather than as part of an organized corporate approach. For example, individuals within an R&D, NPD or marketing function tasked with creating or developing new products engage with and develop relationships with the suppliers that have something to offer here. This is good, but the problem is suppliers gain power through relationships with designers and it is in the supplier's interests to develop these relationships; if they can get their product, service or technology incorporated at the design or concept stage, and especially if they can get it defined in a specification, then it almost guarantees a future revenue stream. Purchasing rarely get invited to be part of such discussions, and by the time they do, the supplier is mandated leaving little ability to influence commercial terms. Effective *sourcing* and the relationships with suppliers therefore need to be much more coordinated and managed if we are to secure the value we need beyond that we currently get. Furthermore there must be a strong linkage to how the organization develops its value proposition to the customer, otherwise any supplier interactions will only ever be supporting an 'inside out' strategy based on convincing the customer to buy what we want to sell. What is actually required is an approach that connects the value of supply chain possibilities with the value proposition that satisfies the customer and this means the convergence of *sourcing* and *satisfying* with organizational *strategy*.

Shaping strategy

Strategy is a much-used and misused word in business. It is derived from the Greek *strategos* meaning *office of general command, presidency, army leader, period of command or campaign or a force of men* (Liddell and Scott, 1940). It was this leader who would single handedly, or together with others, determine military direction and organize activities such a calling up citizens for military duties or maintaining ships to support this. Sun Tzu (circa 2000BC), the ancient Chinese military general, strategist and philosopher from the Zhou Dynasty, is famous for his writings around military tactics and strategy contained in *The Art of War*. These continue to influence modern war, and indeed business tactics because they define a series of courses of action to gain or retain advantage according to certain situations. Strategy is therefore about the direction we take and today our use of the term is more about *direction* than a *leader*. Just as in war when the highest ranking leader might set the direction according to the threat and organize resources according, in organizations' strategy it is about supremacy of direction setting; the single direction that the firm will take, aligning everything else to support this and according to the situation it finds itself in. This is summarized nicely by Johnson and Scholes (1993), who describe corporate strategy as the *direction and scope of an organization over the long term: ideally, which matches its resources to its changing environment and in particular its markets, customers or clients so as to meet stakeholder expectations.*

Corporate strategy is only effective if it can be implemented. Therefore strategy has to be translated so each part of the business can play its part in following the overall direction set. Figure 3.4 gives the typical representation of how corporate strategy gets translated based upon the Johnson and Scholes (1993) model. Here a firm defines its overall direction within a *mission statement* that is then supported by high-level goals and specific measurable objectives. These are then translated into a series of individual strategies and plans or actions for the various functions and resources a firm has and finally controls to ensure actions are properly executed.

Traditionally this has, for most organizations, included a separate translation of strategy into actions for supplier facing functions (eg purchasing) and those who are customer facing (eg sales and marketing). This strategic cascade is – based upon how most textbooks present it and how many firms are organized – one directional; flowing down from the top of the organization.

The problem with a 'top down only' strategic management approach means there is no real need for purchasing to engage with marketing as both take their direction from the top. Indeed functions can exist as silos

FIGURE 3.4   Translating corporate strategy into departmental actions

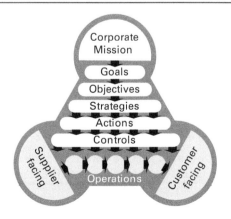

with hand-offs between them. Cross-functional working can help but only if the organization is encouraging this throughout and of course this in itself requires top down remit. Furthermore success depends entirely upon getting the strategy absolutely right including determining all the factors that could cause it to fail and taking advantage of those that can help. This is quite a responsibility for those setting strategy. If we dive back to the military world then history is full of examples where the brilliance of one great leader and the decision made meant battles and wars were won against the odds. History is also not short of examples where great loss of life resulted from the wrong strategy, for example the Battle of Little Bighorn in 1876 or Napoleon invading Russia in 1812. Unless those setting strategy have great and full insight, it can miss the mark and, in today's environment, that could prove catastrophic for a business. So how does strategy connect to sourcing and satisfying? Johnson and Scholes (1993) suggest that strategy must match its resources to its changing environment. The supply base represents an integral part of the firm's resources and so for any corporate strategy to be effective it needs to consider the role of the supply base to support how the organization will achieve its goals. Kaplan and Norton (2004) suggest that the value proposition is part of business strategy and *strategy is based on a differentiated customer value proposition.* As we have already seen the environment that we, our suppliers and our customers exist in is changing and creating new imperatives. Effective corporate strategies must therefore respond to and be determined by the external environment within both the supply base and customer base. This is supported by Gordon (2008) who suggests that when suppliers are viewed as an extension of the customer's enterprise, ideally their importance to the business can be viewed less as cost centres and more as partners with the potential to add value to the business. Strategies are therefore two-way; they inform and are informed by end customer current and potential wants and needs together with what might be possible in the supply base. This is the fundamental concept that underpins and creates a purpose for an effective SRM programme.

The three pillars of SRM

Supporting the *sourcing, satisfying and strategy* philosophy of SRM are three pillars of SRM. These are the three interrelated components that must come together and happen to establish an effective SRM approach (Figure 3.5); as for any structure, all the pillars are necessary to make it whole. The pillars of SRM are *what*, with *whom* and *how*:

- *What...* the organization needs from its supply base in order to realize strategic goals, determined using VIPER macro relationship requirements.

FIGURE 3.5 The three pillars of SRM

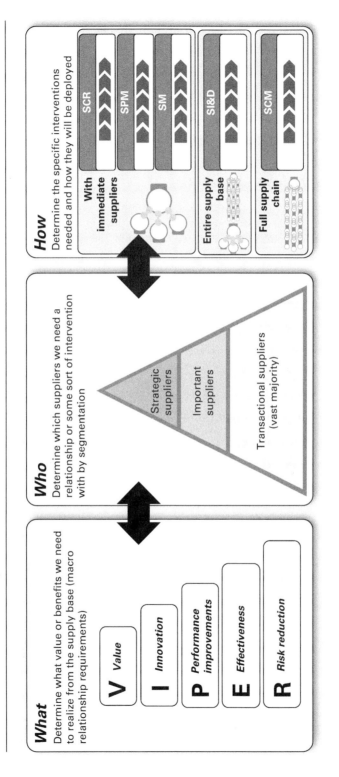

What

Determine what value or benefits we need to realize from the supply base (macro relationship requirements)

V *Value*

I *Innovation*

P *Performance improvements*

E *Effectiveness*

R *Risk reduction*

Who

Determine which suppliers we need a relationship or some sort of intervention with by segmentation

Strategic suppliers

Important suppliers

Transactional suppliers (vast majority)

How

Determine the specific interventions needed and how they will be deployed

With immediate suppliers

SCR

SPM

SM

Entire supply base

SI&D

Full supply chain

SCM

- *With whom...* we need a relationship or some sort of intervention in order to realize strategic goals, defined through supplier segmentation (coming up in Chapter 4).

- *How...* we will deploy specific interventions with the supply base to achieve strategic goals. The majority of this book is devoted to this topic.

We covered 'What' in the last chapter, I will cover 'with whom' and 'how' here.

Not all suppliers are equal

Some are more equal than others. Some suppliers are also more important than others and therefore warrant different types of intervention or relationship. I will devote an entire chapter to segmenting the supply base and defining 'importance' but for now I'll begin with the notion that at the heart of SRM lies the concept that those suppliers who are important in some way warrant special attention. Figure 3.6 shows the pyramid of suppliers that is frequently used in one form or another to represent the suppliers to an organization.

Organizations of a certain size can usually boast many thousands or even tens of thousands of suppliers. Organizations collect and accumulate suppliers in the course of doing business but the vast majority of these will be of little or no importance to the organization beyond fulfilling a simple order, purchase or transaction. The guy who waters the pot plants or the company that disposes of general waste all need to be contracted with in some form, and so become suppliers, but are unlikely to hold any significant importance to the future of the business. At the level of 'unimportant' there are typically many vendors, with whom no special intervention is needed beyond the immediate transaction. As suppliers become more important they diminish in number to just a handful who are vitally important. This pyramid representation of a firm's supply base is helpful to begin to identify, and differentiate, the different types of intervention that are needed according to how far up the pyramid a supplier is. Typically, as we work our way up, suppliers become more important in some way and therefore begin to warrant some sort of extra intervention; perhaps those midway up warrant measurement of performance, driving improvements or management in some form; perhaps the supply chain that sits behind them needs to be understood and managed more closely. Finally, at the top of the pyramid, there may be just a handful of suppliers that are so important that there is good reason to attempt to build a close collaborative relationship with them because together we can unlock great benefits for both parties.

Introducing segmentation

Supplier segmentation is the division of the supply base into groups of suppliers that allow us to determine and apply the different types of intervention that

FIGURE 3.6 Different types of supply base intervention according to importance

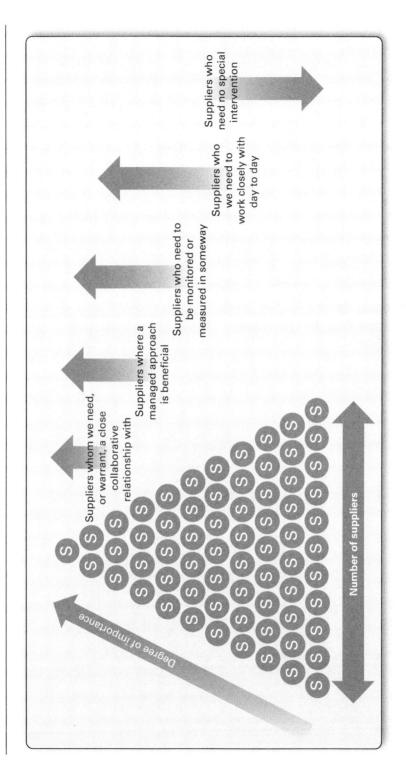

Suppliers whom we need, or warrant, a close collaborative relationship with

Suppliers where a managed approach is beneficial

Suppliers who need to be monitored or measured in someway

Suppliers who we need to work closely with day to day

Suppliers who need no special intervention

Degree of importance

Number of suppliers

are beneficial and worthwhile for each group (Figure 3.7). I'm using three classifications as this seems to be the most widely adopted approach. There are many models and variants out there, using different labels and different demarcations. It doesn't matter which so long as there is a clear rationale for segmentation and everyone understands it. Furthermore, in practice the demarcations are not precise boundaries but more blurred transitions. I will cover this and the full segmentation approach in the next chapter but this simple supplier segmentation model provides a starting point to classify our different suppliers according to how important they are to us. There are three broad classifications. These are:

- *Transactional suppliers* – suppliers with whom no special intervention beyond the immediate transaction is needed.

- *Important suppliers* – suppliers who warrant some degree of management or intervention either because we need to or it is beneficial to do so.

FIGURE 3.7 The supplier segmentation pyramid

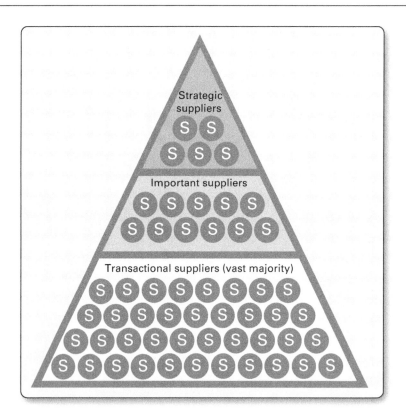

- *Strategic suppliers* – suppliers that are critical or are of strategic importance to us in some way with whom we either need a close relationship to protect our business or who hold the potential to help us realize our organizational goals and achieve greater value together.

SRM: an overarching philosophy and framework

The reason why the term *Supplier Relationship Management (SRM)* seems to carry different meaning depending who is using it, is perhaps because for any given organization, different treatments across the vast range of suppliers are needed according to how important each supplier is to the firm. SRM seems to have become a term coined to describe each and every one of these approaches in one way or another; firms with a regime of only managing certain suppliers claim to be applying SRM alongside those working in close relationships with key partners who are also applying SRM. The little established literature on this subject provides virtually no consistency or clarity here either. The difficulty perhaps is that everyone is right to a degree. Therefore clarity in understanding and defining SRM comes by considering it as the *overarching strategic philosophy and framework* under which different types of supplier intervention across the entire supply base exist. SRM does not replace these but rather it brings order and coherence so as to connect the ambition of the business with the potential in the supply base at a strategic level. Therefore the following well-known and much used approaches all have their place and belong within SRM:

- Strategic collaborative relationships (SCR) – an approach to establish and improve relationships at a strategic level with the critical few suppliers who can add the most value to the organization. The term *collaborative relationship* was popularized by the British Standard BS11000, however this strategic component of SRM is sometimes referred to as *strategic relationship management* (also 'SRM' to really confuse things) or *relationship management* or *strategic relationships*.

- Supplier performance measurement (SPM) – an approach specifically centred around measuring supplier performance and perhaps coordinating improvement initiatives in response to findings.

- Supplier improvement and development (SI&D) – specific interventions with a supplier to drive some sort of improvement or develop supplier capability. Initiatives here might range from simple corrective action to joint initiatives where parties collaborate to reach a new goal.

- Supplier management (SM) – an approach for important suppliers that addresses the day-to-day management, interaction, relationship management, contract management, performance management, review and coordination of improvement initiatives.

- Supply chain management (SCM) – an approach to understand and manage the entire supply chain and possibly even the end-to-end value chain extending to the end customer. Typically concerned with arrangements to ensure flows of information and coordinate logistics, storage and flows of goods right through the supply chain.

Each of these is an established philosophy or approach in its own right and each will be expanded in full within this book and Figure 3.8 shows how each typically aligns to our segmented supply base within SRM.

The focus for these individual components of an SRM is relevant. SPM, SI&D and SM focus on the direct contractual relationship with a discrete number of immediate important suppliers. SCM considers the entire supply chain beyond the immediate contractual relationship and perhaps even follows the chain further on towards the end customer. SI&D tends to focus on immediate suppliers but could also focus on entire supply chains and SCR is the most strategic component here and arguably the one that can potentially unlock the greatest value with a focus on a handful of immediate suppliers that are of strategic importance. The overall focus for SRM is that of the entire supply base and provides a framework to determine and deploy the various different approaches according to need or opportunity. In essence the philosophy of SRM is to ensure a firm has the right approaches, with the right suppliers to achieve corporate goals.

I should point out here that these approaches are not mutually exclusive; in other words SRM doesn't mean you have to choose one or another, it is possible and often necessary to adopt more than one type of intervention. For example, a supplier may require an SM approach but may also need SPM with some SI&D. We will return to this in later chapters.

There is one final dimension here and that is the prioritization of effort against available resources. It is all too easy for an organization to design an elaborate system of supply base segmentation that then demands a range of different interventions according to which suppliers fall into which categories. The problem is then that a small army is required to make it a reality and this is one reason why SRM initiatives often fail to gain traction. In practice, resources in organizations are usually precious and so for SRM to be an effective contributor of value to the firm what resources are available must be directed to the supplier interventions that will have the most impact.

Introducing 'the orchestra' of SRM

So, in summary, the overriding concept of effective SRM is the convergence between the *sourcing* by the business, *satisfying* the end customer and corporate *strategy*. The three pillars of SRM define the major components of an SRM approach that support this overriding concept (Figure 3.9).

FIGURE 3.8 SRM – an all-encompassing strategic framework

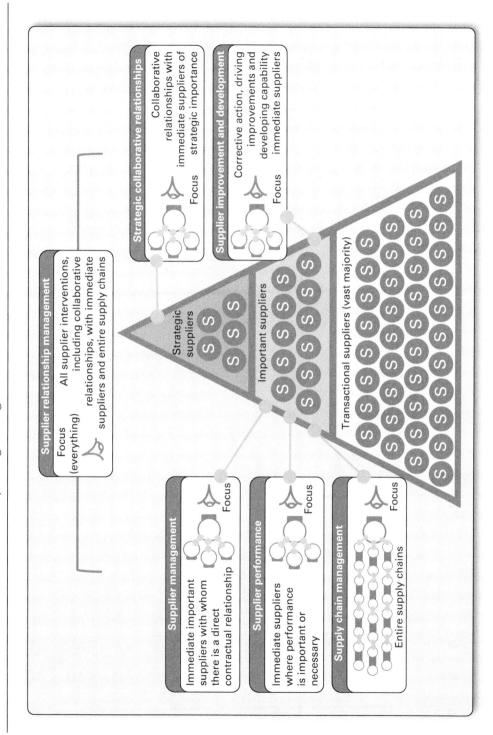

Supplier relationship management

Focus (everything)

All supplier interventions, including collaborative relationships, with immediate suppliers and entire supply chains

Strategic collaborative relationships

Focus

Collaborative relationships with immediate suppliers of strategic importance

Supplier improvement and development

Focus

Corrective action, driving improvements and developing capability immediate suppliers

Strategic suppliers

Important suppliers

Transactional suppliers (vast majority)

Supplier management

Immediate important suppliers with whom there is a direct contractual relationship

Focus

Supplier performance

Immediate suppliers where performance is important or necessary

Focus

Supply chain management

Entire supply chains

Focus

FIGURE 3.9 The major components of SRM

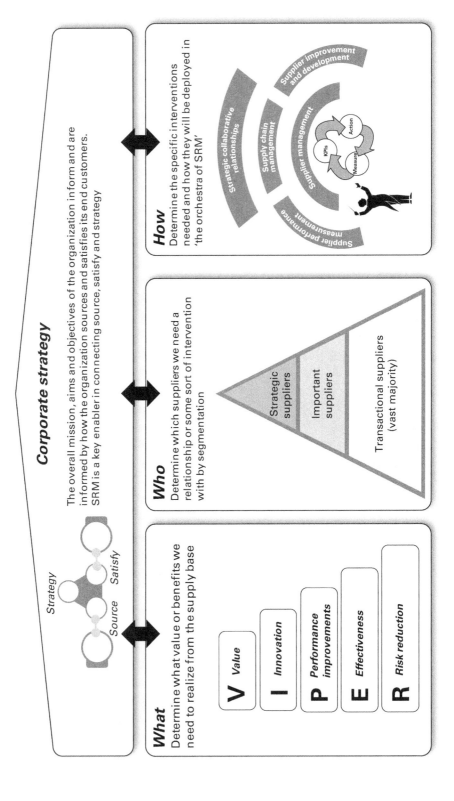

Corporate strategy

The overall mission, aims and objectives of the organization in form and are informed by how the organization sources and satisfies its end customers. SRM is a key enabler in connecting source, satisfy and strategy

Strategy

Source *Satisfy*

What

Determine what value or benefits we need to realize from the supply base

V *Value*

I *Innovation*

P *Performance improvements*

E *Effectiveness*

R *Risk reduction*

Who

Determine which suppliers we need a relationship or some sort of intervention with by segmentation

Strategic suppliers

Important suppliers

Transactional suppliers (vast majority)

How

Determine the specific interventions needed and how they will be deployed in 'the orchestra of SRM'

Strategic collaborative relationships

Supply chain management

Supplier management

Supplier improvement and development

Supplier performance measurement

KPIs Measure Action

A definition of SRM is therefore:

> The overarching strategic approach to determine and implement different supplier based interventions, including the development of collaborative relationships with the critical few suppliers who can make the greatest difference; prioritized against available resources, applied as appropriate across an entire supply base to maximize value to the organization, reduce supply chain risk and enable the organization to achieve its goals and enhance value to the end customer.

Furthermore, several enabling principles required to support an effective SRM programme are emerging. These include adopting an 'end-to-end' value focus, working cross-functionally with the wider organization and integrating the approach with other strategic initiatives such as category management. I will return to and build further on these as we move forward.

There is however one final key concept that is crucial to understanding how SRM works in practice and that is the way all the different components of SRM work together. The philosophy of SRM means it is not something that can follow a linear process or a defined series of steps. Indeed, across the plethora of what is written about SRM, it seems there is a common tendency to attempt to squeeze it into some sort of step-by-step approach, possibly explaining the apparent general lack of consistency or agreement as to what SRM actually is and perhaps why programmes can fail to deliver the results needed. The problem here is SRM is not a step-by-step journey to the right supplier relationships. Such a mindset works against us because every supplier is different, and those that are important are important for different reasons; each requiring a unique relationship or series of interventions according to our circumstances, theirs and what each party needs. One supplier may just need some compliance monitoring, whilst another might warrant a full strategic collaborative relationship. One may need intervention to minimize risk, another might hold latent value if we can work with them to unlock it, and so on.

SRM is in fact like an orchestra. Each of the sections of an orchestra play when needed according to the piece of music, all working in unison and taking their lead from a single conductor. This is precisely how SRM needs to work in order to be successful. Each component of the orchestra of SRM; the areas of focus, the different approaches and interventions, must play as and when needed according to what is appropriate for the circumstances, the current environment and the point in time with the conductor providing a governance framework that guides how the various interventions come in or drop back. Each important supplier has its own piece of music and the melody changes constantly. It is this new mindset for SRM that helps us understand how to build and develop truly effective SRM programmes in practice. It is also the basis upon which the rest of this book is structured. As we move forward I will explore each section of the orchestra of SRM in turn, culminating in a final definition of the entire ensemble and before we end I define how to set the stage for the orchestra to play – in other words all the things an organization needs to do to make SRM happen and deliver great outcomes.

Segmenting the supply base

04

This chapter defines supplier segmentation and provides a practical approach to determine which suppliers are important to us and why. Approaches to determine the right level of intervention, with the right suppliers to deliver the required outcomes are provided.

PATHWAY QUESTIONS ADDRESSED IN THIS CHAPTER

2 Which suppliers are important to us and why?
3 How much resource do we need and if we have only so much resource, which suppliers should we direct this at and why?

Which suppliers should we spend time on?

Some suppliers are more important than others. Some are critical. SRM is about unlocking value from the supply base and to do this we must first identify who the important suppliers are and therefore who we should spend time on and what interventions would help. Surely this is an easy thing to do? Well actually this can be one of the most challenging initial steps within SRM and it is easy to get weighed down by complex process. Get it right and we can have confidence we are directing our precious resource where it will have the greatest impact. Get it wrong and we could miss crucial opportunity and risk or waste precious time and energy in the wrong places.

Defining segmentation

Supply base segmentation is the process of determining which suppliers are important through the application of a set of pre-defined criteria, why they are important and therefore what sort of intervention and relationship would be necessary or beneficial. In our orchestra of SRM, segmentation composes the music we will play with each piece being a unique arrangement specifically for an individual supplier relationship. Segmentation has three components (Figure 4.1) and this chapter expands these in turn:

1 The segmentation criteria.

2 The segmentation process.

3 Determining the relationship or nature of intervention required.

Within these there are three guiding principles that need to drive our efforts here. Effective segmentation should be:

1 *Goal driven* – respond to organizational strategy and goals and ultimately to end customer needs and wants.

2 *Resource driven* – determine and prioritize supplier-focused activity based upon available resources.

3 *Market driven* – be informed by supplier and market understanding so to have confidence we are selecting the right or best suppliers to work with.

Goal driven

The starting point for supply base segmentation is our corporate strategy and goals, how we satisfy our customers and the value we need from our supply base to do this. This is, of course, defined in our VIPER relationship

FIGURE 4.1 The components of segmentation

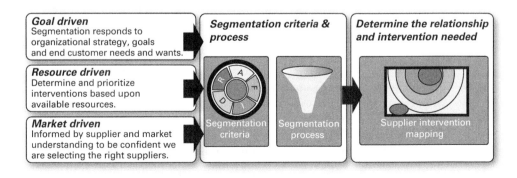

FIGURE 4.2 Segmentation criteria based on VIPER requirements

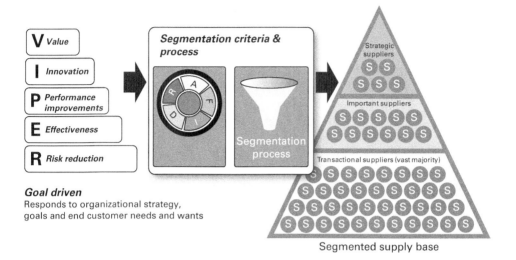

requirements and therefore this must shape our segmentation criteria at a high level and for individual suppliers (Figure 4.2).

Resource driven

It takes resource to unlock value, yet resource is precious and new resources need to be justified so what we have needs to be directed to where it will have the greatest impact. One important supplier may warrant just basic intervention whilst another could need much more; intervention may be necessary today, it may not be needed tomorrow. Segmentation is about determining where and how to direct resources.

SRM programmes can fail through poor or badly applied segmentation and there are some common problems here. An overly inward focus or considering segmentation as a 'once only' activity can yield sub-optimum results, but by far the most common cause of programme failure comes from overly rigid segmentation approaches or where the process creates an unsustainable burden on a business. For example, I worked with a European engineering company who, through segmentation, had determined there were 12 strategic suppliers and 35 important suppliers. A rigid process and procedure for managing each type of supplier was set for the purchasing team to adopt – strategic suppliers were to have assigned performance targets and improvement objectives with quarterly review meetings as well as an annual planning and review session. Performance measurement with an annual review meeting was stipulated for the 35 important suppliers. An initial flurry of activity and a packed diary of review meetings got the new programme off to a good start, but those with assigned responsibility here soon fell behind. Review meetings became more infrequent and the team struggled to keep up with the regime and the day job. The team began to lose interest as many of the supplier meetings were simply seen as a waste of time, adding little value and eventually the programme simply fell into disrepute.

There were in fact three problems here; first, no additional resources had been made available and the team had been expected to 'simply fit it in'; second, the rigidity of the programme meant it in fact required an additional 150 days of time per annum to do it properly; and third, there was no prioritization of what resources were available.

To the supply base and beyond!

The word *segmentation* suggests we are dividing up something, in this case the supply base. Indeed this may be the case. It may be sufficient to simply take our current list of suppliers and divide them up and then treat them in different ways. But what if we don't have the right suppliers? What if there are new suppliers out there who could help transform our business? What happens when we add new suppliers? If we are clear about the value the organization needs from its suppliers (as defined by VIPER), then we could be limiting what is possible by only looking at the pool of suppliers we know. Of course, we may not always be able to switch away from a current supplier easily or there may be good reasons not to, yet there could also be other new suppliers, and indeed entire marketplaces, out there that could change the game. Asking 'how do we manage our suppliers better?' gets us so far, but asking 'who else is out there who could really make a difference to our organization?' gets us further. This check for new possibilities is an important part of the segmentation process.

Checking for new suppliers demands deep market and supplier knowledge, and this requires research that takes time and demands resource. Such knowledge should not be unique to an SRM initiative, but rather something that is core to wider procurement activities. Indeed if the organization has adopted category management or other strategic sourcing approaches then market knowledge would be integral here. There may also be instances where we need to go and conduct new research and data gathering. For example, if the organization decides it needs to gain access to a particular capability or technology to support a new corporate goal, clearly the first place to look would be existing suppliers, but then a judgement is needed as to whether it might be beneficial or necessary to look beyond the current supply base in order to potentially realize a greater opportunity. This is only possible if we understand the market and potential market from which we are sourcing and can determine with confidence if we have the right suppliers on board or not and if not who we might want to approach.

Market and supplier understanding therefore supports effective segmentation.

Segmentation criteria

Segmentation criteria define the basis against which supplier importance is determined. There are different ways to arrive at a suitable set of criteria and different ways to apply it. In this section a generic set of segmentation criteria is provided along practical steps to assess importance for individual suppliers.

Hurt, help or heroes?

There are many factors that drive supplier importance and could therefore be adopted as criterion and basis for segmentation. These include:

- risk;
- spend;
- criticality or business importance;
- future opportunity;
- sustainability;
- ability to innovate;
- market difficulty for the key areas of supply;
- ability or inability to switch suppliers easily;
- proprietary or differentiated nature of goods and services;
- alignment with future goals;
- culture, style and ways of working;
- degree of interest and willingness from the supplier;
- nationality or prevailing religion;
- alignment with business ethics, beliefs and policies;
- established relationships and history of doing business (especially relevant in Eastern and Middle East culture);
- existing obligations or contractual commitments;
- geographical locations;
- distribution channels;
- uniqueness of knowledge or know-how held by supplier;
- affiliations, partnerships, group companies, interests held by key stakeholders;
- accreditations or compliance with regulations; and
- customer or regulatory mandates to use specific suppliers.

This is a big list and clearly impractical as a basis to segment a supply base and only some within this list would be relevant for any given business.

Selecting which criteria we need to use depends upon our organizational goals. For example, if the business has objectives to be an exemplar of sustainability in everything it does then *sustainability* and *alignment of ethical principles and policies* would become key criteria to decide which suppliers were important. Similarly if we need a particular technology or innovation to grow market share, and we don't currently have access to this with current suppliers, then *ability to innovate* would be a key criterion in this case applied to both existing and potential new suppliers.

In simple terms, there are three reasons why we might need or want supplier intervention and that is when a supplier could otherwise *hurt* us, because they could *help* us, or if we work together with a supplier they could be a *hero* for us. Considering supplier importance in terms of who could *hurt*, *help* or be a *hero* provides an easy means to help determine supplier importance and provides the basis upon which a more detailed set of criteria or rules can be developed.

Quick method segmentation

We can choose to make segmentation a meticulous, exhaustive activity applying a series of rigorous tests and evaluations or we can simply take a view. Contrary to popular belief, it is possible to be reasonably effective at supply base segmentation without a complex segmentation system or set of criteria. This can be as simple as asking the question 'if we only have so much resource, time or energy which suppliers should we spend it with, what things should we do and why?'.

An individual who knows the supply base will have a view here, but a group, carefully chosen from across the organization according to the insight they could bring, can provide a more meaningful view still. With debate and discussion the list of nominated suppliers can be narrowed down to arrive at a prioritized list of suppliers. Such a group can even figure our what sort of intervention might be needed for each supplier selected, matched against resources.

This method is quick, simple and can be highly effective. It is based upon the premise that there are individuals in a business who collectively understand the suppliers that need to be kept close. Success requires the right people to be in the room and it helps if the session is well facilitated. It is particularly useful for small or medium sized businesses with limited resources available and a desire to direct it where it will be most effective.

This simple method can be used alone or as part of a more extensive and structured segmentation as a means to validate outputs. Quick method segmentation is therefore included within the full segmentation process that is outlined later in this chapter.

Segmentation criteria

Segmentation criteria are unique to the organization and should be developed according to what the organization is trying to achieve and applied to current and potential new suppliers according to market understanding. It is unlikely that using a single segmentation criterion such as *spend* for example, would cover all the needs of the organization; instead effective segmentation demands a balanced judgement considering a range of factors and therefore demands a range of criteria. That said, complexity should be avoided if possible; the simpler the model the easier it is to apply and the easier it is for groups to understand how it works. Segmentation criteria works at two levels; it defines the things that are important to us in our supply base linked to organizational goals under a series of headings and then provides a means to score or assess individual suppliers against these headings.

Any firm embarking on SRM should consider the segmentation criteria relevant to the organization. Figure 4.3 provides a full generic segmentation model and I shall use this throughout this book. The generic model is based upon five key criteria. These are: risk, alignment (of the supplier's organization

FIGURE 4.3 The generic segmentation criteria

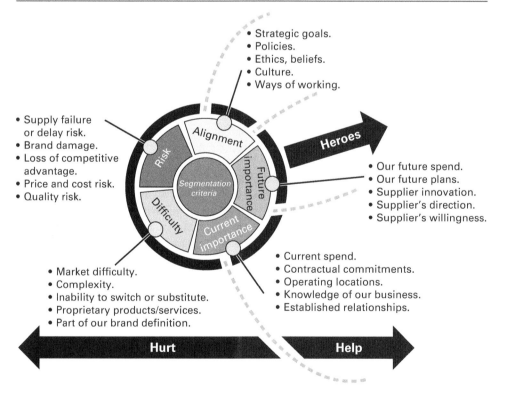

and direction with ours), future importance, current importance, and difficulty (in terms of what is being sourced from a supplier). The model is
divided according to the criteria that relate to a suppliers ability to *hurt*
us, *help* us or be a *hero*. Applying the model requires us to rate each supplier
against the criteria and from there determine the extent and nature of any
intervention required. I will expand on each of the key criterion and then
outline a practical process to do this.

Assessing supplier risk

Supplier *risk* is the degree to which a supplier could hurt us, and the form of
risk to our business of engaging a particular supplier. Risk can take many
forms and depends upon the nature of our organization, or the supplier's,
what they do, how they operate, where they are based and so on. Risk would
almost certainly need to be used as a criterion when segmenting a supply
base, however it is easy to limit thinking here and focus on factors such
as supply chain impact from natural disasters or major catastrophes. The
Marsh Report (2008) suggests that it is more everyday risks such as price
hikes, delivery delays and supplier problems that cause greater concern.
There are five classes of supply side risk (Figure 4.4). These are failure or
delay risk, risk to the reputation of our brand, competitive advantage risk,
price and cost risk and quality risk. Understanding and managing risk is
an integral component of SRM and so we will return to this model again
later in this book. At this stage, when segmenting the supply base, we are
concerned with identifying those suppliers that present risk and so warrant
intervention. That means we are only identifying and assessing risk within
segmentation. Responses to risk, such as mitigation or contingency actions,
are determined later as part of supplier management (SM) and supply chain
management (SCM), covered later in Chapters 9 and 12 respectively.

To assess the risk for a specific supplier as part of segmentation we need to
consider what risks might exist under each supply side risk heading. At this
stage we could do a full risk assessment, having a group brainstorm potential
risks under each heading in turn and then assessing and prioritizing each risk
in turn. (The methodology to do this is provided in Chapter 9 as part of supplier
management and built on further in Chapter 12.) However, with the right
group it is usually enough simply to consider the supplier and then, with discussion and debate, consider if there are significant risks against the five headings. Where a risk is identified as 'likely' the Viswandam and Gaonkar (2008)
classification (adapted slightly here to consider supplier risk not just supply
chain) can help do a quick assessment of the severity of impact, considering
the risk according to whether it holds the potential for:

- Deviation – a minor supply or quality failure, price or cost hikes.
- Disruption – an event that causes significant but recoverable supply
  failure or quality problems, or temporarily impacts our brand or
  competitive advantage.

FIGURE 4.4 The five supply side risk areas

The five supply side risk areas

Failure or delay risk	Brand reputation risk	Competitive advantage risk	Price and cost risk	Quality risks
Risk of complete and possibly permanent supply or service failure or risk of delays in supplying goods or providing a specific service.	Risks that, should they occur, can be disastrous for our brand either due to failure or practices in conflict with our principles and expectations of customers and stakeholders.	Risks of competitive advantage being undermined and include theft of intellectual property, counterfeiting and goods sold on the grey market.	The risk of outturn costs being higher than anticipated or planned for (with or without contractual protection).	Risk associated with quality failures, poor product or service quality and latent defects.

- Disaster – an event that shuts down the supplier, causes irrecoverable supply failure or causes severe damage to our brand or competitive advantage.

Suppliers where risk of disaster or disruption is present are therefore important in risk terms and as such should be scored high within the segmentation process (we'll cover that shortly).

Difficulty of what is being sourced

This criterion is also concerned with the degree to which a supplier could hurt us and is the only criterion to relate specifically to the goods or services being sourced from a given supplier. *Difficulty* is about assessing all the factors that might restrict freedom of choice when sourcing a particular category of spend or group of products or services and therefore might make a supplier important for this reason. Difficulty (based upon Kraljic, 1983) is high if:

- there is an inability to switch suppliers easily;
- only one or a small number of suppliers can supply this;
- what is being sourced is complex, therefore it is necessary to work closely with suppliers before they are able to supply;
- limited availability, eg there is limited supply or capacity in the market, or storage and distribution channels introduce risk in supply; and
- there is competitive demand creating scarcity.

Markets may be difficult but it is also possible to create difficulty by the way we source goods. For example, specifying a brand or buying something that is differentiated in some way limits our market choices to only one supplier. Suppliers will always seek to lock us in with added value, a unique bundle of offerings or something that only they can provide that is proprietary to them. Similarly if our brand relies on their brand then there is only one provider. As long as we are aware and stay in control of what happens here then being locked in with one supplier can be acceptable and even beneficial. For example, a PC manufacturer shipping computers with stickers boasting 'Intel inside' has immediately restricted the ability to swap the chip for another. Yet for this critical component, around which the entire machine is designed, with a partnership arrangement in place this arrangement is just fine.

Many companies find themselves in single or limited source supply arrangements they didn't design and realize they lack choice or the ability to switch. Difficulty with respect to the categories or products being sourced therefore makes the supplier important in terms of segmentation. Again here we are only assessing the situation. If difficulty is high and we cannot influence this then some sort of intervention may be needed with the supplier. However, we may be able to reduce difficulty, maybe changing the specification of what we are buying to something more generic in order to open up choice in the market. Here we might need to switch to using a category management approach.

The tools *Portfolio Analysis* and *Day One Analysis* used within category management can help determine difficulty with great insight and these are expanded in full within my first book *Category Management in Purchasing*, which also provides the full category management methodology.

Within the process of segmentation the level of difficulty is assessed by considering the categories, products and services the supplier provides and the degree of difficulty for any of them and where significant or critical areas of spend are 'difficult' then this supplier should score high for this criterion during segmentation.

Alignment between parties

Alignment is a criterion concerned mostly with the degree to which a specific supplier could help us. Alignment can easily be overlooked when considering which suppliers are important, however alignment is very important and misalignment is even more important as such suppliers could hurt us. For example, one of the objectives of the Kellogg Company states 'as a socially responsible company, [we] aim to nourish our consumers, employees, customers, communities and the environment so that they can flourish and thrive' (**www.kelloggcompany.com**). This policy is supported by a range of initiatives including hunger relief (aiming to provide half a billion breakfasts globally by the end of 2016) and a human rights campaign. So if a strategic supplier whose operations were clearly at odds with these ethics was engaged, this would be misaligned and could hurt the business and damage the brand.

Alignment includes alignment of thinking, principles, goals, ethics, culture, ways of working, beliefs and even language (eg the French like to do business with the French, Germans like to do business with Germans and so on) and if our business brand is founded on principles such as sustainability, fair trade, fair wage, diversity and fair working conditions then alignment of our suppliers in this respect is essential.

So, clearly ensuring there is no misalignment that can hurt is important but once we are clear this is the case then the degree to which alignment is important depends upon how we plan to engage with a particular supplier. It is entirely possible and acceptable to have a supplier who is important to us, say because of high spend, but who is not particularly aligned but, crucially, is not misaligned. Yet if we are looking for a strategic partner to work closely with and grow with then alignment of thinking, ways of working and goals become important. There is little point in attempting to develop a strategic collaborative relationship for the long term with a supplier who is going in the opposite direction, as sooner or later the relationship will need to end.

So assessing alignment is about first checking there is no misalignment and, for the small number of suppliers we are contemplating a close relationship with, then assessing alignment.

Assessing alignment requires us to understand the supplier's goals, aspirations, future direction, who they are and how they operate. We may get some idea here by viewing the supplier's web-presence or checking their annual reports; however, deep understanding only really comes by getting close to suppliers, by visiting them, getting to know the principle players, absorbing what they have to say, spending time with them and so on. We will come back to how to do this later.

Suppliers score high on 'alignment' according to the degree of alignment, based upon what we know about them. Any misalignment that could hurt us should be factored into the risk score.

Current importance

Current importance is all the factors that make a supplier important to us today. It includes spend, contractual commitments, importance due to operating location or geographical coverage, the degree to which the supplier knows our business or has know-how about our processes (and therefore has an advantage) and any established relationships that drive obligation or preference. *Current importance* is mostly concerned with the degree to which a supplier can help us, but there is also scope for the supplier to hurt us, for example if they chose to use any unique knowledge of our business to their advantage and our disadvantage (and so this becomes a risk).

Part of this criterion includes how much we spend relative to our overall spend. Spend is often used as a primary segmentation criterion on its own. Whilst this is a good gauge, as it follows that if the spend is high then the exposure of the business to that supplier is significant too. Using *spend* alone can skew the results. One company I worked with determined that Staples, the office supplies company, was of strategic importance due to their very high spend in this area (due to the nature of the company's business). Other than a high spend there was no other basis to have a special relationship with Staples and there was nothing being sourced that could not be sourced elsewhere immediately if needed. *Spend* has its place in segmentation and needs to be considered but as part of a broader more balanced process of segmentation and so it is included within the broader heading of *Current importance*. A supplier providing temporary labour on demand may have a high spend but might otherwise not be important as there are other companies providing this service readily available. However, if this supplier understands our business and is able to provide specialist capabilities where and when needed then the supplier is more important.

Contractual commitments can mean we are locked into using a particular supplier and therefore we need to manage that supplier in some way. We therefore need to understand what these are and at what point in time a contract will end or expire and therefore the timeframe within which such intervention is required.

Suppliers can amass great knowledge or know-how in the course of an engagement and sometimes this can give them power and therefore make them important. One of the main reasons why outsourcing key functions of a business to a third party can fail is when a company outsources a problem for a supplier to fix without good exit provision. Unique supplier know-how or process knowledge can therefore make a supplier important, however this importance might only be so long as this situation remains. If we understand the issue we can begin to develop actions that alleviate the problem and reclaim knowledge and therefore the supplier will become less important and require less intervention. Once again the degree of intervention becomes something that shifts over time.

The importance of current relationships with a supplier should not be underestimated. If established relationships between individuals work well day-to-day then this is important but crucially making any change to these relationships would need careful management.

Suppliers are scored for this criterion based upon an assessment of all the factors that make a supplier important today, the more factors and the greater the importance the higher the score.

Future importance

Future importance is the degree to which a supplier can help us in the future and is the criterion concerned with finding the future heroes. A supplier that is unimportant today could be of great importance in the future and warrant time and energy to develop the right relationship. Similarly suppliers who are important today may not be so tomorrow.

Our future direction and anticipated future spend are key factors here, but so is what the supplier is doing. Future importance is mainly about asking *which suppliers are working on innovations, or heading in a direction, that could help us in future?* If we know this then we can work out how to get close to these suppliers to capitalize on the mutual opportunity. However, knowing this, or indeed where to look, is not that easy.

If we could predict future innovations then they wouldn't be innovations. Suppliers may share some of their future plans and what they are working on, but there will usually be a deeper secret layer that is not readily shared as the supplier will be protecting their competitive advantage. If we know the supplier already then we may have a view here, otherwise future opportunity can require some detective work to find it. Once again this happens by getting close to suppliers and building trust with them. This takes time, and its not just our current suppliers but potential new suppliers also and here we need market research, understanding and data gathering around supplier capabilities. Here the RFI tool can help to solicit information those suppliers identified as having potential capability.

Future opportunity should be determined based upon the fit with what we need for the future. A supplier may be working on the next generation of rocket motors, but if we are in the business of meat processing then the innovation is not going to help us. Therefore we start with our VIPER macro level relationship requirements and ask three questions:

- Which suppliers posses process, technology, know-how, experience, geographic location, capability to help here?
- Which suppliers have a track record of innovating or being the first to do something new?
- Which suppliers could transition into providing what we need (eg posses similar capabilities or operating locations)?

One final component about future importance is supplier willingness. It is easy to assume that suppliers are always willing to participate. This may be the case but not always and energy to develop a collaborative relationship could easily be wasted if the supplier has other ideas. We will return to this point later.

A supplier scores high for future importance if they hold the potential to fulfil a future need we have identified.

The segmentation process

The process of segmentation is the division of an entire supply base into discrete groups according to their importance through the application of the segmentation criteria, applied supplier-by-supplier to arrive at a segmented supply base. Conducting segmentation ideally requires a cross-functional workshop involving carefully selected participants and facilitated discussion and debate. It is not a once only activity, but once done for the first time should be revisited on a regular basis.

Segmentation might seem straightforward; after all, if we have a good set of criteria all we need to do now is apply it to the supply base and figure out who is important. Easy? No, actually this can be one of the hardest steps within SRM and there are three issues that hinder us here:

- The size of the supply base – if there are, say, 10,000 suppliers in total, and we chose to apply the full segmentation criteria to all suppliers then the process would take about four and half months! Clearly unworkable.

- The degree of depth required to do it properly – determining how individual suppliers stack up against criteria such as alignment and future importance requires close and detailed understanding of specific suppliers and marketplaces. Determining risk requires detailed risk mapping. Research and evaluation to support this takes time and resource. If we attempted this across the entire supply base it could take nearly five years!

- The ability to assimilate lots of information to make sound judgements – when organizations segment their supply base there appears to be a tendency to use some sort of mathematical model that sums scores according to all the criteria met. Such approaches are usually flawed or at best sub-optimum as suppliers only end up being regarded as important if they meet multiple criteria. Suppliers that score low but present potentially show-stopping risk could easily be disregarded.

Applying segmentation criteria to an entire supply base with any degree of depth is unworkable and so we need something a bit more pragmatic. Here Pareto principles apply and we need to be able to exclude the vast majority of suppliers we are certain we are not interested in. This is a bit like how sales teams qualify the leads they are going to spend time pursuing where a 'sales funnel' is used to apply certain tests and carry out certain sales activities with a view to a sale emerging. For our supply base we need to adopt a similar funnel approach, and here our segmentation funnel allows us to make a series of 'passes' where different tests are applied to create or qualify the pool of suppliers against whom the full segmentation criteria will later be applied (Figure 4.5).

Segmentation is most successful when it is performed by an assembled group of those individuals who are close to suppliers, understand the organization and are best placed to have an opinion here. A team of five to seven is about right. Allow sufficient time (ideally an entire day) and ideally the session should be facilitated. For each important supplier identified, the scores against the segmentation criteria should be recorded and the outputs of each discussion and debate about each supplier should be captured as we will need to refer back to both later. Figure 4.6 gives an example segmentation score sheet, using a simple 1–5 score for each criterion together with definitions to aid assigning scores.

With the right individuals assembled conduct segmentation as follows:

1 First pass – quick method 'hurt, help or heroes'. Start with the entire supply base and brainstorm *who could hurt us most, who could best help us, who are the heroes?* Use strict brainstorming rules (no discussion or debate, just ideas until it all goes quiet). Record on a flip chart and 'park it' to revisit later. Aim to spend no more than 10 minutes doing this.

2 Second pass – high-spend check. Again, considering the entire supply base, use spend data to determine those suppliers with whom there is a current high spend or high projected spend. Aim to identify the top 50–100 suppliers here. These will be the group we will focus on but bear in mind there could still be suppliers with low spend who present risk and we need to ensure we don't overlook these. Ideally spend data would be available from a corporate system; if not, there are specialist companies who can carry out spend analysis or analysis of purchase orders or payment records can provide data here.

3 Third pass – who is important. Apply the full segmentation criteria in rapid fashion to the suppliers identified during the first two passes; rating each supplier against each criterion based upon the knowledge

FIGURE 4.5 The process of segmentation

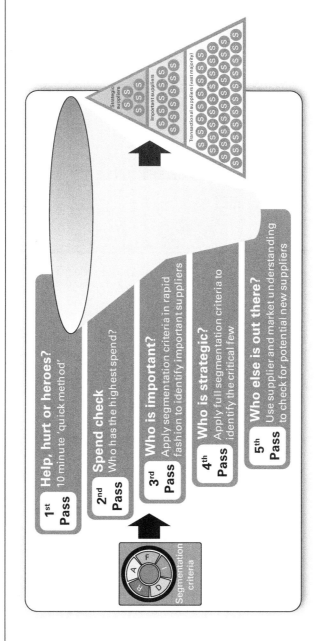

Segmentation criteria

1st Pass
Help, hurt or heroes?
10 minute 'quick method'

2nd Pass
Spend check
Who has the highest spend?

3rd Pass
Who is important?
Apply segmentation criteria in rapid fashion to identify important suppliers

4th Pass
Who is strategic?
Apply full segmentation criteria to identify the critical few

5th Pass
Who else is out there?
Use supplier and market understanding to check for potential new suppliers

Strategic suppliers

Important suppliers

Transactional suppliers (vast majority)

FIGURE 4.6 The segmentation supplier score chart

Supplier Name:

Date:

	1	2	3	4	5
Risk	No discernable risk	Chance of minor risks only	High likelihood of low severity risks occurring with this supplier or in the supply chain	Some likelihood of a high severity risk occurring with this supplier or in the supply chain	Significant likelihood of high severity risk occurring with this supplier or in the supply chain
Alignment	No alignment, conflicting future directions and/or incompatible culture, ethics, policies and ways of working	No apparent misalignment but some aspects of culture, ethics, policies and ways of working are at odds with ours	No apparent misalignment and culture, ethics, policies and ways of working appear compatible	Good degree of alignment of future direction. Compatible culture and ethics, policies and ways of working	Complete alignment of strategic goals, similar culture, ethics and beliefs. Common policies and ways of working
Future importance	No future plans or opportunity with this supplier	Possibility that, with effort, we could unlock future contribution from this supplier	Predicted significant demand from this supplier. Likely high spend in the future	Supplier has potential innovation or know-how that could make a dramatic contribution to our business	Predicted significant demand from this supplier and/or great opportunity for them to make a dramatic contribution to our business
Current importance	Low spend, no real importance	Med-high spend and some contractual commitments	Med-high spend, supplier is important due to location, know-how or established relationships	High spend and contractual obligations	Very high spend. Supplier has contractual obligations and/or is important due to location, know-how or relationships
Difficulty	No difficulty, leverage or acquisition categories and generic, non-complex products. Easy to switch suppliers	Some difficulty of our own creation, eg by our own contracting arrangements. We can switch easily but with effort	Difficult market due to proprietary nature of what we are buying. There is good scope to change this and make the market easier	Difficult market and complexities in what we buy. Difficult but not impossible to switch suppliers	Inability to switch suppliers, little or nothing we can do to change this. Market difficult and/or an essential part of our brand definition

of the group and recording the scores. This pass is about identifying those suppliers who are important or could hurt us, therefore only a superficial assessment of factors such as future importance and alignment are needed at this stage.

4 Fourth pass – who is strategic. Comprehensively apply the full segmentation criteria to the most important suppliers identified during the third pass (perhaps the top 10–20), again recording the scores. Here we are considering who has the potential to significantly help us, or who are the heroes, and any suppliers who could significantly hurt us. Therefore factors such as future importance and alignment need to be considered more deeply. This may involve agreeing fact find actions to verify assumptions made by the group. Aim to identify around 5–10 strategic suppliers in total. If more emerge, challenge the criteria or the way it is being applied. It is possible to conduct the third and fourth pass together in one go.

5 Fifth pass – new suppliers. Until this point segmentation has focused on identifying who is important from our current pool of suppliers. However, if at this stage, and based upon VIPER and what the business needs from the supply base, we either lack something or feel there might be greater opportunity elsewhere in the market, then new suppliers should be considered. This may well involve thorough market research and data gathering actions agreed by the group.

Once all passes are complete, finalize the segmentation and list those suppliers who are important or strategic. Triangulate back with the first pass to check for any suppliers who were initially identified but have not emerged from the detailed segmentation activity. Plan to revisit the list regularly.

Making sense of segmentation

Now that our suppliers are segmented into groups we need to determine the interventions needed for each group. However, in practice, there are degrees of importance and the demarcation lines between one group and another are more blurred (Figure 4.7). Moreover, intervention can take many forms; one size does not fit all so segmentation not only determines who is important, but the outputs from segmentation, and specifically the basis upon which a supplier has been deemed important, determine the degree and nature of intervention required. As we develop approaches for a specific supplier we therefore need to refer back to the basis upon which they were determined to be important. For example, if a supplier is important because there is risk to our brand due to practice in the supply chain then our interventions need to focus on the supply chain (eg through SCM); a supplier who is important due to current knowledge of our business and a high spend might need close management (eg through SM).

FIGURE 4.7   Degrees of importance and blurred demarcations

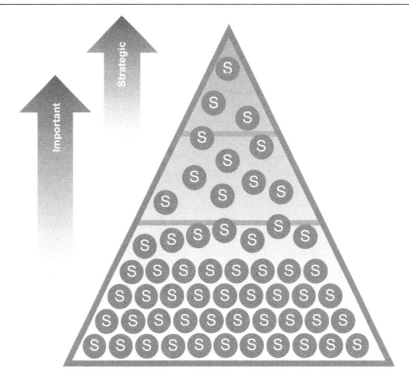

When sat is a room, at the end of a long team-based segmentation workshop, surrounded by flip charts of notes, scores and lists, it is easy to wonder what to do next. It is in fact the discussion and debate amongst the assembled team during the workshop that is the most valuable – the outputs serve as a record of this discussion. Possibly the greatest challenge within segmentation is making sense of these outputs so that the right interventions for specific suppliers can be developed.

The problem is that the segmentation process produces five separate, independent scores for each supplier. Summing these to produce a grand score isn't useful as we could risk excluding a supplier who has a low score overall but yet scores highly against one key criterion such as risk, and therefore requires intervention. Instead our segmentation process must preserve the scores against each criterion for each supplier but we need to be able to assimilate all these scores, across multiple suppliers, in such a way as to prioritize who we should spend time with.

It is possible that a complex mathematical model could do this, however I don't believe I have ever seen one that is completely effective. Segmentation in fact requires good old brainpower and judgement informed by a something that allows us to assimilate and process vast amounts of information. This is not a unique problem; marketeers face similar issues when attempting to analyse a competitor landscape or compare product attributes, so they use visual tools. Typically where complex variables and information needs to be assimilated visual tools tend to be most effective at providing a basis for human judgement. Visual representations of the individual suppliers' evaluations against the criteria help to allow rapid multi-supplier evaluation, ideally performed in a carefully chosen group, to determine who is important and why. This is simple to do and if we take our segmentation score charts and mark up the scores on each, then join these together it creates a unique shape. Figure 4.8 show two suppliers with two very different shapes created during segmentation. On the left, an outsourced partner with high spend who is important today and for the future; on the right, a supplier who presents a significant degree of risk to us and where there is high spend. So which one should we spend time with? Well actually both, but in different ways: for one we need to build a relationship and the other we need to assess and manage risk. The point here is that using a visual method allows us to lay out all the suppliers in front of us and compare one to another to decide who needs what intervention.

There are many other types of graphical representation that could be used here with the segmentation scores and Figure 4.9 shows some examples. A good old bar chart or radar diagram are sound and easily accessible using Excel or similar; however, I favour the 'coxcomb graphic', apparently first used by Florence Nightingale to illustrate levels of mortality over time, but increasingly popular with statisticians and communication experts looking for a good 'infographic'.

Determining intervention and the right relationship

The final step within segmentation is to determine the right relationship for our important suppliers and what intervention is needed matched against available resources. Interventions may not necessarily be permanent and may only be needed for a defined period of time with some suppliers, for example to coincide with contract termination or expiry.

Supply base intervention mapping

By converting supplier segmentation scores into visual representations we can conduct multiple dimension comparison across many suppliers. Here a team-based approach seems to be the most effective means to accomplish this.

Supply base intervention mapping (Figure 4.10) provides a means to use a visual, team-based approach to determine what intervention is needed. It works by drawing out a series of 'territories' where we can place individual suppliers and we do this according to four dimensions: the degree of potential they have to either *hurt* or *help* us (or both), whether they are a *hero* and the

FIGURE 4.8 Example supplier segmentation score outputs with segmentation 'shape' plotted

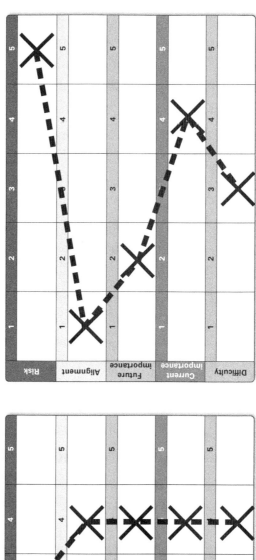
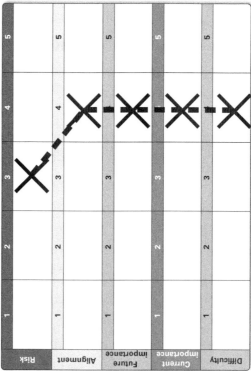

FIGURE 4.9 Examples of other visual indicators for segmentation scores

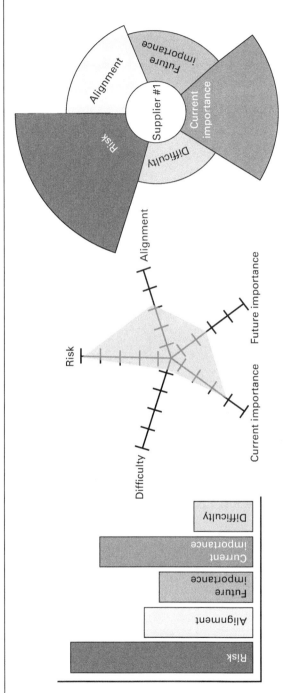

FIGURE 4.10 The supply base intervention map

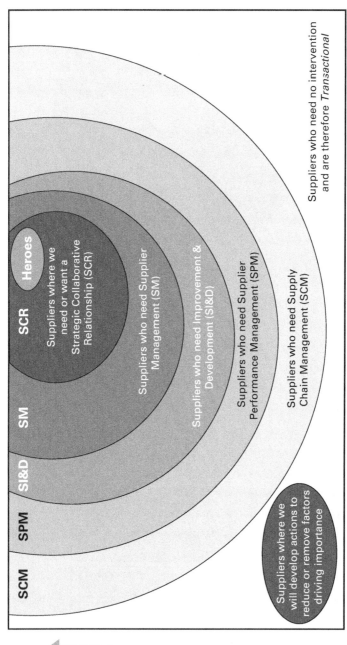

SCM   SPM   SI&D   SM   SCR   Heroes

Suppliers where we need or want a Strategic Collaborative Relationship (SCR)

Suppliers who need Supplier Management (SM)

Suppliers who need Improvement & Development (SI&D)

Suppliers who need Supplier Performance Management (SPM)

Suppliers who need Supply Chain Management (SCM)

Suppliers where we will develop actions to reduce or remove factors driving importance

Suppliers who need no intervention and are therefore *Transactional*

Degree to which a supplier could hurt or help us

Help

Hurt

Degree of business impact (or potential impact)

degree of potential impact they could have (either positively or negatively). Ideally this is something we do on a large sheet of brown paper so our segmentation team can gather around and work on the map.

Each of the territories relates to the different types of supplier intervention. The aim is to plot all the important and strategic suppliers onto the map, placing them in a territory according to the axis and our segmentation scores and outputs for each supplier and the basis upon which we determined the supplier to be important. This is most effective if the summary scores for each supplier are available in a visual form (eg a bar graph or coxcomb graphic), perhaps even cut out so they can be stuck onto the paper by the group and repositioned as needed (Figure 4.11). Equipped with a large intervention map, and a stack of graphical supplier segmentation scores ready to be stuck on, the team can then decide where to place each supplier, and therefore determine what intervention is needed. In a world where most of what we do is online or powered by an 'app', sticking cut-out graphs might seem a bit dated. It is not and it is actually a very powerful approach to secure consensus because it is the discussion and debate during this process that is most important and using a visual means that all can participate in is key here. This discussion might lead to a number of additional outcomes other than simply placing a supplier on the map and here it might be appropriate to include additional notes against each supplier:

- A supplier previously regarded as important might end up not actually needing intervention.
- A supplier might warrant more than one type of intervention.
- We might decide we can negate the need for intervention by developing actions to remove importance, eg if importance is due to *difficulty*, then we might be able to open up choice by changing specification or moving to generic alternatives. There is a special area on the bottom left of the map for these.

Finally, with a complete map it might be appropriate to reposition suppliers according to resources available and then to prioritize how quickly we intend to pursue each intervention. Again this should be done by a team, simply by moving suppliers around on the map until there is consensus. Then the entire map should be converted into an *SRM Roadmap*.

SRM roadmap

The SRM roadmap is a short to medium term programme plan that defines all the specific interventions that will be initiated and when. It is based upon the resources that are available but it also defines the timing of any required interventions with suppliers. A new supplier or one where we are seeking to develop a collaborative relationship will require much energy. Ongoing management of performance for a repeat requirement requires a fairly 'steady state' approach. The need for an intervention might also end or reduce.

FIGURE 4.11 An example supply base intervention map

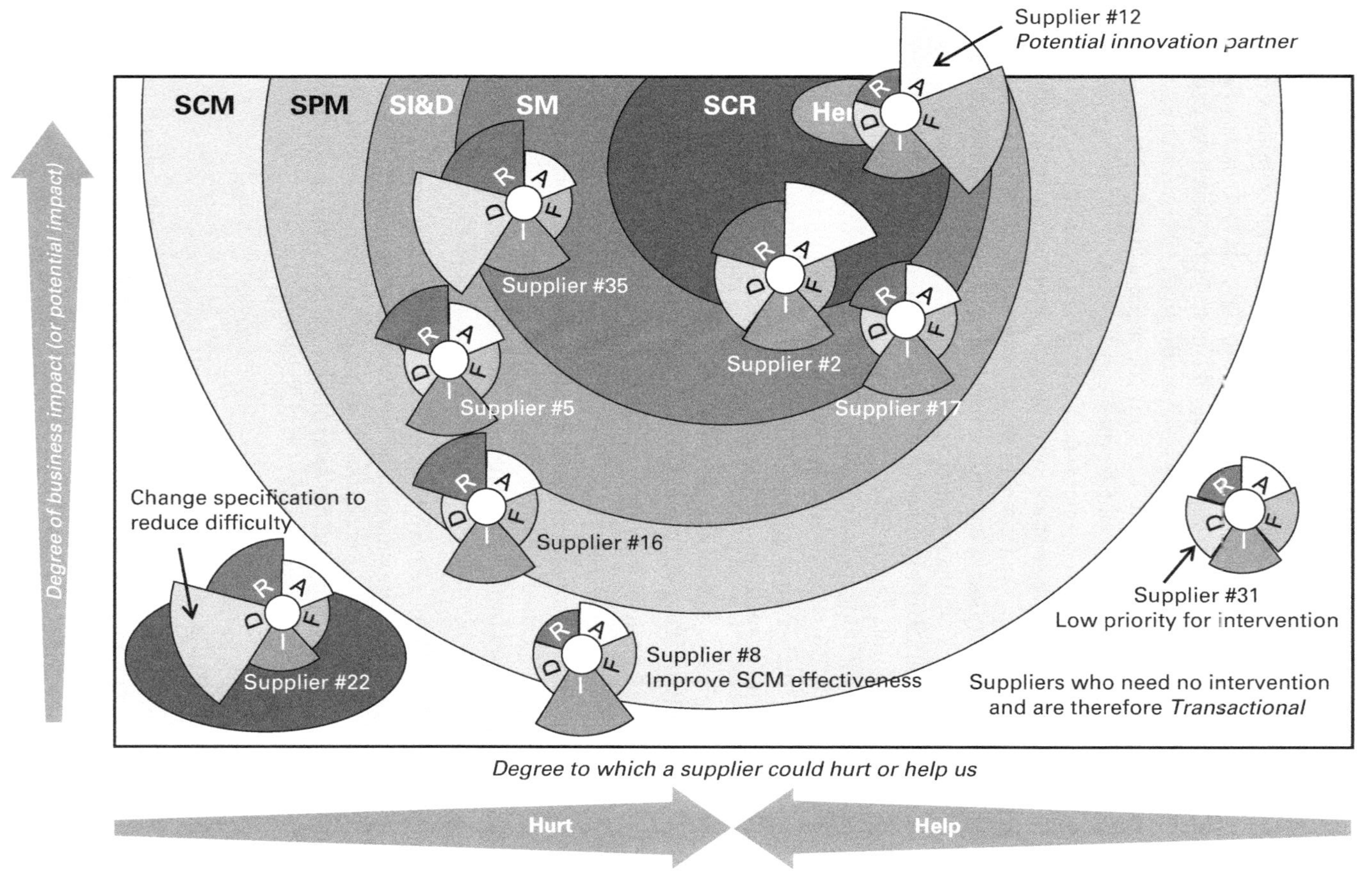

Supplier #12
Potential innovation partner

Supplier #31
Low priority for intervention

Suppliers who need no intervention
and are therefore *Transactional*

SCR

SM

SI&D

SPM

SCM

Help

Held

Supplier #2

Supplier #17

Supplier #35

Supplier #5

Supplier #16

Supplier #8
Improve SCM effectiveness

Change specification to
reduce difficulty

Supplier #22

Degree to which a supplier could hurt or help us

Hurt

Degree of business impact (or potential impact)

For example, if we are in a single source scenario with a supplier due to the specification we have defined then we may need to have a relationship with that supplier. If we change our specification to make our requirement more generic and therefore open up the market then we may no longer need the intervention we had before. A contract expiry may also drive a similar reduction in need for intervention.

The SRM roadmap is therefore a vehicle to define what we will do, with whom and for how long and recognizes there are three states of supplier intervention: *initialization*, *steady state* and *concluding*. Figure 4.12 gives an example of an SRM roadmap and this should be part of a broader approach to manage outsourcing projects such as category management initiatives as part of governance (we will return to that later).

Keeping the transactional suppliers at 'arm's length'

So far the thousands of transactional suppliers segmentation leaves us with have had little mention. That is because SRM is really unconcerned with these suppliers beyond ensuring these suppliers fulfil what they are contracted to do. The process of segmentation seeks to identify and confirm suppliers who are important or even strategic, so what about the rest? If we are clear these suppliers hold no special importance then the organization needs to put in place arrangements to manage this spend effectively and efficiently with the minimum of intervention. This might include:

- Minimizing the need for intervention – all suppliers will demand time and request meetings; however, if those in the organization who interface with suppliers clearly understand who they should, and should not, be spending time with, then saying 'no' to supplier requests becomes recognized good practice.
- Catalogue buying – simple but controlled process for people across an organization to buy from suppliers. Traditionally, organizations with decentralized purchasing found that people with the authority to place an order would do so with the, often local, suppliers they favoured, affording little overall control over the organization's procurement. Today, with modern Enterprise Resource Planning (ERP) systems, the use of catalogue buying enables simple ordering to an agreed type and specification
- Purchasing cards (P-Cards) – like a credit or charge card but billed to the company and often with limitations on where it can be used. It can cost a big organization anything from \$100–\$300 to raise a purchase order and process a payment. P-Cards can reduce this dramatically.
- Clear specifications and statements of work – company standards that promote generic rather than proprietary products or services where possible.

FIGURE 4.12 An example of an SRM roadmap

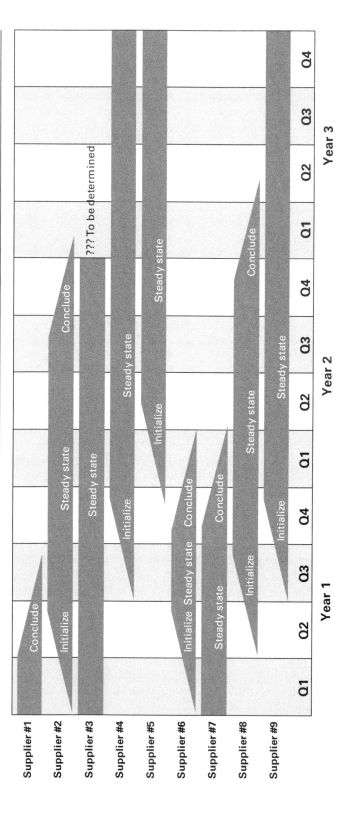

- Teach the organization – the vast majority of people in organizations have never been taught how to manage and interface with suppliers; an omission suppliers will readily exploit. A simple 'do's and don'ts' for anyone engaging with suppliers can make a wealth of difference.

Segmentation and the pillars of SRM

So segmentation is driven by our goals, available resources and supply market possibilities. This informs how we develop our segmentation criteria, which is then applied using a series of different passes to arrive at a shortlist of suppliers who are deemed important. From here we determine the intervention(s) we need as part of an overarching SRM approach. With this, the music is written ready for our orchestra of SRM to play. Our segmentation process therefore underpins and enables the key components of SRM as defined in the three pillars and we can now further build our picture that defines SRM in Figure 4.13.

FIGURE 4.13   Segmentation and the three pillars of SRM

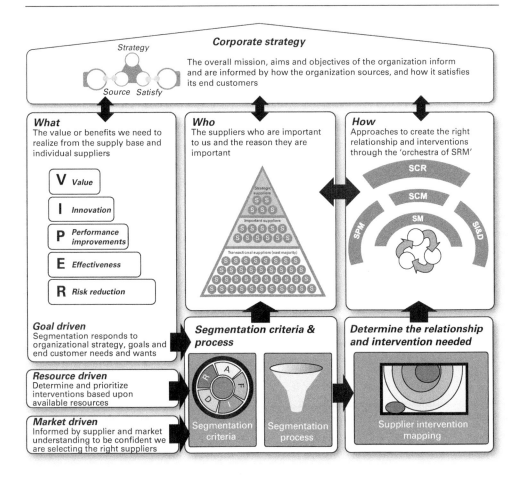

Supplier performance measurement

05

In this chapter we begin to explore specific interventions appropriate for important, and possibly strategic, suppliers. We explore what supplier performance measurement is, types of measurement and ways to measure a supplier or groups of suppliers effectively in a way that produces meaningful results.

PATHWAY QUESTIONS ADDRESSED IN THIS CHAPTER

4 How are our suppliers performing?

5 Are we getting the most from our suppliers and how can we be sure?

Why measure?

It is easy to overlook the importance of measurement in our lives and the way we use measures to inform our decisions in order to protect and enrich us in everything we do. Measurement is a cornerstone of life; without it the moon landing might have undershot, Marconi may not have picked up the first transatlantic radio signal and The Pyramids might not be pyramids. Measurement ensures we take just the right amount of medication, that we know whether or not we need to stop for gas at the next gas station, that clothes will fit us and so on. In fact, in our personal lives we are pretty good at knowing just what measures to use and then using these measures to direct and improve our lives. We are able to make quick judgements about which size pack on the supermarket shelf offers greatest value for money, about the car that has the least environmental impact or the school that is best for our kids based upon league tables of past results. We do this without thinking about it, that is until the gas gauge gets stuck on our car and we find ourselves sitting by the roadside waiting for help to arrive.

Supplier performance is a business measure

In purchasing we seem to be very keen to measure things. Traditionally purchasing functions have concentrated on measuring the overall contribution of purchasing function using umbrella metrics such as price savings achieved or other efficiency based measures (Cousins *et al*, 2008). This is good, especially if the organization needs purchasing to demonstrate how it adds value. Yet other indirect functions typically don't seem to be held quite so accountable; I don't know of too many legal functions that need to demonstrate how good their contracts are or HR functions required to prove just how effective they are at implementing policy. It seems purchasing still has something to prove here and perhaps needs to increase its accountability in order to strengthen its position at the board of directors, leaving purchasing professionals searching for tools to measure purchasing performance (Lardenoije *et al*, 2005). Purchasing might typically need to account for what it does through financial efficiency indicators such as:

- *Purchase Price Variance (PPV)* – a measure of the difference between what the organization budgets for cost of third party spend and what it actually spends. PPV is a financial measure that helps organizations budget and plan.

- *Price savings* – a measure of reduction against previous spend, again a variant of PPV but linking the reduction to some form of intervention.

- *Cost savings* – a similar measure by focusing on more than acquisition price but cost to the organization, perhaps over the life of the product/service.

- *Contribution to EBITDA (Earnings Before Income Tax, Depreciation and Amortization)* – another variant of PPV and price savings – if purchasing intervention can directly reduce price and cost then this reduction will positively impact the bottom line profit.

- *Cash retention* – through negotiating payment terms that favour the organization.

- *Return on Investment (RoI)* – savings and benefits against cost of purchasing function.

- *Cost of inventory* – where stockholding is part of the business; the value of stock and cost to hold and manage it.

However, efficiency measures alone do not reflect the full extent of purchasing activities, in fact the preoccupation with such measures may detract from more useful indications of how purchasing performs (Cousins *et al*, 2008). Furthermore, these typical measures are largely financial and would inform a wider business financial management system.

Crucially though, measuring the performance of the purchasing function does not necessarily ensure we are measuring supplier performance. It may follow that the measures for the purchasing function flow down to suppliers who are then required to demonstrate savings or cash retention, but alone these measures serve only to enable the purchasing function to hit targets. However, suppliers don't typically serve a purchasing function, they serve an entire business and have relationships and stakeholders across the entire firm. Other parts of the business are interested in supplier performance and so might look to purchasing to measure the supplier in other areas such as delivery or quality compliance.

Supplier performance measurement is therefore distinct from purchasing function measurement and so is a business measurement approach not a purchasing function approach, but likely to be coordinated by the purchasing function. It may include measures of purchasing efficiency but together with wider business measures too. Adopting the mindset that supplier performance is a 'business measure' not just a purchasing measure is important to ensure we develop the right approach. It helps shift our focus to the wider organization and demands cross-functional involvement and engagement in order for supplier measurement to be effective for the entire organization.

Organizations measure many things, and each function has its own suite of measures that help demonstrate effective contribution overall and suppliers, the supply chain and purchasing are part of the big measurement story. Figure 5.1 shows some of the common measures used across an organization.

Why measure supplier performance?

A worthy question to ask because whilst some supplier measurement is essential to guide outcomes, it is equally possible there is no benefit to be served by measuring the performance of a supplier and therefore no point in expending the energy.

As individuals and purchasing professionals it seems we are conditioned to believe that when we engage a supplier who is important that we must measure them, and measure as many things as we can. Across the many companies I've worked with, I find that people like to proudly demonstrate their measurement system; perhaps boasting comprehensive supplier scorecards with as many as 20 or 30 measures or indicators on them. Others who lack this will usually claim to be working towards such a system.

It seems there is a commonly held belief, reinforced by some textbooks and training, that best practice means having an extensive regime of supplier measurement with detailed scorecards covering wide and varied aspects of

FIGURE 5.1 Common measures used across an organization

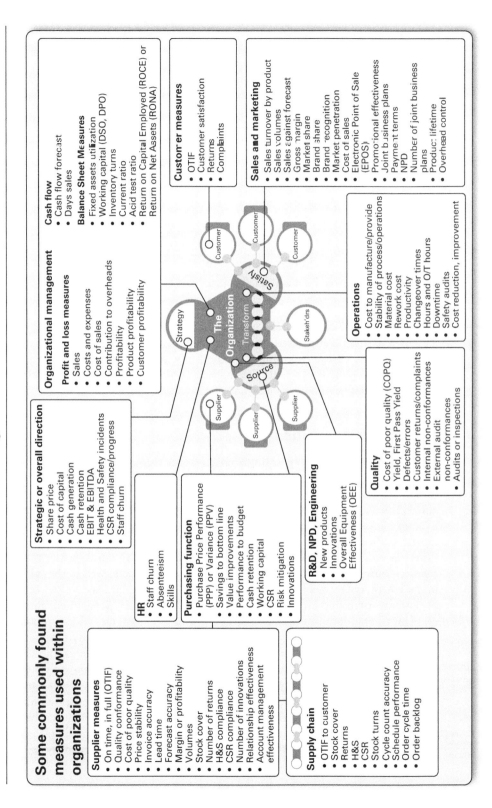

Some commonly found measures used within organizations

Supplier measures
- On time, in full (OTIF)
- Quality conformance
- Cost of poor quality
- Price stability
- Invoice accuracy
- Lead time
- Forecast accuracy
- Margin or profitability
- Volumes
- Stock cover
- Number of returns
- H&S compliance
- CSR compliance
- Number of innovations
- Relationship effectiveness
- Account management effectiveness

HR
- Staff churn
- Absenteeism
- Skills

Purchasing function
- Purchase Price Performance (PPP) or Variance (PPV)
- Savings to bottom line
- Value improvements
- Performance to budget
- Cash retention
- Working capital
- CSR
- Risk mitigation
- Innovations

R&D, NPD, Engineering
- New products
- Innovations
- Overall Equipment Effectiveness (OEE)

Supply chain
- OTIF to customer
- Stock cover
- Returns
- H&S
- CSR
- Stock turns
- Cycle count accuracy
- Schedule performance
- Order cycle time
- Order backlog

Quality
- Cost of poor quality (COPQ)
- Yield, First Pass Yield
- Defects/errors
- Customer returns/complaints
- Internal non-conformances
- External audit non-conformances
- Audits or inspections

Operations
- Cost to manufacture/provide
- Stability of process/operations
- Material cost
- Rework cost
- Productivity
- Changeover times
- Hours and O/T hours
- Downtime
- Safety audits
- Cost reduction, improvement

Strategic or overall direction
- Share price
- Cost of capital
- Cash generation
- Cash retention
- EBIT & EBITDA
- Health and Safety incidents
- CSR compliance/progress
- Staff churn

Organizational management

Profit and loss measures
- Sales
- Costs and expenses
- Cost of sales
- Contribution to overheads
- Profitability
- Product profitability
- Customer profitability

Cash flow
- Cash flow forecast
- Days sales

Balance Sheet Measures
- Fixed assets utilization
- Working capital (DSO, DPO)
- Inventory turns
- Current ratio
- Acid test ratio
- Return on Capital Employed (ROCE) or Return on Net Assets (RONA)

Customer measures
- OTIF
- Customer satisfaction
- Returns
- Complaints

Sales and marketing
- Sales turnover by product
- Sales volumes
- Sales against forecast
- Gross margin
- Market share
- Brand recognition
- Market penetration
- Cost of sales
- Electronic Point of Sale (EPOS)
- Promotional effectiveness
- Joint business plans
- Payment terms
- NPD
- Number of joint business plans
- Product lifetime
- Overhead control

supplier performance and that the ready availability of every measure you could ever need will in some way make performance better. This is not the case.

When presented with a comprehensive supplier scorecard I find that one of the hardest questions for purchasing people to answer is 'so why do you measure these things?' or 'how does measuring these things add value?' Sometimes there are good answers, but often people respond by searching for a reason rather than stating what they believe and know. It seems that supplier measurement systems spring up in purchasing because:

- books on the subject advocate doing this;
- my boss wants me to demonstrate performance;
- belief that an important supplier must have a scorecard;
- everyone else has scorecards with lots of measures on them;
- if you measure something then it improves the outcome;
- everybody needs a dashboard right?
- ease of measurement – if something is easy to measure we will probably end up measuring it.

So why measure? Well, measurement is a vital component to guide an organization and its various enabling functions towards its overall goals. This includes measurement of the purchasing function and some supplier activities but it is important to ensure the right things are being measured.

You are what you measure

So the old adage goes, suggesting that if we measure something then that will in some way drive outcomes. This is true to some extent – if we measure something we tend to do something about what we find. Indeed Cunningham and Fiume (2003) suggest that measurement affects behaviour. We see this in action in our daily lives when we look at how fast we are driving or stand on the bathroom scales in the morning. The same is true within organizations but it doesn't follow that measurement drives behaviour to achieve the required outcomes; rather it drives behaviour to hit targets. Within the NHS in the UK there is a healthcare target that stipulates that 'at least 98 per cent of patients attending an Accident and Emergency (A&E) department must be seen, treated, admitted or discharged in under four hours'. I can report that on every occasion where I have had to take a member of my family to A&E the hospital has hit this target: we have indeed been *seen* within the four hours, but by a triage nurse who has had a quick look, made an initial assessment and sent us away to await a doctor's availability. *Treatment and discharge* comes perhaps five, six or seven hours later. Yet this hospital, like others across the UK is hitting their targets and it is the measure, rather than the patient outcome, that drives behaviour. Cunningham and Fiume (2003) suggest there are three ways to get better figures within a measurement system:

We can improve the system, distort the system – get the required results at the expense of other results – or distort the figures. Therefore if a supplier is managed using a comprehensive suite of measures the supplier will organize itself to hit the targets. Great if these fully articulate the entirety of outcomes required of the supplier, but in practice there is much more potential to be had from some supplier relationships than target hitting and so measurement alone may not be enough. Suppliers will focus on measures if that is how you mange them, even more so if they are contractual – nothing focuses a supplier like a contractual term! If a construction contractor signs up to a penalty term in a contract for late delivery or being over budget then they will orchestrate their entire efforts to achieve this first and foremost. This is a good thing right? It certainly drives the required results and hits the target, but does it always achieve the right outcomes? Perhaps, but it is also likely to focus the supplier into finding ways to undermine the arrangement by watching for any sort of unplanned event or change in requirements that might allow them to suggest 'things have changed' and therefore transfer the blame for not hitting a target back to something the client did. Hitting targets and meeting contractual obligations can easily become the primary driver and motivator leaving little incentive for collaboration or maximizing mutual benefits. Therefore the design of any measurement system with a supplier must consider what is actually needed from a supplier. You are what you measure? Yes and if you measure the wrong things or too many things with a supplier then you will get what you measure.

You are what you measure is relevant to us also. If our focus is having lots of measurement information about suppliers made available to us then our energy will be directed to doing this. Maybe this is just what is needed, or maybe that energy might be better served working more closely with a supplier to move something forward.

If suppliers are managed using a extensive scorecard of measures, then their behaviour and indeed the organization's behaviour will centre around achieving these measures. I worked with an organization where the CEO had decreed that he wanted to see 'all suppliers of direct material achieve 99 per cent on-time delivery'. Buy why? Simply his background was high-volume production where on-time in full delivery was critical and he believed that measurement was an essential part of achieving this. However, in this organization the purchasing team responded by directing resources at putting the necessary systems in place and working with suppliers to hit the target. Yet the company was not an automotive business, or one where the production line would stop if one component was missing; in fact most of their work was project related and whilst a late delivery would be a problem, it would usually be a problem that could be accommodated within the overall timeline of the project or by switching project priorities. There was in fact no real need for 99 per cent on-time delivery from all suppliers and the effort to hit the target prevented the firm working on more value-adding activities elsewhere.

A further common reason for measuring something is ease of obtaining good quality data and measurements. Hughes (2005) suggests 'Whatever you can measure most easily and accurately is what you end up measuring.' Some measures are easier than others to obtain, and if something is easy then why not do it? Especially if we believe it helps. It is easy to measure things where there are visible tangibles or available data; on-time, in full delivery performance, number of people served per session, conformance to specification. It is much harder to measure how customers feel, how keen they are to recommend us or how well a supplier relationship is helping us innovate. It is these latter, and more difficult measures that can sometimes be most useful. The other issue with measuring because it is easy is, once again, when you measure something you tend to then want to do something about it. It is easy to end up committing resources just because we have measured something. It is easy to demand that a supplier provides a monthly report of certain performance metrics, the report might somehow give us confidence or make us believe we are doing what we should be doing, but what is easy for us will have a cost somewhere and could prevent more benefit through doing something else.

It would be easy at this point to think that maybe measurement serves no useful purpose and we should give up. This is incorrect as measurement can be both essential and helpful, but to be so, we must consider carefully what we measure and the way we measure, but also how these measures can be used to drive the outcomes we strive after.

Open and closed loop measurement

Measurement must have a purpose. Measurement is not an end in itself, but a tool for more effective management (Amaratunga and Baldry, 2002). Even with good measures in place, sharing the information, interpreting them, knowing how to respond, being able to convince others and having the ability to take action all present challenge. It is all too easy to design a measurement regime that will consume great energy but it is harder to design one that is effective. If resources are precious then this is a problem suggesting measurement needs to be focused and it needs to have clear purpose and add value. This is true for measurement within organizations at large, but also for the way we measure supplier performance.

Any system of measurement needs to be developed with a purpose in mind; a reason to measure but also including how the measures are acted upon. If the purpose of measurement is academic, to see how we did, then an *open loop* system is enough (Figure 5.2). If a child runs a race at school and is the third fastest then gets a certificate that describes the achievement, this is a measure of her ability on that day, it is a record of achievement and something to be proud of, but it is no more than that. In an open loop measurement system, the measure is just that – a measure and one that doesn't influence future outcomes.

FIGURE 5.2   Open loop measurement system

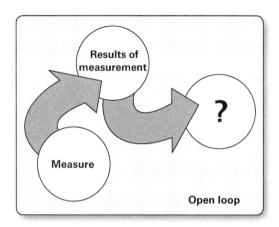

If the same child decides she wants to win the race next time and works to try and be able to run faster then the child has used the measure as a basis to drive improvement. Athletes will train in this way; measuring their time then responding by training harder, adapting technique, measuring again and so on; creating a continuous feedback and correct or improve loop so that measurement is used to drive action to improve future outcomes which are then measured again. This is a *closed loop* measurement system (Figure 5.3) and is the basis for any effective measurement or control system.

FIGURE 5.3   Closed loop measurement system

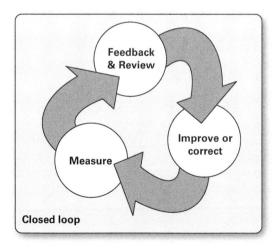

Measure is the arrangements for measurement of the right things at the right time. *Feedback and review* is the way these measures are accessed, outputted, presented, and shared and digested to ensure the right response and *Improve and correct* is the specific actions in response to the measures. Together these three steps within a circular process define supplier performance measurement (SPM) and form an integral component of supplier management (SM). In this and the next chapter we shall explore *Measure* and *Feedback and Review*. In Chapters 7 and 8 we will deal with *Improve and correct*.

Introducing SPM

SPM is part of an overall SRM approach and is concerned with the arrangement to measure individual and collective supplier performance and to use the results to drive appropriate interventions and improve outcomes with suppliers in line with organizational goals.

Once again we see different terminology in this space. Gordon (2008) defines SPM as supplier performance *management* (instead of measurement) and defines it as 'The process of evaluating, measuring and monitoring supplier performance and supplier's business processes and practices for the purposes of reducing costs, mitigating risk, and driving continuous improvement'. This is a good definition. Note that it suggests we should measure both suppliers' capability and outputs. However, it misses the role measurement can play in enabling a supplier to help us work towards specific goals (as opposed to continuous improvement from a current position). Reducing costs, mitigating risks and driving continuous improvement are good aims, but assume this is what an organization needs. Instead, the purpose of SPM as a business-wide approach is to support the achievement of business goals, which could be different. Furthermore, for any SPM approach to succeed and add value it must include a degree of targeting of resources and effort to those suppliers who are important in some way and with different levels of measurement within these. Therefore SPM is defined as:

> The process of targeted evaluation, measuring and monitoring of supplier performance and supplier's business processes and practices for the purposes of achieving desired business outcomes and goals.

Implied within this definition is the fact that measures drive action (or there would be no purpose). SPM must therefore be part of a wider SM regime. Therefore it doesn't matter whether we call it supplier performance *measurement* or *management* as both mean the same thing and thankfully share the same acronym; so we all stand a good chance of knowing what we are talking about when we discuss SPM.

One size does not fit all

There are different supplier performance measurement approaches we could adopt and the relevance or usefulness of each depends upon how important the supplier is. One size does not fit all! Key to SPM is the concept of the right amount of measurement, of the right things, used in a way that helps achieve the required outcomes. A problematic vendor may need goods or services to be checked before acceptance to ensure we have got what we need; other suppliers may only need some form of measurement when something goes wrong. Yet for some suppliers an ongoing regime of measurement and review of various measures may be needed or desirable to help us reach our goals. There are in fact four degrees of measurement we could adopt. The degree of measurement needed typically, but not always, correlates with the degree of importance of a supplier (Figure 5.4). These are:

- *Don't measure* – appropriate for the vast majority of transactional suppliers.

- *Measurement by exception* – measure only when things go wrong, for example a supplier becomes problematic and so we start measuring their performance or measure when there is a problem or cause for concern in order to understand and fix the issue.

- *Compliance measurement* – regular measurement of one or more parameters to verify compliance against a defined level of supplier performance. Compliance measurement typically takes place at the point of goods delivery or service provision so there is a facility to reject anything that does not comply beforehand. Arguably the process of compliance measurement is more checking than measurement, however there may be a measurement dimension, for example in a safety critical industry certain raw materials may need to be measured against key parameters. Compliance measurement may use sampling to check a defined percentage of an overall batch, consignment or service provide by a supplier. It may be a single event or ongoing regular and repeat activities in which case maintaining a record of past performance might enable sample sizes to be varied according to overall performance trends.

- *Multiple parameter, past performance* – the selection and presentation of measures across multiple parameters that collectively represent a supplier's performance to date. This type of measurement approach is backward looking, considering past performance but also identifying trends to help guide decision making.

- *Measuring progress towards joint goals* – a measurement system based upon determining the distance from and the degree of progress towards joint goals. Such a system will use measures of past performance but interpreted to create leading indicators. In fact best practice performance measurement is about linking supplier

FIGURE 5.4 Measurement approaches according to supplier importance

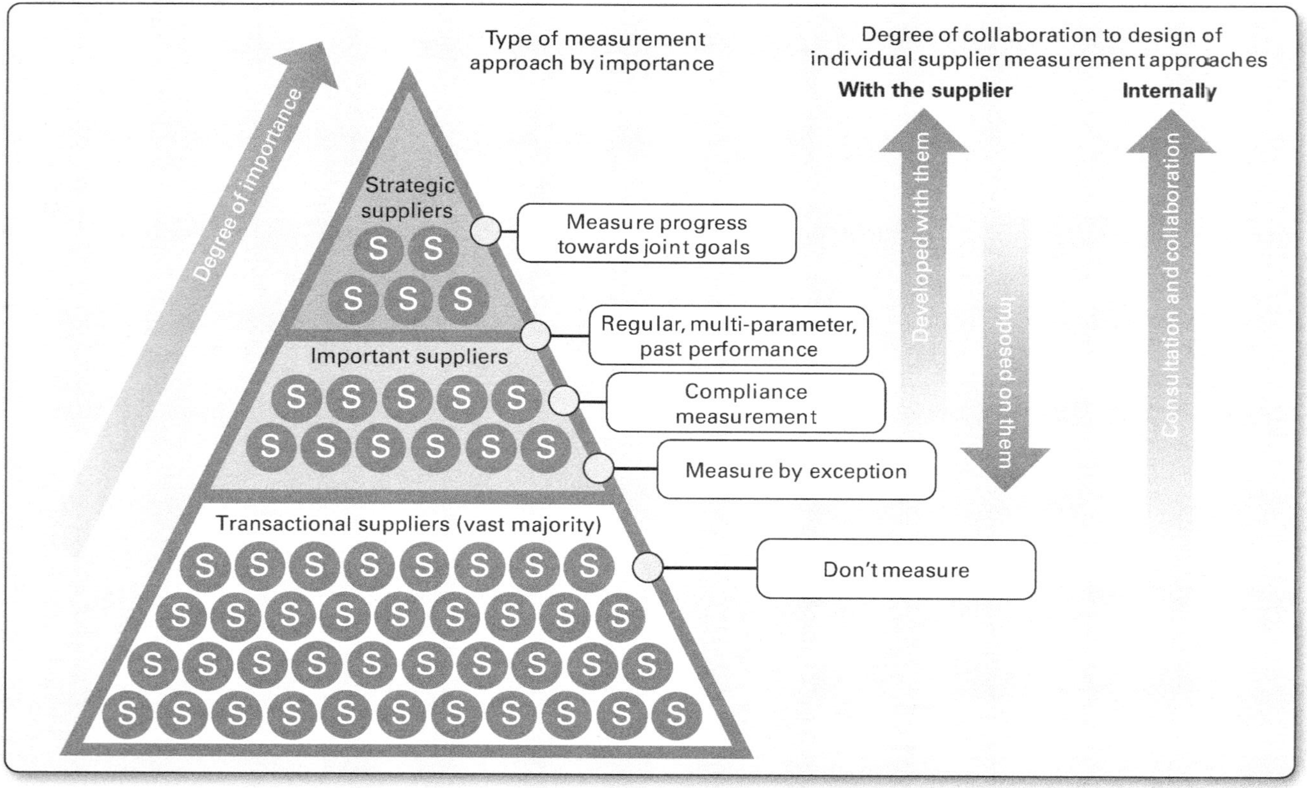

Type of measurement approach by importance

Degree of collaboration to design of individual supplier measurement approaches

With the supplier   **Internally**

Developed with them

Imposed on them

Consultation and collaboration

Measure progress towards joint goals

Regular, multi-parameter, past performance

Compliance measurement

Measure by exception

Don't measure

Strategic suppliers

Important suppliers

Transactional suppliers (vast majority)

Degree of importance

performance to our customer performance (*sourcing* and satisfying) so that if we do well the supplier knows about it and the supplier can then be measured based upon how they are contributing to our overall success.

The degree of collaboration needed to design the measurement system changes with importance too. For a supplier where we need compliance measurement, or measurement by exception, these would typically be measures we determine and impose; *this is what we expect yet this is what you are providing.* This is entirely appropriate for many important suppliers, but not all as such imposing measures provides scope for dispute and will only drive the behaviour needed to satisfy measures. For the most important and strategic suppliers effective measurement requires collaboration and therefore the joint development and agreement of the measurement system; *this is what we agree and we will work together to get there.* Collaboration is not limited to that with the supplier, but with internal stakeholders also.

Common performance measurement approaches

Supplier performance measurement could be stand alone, but where the wider organization has an established performance measurement system in place it should integrate with or at least inform this. Therefore, before we can explore SPM further, we first need to explore the common approaches for organizational performance measurement as any SPM system would naturally form part of this.

Measurement is a vital component to enable organizations to function, and for others to determine how well the organization is functioning. Indeed the strength of entire economies is determined by examining collective performance of groups of companies. Where measures are essential to protect and comply, organizations tend to be pretty good at ensuring the necessary arrangements are in place, after all the risk of not doing this is too great. However, when it comes to measuring less tangible things, the use of effective measurement systems becomes harder to find within firms. Ask senior individuals within a business how effective the organization is at, say, responding to and aligning itself to corporate strategy and they may well struggle to point to any robust or definitive measures here beyond standard financial management information.

Whilst most organizations will use measurement of some sort, effective measurement, which adds value, is often harder to find. The problem is it is easy to measure the wrong things, to measure too many things, to not measure enough or only measure what has happened not what is happening. Add to this the fact that multiple things need to come together to make an organization successful: people, processes, customers, funding, infrastructure and of course suppliers and knowing what and how to measure efficiently becomes a challenge.

Neely *et al* (1995) define performance measurement in organizations as 'the process of quantifying both the efficiency and effectiveness of actions' whilst Dumond (1994) suggests it is necessary 'to support the achievement of goals with the intent to motivate, guide and improve an individual's decision making'. Performance measurement is the way firms determine, on an ongoing basis, that they have the capability to prevail and achieve. The concept has been around for over a century now and originated as accounting systems, mostly developed in the early 1900s to support manufacturing products in batches (Cunningham and Fieume, 2003). Since then measures based upon financial accounting have been the primary means by which organizations have understood and corrected performance. The shortcomings of these existing 'finance only' type approaches are well documented (Kaplan and Norton, 1996; Neely *et al*, 1995; Johnson and Kaplan, 1987; Dixon *et al*, 1990). So for performance measurement to be effective it must consider more than financial measures.

There are many different approaches for organization-wide measurement as well as for the purchasing function or for individual supplier relationships. I will explore eight models or methods that seem to be commonplace. These are top down measurement, the Balanced Scorecard, the Business Excellence Model, the Dashboard, the Performance Prism, the Results and Determinants Framework, crowd measurement and good old gut instinct. I will explore each in turn. Crucially these are approaches for measurement for an entire organization and it is important to explore these in order to figure out how supplier and supply base related measures might integrate in each case.

Top down measurement

In Chapter 3 we considered the role of SRM to connect supply base possibilities with corporate goals so as to inform and be informed by the strategy of the organization. Johnson and Scholes (1993) provide possibly the most commonly accepted model for structuring an organization to succeed. Here the overall direction of the business, articulated within a *mission statement* that is then translated into high-level goals, measurable objectives. These then cascade down through the organization so that each function is then organized with goals, measures and controls that support, align with and contribute to achieving the high-level goals. The Lynch and Cross (1991) Performance Pyramid System advocates a similar approach where strategic goals cascade down through the organization with a reverse flow of information upwards. This model, however, does not directly recognize the contribution of the supply base.

The concept of top down measurement systems is to connect organizational goals to operational activities and work by taking what the organization wants to achieve and developing goals at each level, with measures and

FIGURE 5.5   Top down performance measurement

feedback upwards. Here supplier performance becomes one of the measures alongside internal measurement and customer satisfaction (Figure 5.5).

This is how many companies operate and is possibly the easiest system to put into action, presumably accounting for its widespread use. It assumes a degree of responsiveness from the organization, ie if the executive team define a target, the organization is able to respond, organizing itself as needed and with the capability required. By its very nature top down measurement converts strategic measures into operational measures, supplier measures and customer satisfaction measures, bringing some convergence to *sourcing*, *strategy and satisfying*.

The Balanced Scorecard

The Balanced Scorecard was developed by Kaplan and Norton (1996) as a means of measuring the performance of a firm so that it is guided by not only the financial indicators of performance but also by other value drives that enable the organization to be successful and achieve outcomes. *Balanced* means the approach deals with the challenge that no single type of measure can provide a clear focus for attention and so strikes a balance between disparate strategic measures. It is a scorecard because, just as a scorecard is used in sport to enter scores, in business it is a card, sheet, book, spreadsheet or electronic measure; a place where a measure of performance is entered.

Kaplan and Norton (1996) propose four perspectives to measure organ-izational performance within the Balanced Scorecard approach (Figure 5.6). These are:

- *Financial* – how a firm appears to its shareholders, typically using financial indicators such as the profitability indicator EBITDA (Earnings Before Income, Tax, Depreciation and Amortization), Return on Investment (ROI) or Return on Capital Employed (ROCE).

FIGURE 5.6   The Balanced Scorecard (Kaplan and Norton, 1996), adapted to include a fifth 'supplier' dimension.

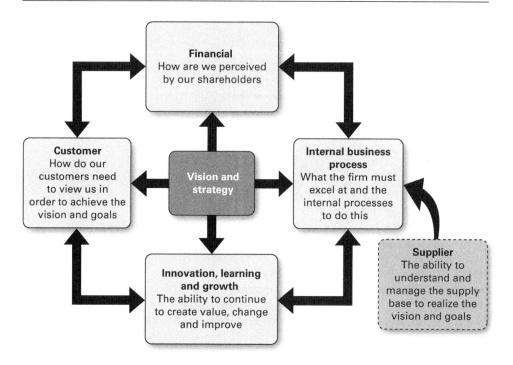

- *Customer* – how the firm should appear to customers in order to achieve the vision and goals. This might include measures of customer satisfaction or market share.

- *Internal business processes* – what the firm must excel at and the internal processes that will have the greatest impact on both customer satisfaction and financial performance.

- *Innovation, learning and growth* – the ability of the firm to continue to create value change and improve. This means the infrastructure needed to secure innovation, long-term growth and ongoing improvement through people, systems and ways of working.

Balanced Scorecard is an organization-wide measurement system. Purchasing effectiveness would be considered within *internal business processes*. The contribution of suppliers would be considered under this heading also (the activities of suppliers being viewed as an extension of what the firm does), but also under *innovation, learning and growth*. However Cousins *et al* (2008) have suggested a fifth dimension to the Balanced Scorecard: 'Supplier perspective' and propose an adapted model specifically to include purchasing function.

Whether balanced or not, the use of a 'scorecard' is commonplace, and terminology that is widely understood.

The Business Excellence Model (EFQM)

The Business Excellence Model (Figure 5.7) is a framework and for organizational management systems promoted by the European Foundation for Quality Management, a European not-for-profit organization founded in 1989 to increase the competitiveness of the European economy. It is a highly practical tool designed to help guide organizations towards the goal of 'business excellence' and as such provides a basis to identify the gaps and measure progress toward this goal. The model is designed to be applied to any organization of any size. The definition of excellence could be many things, depending upon what the organization needs to achieve. EFQM suggest eight fundamental concepts including adding value for customers, creating a sustainable future, developing organizational capability, harnessing creativity and innovation, leading with vision, inspiration and integrity, managing with agility, succeeding through the talent of people and sustaining outstanding results (**www.efqm.org**).

The model is based upon nine criteria, of which five are *enablers* describing what the organization does and how it does it in order to achieve excellence, and four are *results* criteria that cover what the organization achieves. The model is dynamic and based around the principle that if the nine criteria are met then the organization has the ability to learn, innovate and be creative, thus in turn helping to improve the enablers that in turn lead to improved results.

FIGURE 5.7   The EFQM Business Excellence model, adapted from EIPM (2006)

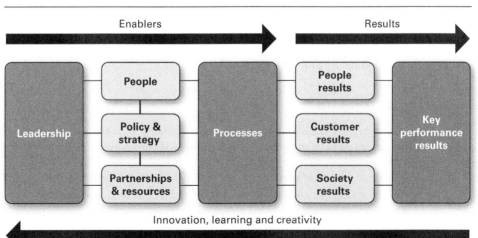

Once again supplier and the contribution of the supply base are not called out within this organization-wide model. However, suppliers form part of a firm's external resources under the enabler *partnerships and resources*. The European Institute of Purchasing Management (EIPM) together with EFQM suggest a growing importance in an organization's external resources with benefits from excellence in managing these external resources. They suggest these include reduced time to market, improved flexibility (cycle time), greater agility to adapt rapidly to new markets or threats from a firm's environment and improved profitability as well as improved CSR in the supply chain.

If the organization has selected the EFQM model as the framework to achieve business excellence, then SPM, and indeed SRM as a whole become important enablers. They do not fit into any one box within the model, but echo everything this book has presented so far about effective SRM being a company-wide philosophy, not just something a purchasing function does, in particular connecting *sourcing* with *satisfying* and *strategy*. SRM therefore runs through the entire EFRM framework. This includes (adapted from EIPM, 2006):

- Leadership extends to the development of vision, mission values and ethics, and the arrangements for the management of external resources.
- Policy and strategy must be dynamic considering supply base capability and performance and current and future supply market possibilities.
- People and resources need to be available, capable and focused on managing external resources.
- Effective relationships, interaction and communication are needed with external resources.
- The supply base needs to be managed at a strategic level using approaches such as category management and SRM.
- How external resources impact customer results, the performance of the people who support the management of external resources, the impact on society and key performance results are measured and acted upon.

The dashboard

The concept of a dashboard is to provide a brief and to the point overview of key parameters to support decision making (Epstein and Manzoni, 1998). The concept seems to have originated as a performance measurement concept in France in the 1930s as the *Tableau du Board*, literally meaning *dashboard*. The more widely known explanation is to use the analogy of an aircraft cockpit. Here there are many hundreds of instruments and indicators providing measures and information. All are necessary at some point and for certain situations, however (and assuming the plane is being flown manually rather than under computer control), under normal flying conditions only a handful are actually used to fly the plane.

The dashboard is less of a framework for what or how to measure things but rather a concept around the selection and presentation of measures and information. Its early use was by process engineers seeking ways to improve production processes and so the means to monitor cause and effect in real time or near real time was devised.

Dashboards are commonplace in organizations and with the right dashboard design, provide an essential management tool to 'keep the firm flying just right and on the correct heading'. The dashboard concept supports other performance measurement systems. As in the balanced score card, measures must be more than just financial but balanced, and as for top down measurement, different 'nested' dashboards become appropriate at each level or within each function.

The Performance Prism

The Performance Prism is a concept developed by Neely and Adams (2000) and is a performance measurement system organized around and based upon combining five perspectives of performance (as if the faces of a prism). These are:

- *Stakeholder satisfaction* – the needs and wants of stakeholders and customers; who they are and what they want.
- *Strategies* – the strategies required to satisfy these.
- *Processes* – the processes needed to execute these strategies.
- *Capabilities* – the capabilities to operate and enhance these processes.
- *Stakeholder contribution* – the contributions required from stakeholders in order to maintain and develop capabilities.

The Performance Prism recognizes that a performance measurement system needs to consider wider stakeholders, beyond customers and employees, and this includes suppliers (Figure 5.8). Successful deployment seems to centre around establishing a good degree of interrelationship between the five perspectives.

Measuring service organizations

The Results and Determinants Framework (Figure 5.9) was developed through a Chartered Institute of Management Accountants (CIMA) funded research project examining service-based businesses in the UK (Fitzgerald *et al*, 1991). The model proposes six dimensions to performance; *results* given by competitiveness and financial performance enabled by the *determinants* of quality, flexibility, resource utilization and innovation. The model is particularly suited to service-based industries where success is often intangible but rather a perceived benefit of level of customer satisfaction.

FIGURE 5.8 The Performance Prism, adapted from Neely and Adams (2002)

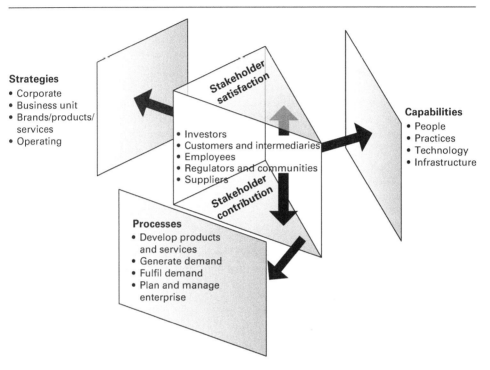

Strategies
- Corporate
- Business unit
- Brands/products/ services
- Operating

Stakeholder satisfaction

- Investors
- Customers and intermediaries
- Employees
- Regulators and communities
- Suppliers

Stakeholder contribution

Capabilities
- People
- Practices
- Technology
- Infrastructure

Processes
- Develop products and services
- Generate demand
- Fulfil demand
- Plan and manage enterprise

FIGURE 5.9 The Results and Determinants Framework

Performance dimensions	Types of measure used
Results Competitiveness Financial performance	• Market share and position. • Sales growth and measures of customer base. • Profitability. • Liquidity. • Capital structure. • Market ratios.
Determinants Quality of service Flexibility Resource utilization Innovation	• Reliability, responsiveness, aesthetics/ appearance, cleanliness/tidiness, comfort, friendliness, communication, courtesy, competency, access, availability, security. • Volume flexibility. • Delivery speed flexibility. • Specification flexibility. • Productivity. • Efficiency. • Performance of the innovation process. • Performance of individual innovators.

Again suppliers are not called out in this model, but where a service business is utilizing suppliers, especially service-based suppliers then all of the determinants apply to the way suppliers are engaged, managed, measured and contribute to the overall quality and performance of the service.

What do the people think?

An approach worth touching on is the concept of measurement based upon what 'the people' think. New ideas such as crowd sourcing and crowd funding, based on tapping into the power of many individuals, each making a small contribution, for collective provision of information, ideas, funding, answers, innovation and decision making are emerging. The basis for these ideas seems to be that a group of people is, on average, more knowledgeable than an individual. It is hard to find much empirical evidence to point to regarding the effectiveness of this approach, yet much is written around crowd-based activities and indeed it is all around us. Wikipedia is founded on this principle. Crowd measurement is therefore a real possibility.

ProMES (Productivity Measurement and Enhancement System), developed by Professor Robert D Pritchard of University of Central Florida (Pritchard *et al*, 2002), is an approach to measuring and improving the productivity, effectiveness and overall performance of people within an organization that seems to be based around crowd principles. Within such a system people decide for themselves what they will work on. People are assumed to be motivated based upon the difference they can make to the output for the effort they put in. The measurement is how individuals judge the output of their efforts as good or bad, ideally leading to personal satisfaction, feeling of accomplishment and new motivation for the next thing.

Arguably this is less of a performance measurement system but rather a concept for a new type of motivation to drive an output focused work behaviour. However, I have included it because there is something within the concept of self-motivation, management and measurement in pursuit of a goal that has its place within a collaborative supplier relationship. It is not empirical, has no dashboard, is very much bottom up not top down but could be just the approach that is needed to secure the next new thing from a small creative supplier. Sounds crazy and implausible? Perhaps, but this is just how the Washington-based games developer Valve operates. There are no bosses and no hierarchy, people decide each other's pay and people are free to choose to work on whatever they think is interesting. All the desks have wheels so people can just wheel their workstation to wherever and by whoever they want to work on whatever they want. Yet Valve are a highly successful games developer and architects of the Half-Life series, Team Fortress and Counter Strike. If a company like Valve was a key supplier and source of innovation, measuring and managing them with traditional measurement approaches could be counterproductive and limit potential.

Gut instinct

I can't leave this section without including *gut instinct*. This is not some-thing that tends to find its way into scientific books about measurement; however, it should not be ignored and is the way many people, and indeed organizations, make decisions. Gut instinct is the way someone with experience in a particular area is able to assimilate complex and varied cues and inputs to identify an issue or know a course of action to take, presumably through a series of thought processes based upon their experience they are unaware of and do not understand.

Sometimes, despite all the empirical data that might be available, having a sense that something is not right in a function or supplier relationship may well be an indicator that suggests further exploration is needed. It is difficult to use gut instinct alone as a basis for action or indeed convincing others, but it is the basis to ask questions or instigate investigation, review, check, verification and so on. In the absence of any other measurement system gut instinct often comes to the fore.

So where does that leave us?

Any and all of these approaches could be used as the basis for measurement within an organization, and if we are to put in place effective SPM then what we do must surely integrate with any organization-wide approach in place or being worked towards. Yet across these models supplier performance is notable by its absence, leaving the reader to figure out how it fits.

The Balanced Scorecard has been criticized for its empirical nature and the fact that it simply provides a list of metrics; it therefore requires interpreta-tion. Here we could use a dashboard to help. Dashboards can be very power-ful to support decision making providing they indicate the right things. Modern information systems make dashboards much more accessible; if the information can be extracted then there will almost certainly be an app for a smartphone somewhere. Lardenoije *et al* (2005) suggest there is little evidence that the Performance Prism works in practice other than that presented by Neely *et al* (2001), yet its focus on capability and process and not just output is an important step forward. Top down measurement assumes the organization is responsive and crowd measurement may have its place for some organizations, but is presently alien to how the majority of firms are structured and organized. Gut instinct can be great; few CEOs would bet their future business on someone else's sense of things.

Before we write off the majority of this chapter, it is important to note that these different approaches to performance measurement are not, in fact, separate in the sense that a firm needs to choose one or another, weighing up which one might be best, but they are perspectives on aspects of organizing a measurement system and all have their place. Indeed Kaplan and Norton (1996) suggest that the power of the Balanced Scorecard system comes when it is used as more than a measurement system, but rather a management system; used to clarify and gain consensus about strategy, to align department and personal goals to the organization and communicate strategy. EFQM works because the organization organizes itself to deliver against the nine criteria and so on. Where the organization has adopted or is working towards a specific framework, SRM and SPM should be integrated into this. Where this is not the case then our approach to SPM should be one based upon an amalgam of what works; taking the bits that are effective from each of the methods outlined above. For example, a scorecard of measures for key suppliers, developed top down and aligned with corporate goals, with an executive dashboard and so on.

Irrespective of whatever framework or model is being used, one thing that is certain is how we plan and structure measurement and intervention with the supply base needs to be carefully designed if it is to work at all, let alone be effective. There does not appear to be a strong body of knowledge or guidance to help here and many of the architects of the famous models seem to not specifically include this aspect. Therefore we need to interpret what is available specifically for the context of external resources. We need to design an SPM system that will be effective and can integrate with any established organization-wide approach to measurement, and we will explore just how to do this in the next chapter.

Building a supplier performance measurement system

06

In this chapter we explore how to design and implement an SPM system. We will consider the characteristics of the perfect SPM system and explore what needs to happen to determine good KPIs and how to use these to drive appropriate supplier specific interventions.

PATHWAY QUESTIONS ADDRESSED IN THIS CHAPTER

4 How are our suppliers performing?

5 Are we getting the most from our suppliers and how can we be sure?

The SPM system

The perfect SPM system carefully targets resource to measure just the right things, at the right time, with the right suppliers and outputs information in the most useful and meaningful way. Sounds straightforward enough but organizations frequently seem to get lost in the process of translating this into action, resulting in over-engineering of measurement approaches.

FIGURE 6.1   The SPM system

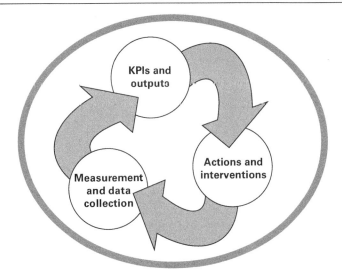

Measurement needs a purpose and the purpose is the precise targeting of supplier invention. Therefore effective SPM requires a *closed loop* approach to measurement and so the system of supplier performance measurement, and indeed management in response to measures, is given in Figure 6.1.

If we are to implement an SPM system then we need put in place arrangements for each of the three steps in the cycle. There are different considerations, options or possibilities here and these are expanded through the rest of this chapter; however, before exploring the practicalities we shall consider the characteristics of a good SPM approach.

Reasons SPM systems fail

There is no shortage of SPM systems that have simply failed to get going, keep going or demonstrate meaningful contribution. Supplier measurement regimes can easily take on a life of their own, becoming little more than data collection exercises or ones where good information is simply ignored. One US-based company appointed an individual with the role of analysing and measuring supplier performance. Each month he produced a thick report, circulated to all, that provided supplier-specific data on delivery and quality and performance together with vast market data providing price trends for commodity and key indices. The report was an impressive piece of work; however, in my subsequent discussions with different individuals in the team I asked how people managed the performance of the suppliers they looked after. From a team of 38, only a handful mentioned the report they received, the majority of the remainder did remember the report when prompted but it was apparent the information was serving little purpose.

Reasons why SPM systems fail or end up sub-optimum include:

- measuring the wrong things;
- measuring too many things;
- overburdening system data collection;
- bad data or inputs;
- difficulties securing data or information from disparate systems;
- the important things are hard to measure;
- lack of goal congruence – not linked to goals, or linked to the wrong goals;
- results don't highlight things to act upon;
- outputs don't tell the whole story;
- failure to act;
- suppliers dispute measures or data integrity; and
- measures used punitively, driving defensive behaviour.

Just one of these can be enough to render an entire SPM system worthless or to bring the effort being spent on it into question. Yet all of these are in fact easy to avoid with the right thought and effort at the outset.

10 Characteristics of best practice SPM

There are 10 characteristics that define best practice for any SPM system. Each responds in some way to established best practice, what has been proven to be effective or the published wisdom in this space. These are:

10 Characteristics that define SPM best practice

1 *Unique to the organizational context* – every organization is different and therefore the SPM system must be designed around the organization, the nature of its supply base and what it is trying to achieve overall.

2 *Supplier specific* – whilst a company may have an overarching approach to SPM approach, SPM systems must, in fact, be supplier specific also and therefore tailored for an individual relationship. One size does not fit all.

3 *Goal alignment* – what gets measured and specific supplier interventions are value and outcome driven, aligned to the aims and goals of the organization as informed by customer needs and desires.

4 *Business-wide approach* – alignment to stakeholder expectations and the way the organization does things; using cross functional-engagement to incorporate the needs and wants of internal stakeholders, and perhaps external stakeholders.

5 *Supplier involvement as appropriate* – depending upon the degree of importance of the supplier, the potential involvement of the supplier in agreeing what gets measured and how the measures will be used in practice.

6 *Focused resources* – measurement and intervention resources focused carefully according to the nature and degree of importance of the supplier relationship.

7 *Balanced* – meaningful, valuable and balanced measures, interpreted where needed and based upon accurate data, using different data sources and comparable to others.

8 *Scarcity* – keep it simple! The measurement system is designed as if 'measures were scarce' so what gets measured and outputted makes a difference in some way and is easy to understand and act upon.

9 *Fosters positive behaviour* – designed to foster the required behaviour rather than hit targets.

10 *Meaningful outputs* – measures are interpreted, presented and made available where, when and to whom as appropriate in order to influence outcomes and enable actions and informed decision making.

Five steps to put SPM in place with a supplier

The five steps to implementing SPM for a specific supplier (Figure 6.2) are as follows; each is expanded over the next five sections in this chapter:

1 *Determine SPM aims* – what are we trying achieve overall by measuring this supplier?

2 *Determine requirements and targets* – what supplier-specific requirements and targets do we need to satisfy and achieve?

3 *Determine KPIs* – determine the measures, indicators and KPIs that will best demonstrate how the supplier is meeting and working towards the requirements and targets.

4 *Measurement system design* – design and implement the arrangements needed to collect data and produce the KPIs.

FIGURE 6.2 Five steps to developing an SPM approach for a supplier

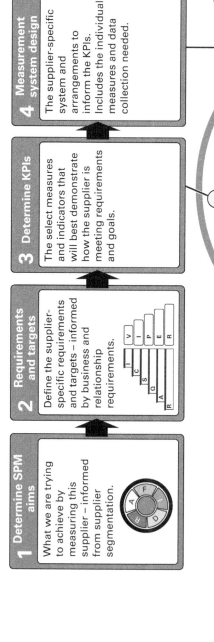

1 Determine SPM aims

What we are trying to achieve by measuring this supplier – informed from supplier segmentation.

2 Requirements and targets

Define the supplier-specific requirements and targets – informed by business and relationship requirements.

3 Determine KPIs

The select measures and indicators that will best demonstrate how the supplier is meeting requirements and goals.

4 Measurement system design

The supplier-specific system and arrangements to inform the KPIs. Includes the individual measures and data collection needed.

5 Output

Means to output the KPIs together with supporting measures or detailed indicators so they are visible to the right people, or at the right points in the process, at the right time to enable action an intervention as needed.

KPIs and outputs

Actions and interventions

Measurement and data collection

5 *Output* – develop a means to output the KPIs together with supporting measures or detailed indicators if required so they are visible to the right people, or at the right points in the process, at the right time to enable action and intervention as needed.

These steps are unique to a supplier because each supplier is important for different reasons and therefore each requires a unique and tailored measurement approach.

Step 1: Determine the SPM aim

SPM for a supplier starts with being clear about what we are aiming for, what we are trying to satisfy or the problem we are attempting to solve. This works at two levels:

1 *Organizational aims* – the aims and objectives of the organization and what it needs from its supply base overall as defined in the macro level relationship requirements (back in Figure 2.7). This is the value the organization needs from its entire supply base. In practice this is done once and then guides how the individual supplier SPM arrangements are put in place.

2 *Supplier-specific SPM aims* – the aims and objectives for the specific supplier relationship, informed by the output of segmentation, especially *risk*, *current importance* and *future importance*. If there is risk with a specific supplier, because we lack confidence, then the SPM objective is a measurement system that provides confidence, perhaps through compliance measurement. Similarly if there is great future opportunity then the SPM objective might be to develop an SPM approach that allows both parties to move towards a shared common goal. Therefore, in deciding the SPM aim we are also determining the degree of collaboration required both internally and with the supplier to develop the approach.

Step 2: Supplier-specific requirements and targets

Alice: 'Would you tell me, please, which way I ought to go from here?', 'That depends a good deal on where you want to get to,' said the Cat.

(Lewis Carroll, 1865)

Climbing the mountain

Scafell Pike is the highest mountain in England standing at 978 metres located in Lake District National Park in Cumbria. Imagine we are setting out to climb this mountain and reach the highest summit (our goal). Within our party people want different things: some want to take the steepest route, others the more scenic route. Some want to stop at certain points along the way; others prefer to keep going. Through discussion we have agreed how we will all ascend together (our requirements). From these we've determined the route of ascent we will take (our strategy) and we're setting out with all the equipment we need or might need (our processes). We also know the prevailing conditions can change suddenly so we know we must ensure we are safe and that we can achieve our goal and return safely before nightfall (our external environment).

If we have no goal in mind we are just wandering aimlessly, clearly a waste of time and dangerous as we could end up anywhere. However with a goal in mind we can then check aspects of our progress to help reach our goal (our measures). Just like climbing a mountain, if we are going to implement a measurement approach for a supplier we must start with an overall goal in mind and then the detailed requirements for the supplier and what we source from them. This, of course, must be informed from the business requirements (RAQSCI) for the categories and products this supplier provides and the relationship requirements (VIPER).

Deciding what mountain to climb with our supplier is a crucial step and there are many interested parties here. Finance may want purchasing and supplier performance to deliver against certain cost metrics. Operations or service functions may demand suppliers demonstrate a certain ongoing capability or level of compliance to prevent risk and perhaps marketing want to highlight the sustainable nature of an offering and need supplier performance information to support this. Everyone has different needs and this is typical yet as we have seen measurement must align with internal and external stakeholder needs and expectation. It must also align with the overall goals of the organization. It is at this point where SPM can fail to get going because to actually achieve this in practice, starting out from a zero base, requires considerable effort, engagement across the business and beyond and agreement of what is important between parties. However, depending upon how mature the organization is in terms of strategic procurement, chances are we already have what we need here. Assuming we have a robust set of RAQSCI for what we buy, which would be developed as part of a Category Management programme, together with our VIPER, then collectively these form the basis to set individual supplier SPM targets. Remember, the business and relationship requirements represent the definitive summary of what the entire organization needs and wants from a supplier and the categories or products/services they provide. If these are robust then they should:

- embody the overall ambition, goals and objectives of the organization and translate these into specific statements of requirement for the category and supplier;
- have been developed cross-functionally and represent the needs and wants of the entire business;
- synthesize, consolidate and establish consensus for differing or opposing needs and wants;
- have involved some challenge of what stakeholders believe they need, to be certain this is the right need for the organization; and
- include any needs or wants around process and capability that are essential.

If our business and relationship requirements meet these tests then they are a solid basis from which to develop SPM targets. If not, more work is needed here. Business and relationship requirements are converted into SPM targets as follows:

1 Extract those requirements where SPM will help ensure this requirement is met or will add value in some way.

2 Consolidate and summarize as needed to create simple targets.

3 Redefine statements of requirement into targets where needed.

The aim is to identify the targets that will make the biggest difference if we can understand the degree to which we are working towards them. There will be many entries within a typical list of business or relationship requirements that are not relevant to measurement. For example, we might have an *assurance of supply* requirement that the supplier has a presence in certain countries or a *quality* requirement that the supplier holds ISO9001 accreditation. These are not things we need to measure ongoing, but rather a requirement that would form part of a supplier selection or qualification process. We can ignore such requirements when developing the SPM approach.

Therefore, this step is not about converting all the business and relationship requirements into targets; that is how organizations end up with lengthy scorecards that do little. Instead success depends upon extracting the fewest most useful of measures (Figure 6.3). In fact measures alone may not be enough, we may also need a means to interpret or combine measures to create more useful information. It is here where *indicators* become important.

Step 3: Determine KPIs

The third step is about developing the key performance indicators (KPIs) for this supplier relationship.

Why are we talking about 'key performance indicators' and not 'key performance measures'? Simply because measures often require interpretation

FIGURE 6.3 Extracting measures from business and relationship requirements

Business requirements

	Need	Want
Assurance of supply		
• FDA compliance	✓	
• CSR compliance	✓	
• Sufficient capacity		✓
Quality		
• 99% defect free	✓	
• ISO9001	✓	
Service		
• 98% on time, in full	✓	
• 24/7 support	✓	
• Monthly reporting		✓
Cost & commercial		
• 5% cost reduction	✓	
• 30 days terms	✓	
• Open book	✓	
Innovation		
• Joint workshops		✓
• Next generation s/w		✓

Measures & indicators

1. Defect rate.
2. Delivery performance.
3. Relationship effectiveness.
4. Reduction in impress stocks.
5. Cost reduction targets.
6. Innovation projects delivered.

Relationship requirements

	Need	Want
Risk		
• Annual audit	✓	
• CSR compliance	✓	
Effectiveness of ops		
• Joint working team	✓	
• eCommerce	✓	
• Demand forecasts	✓	
Performance		
• 9% delivery performance	✓	
• No impress stocks	✓	
• Effective relationship	✓	
Innovation		
• The new ideas/year		✓
• Joint workshops		✓
Value		
• Reduce costs	✓	
• New joint venture		✓

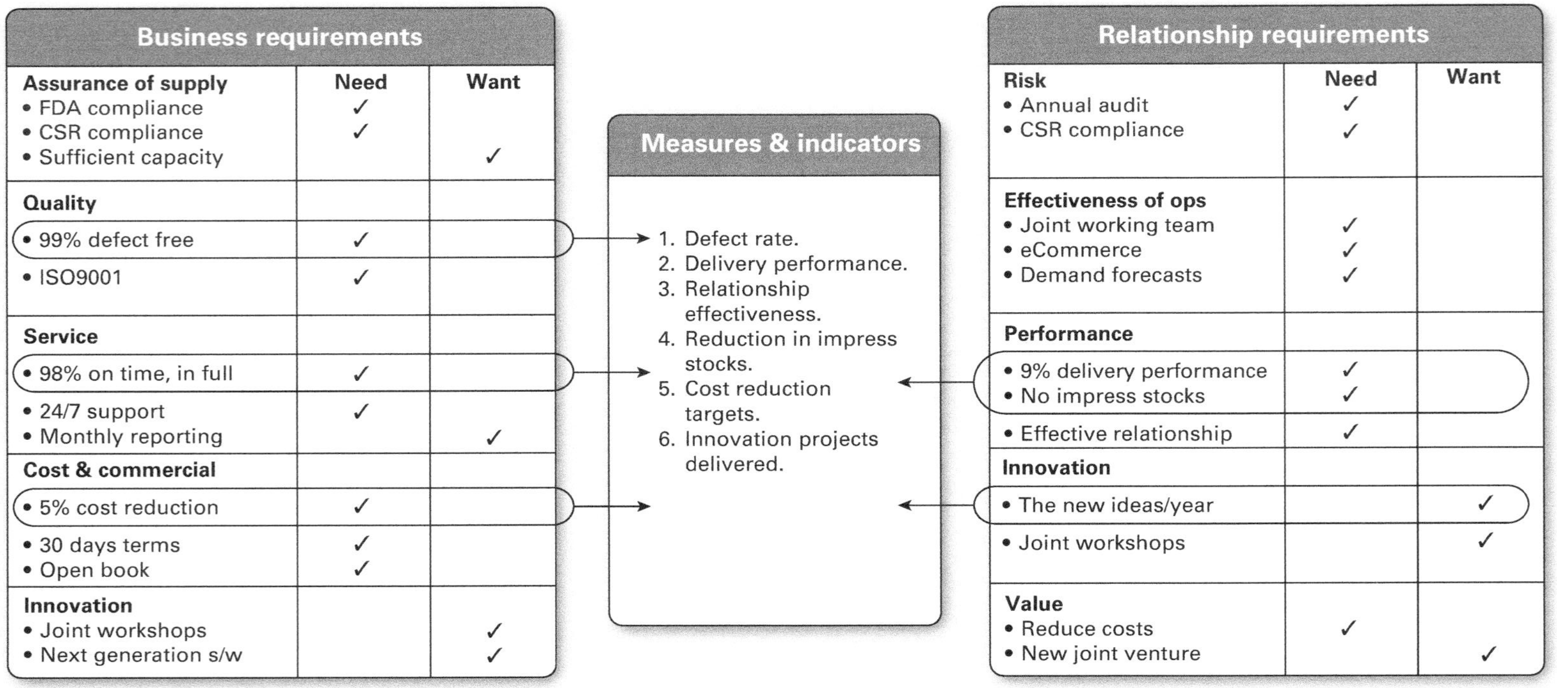

in order to be useful. Nonetheless the term 'KPI' seems to be misused somewhat. KPIs should be both those measures and indicators that will succinctly provide just the right amount of information necessary to guide a business, function, task or activity towards a stated goal or highlight a problem that needs attention.

The problem is, it is easy to end up making everything a KPI! If a supplier scorecard boasts 20 or 30 KPIs covering every aspect of supplier performance relationship then it is questionable if these are all 'key' to managing that supplier. Perhaps they are nice to have; perhaps some are more detailed measures or indicators that are used when things go wrong; perhaps there is a belief they are necessary in some way.

Building a good and useful set of KPIs is nothing short of an art form and before we look at this, there are some further considerations here to explore first.

Looking back, looking forward

'If you can't measure it, you can't manage it' is a quote frequently attributed to Peter Drucker, the renowned management consultant, educator and author. Yet Edward Deming said 'the most important things cannot be measured'. He was describing the issues that are most important or long term or that cannot be measured in advance. With measurement we can manage specific aspects of a supplier's performance such as delivery or quality compliance, and there may be good reasons to do this, but often other measures could be more useful. Rudzki (2007) suggests that when organizations use measurements around what has happened it is 'like looking in the rear view mirror. It's useful information about where you've been, but it's dangerous to steer by it.' A more potent measure would be if we could somehow measure how effective a supplier *will* be, how much they *will* help us innovate or realize our business goals, yet there are no such measures, but we can use measures to help us predict if we are moving in the right direction.

Remember the mountain we are climbing? There are many measures we could use here to help reach our goal, but imagine if we tried to check progress by reviewing the walk so far; how far we have travelled, how high we are, how many times we have stumbled, number of wrong turns taken and so on. This information is interesting and can help us, to a degree, check that based upon our performance so far, if we continue as we are we will reach our goal. This is in fact how many organizations set about measurement, measuring what *has* happened; focusing on things like past delivery or quality performance which typically are the easiest things to measure.

As we ascend, what is more useful is to know if we are heading in the right direction, how far away we are, if there is sufficient daylight time remaining based upon our predicted progress, if the weather conditions will remain favourable and so on. If the mist comes down we can easily lose our sense of direction and the checks we have been making may no longer be helpful.

Instead we may now need to refine our goals. Getting off the mountain safely rather than reaching the peak may become the new priority demanding new measures.

Not every supplier relationship is like a mountain; some are more like small hillocks and just call for a simple measure of achievement. But where there is a mountain to climb then the value of using measures that help us move towards the goal can be useful.

Measures vs indicators

A measure alone is not always useful. The gas tank on my car holds 90 litres or around 24 US gallons; a measure of capacity and an interesting measure but not one that I will use every day. The gas gauge is more useful and together with the transducer in the tank is a system that provides a measurement of the level of fuel in the tank. This measure is more useful as it guides my decision making about when I need to fill up. The gauge tells me I have about an eighth of a tank left. I know fuel is getting low but is that enough to reach my destination in a hurry without the need to stop? Beside it, the car's computer displays a reading that suggests 52 miles until empty; another measure? No, an indicator and one that is providing information about what might happen based upon measures of what has happened – combining data from the fuel tank transducer with current and recent distance, speed and time data to provide an estimate, based upon current driving style, for when fuel will run out. The problem is that I know, from bitter past experience, that it is not that accurate. If the terrain or how I drive changes then this indication will be incorrect. The system will of course recalculate as I go, but this is not helpful if I have already made the decision to drive past the gas station and keep going. Somewhere else on my dashboard a 'low fuel' warning light has just come on: another indicator, and one that tells me that the current status of fuel has reached a point where action is needed soon but no more than that. This indicator alone doesn't tell me how urgent action is needed, or how long the light has been on for; to find out this I need to look at the other gauges and indicators for more information.

An indicator is therefore distinct from a measure. Indicators provide information, typically using one or more measures and interpretation to provide something that is more useful than the measures alone. By their very nature indicators may lack the precision and accuracy of a measure as the process of interpretation can introduce a margin of error as can any uncertainty, for example not knowing the terrain we will drive on or our future driving style in estimating 'miles until empty'.

Indicators can be more useful than measures alone in helping us achieve our goals. In practice we might need to select an array of both measures and indicators according to the circumstances. We can also develop indicators that look back at past performance, perhaps providing trend data about a series of measurements or we can develop indicators that look forward.

These are called *leading* indicators and *lagging* indicators. Both are relevant to organization-wide and supplier performance measurement:

- *Lagging indicator* – indicators that show what has happened, eg how full the gas tank is, quality or delivery performance, number of people served etc. Whilst lagging indicators have the inherent weakness of looking only at what has happened it may be the only type of indicator available or possible in some situations.

- *Leading indicator* – indicators that predict or drive outcomes, eg miles until empty or current wait time before we answer your call. For example, in economics leading indicators are used to predict how an economy as a whole will change; compiled from factors such as number of people seeking unemployed benefits, new orders received by manufacturers, average weekly hours worked and permits issued for new building projects. Leading indicators typically convert lagging indicators or measures to predict future state, adding interpretation of trends.

The most important things cannot be measured

So indicators developed from measures can be more helpful, but what about the things that can't be measured so easily if at all; things like how someone feels about something. Back to my car and whilst I have a dashboard of measures and indicators, my decisions about driving are also, and more so, informed from other factors such as road conditions, weather, how the traffic is moving, perceived space from the car in front, risks, the 'feel' of the car on the road and so on. These are more than responses to measures or indicators but a complex series of judgements I make without fully understanding or being conscious of how. As Edward Deming said the most important things cannot be measured. Similarly you can't measure a relationship but you can say how it feels. This is a crucial point if we are to measure supplier performance. It is easy to focus on measuring aspects such as on time, in full or conformance to specification. Such measures may be important or necessary, but if we are seeking more value from a supplier relationship, higher up the VIPER hierarchy then we need to develop a relationship and that means we need to understand how it is working, despite not being able to directly measure it.

Whilst we cannot measure a relationship or how something feels or is working directly we can however solicit feedback about such things and, if we ask the right questions, convert feelings into some sort of measure. This, of course, is the basis for how customer surveys work.

Key performance indicators (KPIs)

A performance indicator is just that, an indicator that shows the performance of something. A KPI is an indicator that has been identified as more important or relevant than all the other indicators. KPIs exist throughout businesses and might typically be presented on some sort of scorecard. They are used as indicators of performance in many areas including performance of the organization, a specific project or individual suppliers.

A KPI scorecard typically contains both direct measures and indicators, but all called KPIs. This is normal; the point is what information is being presented and acted upon is that which is needed to guide the business. In my car, current speed is a pretty important (measure) as is 'miles until empty' (indicator). Both are *key* to help me drive. A measure of engine temperature is useful but an indicator that tells me to stop due to over temperature in the engine to prevent damage is essential.

Determining what is key is an important concept within performance measurement – have too many measures and the system will consume great resource but will not add value and any scorecard will become meaningless and confusing (Gordon, 2008). Too few and decision making could be impaired or outcomes could be compromised. Measurements should be relatively few in number, focused on the activities that will yield the greatest results (Cunningham and Fiume, 2003). The point of *key* performance indicators is therefore to identify the handful of indicators that will guide actions effectively and efficiently. Cunningham and Fiume (2003) suggest outputs should offer the most relevant information to the reader and be the ones that any employee can relate to.

KPIs should be developed as if scarcity was a key consideration; as if every KPI used comes with a high cost. This doesn't mean that only a few things should be measured, but rather is concerned with what gets presented, shared and drives action. Behind this there could be a vast array of further measures and indicators to drill down if further information is needed. Back to my car example and imagine that you could buy a new type of car that was half the price of other cars, but you had to make some compromises and one of these meant that you could only have one indicator (or measure) on the dashboard. What would you choose? Speed, gas level, miles until empty or just a big light that came on to tell you that you needed do to something, perhaps driving slower, gas was low, there was a problem with the engine. It wouldn't be the most useful of indicators, but if you could have only one then perhaps it would be a good compromise. Asking 'if we could only measure or indicate one thing... what would it be?' is a great place to start in determining KPIs as it forces us to debate what is really important. Therefore the process of developing KPIs is most effective if there is discussion and debate from those involved to challenge what is essential and resist the temptation to measure too many things.

KPIs are defined as:

> The essential measures or indicators necessary ongoing to guide a business, function or individual towards a stated goal, or to provide an alert of a state that might prevent, or hinder reaching, the goal.

Service level agreements (SLAs)

It is worth touching on SLAs as these are often referred to alongside KPIs as another measurement approach. This is in fact not entirely correct, as an SLA is actually part of a contract, specifically for a service or the service aspects associated with a product. SLAs are negotiated between two or more parties, where the targets and the requirements for how services must be delivered, responsibilities, remedies and performance are defined in plain English with the intent of establishing a common understanding about expectations. Depending upon how they are written SLAs can be legally binding, with remedies or agreed courses of action for failure to meet defined targets.

A SLA is therefore not a measurement system but a means by which performance targets can be defined and formally agreed. Examples might include '80 per cent of calls to be answered within 15 seconds', 'System uptime of 99 per cent to be maintained' or '95 per cent of all emergency call outs to be attended within two hours'.

If we have identified what needs to be measured with KPIs that help to achieve our outcomes, SLAs become the guiding expression of the targets that sit behind this.

Step 4: Measurement system design

Step 4 is concerned with determining the inputs and arrangement for data collection and analysis necessary to inform our KPIs. Note that our SPM process didn't start with this but rather it is here, all the way at step 4 and that is because we are starting with the outputs in mind then designing the measuring system to achieve this. If we were to start with available data or measures and build KPIs from here then our SPM system will only be as good as the things we can measure easily.

What to measure

There are many things we could measure, and many different sources of information. This step requires a degree of creativity to determine the most efficient way to secure data that will inform a KPI and it is possible that the practicalities of measurement may require us to reframe or redefine our KPIs. After all, there is little point designing a brilliant scorecard of insightful KPIs if we can't secure the inputs needed to produce them. Designing a measurement system is therefore somewhat iterative in order to get it right.

It is important too, to look beyond the obvious measures. There is often a tendency to look for measures of how effective something is, ie on-time, in full deliveries or conformance to specification. However, Van Weele (1984) suggests there are two dimensions to measuring performance and we should consider both efficiency and effectiveness. Efficiency is the relationship between planned and actual sacrifices that are made to achieve the goals. Effectiveness is the extent to which a goal can be met using a chosen course of action. Gordon (2008) also suggests we should measure the supplier's business practices and processes as well as their performance. So in designing a measurement regime to collect and analyse specific information in order to create a scorecard of insightful KPIs, it is possible we need to consider a range of different sources, types of data collection, ways to interpret data, analysis techniques and data presentation methods. Table 6.1 provides an extensive list of the sorts of things that get measured for different areas of supply and supply chain performance. Many of these are measures, some are indicators but this table can help to consider where data and insight can come from.

Two-way measurement

For some important suppliers, measuring their performance may be enough, but for others, where the ability to collaborate is key, understanding how we are performing within the relationship is equally important if the relationship is to be effective. This dimension is frequently ignored and seems to be a product of mindsets such as 'the supplier is there to serve us' or 'the supply can absorb this'. However, poor performance on our part could hinder a relationship and worse still we could remain blissfully ignorant as suppliers rarely voice such issues unless they are confident in the relationship (we will explore 'voice of the supplier' in Chapter 11). This drives protectionist behaviour in the supplier who might put in place arrangements to work around, compensate for our poor performance, stockpile, build in contingency and so on, all of which increase their costs and so we ultimately end up paying for this. Typical areas of poor performance on our part that can hinder a relationship include:

- poor, conflicting or late communication;
- inaccurate forecasting;
- delays, cancellations and postponements;
- difficult interpersonal relationships;
- lack of flexibility or unrealistic demands;
- late payment, payment issues, excessive challenge of fair invoicing; and
- administrative and bureaucratic burdens placed on the supplier necessary for them to retain business (eg admin processes, audit questionnaires or entry onto new ERP systems).

For the critical few where two-way measurement is appropriate and necessary, this enables us to take an interest in how efficient and effective we are within the overall relationship, but there is an art to doing this effectively. Two-way measurement systems must be designed so they help suppliers to have a voice. Simply sending a questionnaire asking the supplier to rate our performance is unlikely to produce anything meaningful as they may well just tell us what they think we want to hear. Questions such as 'rate our

TABLE 6.1 Measures/indicators for different areas of supply and supply chain performance

Area	Possible Measures and Indicators	Type	Possible KPIs
Financial and cost performance	• Cost of goods or service	M La Quan	• Progress towards cost target (In La Le Quan)
	• Reduction of cost	M La Quan	• Total acquired cost (In La Quan)
	• Cost per transaction	M In La Quan Qual	• Total cost of ownership (In La Quan)
	• Research and development costs	M La Quan	• Absolute working capital available (M Le Quan)
	• Labour costs	M La Quan	• Improvement in working capital (M In Le Quan)
	• Cost of waste	M La Quan	
	• Cost of rework, repair and scrap	M La Quan	
	• Inventory costs	M La Quan	
	• Working capital	M La Le Quan	
	• Days Payables Outstanding (DPO)	M La Quan	
	• Environmental compliance costs	M La Quan Qual	
	• Shipping and delivery costs	M La Quan	
	• Manufacturing cost	M La Quan	
	• Operating costs	M La Quan	

TABLE 6.1 *continued*

Area	Possible Measures and Indicators	Type	Possible KPIs
Safety and quality of goods and services	• Number of safety incidents or near misses	M La Quan	• Lost Time Injury Frequency Rate (LTIFR)
	• Cost of poor quality	M La Quan Qual	• Progress towards quality targets (In Le Quan Qual)
	• Assembly or finished goods quality	M In La Quan Qual	• Combined quality performance (In La Quan Qual)
	• Raw material quality	M La Quan Qual	• Future predicted quality (In Le Quan Qual)
	• Quality of service	M In La Quan Qual	
	• Customer satisfaction	M In La Qual	
	• Fitness for purpose	M In La Quan Qual	
	• Compliance to specification or requirements	M In La Quan Qual	
	• Delivery quality	M In La Quan Qual	
	• Number of rejects	M La Quan	
	• Complaints	M In La Quan Qual	
	• Warranty returns	M La Quan Qual	
	• Sales returns	M La Quan Qual	
	• Field service calls and visits	M In La Quan Qual	
	• Repairs	M La Quan Qual	
	• Defect rates	M La Quan	
	• Rework	M La Quan	
	• Scrap	M La Quan	
	• First pass yield	M La Quan	

TABLE 6.1 *continued*

Area	Possible Measures and Indicators	Type	Possible KPIs
Delivery performance	• On-time supplier delivery • Accuracy of delivery – in full • Lead-time • Delivery performance • Packaging	M La Quan M La Quan M La Le Quan M In La Quan M In La Quan Qual	• On-time in full delivery performance (In La Quan) • On-time in full in specification performance (In La Quan Qual) • Reduction of packaging to new target (In Le Qual) • Progress towards new lead time goals (In Le Quan Qual)
Effectiveness measures	• Inventory turnover • Inventory efficiency • Reduction in inventory • Excess/obsolete inventory • Forecasting and planning accuracy • Cycle times • Decision making time • Unplanned orders • Schedule changes • Overdue backlogs • Data accuracy • Productivity • Motivation of staff • Asset utilization • Asset efficiency • Amount of waste	M La Quan In La Quan M La Quan M In La Quan M La Quan Qual M La Quan M In La Quan M La Quan M La Quan M La Quan M In La Quan Qual M In La Quan Qual M In La Qual M In La Quan Qual M In La Quan Qual M In La Quan Qual	• Progress towards efficiency improvement (In Le Quan Qual) • Cycle time reduction (In La Quan) • Combined supplier efficiency (In Le Quan Qual) • Reduction of waste (In Le Quan Qual)

TABLE 6.1 *continued*

Area	Possible Measures and Indicators	Type	Possible KPIs
Supplier management systems & capability	• Accreditation to international standards	In La Le Qual	• Overall supplier compliance (In La Le Qual)
	• Suitability/effectiveness of supplier's management systems	M In La Le Qual	• Process capability improvement (In La Le Quan Qual)
	• Audit scores	M In La Le Qual	• Progress towards CSR goals (In Le Qual)
	• Procedures in place and being followed	M In La Qual	
	• Arrangements for corrective and preventative action	In La Qual	
	• Capability of people	In La Le Qual	
	• Process capability	In La Le Quan Qual	
	• CSR performance	M In La Le Qual	
Relationship	• Risk management and mitigation	In La Le Qual	• Relationship performance (In La Le Qual)
	• Relationship effectiveness	M In La Qual	• Risk reduction to target (In La Le Qual)
	• Information exchange and sharing	M In La Qual	• Total value from innovations (In La Quan Qual)
	• Timely communication	M In La Qual	• Supplier contribution to business growth (In Le Qual)
	• Follow through, delivery of actions and promise fulfilment	In La Le Qual	• % invoices correct and on-time (In La Quan Qual)
	• Investment in relationship development	M In La Quan Qual	
	• Investment in inventory	M In La Quan	
	• Minimum order levels	In Le Qual	
	• Resource management	In La Qual	
	• Range development	In Le Qual	
	• Customer and supplier education	M In La Le Qual	
	• Emergency response	M In La Quan Qual	
	• eAuction success	M La Qual	
	• New innovations or ideas offered	M In La Qual	
	• Value derived each new innovations and ideas	M In La Le Qual Quan	
	• Invoice accuracy	M In La Quan Qual	

KEY – M – Measure   In – Indicator   La – Lagging   Le – Leading   Quan – Typically based on quantitative data or research   Qual – Typically derived from qualitative data or research overall relationship' or 'rate how well we communicate key information' are unlikely to get a supplier to reveal concerns as a low score triggers questions that might lead to needing to reveal a problem with a specific individual. Two-way measurement must therefore first give the supplier a voice and make them feel safe about sharing concerns, and then needs a means to solicit information in a focused way about specific aspects of the relationship. Questionnaires have their place, but sometimes better quality information comes face-to-face between individuals, one either side, who have come to trust each other. Where questionnaires are used the questions need careful thought. Success comes through positive and constructive questioning, which in turn will highlight issues but without needing to make accusations or cause loss of face. Questions such as 'what things would make communication more effective?' or 'how can we become even more effective at working together?' can help. This type of questioning is less quantitative and requires interpretation but can be more useful overall and opens up channels to discuss improvements. From here parties may be able to work towards jointly developed KPI that measure specific aspects of a relationship where needed.

Measuring process, practices, behaviour and culture

Some aspects of supplier performance cannot be ascertained by asking them, as they may not be aware. Gordon (2008) states that a lot of insight is needed into not only supplier performance using quantifiable performance metrics but also the means by which this performance is achieved. This includes the supplier's processes, practices, behaviour and culture. However, if we accept that by forging the right relationship with certain important suppliers we can add value, then it follows that we must also measure processes, practices, behaviour and culture; theirs and those that are joint between us.

There are measures we can develop for aspects of process efficiency and effectiveness, but practices, behaviour and culture are much more subjective. In a close personal relationship norms around practices, behaviour and even culture develop. There may not be a specific discussion around this but in a healthy relationship practices get agreed based on what works for both, behaviour gets shaped through parties agreeing what is mutually acceptable and where boundaries lie and if all these things happen the relationship takes on its own positive culture over time. Split up and meet someone new and the process begins over. The same happens with a supplier relationship, except companies rarely seek to agree what practices and behaviours are appropriate or expected, yet if we do this we then create the basis to measure it or at least check it feels right. In Chapter 11 we will explore the *Relationship Charter*, a means to define expected practices and behaviours and thus a basis to them measure the degree to which parties emulate this.

Collecting and analysing data

KPIs typically demand different data types, from different sources. Collecting data to create KPIs could be an automatic process in real time, perhaps using a corporate system or well-designed app, or perhaps it requires a regular or even irregular activity to produce the latest set of KPIs. We could do this or we could get the supplier to do this, or a combination of both.

Securing data to create KPIs is not easy. In fact, the Aberdeen Group (Limberakis, 2012) suggest that for the companies they identify as 'best in class' only 40 per cent of these have the ability to access a 'single source of truth' for all supplier information.

There are two forms of data within any measurement system, these are quantitative or qualitative:

- *Quantitative* – data, research or measures based upon the collection of numbers or hard data, eg the man's height is 1.88m, I travelled for 12.5 miles.

- *Qualitative* – based upon opinion, perception, observation or how it feels, eg the man is tall, his eyes are a bluely green colour, the road feels wet and slippery. In order for qualitative measures to be useful, to have any scientific value or be credible they need to be quantified and converted to quantitative measures to remove subjectivity.

Furthermore, there two types of data source available:

- *Primary data* – data or measurements that are directly collected by the individual or company and might include actual measurements of an aspect of a product, service or delivery compliance (quantitative) or asking a stakeholder for feedback about an engagement with a supplier (qualitative).

- *Secondary data* – data or measurements that are collected or made available by a third party. Again these could be quantitative, eg published raw material price indices, exchange rates or supplier provided test results; or qualitative, eg 'I heard that...'.

It is easier to find quantitative things to measure for suppliers who provide goods, but for service suppliers this can become more subjective as more relies upon what individuals do and what is experienced rather than what can be seen, held, touched, counted etc. Yet it is through this type of approach that we can measure soft factors such as relationships with suppliers, levels of service, end customer enjoyment of an experience and so on. Therefore the means by which subjective opinion is quantified and converted to give us hard data is crucial. For example, if you complete a customer satisfaction survey, whilst you might be invited to describe how you feel about something you will probably also be asked to rate your satisfaction, which of course is subjective and personal to you, using a scale against which there are precise definitions which convert your opinion into a comparable rating. If an airline employed contract cleaners to pre-prepare aircraft cabins before a flight then it is possible to measure turnaround time or check all the safety cards are present and in the right place. However it is the subsequent customer experience of 'cleanliness' that is the true test, and customers are likely to only complain if something is really bad, like finding someone's used ear plug or chewing gum in the seat pocket. Merely finding an old napkin or noting how dirty the footwell is would most likely only cause the passenger to think poorly of the airline. Perhaps it might even influence choice as to whom they fly with next time. Qualitative data and how we convert it is therefore an important consideration in designing supplier measurement systems. Figure 6.4 provides an example of a stakeholder survey used to collect information about supplier performance and how a

FIGURE 6.4   An example stakeholder survey tool

Supplier Relationship Survey

Supplier   *The Wise and Wily Widget Company*

Please take five minutes to complete each question; tick one box for each and provide any comments you wish then return to Jake Anderson in Purchasing before 31 May. Any questions please call. We will circulate the results on 6 June.

1 – Response to problems
When there is a problem the supplier responds immediately

☐ Strongly disagree   ☐ Disagree   ☐ Agree   ☐ Strongly agree

Comments

2 – Contacting the supplier
When I need to contact the supplier I often struggle to get hold of who I need to speak to

☐ Strongly disagree   ☐ Disagree   ☐ Agree   ☐ Strongly agree

Comments

3 – Helpfulness for new projects
The supplier could be more proactive in offering help and support for new projects

☐ Strongly disagree   ☐ Disagree   ☐ Agree   ☐ Strongly agree

Comments

4 – The Relationship overall
Overall this supplier does everything I would expect to maintain an effective relationship

☐ Strongly disagree   ☐ Disagree   ☐ Agree   ☐ Strongly agree

Comments

relationship is working overall. Indeed the design of data collection such as questionnaires or online surveys is a subject all of its own and so further reading is recommended here.

The SPM system for a specific supplier or group of suppliers needs to be as efficient as possible; capable of producing the ideal suite of KPIs when needed with minimal resources and effort. Ways to achieve this include to:

- utilize corporate systems – ERP, purchasing or eSourcing systems may include performance measurement capability;
- maximize available secondary data (assuming confidence in its validity);
- have the supplier measure and supply KPI data – whilst this has a cost to them, it may be more efficient for them to do this;
- use specialist providers – companies who can analyse available corporate information to extract spend or performance data; and
- find an App! There are smartphone or tablet apps for most things today. Someone, somewhere, may well have created a simple program that can help you.

Measurement system responsiveness

Measurement systems have different degrees of responsiveness, either in terms of obtaining feedback about the measurement or the time taken to be able to effect improvements. In order to prevent, or achieve timely correction of, a supplier problem we must understand our system responsiveness how quickly we can effect a correction. Imagine driving a car where the system of speed measurement took 10 seconds to display the current speed or worse you had to push the brake pedal five seconds before it would operate. Whilst not ideal, if you were aware, adaptation of driving style and planning breaking very early, would be possible.

In the UK radio industry, advertisers make decisions on whether or not to buy commercial airtime based upon listener ratings and the demographic profiles of the listeners. Until very recently the only way to measure this was for a small army of researchers to recruit a representative sample of listeners from across the nation who would then be paid to maintain a small log book of what stations they listened to and when over a set period of time. The results (known as RAJAR – RAdio Joint Audience Ratings) would be compiled and published quarterly and radio station executives and presenters would pore over the results to see how they performed three months ago. Historically, the only way to measure what happened in individual households was to go and ask people, which meant it took time to obtain meaningful feedback about the individual measures.

Where we can obtain a measure instantly it can take time to respond to it – like getting a large ship to respond; by the time it is apparent that the vessel is moving off course corrections can be made, but it is some time before it responds. This demands skilful anticipation and why most large ships are driven by computer control today. If customer satisfaction results suggest service from a supplier has dropped, this will need to be investigated, understood and a programme of retraining instigated and perhaps action to tackle morale, behaviour and organizational culture. This all takes time.

Furthermore, if it takes time to access and compile measures into a form that enables something to be done (just like the radio audience ratings), then it can take even more time to do something in response to a KPI.

The responsiveness of a measurement system impacts organizations and our relationship with suppliers. Despite the benefit of new IT solutions, measurement and improvement systems can still be complex and slow, but may also be the only way possible to guide and improve business outcomes. However, if we understand responsiveness we can at least manage supplier improvements and interventions accordingly.

SPM system maturity

So there are many different considerations in designing a SPM system for a supplier and developing KPIs that will be useful to us. This of course depends upon our SPM aims for this relationship. Sometimes a set of lagging measures may suffice, for others we may need outcome driven performance management using hard and soft measures to support a collaborative relationship. There are therefore different degrees of SPM and we can select different levels of SPM maturity according to the outcomes needed. These are given in Figure 6.5.

Step 5: SPM outputs

Step 5 is the way our measures and KPIs are outputted so as to be meaningful, timely and in a form that enables effective supplier management and improvement.

The perfect scorecard

Is actually quite small, displaying just the handful of KPIs needed and is something that provides an instant, easy to understand, view of supplier performance. There are many ways of outputting indicators and measures so they can be useful. The *scorecard* is probably the most common method of collecting and displaying supplier performance information (Gordon, 2008). A *scorecard* is therefore a simple output mechanism. Another output mechanism is, of course, the dashboard. Scorecards could in fact be viewed as mini dashboards, however it would not be uncommon to have both these used side by side with scorecards being used at a detailed supplier level and a dashboard providing a senior team with summary information.

Scorecards in SPM derive from the original Kaplan and Norton work and typically is an approach used to collate a range of different indicators, linked to business and relationship requirements, for one or more suppliers (Figure 6.6).

FIGURE 6.5 Levels of SPM maturity

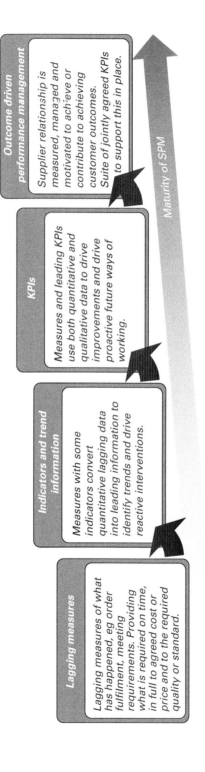

Lagging measures

Lagging measures of what has happened, eg order fulfilment, meeting requirements. Providing what is required on time, in full to agreed cost or price and to the required quality or standard.

Indicators and trend information

Measures with some indicators convert quantitative lagging data into leading information to identify trends and drive reactive interventions.

KPIs

Measures and leading KPIs use both quantitative and qualitative data to drive improvements and drive proactive future ways of working.

Outcome driven performance management

Supplier relationship is measured, managed and motivated to achieve or contribute to achieving customer outcomes. Suite of jointly agreed KPIs to support this in place.

Maturity of SPM

FIGURE 6.6 An example scorecard

Supplier Score Card – For *Entreprise Gadget Logiciel, France*						
Lagging Measures or KPIs	Result area and information source	Target	Q1	Q2	Q3	Q4
Safety – Lost Time Injury Frequency Rate	Number of incidents or near misses at supplier, with product or during delivery	Zero	0	0	1	0
Assurance of supply – Delivery on time, in full, in specification (DOTIFIS)	DOTIFIS report from ERP goods receipt + Internal rejections	98%	98%	100%	99%	92%
Relationship performance – delivery of actions, support and communication	Stakeholder survey results, complaints from stakeholders	90% Very satisfied	90%	100%	95%	82%
Leading Measures or KPIs	Result area and information source	Target	Q1	Q2	Q3	Q4
Growth and innovation – supplier contribution to business growth	Number new ideas delivered and total delivered value for both parties from them	2 ideas $50k/idea	0 ideas $0k/idea	3 ideas $78k/idea	2 ideas $10k/idea	2 ideas $60k/idea
Waste reduction – to meet corporate waste minimization goal	Production scrap rates, energy usage, packaging volumes and assessment	2%	5%	4.5%	4.2%	3.4%
CSR goals and compliance – to meet all supply chain CSR policies within two years	Audit reports	100% in 2 years	78%	82%	82%	82%

Scorecards should not be considered as a 'once only' activity, but rather as something dynamic with the KPIs and measures used changing to reflect the changing customer and environmental needs.

The perfect dashboard

A dashboard is an alternative approach to outputting supplier data. The perfect dashboard provides a current summary of the status of supplier performance – not all aspects but just enough to provide the vital information needed. A dashboard could be a report, online display, smartphone app or other means to provide the vital information where and when needed. If we have a scorecard in place for a supplier relationship, we probably do not need a dashboard also as it would be a duplication. However, the dashboard concept tends to be more suited to situations where summary information is needed, either summary performance information about a single supplier, supported by extensive scorecards detailing different aspects of day-to-day performance or more commonly to provide summary supplier performance information for senior staff relating to all or a group of suppliers, or overall progress towards a specific goal. Figure 6.7 gives an example.

Again it is all too easy to design supplier performance dashboards that start to look like the cockpit of a Boeing 747, but efficiency and effectiveness comes from focusing on just what is needed by those who are accountable or need to make informed decisions.

Making outputs compelling

If the outputs of our measurement system fail to communicate the message, fail to highlight where action is needed or are simply too complex to understand then they are worthless. The example of the scorecard in Figure 6.3 includes a visual dimension through the Red/Amber/Green status accompanying each measure, directing the reader as to where attention might be needed. This is great for KPIs, where we have perfected the timely creation of the right key indicators informed by good data collection and measurement. However, we may need additional supplier performance information, perhaps to investigate a specific problem, inform a strategic sourcing or category management project or help create the KPI in the first place. Here, the way measurement data gets presented can make all the difference as to whether the reader gets it or not, and if we are trying to convince budget holders or stakeholders to act this is crucial.

Some people have the sort of brain that can look at a table of data and 'see' what it is saying in double quick time, but for most, tables of data or statistical information require interpretation or explanation. Converting data into visual information allows it to be accessed more widely but also enables the story of the data to be told; conveying trends and key points to the reader. Such examples are all around us – government publications

FIGURE 6.7   An example executive level supplier dashboard

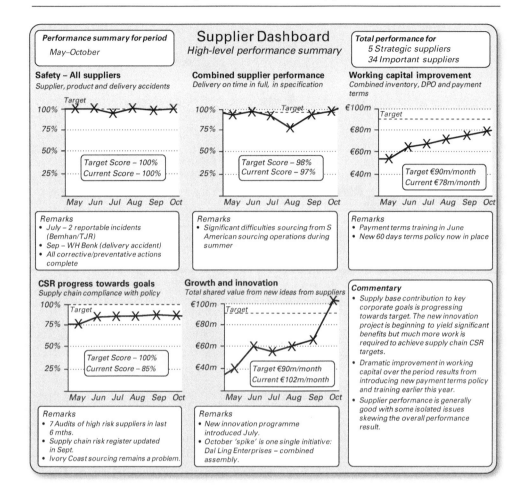

packed with 'infographics' convert complex statistical data into digestible images that show things like population, employment or migration as different sized clusters of little people superimposed on a map. Coxcomb graphics show variation in segments, bar charts show trends and so on. Applying similar creativity to how we portray key supplier performance data can really help to galvanize support from the wider business to a certain cause. For example, imagine a scenario where the business favours a certain pump supplier because it is cheaper, yet our supplier performance data reveals the total cost of ownership is actually much higher overall, and we would be better served switching supplier. Here, presenting total cost of ownership data visually can help educate stakeholders and win their support for change (Figure 6.8).

FIGURE 6.8   Total cost of ownership data for a pump

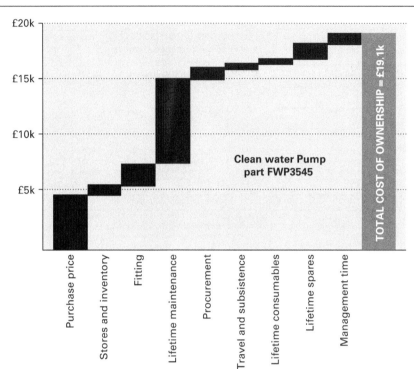

Revealing trends within supplier performance is also important as this converts lagging measures into leading indicators and visual outputs can help here also. Cunningham and Fiume (2003) suggest it is important to 'show trend lines', suggesting KPIs can show not only the actual results and goal for this period but also the trend over a longer period of time to demonstrate continuous improvement. It can also show where intervention is needed. For example, consider Figure 6.9. Here we have performance data for a supplier over a 12-month period shown as a pie chart. The size of each segment represents the performance for that month. What does this tell us? Not much unless we study the relative size of each segment. More useful is to convert this into a simple bar chart and then overlay a trend line with some commentary.

Finally, consider being creative with supplier performance measurement. If the goal is to convince others or drive change then consider ways to communicate complex performance information so others get it easily. It doesn't follow that measurement information always needs some sort of bar or pie chart. There is a world of visual information techniques – indeed this is an entire topic all of its own with many books on the subject available. Shifting the mindset away from 'how to I reproduce this data in graph

FIGURE 6.9 Less and more useful approaches to presenting supplier performance information

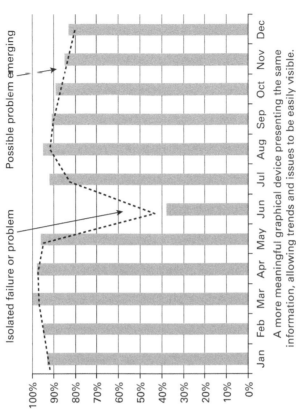

A more meaningful graphical device presenting the same information, allowing trends and issues to be easily visible.

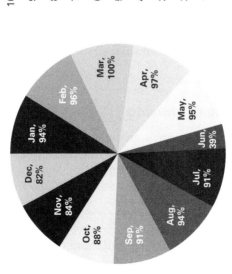

A less meaningful representation of monthly performance data – the pie chart fails to reveal problems and trends

FIGURE 6.10 Using a Minard graph to show where cost is added in a supply chain

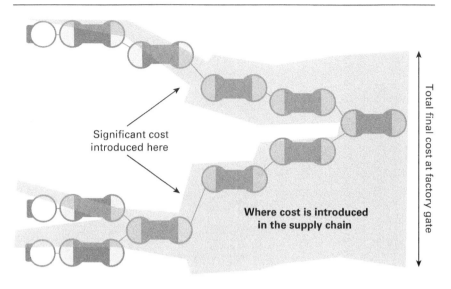

form' to 'how do I show the story this is telling me' can make all the difference. The London Underground map, is actually not a map. It is a graphical representation of the sequence of stops and where lines connect, which is everything the traveller needs to know to navigate the system. It bears little relationship to how lines are actually routed – a concept developed by Harry Beck in 1931.

Figure 6.10 gives an example of a Minard Graph (developed by the civil engineer Charles Minard who pioneered the use of graphics in engineering) used to show where cost is added within a supply chain – providing an instant visual message of where to look first.

The importance of sharing

There is little point measuring something if we do nothing with the results. Clearly if we measure a supplier's performance but don't provide them with the results there is no opportunity for them to improve or correct. Yet this is often exactly what happens – KPIs and scorecards end up being kept secret for a number of reasons:

- Assuming no need to share anything other than a problematic result.
- Not making the time to meet and share.
- Simple forgetfulness.
- Fear the supplier will try to take an advantage from positive performance data.

- Knowledge is power.
- Not risking supplier challenge.
- No consequences – no one else will know data is not being shared.
- Apathy.

Cunningham and Fiume (2003) suggest that 'if it is worth measuring, it should be displayed in a way that everyone can see'. Just like at a sporting event where people watch both the game and the scoreboard. 'Doing something' with measurement is not only about sharing with the supplier, but can also be about sharing data internally. If supplier measurement is regarded as something procurement does in isolation then there will be no value beyond a report satisfying the individual who looks after such things. Yet supplier performance is a business-wide concern, so sharing performance should also be business wide as appropriate. Metrics shape behaviour. If someone's salary bonus is dependent upon achieving a certain level of sales or savings or compliance to budget, their behaviour will be aligned behind this. So if we want good or improved performance then everyone who plays a part in the buyer–seller relationship needs to know what is going on. This is supported by Gordon (2008) who suggests that SPM might be more appropriately viewed as business relationship management including how effectively the firm ensures a two-way flow of understanding between the company and its suppliers in terms of meeting performance expectations.

Sharing measures with suppliers and internally is really very simple. It involves giving them the scorecard and this can be done during a supplier review meeting, perhaps involving internal stakeholders as appropriate. We will cover how to do this in Chapter 9.

Acting upon measurement

07

This chapter explores the process of driving corrective and preventative action, and driving improvements with suppliers in response to supplier measurement or as a standalone activity. The different levels of intervention are outlined and approaches for managing improvements are explored and a comprehensive improvement process is provided.

PATHWAY QUESTION ADDRESSED IN THIS CHAPTER

6 What supplier improvements would make a difference to us and how can we drive these?

How much improvement?

Supplier improvement and development (SI&D) are integral components within an overall SRM approach. SI&D can mean many different things ranging from simple intervention to have a supplier fix a problem related to what they provide through to working collaboratively with a supplier to develop capability across an entire process to the benefit of both parties. Similarly to SPM, each SI&D approach is also unique, matched to the supplier, what is being supplied and the prevailing environment and conditions. Flexibility is essential in order to select and deploy the right approach for each scenario.

Interventions here fall into one of two categories according to the degree of importance of a supplier and the outcomes we need:

- *Supplier improvement* – corrective action, preventative action and continuous improvement. Interventions are developed to move from a current position, perhaps based on past performance, towards a new improved position. Supplier improvement is most relevant to our middle tier *important* suppliers and perhaps even some *transactional* suppliers and is mostly, but not completely, reactive.

- *Supplier development* – working with the supplier to advance towards an agreed goal. Interventions are collaborative with the supplier and seek to develop new capability thus enabling the supplier to work towards a new goal that would otherwise be unrealizable. Supplier development is most relevant for *strategic* suppliers and is typically proactive.

SI&D intervention may be necessary and appropriate for many different reasons. This includes:

Supplier improvement (reactive)

- Fix a supplier related problem.
- Reduce or eliminate a known risk.
- Reduce cost.
- Improve process effectiveness or efficiency.
- Improve performance.

Supplier development (proactive)

- Develop capability.
- Develop a new product or service.
- Create a new differentiator.
- Increase market penetration.
- Enter new markets.
- Release new value that benefit both parties.

SI&D action could be an isolated, standalone activity, perhaps in response to a simple supplier issue. It is more effective when as part of a wider SRM approach with improvement initiatives responding directly to KPIs and development initiatives determined according to what the organization needs from its supply base. SI&D is an integral component within a wider SRM approach with a mightiness that comes from the way it works together with the other components. SPM informs SI&D, which shapes SM and SCM and becomes part of SCR and so on. SI&D is defined as:

> Supplier-specific reactive and proactive intervention, ideally within an overall SRM approach, to drive specific corrective actions, improvements and, for the most important suppliers, to further advance and develop the supplier and its capabilities in line with our goals and perhaps joint, shared goals.

Acting upon measurement

On 16 July 1999, John F Kennedy Jr died, along with his wife and sister-in-law, when the aircraft he was piloting crashed off the coast of Massachusetts. The investigation into the crash by the National Transportation Safety Board determined the cause to be due to 'spatial disorientation' (NTSB, 2000); in other words, when a pilot's perception of direction does not agree with reality. A visible point reference such as the horizon enables a pilot to determine the attitude, altitude and airspeed of the plane. Without a reference point it is possible to inadvertently descend whilst flying upside down believing the plane to be either flying straight or ascending as the effects of rapid descent will keep the pilot in the seat as if the right way up. Indeed, in such a situation a pilot can be completely oblivious to the fact that he is flying upside down. On this day visibility was poor and other pilots had reported 'no horizon' due to mist and haze. In order to fly safely in such conditions pilots need an 'instrument rating', which Kennedy did not possess, and protocol would require the pilot to fly by, and completely trust instruments rather than perceptions, which goes against our natural human instinct. It is reasonable to assume that the indicators in front of Kennedy were presenting the correct information about how the plane was flying (as the investigation did not find anything to suggest otherwise) and so perhaps this information was either not believed or understood and was not acted upon.

This tragic case highlights the need to be able to understand and act upon certain key indicators. Measurement is only effective if something meaningful is done with the results. If we have developed our KPIs effectively then these will provide the precise measures and indicators to help us move towards a stated goal or outcome. For this to happen the outputs of our measurement system must be shared and available and we must be organized so as to review and act upon these outputs. However, KPIs as part of SPM is just one trigger for SI&D initiatives. It is entirely appropriate for improvement or development activity to be required and necessary where there are no KPIs but because we see an opportunity to drive an improvement or development with a supplier to help us reach our goal.

How much improvement do we need?

The Aberdeen Group (Limberakis, 2012) suggest a key factor that characterizes best-in-class suppliers is the ability of an organization to track progress of corrective actions and improvement plans with suppliers.

Intervention here can take many forms and we need to be able to select and deploy the right approach. For most transactional suppliers it would be entirely appropriate not to invest any effort in fixing a supplier related issue. If the contractor who is employed to do grounds maintenance fails to turn up we can simply call someone else. If goods or services are not what we ordered we might demand a replacement, rework, rectification or refund as appropriate. These are simply the vast majority of suppliers, perhaps serving a great number of individuals within a business, where there is relatively low spend and low risk. If there is a supplier related problem somebody will instigate corrective action with the supplier, just as if it were something we had bought personally and needed to take back.

Corrective action alone may not be sufficient for issues with our important suppliers, especially those where we determine significant risk exists, and so we might need greater confidence for the future by seeking both corrective action and action to prevent reoccurrence.

Action and intervention could be standalone, perhaps a user rejecting something that is not satisfactory or a response to outputs from our SPM system such as a goods inwards inspection department in a factory. Again such intervention is typically reactive, but for our very important and strategic suppliers if we can move beyond reactive approaches we can find greater opportunity for new value from the supply base, and with collaboration with key suppliers significant growth and competitive advantage can be realized.

It is possible to get beyond correcting and preventing supplier problems for the critical few strategic suppliers and instead drive supplier improvement and development, to achieve new goals. We still need to decide what sort of intervention is needed to get there and this must be matched against our ability and the ability of a supplier to deliver here. For our important and strategic suppliers this might range from simple improvements up to full collaborative programmes with the supplier supporting joint advancement towards mutually agreed goals, perhaps even demanding effort from us to help develop the supplier's capability also. Figure 7.1 shows the different approaches to improvement and development according to importance in terms of how improvement goals are defined, arrangements for measurement and types of interventions.

The six degrees of supplier intervention

There are six degrees of action and intervention with suppliers possible (Figure 7.2) and how much we need and what we choose to do depends upon how important the supplier is, our goals and what the KPIs tell us. Our six choices are as follows. The first three are largely reactive:

1 *Don't improve* – accept the situation. Appropriate where there is an issue or performance is below what is required but the impact of the situation is tolerable and/or it is not worth expending the effort to address the issue or you can simply stop using the provider.

2 *Corrective action* – specific intervention to fix a problem or correct performance. Appropriate for apparent isolated problems, or where there is no chance the problem can be repeated. Corrective action fixes a single problem; it does not enable us to learn from the problem.

FIGURE 7.1 Goals, measures and interventions according to supplier importance

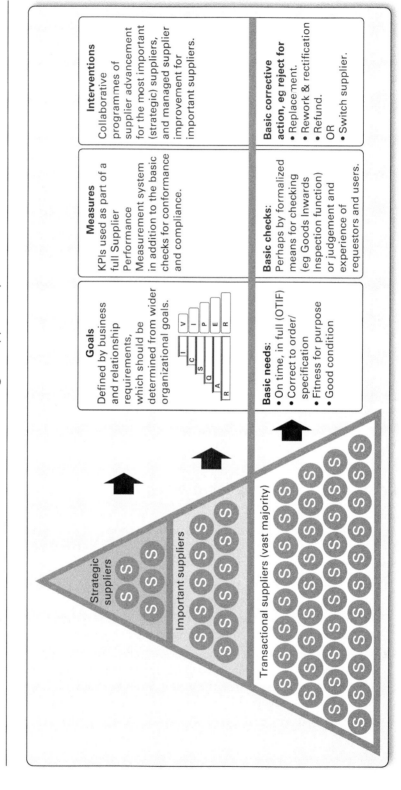

FIGURE 7.2 The six degrees of action and intervention

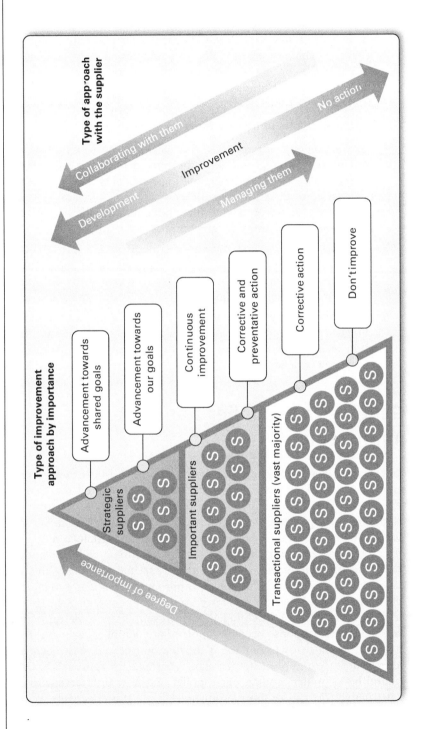

3 *Corrective and preventative action* – here the problem is fixed or performance corrected and then actions to prevent reoccurrence are implemented. Preventative action may not always be possible, but the deliberate step to review and consider the possibility helps realize learnings where they exist. Where companies have implemented ISO9001 the concept of corrective and preventative action will be well understood both internally and with suppliers as it forms an integral part of the standard.

The final three degrees of intervention tend to be more proactive:

4 *Continuous improvement (CI)* – an ongoing effort to improve overall supplier performance that looks beyond corrective and preventative action, but seeks to make ongoing improvements from our current position to products, services, processes or capability. Improvements are typically incremental over time, but could equally be a breakthrough or game changing improvement all at once.

5 *Advancement towards our goals* – distinct from CI; CI is about improving from where we are (ie setting goals based upon looking backwards), instead here we consider advancement towards our goals with interventions and supporting KPIs to help achieve this.

6 *Advancement towards shared goal* – here our goals are mutually agreed with the supplier and there is a jointly designed, owned and executed programme of intervention to move towards this, supported by leading KPIs.

Gauging the supplier's appetite for improvement

Where a supplier fails to hit a performance target it is just that – a fail. The supplier gets a black mark and is told how disappointed the company is with them. There are occasions where this approach is appropriate; for example a poor performing subcontractor may need to be managed in this way. However, generally a regime based upon performance measurement or failure to meet performance is a bit like berating a child for not getting the grades the parent expected. As many parents will testify this can be counterproductive. A more productive approach is to attempt to understand what is preventing the child from performing or encouraging the child to do better, unless of course the child has decided simply not to perform in which case a different response becomes appropriate. Suppliers are no different – if we are poised ready to pounce at the first hint of failure the supplier will adopt a defence and protectionist stance. Instead, an approach based more around better understanding our supplier and how to intervene in a more constructive way can be more productive. To do this effectively we need to gauge the supplier's appetite for improvement.

Suppliers will typically want to correct things that fall short. They are also likely to want to seek to improve and develop, after all survival and growth depend upon it. Suppliers may well determine and implement improvements based upon their own business aims and goals. These may well benefit us too so we certainly need to understand them if the supplier is important to us. However, here our role is passive; we are simply *observing* supplier-led improvements. This may be enough for less important suppliers, however for those suppliers who are important to us observation may not be enough as we cannot be sure the supplier's intervention is aligned to what we need. Instead for important suppliers we need to *drive* supplier improvements; to assume responsibility to make some sort of corrective action, improvement or advancement with a supplier happen. This is an important mindset within an overall SRM approach as remaining passive will not drive the results and outcomes we seek.

It doesn't follow that if you tell a supplier how you want them to improve that they will do so. Maybe they will, maybe they don't want to, maybe they need help to change. If I buy something from a shop that turns out to be defective then if I take it back they will almost certainly fix the problem, perhaps with a refund or replacement. Why? Well, they have legal obligations here and would most likely want to make sure I am satisfied and so preserve their reputation and brand. I may also be a good customer and one they don't want to lose. However, if I ask the same shop owner to alter his range or make changes to the way things are stocked he may listen, may be interested or may simply politely thank me and do nothing. Yet if with these changes came some certainty of increased business the level of interest would increase.

There are three things that will compel a supplier to respond to a call to improve or develop. These are:

- there is something in it for them;
- if they don't they will be worse off; and
- if it isn't a burden for them.

If we require supplier improvements and developments we therefore cannot assume suppliers will respond but rather we need to assess the degree to which they will be receptive and interested. Here we turn to two key strategic tools from category management – portfolio analysis and supplier preferencing.

Using portfolio analysis to understand our position

Portfolio analysis (Figure 7.3), based upon the work of Peter Kraljic (1983), is a means to determine the most effective strategic approach to source categories of spend (categorized to reflect how markets are organized) according to how difficult the market is and the potential to impact our profit, ie impact on profit is high if a small percentage improvement for each unit sourced will have a great impact on our profit – typically where there is high spend or we buy high volumes. If the categories a supplier provides sit

Little   Supplier interest in improvement/development   *Strong*

Critical

The supplier has power here as we cannot easily switch supplier.

Supplier interest – Little beyond basic obligations, eg corrective action unless we have great strength in the market.

Strategic

We need them and they need us. If we manage the relationship well then there should be shared power with mutual goals.

Supplier interest – Strong, willingness to improve and also to collaborate with us to develop capability and effectiveness.

Acquisition

Our power is diluted but we still have choice and ability to switch. Here we should automate our buying as much as possible.

Supplier interest – Little beyond basic obligations, eg corrective action.

Leverage

We have choice and the power of alternatives; we can switch suppliers if we don't get what we want.

Supplier interest – Strong, willingness to improve in order to secure and maintain future business.

Power balance

Power balance line shifts right if we have low strength of position in the market (eg we are a small company), but shifts left if we have high strength of position in the marketplace (eg we are a major global player), affording us power even for categories in *Critical* in some cases and therefore increased interest from a supplier to drive improvements.

Degree of market difficulty

Degree of profit impact

Buyer power

Supplier power

in *Critical* then they hold the power here for this category. In *Leverage* we hold the power as we can switch supplier (low market difficulty). In *Strategic* ideally we both need each other and so power is mutual. Portfolio analysis helps begin to identify if any improvement or development initiative will have potency, but we also need to use it together with supplier preferencing.

Using supplier preferencing to understand their position

Supplier preferencing (Figure 7.4) comes from the world of sales and marketing and is a tool used to 'place ourselves in the supplier's shoes' and determine how they will, most likely, be viewing our account and therefore the degree of interest they may have in working on improvements for us or advancements with us. Supplier preferencing considers how attractive our account might be to a supplier based upon factors such as high spend, profit margin, payment terms, kudos from association with our brand, future opportunity and ease of doing business. It also considers the value of our account relative to the supplier's overall turnover. If a supplier sees us as *Development* then we are attractive and represent an account the supplier wants to grow in

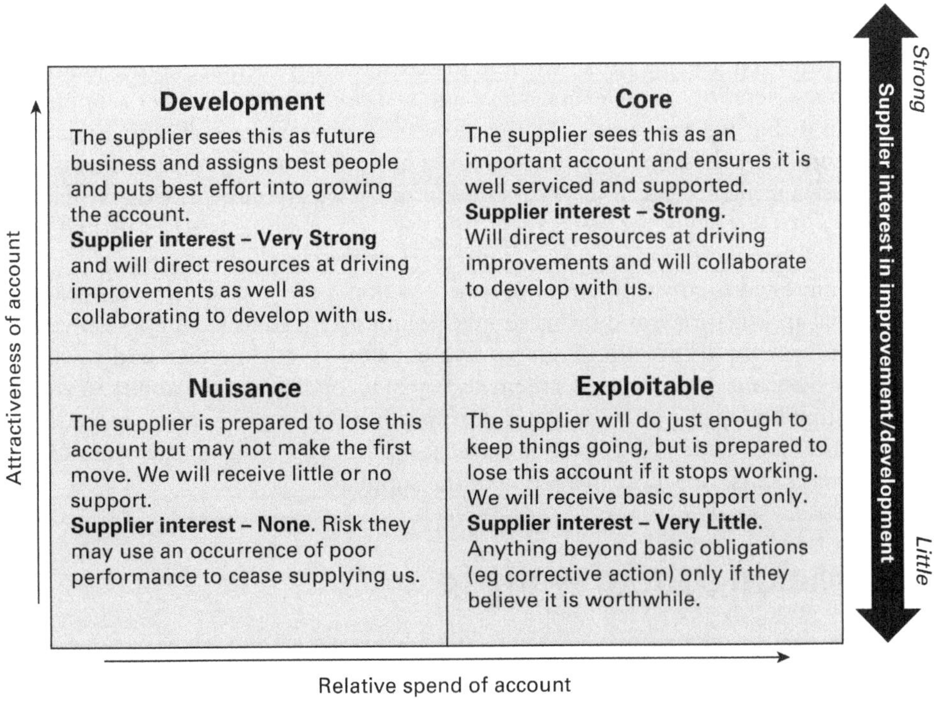

FIGURE 7.4   Supplier preferencing and the supplier's appetite for improvement and advancement

terms of spend. They will therefore be at their most attentive and responsive if we are in this quadrant and have their best business development people looking after us. Similarly in *Core* the supplier will have their most experienced people looking after the account and so will be prepared to put effort into improvement and advancement programmes. However, in *Nuisance* or *Exploitable* the supplier is less interested as our account is not attractive. So long as we continue to spend money with them (*Exploitable*) they will do just enough to keep things going, but are unlikely to be ready to put much effort in beyond this. So the degree of supplier interest will be directly linked to how attractive our account is to the supplier. Supplier preferencing and portfolio analysis are expanded much more in *Category Management in Purchasing* (published by Kogan Page).

Combining portfolio and preferencing to determine the right response

Once we have classified our position within portfolio analysis and supplier preferencing, it is the combination of the two tools that enables us to determine the supplier's overall appetite for improvement and more important how we should approach and shape any intervention with them. Figure 7.5 gives the ideal responses for the combined outputs of both these key tools. For certain combinations our way forward is clear, eg in *Strategic* and *Core* interventions should focus around *continuous improvements* or perhaps *advancement towards goals*. However, other combinations within this analysis can suggest that we don't actually have the option of driving interventions with a supplier, but rather we need to take alternative action in order to protect ourselves. For example, in *Critical* and *Development* the supplier is interested in us but we are at risk. We therefore need to work on building a relationship with them, perhaps encouraging and incentivizing improvements and advancements. But in *Critical* and *Nuisance* we are more at risk, we cannot switch suppliers, we need them but they are not interested in us and may well be ready to move away from us. Here the supplier will certainly not be interested in any sort of improvement action, perhaps with the exception of basic obligations, and if this supplier is important to us we must resolve this imbalance. In practice we have two choices – we can either find a way to reduce our dependency on them and open up choice and the ability to switch suppliers, perhaps by making our specification more generic, considering alternatives or substitutes, or eliminating the need altogether, or we need to make ourselves more attractive to the supplier.

Making them want to...

For situations where we seek improvement but the supplier lacks the appetite we should work on making ourselves more attractive and/or incentivizing

FIGURE 7.5 Determining supplier intervention responses by combining portfolio analysis and supplier preferencing

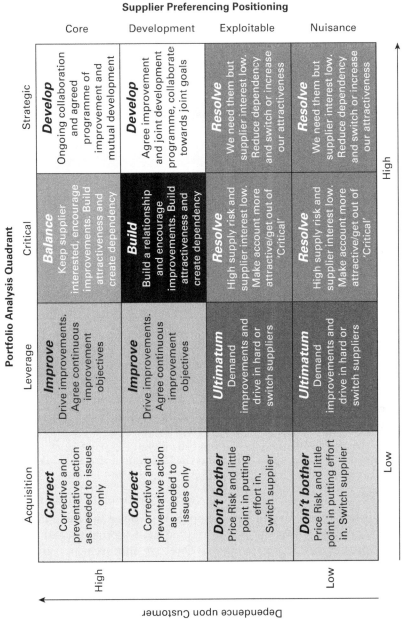

them. This can feel at odds with traditional buyer mindsets that might consider suppliers as *serving* us but it is sometimes necessary to face the fact that there are situations where we need the supplier more than they need us. In such instances, unless we can switch suppliers, our only course of action is to try to make them more interested in us. This can happen through effort on our part around *attractiveness, involvement* and *incentivization.*

Making us more attractive to them

We can make an account more attractive to a supplier in number of ways. Often we have more ability to do something here, and perhaps more leverage, than we realize. Perhaps the most under-utilized source of power around attractiveness is the kudos of being a supplier to a reputable, known brand business. Ways to increase supplier attractiveness include:

- increase spend or volumes;
- agree increased margin;
- more attractive payment terms;
- make doing business with us easier; and
- give things they will value, but are easy for us to provide, for example promote them, allow them to say they are a supplier to us in their marketing material etc.

Involving the supplier

If a supplier is not involved they cannot begin to be interested. Simply involving the supplier can be an easy way to galvanize interest and support to work towards a specific outcome, especially if in doing so they begin to see future potential for the account. The most effective improvements happen when we create a shared objective with the supplier, but only if they are interested. This means that traditional directive approaches to get a supplier to improve may fall short. There are in fact four degrees of involvement; each has its place according to the supplier scenario.

- *No involvement* – the supplier can't do it or won't do it so we do it.
- *Directive involvement* – the supplier is involved by telling the supplier what to do, perhaps in response to a problem, and the supplier is expected to respond. Directive improvements often come to the fore within a deteriorating supplier relationship, sometimes with threats of penalties or legal remedies.
- *Positive involvement* – positive action to involve the supplier in what we need to achieve with the aim of winning their interest and motivating them to drive improvements.
- *Collaborative involvement* – parties jointly decide and work towards agreed improvements sharing the benefits in some way.

Making a shift from *directive* to *positive* involvement increases the likelihood of a willing response, especially if we hold little power in the relationship.

Incentivizing the supplier

Hannabarger *et al* (2007) suggests 'you get what you reward'. When it comes to driving supplier improvement and development, incentivization is a powerful means to stimulate their interest, especially if there was little to begin with. Suppliers can be incentivized through either punitive or beneficial consequences of achieving certain outcomes, and work by providing reward, recognition or support:

Punitive

- contractual obligations; and
- penalties.

Beneficial

- gain share arrangements linked to defined level of benefit or improvement;
- payment by reward for hitting agreed goals;
- supplier recognition and certification programmes; and
- go help them, provide resources and expertise to help them develop.

Punitive incentives will drive certain supplier behaviour around ensuring agreed obligations are met. They will be effective and even collaborative only to the extent of meeting these obligations and nothing beyond this. For a construction project that must be completed on time this type of incentive is entirely appropriate. However, punitive incentives will fail to drive a supplier to help innovate with us, instead here incentives must be more beneficial to them.

Supplier incentivization requires clarity in terms of how the incentivization mechanism works and how success will be measured. Contractual provision is essential, so too are an agreed set of KPIs that will be used to measure success.

Learning from common improvement methodologies

There are many improvement methodologies out there and many we could adopt: four, five, six, seven, eight and ten step processes abound. Typically these originate from the worlds of manufacturing, business process improvement, change management and business development. An internet search here could well leave the enquirer bewildered and confused about how to set about driving some sort of improvement. *Improvement* is a science all of its own, firmly embedded within movements such as Total Quality Management (TQM), Lean, Six Sigma or Kaizen, each having earned recognition for proven improvement results in certain industrial environments, mostly manufacturing and the associated processes. Despite great success here, application of these methodologies with suppliers or within the supply chain demands adaptation and interpretation for this environment. Furthermore practitioners in this field tend to reside within manufacturing, process or quality functions.

Martin (2007) suggests that the full analytical potential (of these Lean, Six Sigma approaches) has not been realized because users are not familiar with supply chain work streams. It is rare to find individuals that are both highly competent in making these improvement philosophies a reality whilst having a deep understanding of strategic purchasing and how supply chains work. Such a combination is mightily powerful and such an individual is an asset to any purchasing function and arguably this is a skill set procurement functions need much more for the future.

Perhaps there is a Lean, Six Sigma or Kaizen (Continuous Improvement) team in our organization already, perhaps even an established improvement methodology applied regularly for manufacturing projects. Such teams can be keen to get involved in applying their knowledge beyond the bounds of a firm's manufacturing or process environment and working with purchasing on the supply chain. Therefore these experts have a lot to offer and should be invited to help develop supplier improvements; they will, most likely, have a vast toolbox of techniques that can help. Remember, however, that typically such teams will lack the understanding of strategic procurement and so the need to work together is key to success.

The mainstream methodologies that have the most relevance for supplier improvement are PDCA (Plan-Do-Check-Act), Lean, Six Sigma, Voice of the Customer (VoC), Kaizen and Continuous Improvement and DMAIC (Define, Measure, Analyse, Improve & Control). No one approach is necessarily better than another; they are all well proven and pretty much all of the methodologies would be effective for supplier improvements if deployed well. George (2002) suggests 'more organizations fail from a lack of creating the right culture and infrastructure than from using the wrong tools'. I will briefly explore each in turn and how they can support supplier improvement programmes, however each is an entire concept all of its own and so further reading is recommended if one ore more of these is to be adopted. Alternatively, in the next chapter I will outline the STPDR (Situation, Target, Plan, Do, Review) supplier improvement process – built upon the core principles from across these mainstream improvement methodologies, but specifically designed for driving supplier and supply chain improvement.

FIGURE 7.6   The Deming cycle – Plan-Do-Check-Act

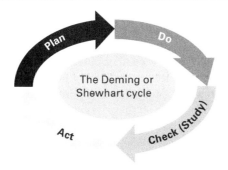

Plan-Do-Check-(or Study)-Act

Perhaps the most widely known improvement process, and one where most others can be boiled down to, is the Plan-Do-Check-Act (PDCA) process (Figure 7.6), also known the Deming cycle (Deming, 1982), as it was popularized by Edward Deming in Japan in the 1950s having been based upon earlier work by Walter Shewhart in 1939 (Shewhart, 1986) and therefore may also be known as the Shewhart cycle.

Plan   – establish objectives and determine how to achieve outcomes.

Do   – implement the plan.

Check – Deming later switched *check* to *study* in his model which is what this step is concerned with; studying the actual results against the expected results.

Action – if objectives were not met, analyse why and determine the action needed. However, if objectives were met then build on this and set standards for future performance.

Variants of PDCA include PDSA (Study not Check) and OPDCA, where an additional *Observation* step is included to ensure the current condition is fully understood before embarking on planning.

Learning from Lean

Lean (lean manufacturing, lean enterprise, lean production and of course lean supply chain) is based upon the concept that using resources for any other purpose than the goal of creating end customer value is a waste and should be eliminated, ie preserving value with less work. *Lean* originates from the Toyota Production System (Womak *et al*, 1990) and seems to have become mainstream and identified as *Lean* in the 1990s. However, the principles of *Lean* can actually be found as early as the 18th century when the Royal Navy developed 'Standard Ops' and 'Quick Changeover' methods to enable the delivery of a broadside twice as fast as other navies (Bicheno and Holweg, 2009). Deming emphasized the need to focus on waste reduction during the 1950s, but it was Taiichi Ohno, the father of the Toyota Production System and JIT, who assembled the seven wastes (called *Muda*). These *wastes* represent areas where resources can end up being used for purposes other than creating customer value and by focusing on these it is possible to make an organization and supply chain more effective. The original seven wastes by Ohno (which handily form the acronym TIM WOOD) are:

- *Transport* – moving goods or services that are not required to process.
- *Inventory* – carrying additional inventory or work in progress.
- *Motion* – of people or equipment over and above what is needed for processing.
- *Waiting*.
- *Over-production*.
- *Overprocessing*.
- *Defects* – and the cost of poor quality.

However, Womack *et al* (1990) introduced an eighth waste defined as:

- Waste of making the wrong product efficiently – goods or services that do not meet customer demand or specifications.

Furthermore Bicheno and Holweg (2009) also suggest that today it is appropriate to add to Ohno's famous list and propose new additional wastes, which are:

- waste of untapped human potential;
- waste of excessive information and communication;
- waste of time;
- waste of inappropriate systems;
- wasted energy and water;
- wasted natural resources;
- waste of variation (called *Mura* within Lean);
- waste of no follow through; and
- waste of knowledge.

Lean comes from the world of manufacturing and in this context effective application of Lean does not mean practitioners must embark on a quest to remove all the 'wastes' they can find. What is, and is not, waste is solely determined by the customer, not the Operations Manager on the shop floor!

(Bicheno and Holweg, 2009). The same applies if we adopt Lean principles with suppliers, for example holding inventory might seem at odds with Lean principles, but if that inventory is a customer stipulated requirement and it provides vital reassurance and confidence to the customer, then it is not a waste. Once again we find ourselves needing to focus on value, as ultimately defined by the end customer and what does not contribute to value is waste. The published wisdom on Lean tends to adopt an inward focus to identification and reduction of *waste*; waste on the shop floor, waste in inventory and so on. However, a shift of perspective to consider what the customer might consider waste can help us form a better definition of the value we should pursue. For example, if you phone a call centre and the automated system asks you to enter your account number, but when you get put through to an operative she asks for the very same information again you have wasted time and effort. If we queue multiple times, have to re-enter information online more than once, or arrive to be told something is out of stock or get told the wrong information then waste in terms of time, delay, duplication, poor communication is forced upon us. This thinking allows us to consider waste within a supplier or supply chain process or indeed in the context of what the customer values and reinforces the importance of taking an 'end-to-end value chain' perspective and ensuring what the customer needs and wants are get properly understood and articulated within our business and relationship requirements.

Lean is a tool to improve an organization's supply chain and logistic performance (Myerson, 2012). Lean within a supplier improvement initiative is concerned with preserving and improving overall supplier and supply chain value. In practice this might involve specific initiatives such as mapping all the steps in the supply chain to see if we can become more efficient and reduce *motion*, looking for ways to reduce or improve packaging to reduce *defects* and unnecessary *transport* or changing a specification to reduce *over-production*.

One of the most popular tools in Lean is 5S, which is a simple tool used to help reduce waste, variation and improve productivity. Originally named after the Japanese 5 Ss, which are *Seiri, Seiton, Seiso, Seiketsu and Shitsuke*, these are commonly translated into:

- *Sort* – throw out what is not used or needed.
- *Simplify* – put what is left in its rightful place.
- *Scan* – to look for things that are out of place and 'tidy up'.
- *Standardize* (sometimes stabilize) – make the improvement permanent and put standard procedures in place.
- *Sustain* – ensure the improvement sticks and to continue the habit.

The improvement philosophy behind 5S can be best understood by applying the model to an everyday process such as tidying a desk or reorganizing a room and forms a neat improvement process. Once again this is a model that can help with supplier improvement – *sort* the suppliers who have the best potential to build end customer value, ditch the rest; *simplify* how we work and interact together to make it more effective; *scan* supplier performance using KPIs derived from customer expectations and act where needed; *stabilize* with new processes, procedures and ways of working; and *sustain* through ongoing monitoring, measuring and review.

How Six Sigma can help

Six Sigma is a set of approaches, tools and techniques for process improvement and seeks to improve the quality of process outputs by identifying and removing the cause of defects, errors and minimizing variability. The concept was developed by Motorola during the 80s and famously adopted as the means by which Jack Welsh, CEO of General Electric, used to transform the business (Tennant, 2001). Six Sigma originated as concept to improve manufacturing using statistical modelling of manufacturing processes (a six sigma process being one free where 99.9999998 per cent of products being manufactured are statistically expected to be from defects) and whilst the concept may not be entirely relevant to supplier improvements and developments, some of the tools used and indeed the knowledge of Six Sigma champions is relevant and can help us.

It seems Lean and Six Sigma sometimes seem to compete as improvement philosophies; however, the more enlightened companies see them as partners. Combining Lean with Six Sigma means we can consider improvement in terms of the removal of waste and reduction of variation, two of the main themes that W Edward Deming pursued during his career (Bicheno and Holweg, 2009). Within Lean we can simplify processes, eliminate waste and increase speed. Within Six Sigma we can reduce variation, eliminate defects and sustain the gain.

Six Sigma makes sense when you see what happens in organizations and supply chains as a series of processes that flow across departmental and contractual boundaries and the entire methodology is structured around meeting the requirements of the customer. GE's version of Six Sigma is built upon six guiding principles (Bicheno and Holweg, 2009). These are:

- *Critical to quality* – everything must be driven from what the customer needs and wants and so the starting point is to understand this.
- *Defect* – anything that doesn't deliver customer needs and wants.
- *Process capability* – processes must be designed so they have the necessary capability to deliver customer needs and wants.
- *Variation* – as experienced by the customer.
- *Stable operations* – to ensure consistent, predictable and reliable processes to deliver customer needs and wants.
- *Design for Six Sigma* – design must meet customer needs, wants and process capability.

Six Sigma can help be effective at driving supplier improvement and once again we are reminded how essential understanding customer requirements are and the role good business and relationship requirements play in the improvement process.

Hearing the Voice of the Customer (VOC)

A major 'customer value' focus within Lean Six Sigma is that of understanding customer requirements through Voice of the Customer (VOC) where improvement initiatives consider the impact of the project in terms of its eventual solution on the external customer. VOC is also found in marketing, market research and IT and can use a variety of tools, methods, techniques and approaches to capture and understand customer expectations, preferences and aversions and analyse overall customer needs and how customers value those needs. One of the biggest challenges with VOC is that of truly understanding the customer as it is easy to inadvertently substitute our voice for theirs.

Within SRM and specifically supplier improvement VOC is highly important as our improvement interventions need to respond directly to VOC. Here our customers are those in the firm who have an interest in what our suppliers do and how our supply chain operates as well as our customer and the ultimate end customer. Within SRM VOC is articulated through the business and relationship requirements, therefore providing these are robust, have been well developed with thorough research and consultation and are regularly reviewed then it follows that our KPIs and supplier improvement intervention will be aligned with VOC.

Kaizen (continuous improvement) has its place

Kaizen (*kai* = change and *zen* = good) means 'good change' and refers to any sort of improvement – one off, continuous, breakthrough or small. However, *Kaizen* has come to stand for *continuous improvement* or *philosophy of improvement* following the way the label has been used widely in Japan and by pioneers of the movement. Kaizen is described by Imai (1986) as the 'the key to Japan's competitive success'.

Kaizen is a philosophy centred around continuous improvement of processes in manufacturing, engineering and business management and seeks to involve the entire business as well as the supply chain (Imai, 1986). Kaizen seeks to improve standardized activities and processes as well as eliminating waste and integral to the concept is the idea of nurturing human resources and having those involved participate in driving continuous improvement. This could be a formal large team improvement initiative or simple approaches where those involved in a process or delivery are encouraged to make suggestions for improvement.

Continuous improvement is frequently cited as the same as or originating from Kaizen, which is true in part however the concept is also found in work from other pioneers such as W Edwards Deming, where principles of continuous improvement are embedded within a system to improve towards goals informed by ongoing feedback from customers and form the process.

Continuous improvement with suppliers is therefore an ongoing effort to improve products, services, performance, capabilities or processes through incremental improvements over time or breakthrough (all at once).

Adopting a multi-step process such as DMAIC, Juran or Kotter

It seems there is an improvement process of one sort or another for every possible occasion. Search on 'improvement process' and you will be spoilt for choice. Many of these are processes created or adapted for a particular industry or group of people with steps modulated to the area in question: five steps to improve healthcare outcomes, six step high school improvement process, 10 steps for automotive process improvement and so on. The point here is it seems the process of driving improvement needs to be designed with the purpose in mind. Across all of these the underlying steps are generally common but modulated differently to purpose and number of steps. In fact, after more than 70 years, it is still hard to question the utility and elegance of Deming's Plan-Do-Check-Act approach that, as I said earlier, can be seen behind most improvement processes out there. Three notable and perhaps the most common are DMAIC, Juran's six steps, the 8D's and Kotter's eight steps.

DMAIC – (pronounced Duh-May-ick) is a data driven problem-solving and improvement tool from the world of Six Sigma. Motorola recognized that there was a pattern to improvement (and use of data and process tools) that could naturally be divided into five phases of problem solving (George, 2002) as follows:

1 *Define* – the problem, goal, scope, available resources and any time constraints. Typically this would be captured within a Team or Project Charter.

2 *Measure* – using facts and data to establish and measure the current position to give a base line and identify the gap between current position and the goal.

3 *Analyse* – identify the root cause of the problem, what is constraining or preventing improvements or what would need to change to enable improvements.

4 *Improve* – determine, plan and implement the required improvement.

5 *Control* – sustain and monitor the improvement and embed as needed.

DMAIC is useful as it expands Deming's *plan* step much more to be clear about what we are setting out to do, to analyse the current position, to identify root causes or constraints before planning what we are going to do. This is a crucial sequence of activities for supplier improvement as it guides our intervention so as to respond directly to what needs to be improved, perhaps based upon our KPIs, business or relationship requirements.

Juran's Six Steps – Juran's six steps of problem solving originate from the world of quality improvement and is typically applied as part of a quality improvement project within an organizational culture that supports such an approach. Success demands the use of effective cross-functional team working to deploy the approach and adopting a 'breakthrough attitude', two key factors in SRM and supplier improvement as well as in category management. Juran's six steps are (Juran Institute Inc, 2013):

1 *Identify project* – adopting a breakthrough attitude.

2 *Establish the project* – set and verify a clear goal, form a cross-functional team.

3 *Diagnose the cause* – analyse symptoms, confirm the goal and establish root cause of the problem.

4 *Remedy the cause* – identify options then select, design and implement new arrangements so to eliminate, reduce or neutralize the root cause.

5 *Hold the gains* – introduce controls to maintain process and new arrangements.

6 *Replicate and nominate* – apply the results and learnings more broadly.

The 8Ds – an improvement cycle commonly used and probably originating from Ford (Bicheno and Holweg, 2009) is the 8Ds or *Disciplines*:

1 Form a team.

2 Contain the symptom.

3 Describe the problem.

4 Find the root cause.

5 Verify the root cause and select the corrective action.

6 Implement permanent corrective action.

7 Prevent reoccurrence, make the solution standard.

8 Congratulate and celebrate.

Kotter's 8 Steps – finally, driving improvement of any kind involves change. Poor change management and specifically failing to understand and reduce the impact of resistance to change is one of the leading reasons why projects fail. John Kotter's 8 steps for leading change (Kotter, 2012) focus on how organizations need to link with individuals, groups for change to be successful. The Kotter 8-step model therefore provides the steps for effective change management with an emphasis on acceptance and preparedness for change.

1 Establish a sense of urgency.
2 Create a guiding coalition.
3 Develop a clear shared vision.
4 Communicate the vision.
5 Empowering people to act on the vision.
6 Create short-term wins.
7 Consolidate and build on the gains.
8 Make it stick – institutionalize the change.

This process is very different from that used to solve problems as it can help create a shared vision with the momentum to realize it between a firm and a supplier, and between purchasing and its stakeholders. Effective change management is therefore an essential component for supplier improvements and indeed supplier developments beyond basic corrective actions.

So where does this leave us?

Supplier improvement and development (SI&D) needs a process to drive it effectively. Any one of the approaches above would work; however there can be limitations when some of these are applied to suppliers. Many are overly process focused due to their manufacturing origin and so not immediately suited to aspects of developing supplier relationships. All have been developed either for *improvement* or *problem solving*, yet across the literature architects of these processes or commentators seem to use both terms interchangeably, however for suppliers there is a need to be clear about what we are trying to achieve; to solve a problem or make something good into something better. It seems in fact that the differences across the various methodologies out there are where we start, what is important, who is involved and what sort of outcome we need. Therefore utilizing established improvement processes requires some interpretation and adaptation for the supply base.

Alternatively we can use a new improvement process and one that takes advantage of and builds upon that which has been proven to be effective within the established approaches but also provides for the nuances of SI&D with individual suppliers and throughout a supply chain, specifically:

- adaptability – relevant for fixing simple problems or helping achieve dramatic step change improvement;
- preserving the end customer focus through business and relationship requirements;
- making it a business-wide concern with cross-functional contribution;
- adopting Juran's breakthrough attitude;

- incorporating sound change management principles; and
- simple and accessible for those of us who are not experts and something that can be deployed without the need for a black belt in something that sounds Japanese.

The STPDR process (Figure 7.7) seeks to incorporate these success factors based upon what is proven to be effective and this is explored in full in the next chapter.

FIGURE 7.7   Introducing the STPDR process

Supplier improvement and development

08

This chapter outlines the SRPDR process for supplier improvement and development founded upon the best practice improvement approaches. Each step of the methodology is expanded together with practical help to apply the process to a range of supplier problem, improvement or development scenarios.

PATHWAY QUESTION ADDRESSED IN THIS CHAPTER

6 What supplier improvements would make a difference to us and how can we drive these?

Introducing 'STPDR'

The STPDR supplier improvement process (Figure 8.1) is a simple and straightforward approach for driving all types of supplier improvement. STPDR is a five-stage improvement process that can be applied to a variety of situations. The five stages are study, target, plan, do and review.

Supplier improvement and development (SI&D) requires a process and one that is supported by the right structure and commitment to ensure it is effective. SI&D must be firmly embedded within an overall SRM approach, sanctioned by the business and aligned to corporate aims and objectives. To do this we can use the STPDR supplier improvement process (Figure 8.1), linked to our KPIs, business objectives and the needs and wants of key stakeholders.

FIGURE 8.1 The five-stage STPDR supplier improvement process

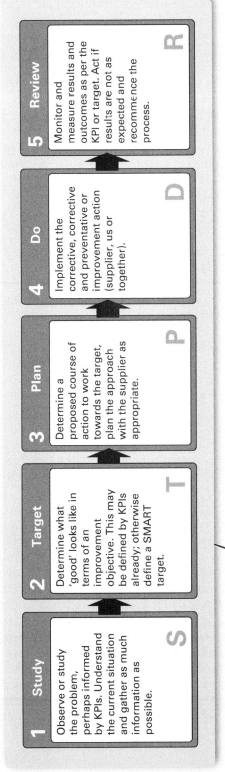

1 Study **S**

Observe or study the problem, perhaps informed by KPIs. Understand the current situation and gather as much information as possible.

2 Target **T**

Determine what 'good' looks like in terms of an improvement objective. This may be defined by KPIs already; otherwise define a SMART target.

3 Plan **P**

Determine a proposed course of action to work towards the target, plan the approach with the supplier as appropriate.

4 Do **D**

Implement the corrective, corrective and preventative or improvement action (supplier, us or together).

5 Review **R**

Monitor and measure results and outcomes as per the KPI or target. Act if results are not as expected and recommence the process.

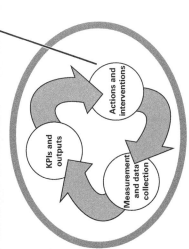

Actions and interventions

Measurement and data collection

KPIs and outputs

One of the simplest and most elegant tools to help determine 'where to go from here' is the STP (situation, target, proposal). Those familiar with my previous two publications, *Category Management in Purchasing* and *Negotiation for Purchasing Professionals*, will know that I am a great advocate of this because this simple tool is highly effective at enabling individuals and teams to figure out exactly where they are, where to go and how to get there for any problem or opportunity and using the tool requires the full contribution and alignment of a team to do so. I have observed teams in businesses all over the world use the STP tool to great effect – it is beautifully simple and it just works. It is therefore no accident that our supplier improvement tool incorporates an STP, except here we *study the situation* and our proposal becomes our *plan* for reasons I will expand on shortly, and, as the other methodologies out there would suggest, we need to add some further steps if our improvements are to be realized and embedded.

Step 1: Study the situation

STPDR Step 1 is about determining where we are now and is concerned with studying the precise nature of the problem we are attempting to fix or the area where we need improvement. *Juran's Quality Handbook* states 'Diagnosis should precede remedy otherwise biases or outdated beliefs can get in the way' (Juran and Godrey, 1999).

If we are to solve a problem then the diagnostic journey starts with analysing the symptoms, just as a doctor would start by asking where does it hurt. If we are solving a problem with a supplier then our symptoms might be expressed as late delivery, poor quality, incorrect quantity, not to specification or poor service. Here we need to start being precise. When you tell the doctor it hurts, he will ask 'where exactly? For how long? Does it hurt more if I squeeze here?' Similarly we need to look further: poor quality – compared with what? How late? How short? And so on.

If we are faced with a simple delivery issue then the problem may well be readily apparent, however not all supplier related problems are that simple and it may not be until later that an issue surfaces. Imagine buying several tins of paint for a home improvement project which all appear to be identical, but once applied it turns out there is a slight variation in colour from one part of our painted wall to another. Here the problem only becomes apparent after use and we would then need to study the problem; to attempt to identify if it is a problem with the paint, the wall or the application; to check which tins are different, if they have batch numbers and if so if there is a variation or anything that might tell us what has caused the problem. Only then could we begin to figure out what we need to do to remedy the problem.

The *Study* step therefore requires us to first define the problem and then, if the cause if not obvious, to study the situation or problem in order to determine its root cause, as if carrying out some sort of autopsy. The word autopsy is derived from the Greek *autoptēs*, which means 'self seen' or 'eyewitness', and this is why this step is called *study* because it is vitally important to take the time to properly comprehend and understand the problem before attempting to fix it; to *see* precisely what the issue is. We can waste a lot of time, effort and energy acting upon what someone told us, what the problem might be expected to be or on a single theory alone. If we decide the paint is defective and secure replacement tins we have wasted our time if the problem turns out to be due to a reaction with the wall's surface. Similarly a stopped production line due to a supplier tacking the wrong problem to try and fix an issue could be costly.

My first job was that of a Goods Inwards Inspector for a large electronics company. I frequently found myself out on the production line working with the production teams to solve a manufacturing issue. Often the problem would not be readily apparent and would require investigation to truly understand what the issue was. Perhaps two parts that were perfectly acceptable on their own might cause an unexpected issue when assembled together, perhaps slight variations in paint finishes, parts at extreme ends of their tolerances but still within specification. It was not uncommon for the part that seemed to be causing the issue to not actually be the cause of the problem. Truly understanding the problem often required investigation, gathering data, taking measurements and sometimes getting the supplier involved.

Juran (Juran Institute Inc, 2013) state one of the necessary elements for effective problem solving is data and hard facts; otherwise we are merely guessing at the causes and our efforts will be hampered by our lack of knowledge. They also state we need tools to solve complex problems and to help organize and understand the data and facts available, and structure in order to achieve breakthrough. Structure means cross-functional teams, chartered and empowered to work on a project and following a logical sequence of problem solution steps.

Supplier improvement therefore begins with good data and taking the time to really see the problem and understand it fully. We need to establish the root cause and once we know this, figuring out what to do becomes much easier.

Finding the root cause

Getting to a root cause is not as straightforward as it might seem, largely because our biases tend to prevent us seeing other than what we want to see. Factors that hamper us getting to the root cause and can introduce bias in our thinking include:

- *Exclusion* – missing data, not studying all of the problem or process.
- *Interaction* – the process or problem gets influenced as a result of being studied.
- *Perception* – beliefs and attitudes of those involved colour what we see and how we understand things.

Therefore determining a root cause requires us to adopt an approach that prevents bias and here we follow four key steps:

1 *Subject and deviation* – define the unwanted effect? Finlow-Bates (1998) suggests this should be expressed in just two words in *subject deviation* format. For example, paint incorrect, call-handler rude, packaging damaged and so on. Here the discipline of expressing this in just two words means we must focus hard on exactly what the symptom is.

2 *Potential causes* – determine the immediate direct cause or potential causes.

3 *Narrow down causes* – investigate each cause, test and eliminate to arrive at actual cause or causes.

4 *Sequence of causes* – determine the sequence of causes beyond this as far as possible. For example, 'packaging damaged' is caused by inadequate packaging, caused by correct packaging not being available, caused by correct packaging not ordered caused by the packer forgetting to say we had run out and so on.

Fishbone diagrams

A tool that can help with root cause analysis is the Ishikawa or 'Fishbone' diagram tool. Fishbone diagrams originate from the world of quality control and help show the causes of a specific event or problem (Ishikawa, 1968). Developed by Kaoru Ishikawa in the 60s, a fishbone diagram can be drawn to consider all of the potential causes of a particular problem or indeed what would cause an improvement effect and therefore what needs to be tackled to remove the problem or bring about the improvement. Each cause is typically grouped into categories or main cause themes that form the 'bones' connecting to the backbone. In manufacturing these categories might be the '6Ms' or even '8Ms' from the Toyota Production System. These are *Machine*, *Method*, *Material*, *Manpower*, *Measurement*, *Mother Nature* and sometimes *Management* and *Maintenance*. Alternatively the 7 wastes might be used and marketeers may use this technique with the 7Ps of marketing to determine a marketing strategy for a product. Using these high-level cause themes, the potential causes of a problem can then be considered, ideally within one or many group brainstorming sessions, and added to each arm of the diagram. The aim is to identify all the possible things that could have caused the problem, in effect creating a series of mini hypotheses.

Once complete, each potential cause can then be studied, explored, tested and perhaps eliminated, starting with the simplest and working through the entire model and this technique will allow the root cause to be identified for even the most complex of supplier related problems.

The 6Ms or 8Ms may provide a suitable framework, however for supplier related problems the slightly adapted set given in Figure 8.2 might be more

FIGURE 8.2 Fishbone diagram for a complex supplier issue

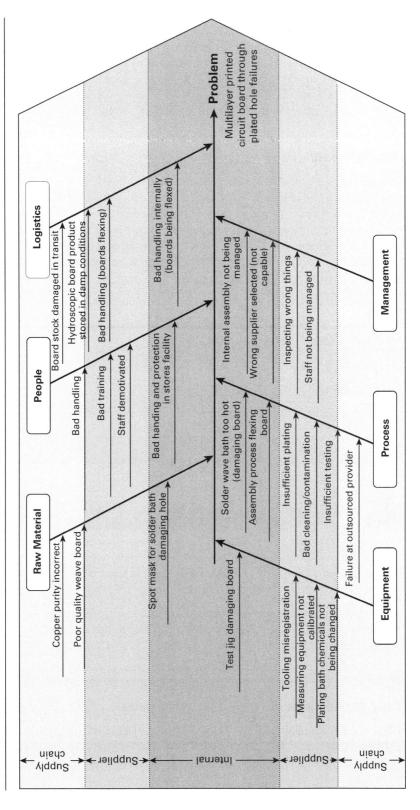

relevant. Note that for a supplier related problem, the factors that might cause the problem could reside with us, with the supplier or with their subcontractors or the interconnectivity between these entities. Therefore Figure 8.2 has been adapted to use a fishbone diagram that spans all entities, clearly differentiating between where a problem might occur.

The 'five whys'

The five-whys technique is another approach to find a root cause and can also help with the development of a fishbone diagram. This is a technique that children learn early on and thankfully we leave behind in adulthood, but is good to getting to the bottom of things. Five-whys is as simple as asking the question *why* five or even more times when presented with a problem or the scenario and the answers progressively get closer to the real reason, for example:

> *The problem* – Police officer: 'You appear to have pulled over and stopped at the side of the motorway.'
>
> *Police officer why number 1:* 'Why?'
>
> *Motorist answer number 1:* 'I'm broken down'
>
> *Police officer why number 2:* 'Why?'
>
> *Motorist answer number 2:* 'My vehicle just cut out on me and I had to pull over.'
>
> *Police officer why number 3:* 'Why?'
>
> *Motorist answer number 3:* 'I've run out of fuel.'
>
> *Police officer why number 4:* 'Why?'
>
> *Motorist answer number 4:* 'I didn't stop to get gas at the last station.'
>
> *Police officer why number 5:* 'Why?'
>
> *Motorist Answer number 5:* 'I wasn't paying attention and forgot I needed to get gas.'

Whilst this approach is very powerful, it is problematic because asking *why* repeatedly can appear a bit condescending. A more subtle approach is to mix *why* with questions like 'how does it do that?' or 'in what way or how does that make that happen?' and so on.

Root causes where there is no problem

So far we have considered the *study* stage in relation to a supplier related problem. This is of course only one reason why we might need to embark upon a supplier improvement activity. Alternatively there may be no problem at all, but rather an opportunity we have identified to improve a product, process, service, relationship, communication or other factor that could deliver a benefit for one or both parties. Here *Study the situation* becomes about understanding all the things that both hinder improvement or might need to happen to drive improvement. Once again we need to immerse ourselves, and ideally others who can help or have an interest, in the situation: to observe and to see with our own eyes what could make things better. Tools from Lean, Six Sigma and Quality Improvement can help here. The fishbone diagram, and more importantly the cross-functional brainstorming sessions that create it, can help us identify areas for improvement. Except here we are not looking for the root cause of a problem, but rather for potential sources of improvement; cause and effect of a problem becomes improvement and outcome. Figure 8.3 gives an example.

Step 1 of STPDR is possibly the most crucial. It is one that is easily neglected. If we truly see and understand a problem or what it takes to drive improvement we can move on to figure out where we want to be. The steps within this stage are therefore:

1 *Form a team* – necessary when we are setting out to fix a complex problem where we need a cross-functional team; one comprising those with an interest or expertise. Team might even need to include the supplier where we are seeking to drive improvements.

2 *Gather data* – collect as much available information, measurements, reports and observations about the problem, current situation or opportunity as possible.

3 *Study the problem/what is preventing excellence* – test, observe, compare, inspect, challenge and evaluate every aspect of the problem or improvement opportunity in order to fully comprehend and understand it.

4 *Develop hypotheses/options for change* – use tools such as the fishbone diagram, ideally developed in a group, to determine all the possible causes of a problem or the options for change for an improvement.

5 *Determine root causes/priorities for change* – test hypotheses and progressively eliminate them to arrive at the root cause or causes or for an improvement determine the priority areas to work on to bring about an improvement.

Step 2: Target for improvement

Step 2 is about determining where we want to be. Here we are looking to set a target that defines the objective for our improvement activity and the specific outcome we wish to achieve. There are three big assumptions here:

FIGURE 8.3 Fishbone diagram for a supplier improvement initiative

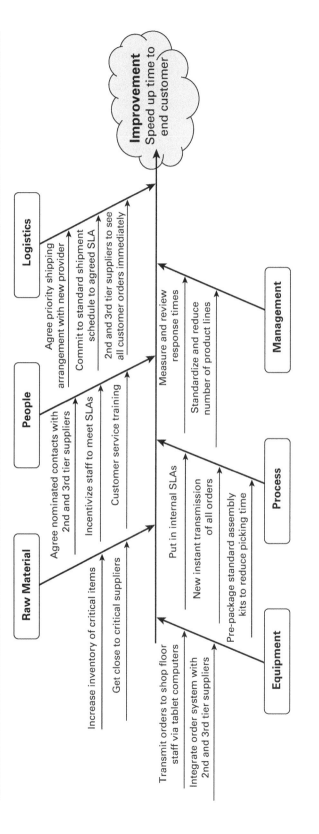

1 We know where we want to be.

2 We know exactly how to get there.

3 We are going to take the time to think about both of these.

It is easy to miss this step or for a target to simply be assumed due to our natural human tendency to cut straight to a solution: 'The paint is the wrong colour' so 'I'll take it back and get some new paint'. An obvious response and we will automatically make similar responses every day without a second thought, but this is not a target, this is actually a proposal or plan of what we intend to do. Our brains have already processed the problem and decided on the course of action. In the case of our tin of paint this may be enough, but if we jump straight to solutions for more complex issues we might lose sight of what we set out to achieve or worse those around us can't see or share our vision of our future direction and end up following aimlessly.

Indeed much of what is published in this space talks of different approaches to simply move towards a goal as if defining the goal was the easy bit; in practice this step can be the hardest. *Target* is the second step because we need the previous *Study* step to help us identify where we need to be, by revealing the root cause or where our improvements will have the most impact and therefore shape the goal, but it doesn't stop there.

Remember we have already defined certain goals within our business requirements and relationship requirements that flow from our high-level organizational goals. These may have been used to develop our KPIs and within our segmentation we may have identified specific opportunities for a supplier. Therefore targets for supplier improvement may not need to be created anew but, in fact, we may already have them.

This means that for everyday supplier related issues, delivery or quality problems we simply need things to return to our stated expectations; restating these targets within our improvement process, for example: 'On-time, in full deliveries to return to 99.5 per cent target figure within 30 days' or 'Return to 80 per cent of calls to be answered in 15 seconds within 7 days'.

For more complex supplier improvements target setting gets harder, especially if our aim is less defined and might involve unknowns such as finding new innovation that we can work on together with a supplier. Even if we can be clear about where we want to be, the journey to get there can be even more challenging. If we are setting out to drive an improvement from an already good place then here we may be setting out a new level of ambition within a supplier perhaps collaborating with the supplier to set the target.

Most literature on target setting will be quick to suggest all targets should be SMART (Specific, Measurable, Achievable, Realistic and Time-related). This helps but sometimes aiming for SMART targets can work against us as it can force us to be overly analytical in our targets. Not every goal lends itself to such an approach, for example targets for an improved relationship using SMART might leave us wondering how to apply the acronym. An alternative approach here is to consider these questions and if we can answer them then we have set a target:

- What specifically do we want?
- Where are we now relative to this goal?
- How will we know we've achieved it?
- Will there be any evidence to know we've achieved it?

The steps within this stage are therefore:

1 *Refer to any existing targets* – is there already a target here?
  If this is a supplier problem chances are we know what good looks
  like. Refer back to the business and relationship requirements and
  any targets that flow from these.

2 *Define target* – restating any existing target or define new. For a
  complex improvement initiative this may involve setting an overall
  goal with interim milestones.

Step 3: Plan

I knew six honest serving men,
(they taught me all I knew);
their names are what and why and when,
and where and how and who.
                    (Rudyard Kipling, 1902)

Kipling's opening lines from a poem accompanying the tale of 'The Elephant's
Child' is more than a century old now but remains an excellent reminder of
what a plan must deliver. If we create a plan that contains these *six honest
serving men* then we will be in good shape to achieve our target.

Step 3 is about planning the specific action to fix the problem or drive in the
improvement in order to meet the target. This may be a simple one-off action
(eg 'take the paint back and get new'), which would typically be expected for
simple supplier problems, or could be a sequence of steps and activities of
varying degrees of complexity. The plan (alternatively known as a *Programme*
by those in certain technical or architectural environments) connects targets
to actions and provides vital alignment, reduces uncertainty, focuses attention
and provides detailed direction for all involved. It guides execution whilst
providing a basis for control of actions to ensure they are delivered.

It is tempting to neglect planning and 'cut to the chase'. If we are working
alone on something simple this may be alright, but where others are involved
everyone needs to understand and be aligned with what is happening, who
is doing what, when and why. Obvious perhaps, yet the importance of good
planning is often missed. Anyone who has ever been part of a team activity
that required all to contribute but set off without a plan may well have experienced the chaos, tension and lack of traction first hand. Project planning
and project management is a subject all of its own and so for complex supplier
improvement projects further reading is recommended.

If we are fixing a supplier problem then we need only a simple action plan using *What, When and Who* format; listing the individual activities needed, when each must be completed by and who owns each action. Action lists should be agreed with those involved, shared and someone needs to take responsibility to ensure actions are delivered as agreed.

For more complex improvement initiatives planning needs to be a bit more advanced if it is to be successful. Here the use of Gantt charts to define the programme of activities and interim milestones becomes more appropriate and forms the basis to assign responsibility and secure resources.

Plans for complex supplier problems or supplier improvements may need to go further than the steps needed to move from one place to another, but may involve other activities too. If our course of action involves significant change within an organization or process we need to make provision to manage the change effectively so those involved understand what is expected but more crucially embrace rather than resist the change. Planning may therefore need to provide for good communication to help people understand *why* the change is happening and *what* is expected of them, procedures might need to be changed, people may need retraining and so on.

Complex improvement activities should be broken down into a series of smaller, more manageable steps, with key milestones identified. A series of smaller, more achievable goals, increases the likelihood of project success and those involved are better able to relate to the immediate task and see progress. It also helps to manage progress. Activities to potentially plan for within a complex improvement project might include:

- internal and supplier communication activity;
- involvement and participation of key players – to create a shared goal and 'felt need' for the improvement;
- executive support or endorsement; and
- change to policies, processes, systems or procedures;
- training and capability development;
- progress reviews; and
- how success will be celebrated.

Planning is best accomplished in a team with those contributing actively involved and a supplier improvement project is no different. If a supplier improvement is to be a success then those involved need to come to 'live and breath' the plan; there must be complete alignment and understanding and all must know what is expected of them. Planning for complex supplier improvements should therefore be a joint activity. Brown paper planning can help – here those involved literally stand around a piece of brown paper with a timeline across the bottom and create the plan. The individual activities are first brainstormed, each written on a separate Post-it note and then placed, with team agreement, on the brown paper to create a giant Gantt chart. The

FIGURE 8.4 The complete STPDR process, with individual activities at each step for either problem resolution or driving a supplier improvement

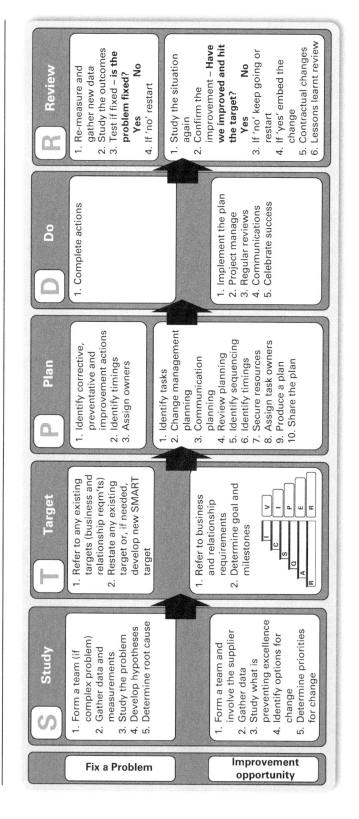

team can work on and reposition activities as needed until there is consensus regarding the finished plan. The addition of separate 'swim lanes' across the length of the brown paper allows planning to be themed, perhaps around supplier activities, internal activities, communication, reviews and so on. The benefit of brown paper planning is the group alignment the process naturally brings.

Steps within the *Plan* stage for supplier improvement are therefore:

1 *Identify activities* – list all the activities and tasks needed to accomplish the goal.

2 *Identify change management activities* – list all the activities and tasks needed to ensure the change is managed effectively and well provided for.

3 *Communications planning* – identify activities to ensure effective communication of the project to those who need to know or where it would help the project and increase buy-in by doing so. Typically this might include activities to identify key stakeholders and deploy regular targeted communications activities to each.

4 *Review planning* – identify the activities needed for good project management including regular review if appropriate.

5 *Identify sequencing* – figure out the sequence of activities required, paying attention to any dependencies, ie where one activity cannot start until another is complete.

6 *Identify the timing* – identify timing for each activity within the overall timeframe.

7 *Secure resources* – identify and secure resources needed for each task.

8 *Assign task owners* – assign and agree owners for each task.

9 *Develop a plan* – using Gantt chart form or an alternative planning approach, develop a plan, ideally as a joint planning exercise.

10 *Share the plan* – ensure all those involved receive the plan and any updates along the way.

Step 4: Do

Maintaining a linkage to the Deming cycle – the *Do* step is just what it says: it is about putting the supplier improvement plan into action. If we have completed the first three steps effectively then this step should be the easiest to get right. Success from *Do* comes through good project management in organizing, motivating and controlling resources and those involved to work towards the target.

Plans fail for many reasons: lack of resources, lack of buy-in, competing initiatives, poor goal setting, resistance to change and so on. However, we can head off many of these simply by making provision for them within the planning process.

For plans to fix a supplier problem, *Do* may be simply a case of ensuring agreed actions with a supplier are implemented, perhaps by keeping track of progress through e-mail, meetings and so. For more complex supplier improvements, *Do* means there could be a series of actions that need to be completed within a set timeframe, maintaining momentum and interest from those involved along the way. It doesn't follow that once a plan is developed and agreed that those involved will do what is required of them. Actions agreed in a meeting can easily drift if there is no apparent pressure, penalty or consequence for non-delivery. Human nature is such that people tend to focus on the need or issue that is closest in the field of view, responding to 'who is shouting the loudest'. The same applies to those internally and within a supplier's organization. So it is essential that we are ensuring our supplier improvement project always remains centre and front to the field of view of all involved. This is particularly important when the supplier may not be as enthusiastic to implement the improvement as we would like, perhaps because we are not that important to them. However, we can overcome this to a degree by sheer hard work, enthusiasm and allowing no slippage. Those leading at this step need the drive to push for delivery, rejecting excuses, abhorring slippage and removing obstacles.

Steps within the *Do* stage for supplier improvement are therefore:

1 *Implement the plan* – execute each activity as per the plan and to the timescales set.

2 *Project manage* – high focus, daily project management with ongoing checks and interactions with all involved to ensure activities are delivered and interventions to prevent slippage.

3 *Regular reviews* – review progress regularly with all involved. Check the project is continuing as planned and on track to realize overall goals. Act upon any issues or changing circumstances. Report and share progress to those involved and who need to know as per the communications plan developed during *Plan*.

4 *Celebrate success* – finally, after a long slog it is good to celebrate success; to thank all for their efforts and inspire people for what comes next. This is particularly important with a supplier and often a step that is neglected as the idea seems to be at odds with the common view of how we should interact with suppliers. However, social interaction is an essential component of effective joint working so if we are driving some sort of improvement with a supplier we must regard them as important in some way, so building social relationships can be a powerful thing to do. Furthermore, the end of a hard improvement projects legitimizes this, within the boundaries of any corporate guidelines and policy here of course.

Step 5: Review

The fifth step is about two things; checking that the improvement have been made and we have reached our target, and about instigating any new arrangements to ensure the improvement sticks, otherwise things may simply revert to the previous state.

Checking we have met the target may involve a repeat of some of the initial activities from step 1: we may need to re-measure, to re-evaluate or to once again study the situation to see if our interventions have been successful; ideally our targets provide a clear and measurable definition of what good looks like. If we are satisfied that our improvement has been successful then the cycle is complete. If it has not been, we can either effect further corrective actions or simply go back and restart the process again, studying the new problem and so on. If we have changed our paint, applied the new paint and all is good then our problem is solved. However, if we do this and we encounter a similar problem we have to once again study what is wrong.

It may be enough just to fixed a one-off simple supplier problem, but for more complex improvements it may be appropriate to put in place new arrangements so to prevent the problem reoccurring and to ensure the improvement is maintained (Lean calls this 'mistake proofing'). In practice this might involve:

- changes to policies, procedures, processes or systems;
- retraining or new training of those involved;
- communicating the details of the new arrangements, and what is expected of those involved;
- ongoing measurement and monitoring, perhaps involving new KPIs; and
- assigning new roles and responsibilities, eg to *own* a new process, monitor effectiveness etc.

Finally, a lessons learnt review is always worthwhile at the end of an improvement initiative. Taking time with those involved to ask the two simple questions: 'what worked well', and 'what could have been better' captures vital knowledge and the simple process of discussing this serves to share this knowledge and align and equip those involved for the next time.

Steps within the *Review* stage for supplier improvement are therefore:

1 *Study the situation* – re-measure, re-examine, gather new data and study the situation once again to see if the problem has been fixed, the improvement realized but ultimately if the target has been achieved as stated.

2 *Confirm* – confirm, with stakeholders and those involved as appropriate, that the target has been achieved and therefore there is no further action to fix the problem or complete the improvement.

If no confirmation is available then gather further data or study some more as needed. However, if it is clear that the target has not been met, and the target still remains appropriate, then the improvement initiative has failed and the process should be restarted.

3 *Embed the change* – implement actions necessary to ensure the improvement sticks and problems are not repeated. This might involve changes to policies, procedures, processes and systems, train and re-train, communicate, set new measurement regime in place and assign new roles and responsibilities.

4 *Contractual changes* – agree and update contractual arrangements or develop new as appropriate to ensure any new obligations or requirements are incorporated.

5 *Lessons learnt review* – conduct a lessons learnt review. Share with all involved and others who may benefit from the knowledge.

Making it work

The full STPDR process, with all activities at each step for both supplier problem resolution and for driving supplier improvement is given in Figure 8.4.

Making supplier improvement work effectively requires more than a process: it demands systems and arrangements around the process to enable it to work. Supplier improvement is a business-wide concern, so the STPDR process should ideally become common practice across an organization for all who interface with suppliers. Furthermore, driving improvements with suppliers requires regular and ongoing interaction to ensure things are progressing. Supplier improvement therefore needs to become part of the way the business operates day-to-day. This doesn't just happen by itself but rather there are arrangements we can put in place to enable STPDR. These include regular reviews with suppliers, a system to report problems internally and ensuring everyone knows what to do when they encounter a supplier related problem.

Reviewing improvement progress with suppliers

In practice, any significant improvement relating to a supplier needs to be driven together with the supplier. Even for the simplest of improvements that the supplier will handle alone, we still need to understand progress and whether our target will be met. Project management during the *Do* step might require us to manage, or be aware of, progress against specific supplier actions. Here making this a topic within regular supplier review meetings can help achieve this; we will cover this in the next chapter.

Supplier Problem Reports (SPRs)

Driving supplier improvements to fix a problem demands that we know about the problem in the first place. Obvious enough, but in a dispersed organization, where local business units manage aspects of day-to-day purchasing operations and hold individual relationships with suppliers it is entirely possible that any issues with a supplier can remain local within the individual business units; indeed it is also in the suppliers interest to sort such problems locally too. Purchasing may have done a good job of establishing some sort of blanket terms or pricing agreement for the business to buy against, however from that point onwards it is then in the supplier's interest to develop local relationships and create dependency with the user community. It is entirely possible, and indeed typically for a purchasing function to remain in blissful ignorance of the true performance of a supplier across a business.

How can we get to know about supplier related problems? If our organization has a company-wide ERP system and any problems with goods detected at the point of receipt get recorded, categorized, then we might have access to supplier performance reports at a push of a button. But what about services? And what if our business is not so well equipped and there is no magic button to access a picture of how a supplier is performing? Furthermore, not all supplier related problems are apparent at the point of receipt of delivery. It may be sometime later that they are detected and understood. There are many challenges here.

The different means by which we can understand supplier related problems include:

- *Corporate systems* – information from corporate systems around delivery or service level information, perhaps forming part of our SPM regime.

- *Ask the supplier* – get them to list issues they have dealt with during supplier reviews. This is useful but there is a time lag, it assumes the supplier will be honest with us and we need to 'pull' the information, which takes effort.

- *Consult stakeholders* – ask them what problems they have been experiencing. Again there is a time lag here and effort is required to do this regularly although arguably this should be part of the role of purchasing anyway. Once again we are 'pulling' information.

- *Problem reporting* – establish a 'supplier problem report' system so people report problems. Here information is 'pushed' to us at the time of the problem which can be more effective if no corporate system data is available, however establishing such a system demands a cultural shift.

The reality around getting to know about supplier related problems in an organization is we need the cooperation from those across the organization to report problems. People across an organization need to know what is expected of them and the role they have to play when they encounter a problem relating to supplied goods or services.

Supplier Problem Reports (SPR) are a means for those across an organization to report and get help for supplier related problems, and the process of implementing an SPR system requires the organization to be educated about the system and how to use it. It works like this:

1 A report can be raised by anyone in the business when they encounter a supplier related problem.

2 The report is raised, perhaps using a simple online system or a standard form, and routed to a central function, perhaps located within purchasing, which then logs the problem and provides some sort of response.

3 The initial response might be to engage with the individual or group who has raised the concern to understand the problem and then perhaps with the supplier to secure an appropriate response. Here the STPDR improvement and development process becomes the means by which the improvement action is progressed.

SPRs can be useful where other information systems are lacking or where those out in the business are not used to getting others involved in problems that occur locally. Such a system enables the organization to see the true extent of any supplier related problem and deal with patterns or reoccurring problems, this serves to reduce supplier risk. Establishing an SPR system requires great effort. It is not enough for a purchasing function to introduce the initiative, instead business-wide promotion and education is needed in order to establish a connection in the minds of those across a the business between encountering a supplier problem and raising an SPR. This might seem like a lot of effort, but unless the organization has good systems for information sharing, the only way to find out about supplier problems is to sell the idea and benefits of volunteering information.

When improvements are not realized

Improvements may not be realized. Problems may not be resolved. The supplier may be unwilling or unable to deliver the improvement we require or they originally agreed to. Our options here are simple and what we do depends upon how important the supplier is to us and what alternatives we might have. We could:

- help the supplier to improve and put effort into developing them;
- abandon the improvement and accept the current position; and
- switch away from this supplier either in part or entirely.

Portfolio analysis and supplier preferencing, together with the outcomes of our segmentation, should be used to determine the right course of action here.

Supplier development

So far we've explored supplier improvement, but there is one final dimension here, appropriate for a small number of important suppliers, and that is supplier development.

Supplier development is deliberate action or intervention aimed at increasing the supplier's capability and performance in line with future business needs. It could be driven in response to a problem or need to improve, especially where we are exposed to risk, but is more commonly driven from an opportunity for both parties to secure greater benefit by helping the supplier develop.

The ISM (Institute of Supply Management) defines supplier development as 'a systematic effort to create and maintain a network of competent suppliers, and to improve various supplier capabilities that are necessary for the purchasing organization to meet its competitive challenges'. This is true; however, supplier development will also require effort on our part; therefore what resources we have available need to be focused to those suppliers where development intervention will unlock the greatest and most valuable results. Gordon (2008) suggests the 'development of key or critical suppliers has come to be seen as an option as increased outsourcing of products and services has resulted in increased dependency on outside suppliers' performance, quality, cost responsiveness, and technology'. Where there is a high dependency and reduced alternatives supplier development may well be preferable over switching suppliers.

Supplier development demands time, resources, money and, crucially, commitment to the relationship and the supplier. This commitment may need to be business wide. Development intervention could be planned and executed in a systematic way and here the STPDR process should be used to structure proceedings. However, development can also be ad hoc and where a relationship has been determined to be sufficiently important to warrant just helping a supplier out where needed. Sometimes ad hoc development effort on our part can help build a stronger relationship; we are in effect giving something for the sake of a prosperous relationship.

Specific things we can do to develop a supplier include to:

- *Train them* – invite them to us or go to them and conduct specific training, sharing our knowledge and experience.

- *Implant people to work with them* – sending the right people with the right skills, experience or abilities to work with a supplier for an agreed period of time can have a massive beneficial impact and can help develop a supplier. Knowledge can be shared and the right person can help the supplier figure out how to improve. Crucial to this working is the selection of the right individual to go do this work and that the supplier is able to organize themselves to realize the full potential of the opportunity. If this support is seen as just another 'pair of hands' the benefit will be short lived, but if the supplier can embrace the opportunity and put effort into extracting as much help and experience as possible then the intervention will have a longer lasting impact. Therefore how people will work with the supplier, what they will work on, what the supplier will do to maximize the benefit and so on need to be figured out at the outset.

- *Have them come to us* – similar development can be possible if the supplier can have their people come and work with us for a while. Again ensuring the right people are given the ability to work in the right areas is critical to success.
- *Consultancy* – if implanting resources in their organization is a step too far then providing focused bursts of help on a consultancy or technical assistance basis can help develop a supplier.
- *Share resources* – sharing certain resources we have, where it is easy for us to do so, could add great value to the supplier. For example, spare building space could be provided to a supplier to support a specific project but make sure you make some sort of contractual provision so there are no assumed rights in the event of a dispute.
- *Develop supplier role models* – where a relationship with one supplier has been developed to be highly effective this supplier can then act as a role model to help other key suppliers develop.

Supplier development demands an investment by us. This investment could be made for free, or there may be some sort of arrangement for the supplier to contribute either directly or as some contra arrangement. Either way the supplier needs to agree to participate and to invest time or otherwise to support it. How much investment should be made is a decision and a choice and this depends upon how worthwhile the investment might be and here the basis for segmentation should guide us. It might be argued that investing in developing a supplier is a waste of time, and something that they should be doing anyway, as if it is 'their problem not ours'. For many suppliers this is true, however there are some scenarios where:

- the supplier is unable to galvanize the degree of development we need without help;
- the supplier does not know how to develop;
- we can see potential they cannot;
- there are great mutual benefits by developing together; and
- the benefits of building a strong relationship negate the effort to get there.

Developing BikeAway: the UK retailer who spotted a unique innovation

When the UK supermarket chain Sainsbury's decided to encourage its staff to cycle to work rather than bringing a car in and parking it in the customer parking spaces, the biggest obstacle seemed to be insufficient secure storage for bicycles. This need attracted the attention of one executive, a keen cyclist who understood the limitations of the standard metal loops typically found outside supermarkets. What he wanted was a solution that allowed the bike to be better secured, so lights and accessories couldn't be stolen and with provision for the cyclist to safely store helmet, wet weather gear and so on. Whilst reading a cycling magazine he came across an article profiling a new design of bike locker by a new company called BikeAway. The article showed a large vertical locker where a bike could be hung vertically inside the locker, together with storage for clothing, bags and helmets. Having found the perfect solution the Sainsbury's executive decided to personally call the company.

Jason Hamlyn, the inventor of the BikeAway locker was working evenings and weekends out of his home to get his new bike locker company off the ground. He had some way to go financially before he could do it full time and so he was still employed full time as a metal fabricator in a factory. The only phone number he could ever give was his work's phone number but didn't really expect anyone to ever call. However, one day a call came over the factory PA system asking Jason Hamlyn to call reception; this he did to be told that they had the MD of Sainsbury's on the phone for him. He took the call. The MD explained his interest and Jason felt duty bound to be upfront and honest about how early in the setup process things were. Unperturbed the MD suggested he had a meeting not too far from where Jason lived soon and could they meet? During the meeting Jason demonstrated the product to the executive. The executive said that it was exactly what he was looking for to equip all his stores and asked Jason to give him a price and consider how long it would take to produce and install several thousand. Jason replied instantly with an ill thought through number and the MD, with quite some experience in this area, suggested that his price was too low and would not be a sustainable proposition for his new business. He asked Jason to go away and develop a more structured price to produce and install lockers at every Sainsbury's store in the United Kingdom over the next two years. This he did and a purchase order quickly followed. Jason quit his job and launched himself into BikeAway full time. To this day his bike lockers are still the product of choice for Sainsbury's and many other retailers, schools, universities, councils and other organizations keen to make provision for cyclists. BikeAway is now a very successful organization, helped to develop by a smart customer who could see the potential and benefits of investing some time, help and ensuring that the commercial arrangement was one that would work long term for both parties.

Supplier management

09

This chapter explores what supplier management is, the components of supplier management, different degrees of management and how an approach to supplier management can be realized.

PATHWAY QUESTIONS ADDRESSED IN THIS CHAPTER

7 Do we know everything we should know about our suppliers?

10 What are the risks with suppliers or back up our supply chains and how is this risk being managed?

17 Are all our efforts with suppliers coordinated and aligned with our corporate goals?

A core activity

In the orchestra of SRM, supplier management (SM) ensures the musicians are all playing the right music, at the same time, so the resultant combined sound is perfect. As such, SM is the section that plays always.

SM is a core activity and one that lies at the heart of any relationship with every supplier that has been determined to be important in some way. SM, as its name suggests, is concerned with day-to-day management of the supplier and any interventions needed to ensure we secure everything we need from a supplier and prevent problems arising.

Defining supplier management

Are you managing your important suppliers effectively? This question can often cause Heads of Purchasing to pause a moment and then provide answers coupled with a caveat of uncertainty. In fact this is a difficult question to answer; what does *effective* mean? What are all the things that we should be doing?

Our starting point is what the organization is setting out to achieve and what role individual suppliers and the wide supply base needs to play to support this, as identified during segmentation. If we deem a supplier to be important, then it follows they need to be managed if we are to realize the full potential from the relationship or prevent things going wrong. Just like a close relationship with a partner, if one party fails to attend to the relationship, fails to communicate, doesn't make time to share then the relationship grows cold and perhaps even comes to an end. Relationships with important suppliers are no different and just because it is a commercial relationship it doesn't mean that we don't need to do anything beyond issuing purchase orders. The degree of management needed depends upon why a supplier is considered important together with any external environmental drivers and impacts. Every supply scenario is different and therefore the nature and degree of management will vary across important suppliers. In the orchestra of SRM, if SM is the section that plays all the time, it can play all sorts of different tunes according to what is needed. SM therefore sits at the core of SRM, it 'wraps' around SPM (Figure 9.1) and supports SCM, SI&D and SCR. It provides the means by which all the different components of SRM are effectively deployed and work in practice.

FIGURE 9.1   The components of supplier management

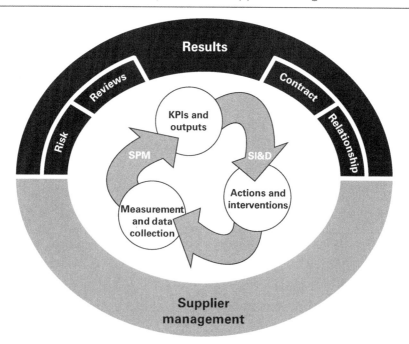

Supplier management has two dimensions: to manage the relationship and interface with the supplier, and to provide a single point of coordination for interventions and initiatives. It is defined as:

> A systematic approach to manage the relationship and all SRM interventions with important and strategic suppliers, working in concert with the wider business to ensure contractual obligations are met, to maximize performance and to minimize risk.

SM has five dimensions (Figure 9.1). Together these ensure we secure everything we need from the supplier ongoing. They are:

- results – managing for results;
- risk – supplier risk management;
- review – supplier reviews;
- contract – contract management; and
- relationship – interface and relationship management.

I shall cover these through this and the next two chapters; *results, risk and review* in this chapter, *contract management* in Chapter 10 and *relationship management* in Chapter 11.

Why manage suppliers?

The *Supplier Preferencing* tool helps us understand how to manage important suppliers (Figure 9.2). If the supplier sees us as an attractive account and one to be developed we will receive their best attention from their best people, but if our account is not attractive, or even not as attractive as other accounts then we can easily end up in the *exploitable* quadrant. Orders will be fulfilled and business will continue as usual but here we simply will not get the most from the supplier. Perhaps other clients will get preference, and we may not benefit from new innovations or developments, furthermore the supplier may be less than interested in our future direction. Perhaps we may even face some assurance of supply risk here.

Irrespective of how the supplier might see us, if we have decided a supplier is important to us then they should be managed; supplier preferencing helps us determine our response. In *Development* or *Core* our response is to take full advantage of the supplier's interest in us, whereas in *Exploitable* we need to manage them hard, leaving them no room to perform averagely but setting high expectations and demanding excellence from them, mindful that this presents risk to us if the supplier sees us as unattractive, as our demands may simply be too much and the supplier may prefer to distance themselves. Supplier preferencing also helps us decide if we need to make our account more attractive to them in order to shore up our position.

FIGURE 9.2   Using supplier preferencing to determine SM responses

	Development	Core
	Development Supplier very interested in us and wants to grow account. **Supplier Management Response:** Take full advantage of our position, build the **relationship** and effective day-to-day management to maintain **results**. **Review** regularly.	**Core** Supplier very interested in us and wants to retain and grow account. **Supplier Management Response:** Take full advantage of our position, build the **relationship** and effective day-to-day management to maintain **results**. **Review** regularly.
	Nuisance The supplier is prepared to lose this account and is disinterested in us. **Supplier Management Response:** Manage **risk** tightly, use **contract** to drive compliance. Manage tightly to secure **results**. Attempt to improve attractiveness or plan to switch supplier.	**Exploitable** Supplier not too interested in us and assurance of supply risk. **Supplier Management Response:** Manage **results** tightly to secure what we need, attempt to improve attractiveness, manage **risk** or be prepared to switch supplier.

(Vertical axis: Attractiveness of account; Horizontal axis: Relative spend of account)

Relative spend of account

Managing for results

Managing for results is about securing the outcomes we need from important and strategic suppliers. It is about ensuring that interventions with suppliers are effective and that the wider organization is aligned with us to a single cause. Just as in any management scenario, SM is less about doing and more about coordination, alignment and ensuring all the right things are happening. It forms the core means by which every other component of SRM is realized. For example, SM is not about performance measurement, that is part of SPM, but it is about the means by which SPM becomes effective by providing the basis for review and action.

Managing for *results* in SM is the overarching management approach for the *risk*, *review*, *contract* and *relationship* components of SM. As such it involves a series of specific activities, approaches and interventions that in turn enable us to manage an entire SRM approach. These include:

- providing the means and forum for performance review within SPM;
- ensuring SPM is effective with the right KPIs and supporting systems for data collection and measurement;
- ensuring we act upon measurement;
- driving and managing supplier improvements and developments as part of SI&D initiatives;

- ensuring the supplier is fulfilling their contractual obligations to us;
- ensuring the relationship with the supplier operates as it needs to for outcomes we need;
- ensuring alignment with the wider organization;
- providing the means to connect supply chain possibilities with end customer needs and aspiration and so help shape future organizational strategy;
- understanding and managing supply chain risk;
- ensuring smooth day-to-day operations;
- creating the environment for joint working, collaboration and innovation as part of an SCR approach; and
- project management activities until completion.

Using a supplier calendar

Managing for results within SM requires management of a series of time-based activities; these include:

- contract expiry or break points;
- supplier review meetings;
- project or improvement initiative milestones or deadlines;
- introduction of new legal or regulatory obligations; and
- points in time when preparation for all of the above needs to commence.

A *supplier calendar* provides a means to capture these events for each important and strategic supplier. It helps to highlight, manage and prompt specific actions ahead of certain time-based activities and providing we regularly review the calendar so to act in response to calendar prompts, we can stay in control of all key supplier activities.

A calendar is required for each important or strategic supplier, and perhaps overall. Calendars are dynamic and should be updated regularly to reflect the changing supplier relationship. They should look near term but at least as long as the longest known event in the future. Individual supplier calendars may be part of a bigger, consolidated calendar that records key events across all important and strategic suppliers and provides key information to support governance and manage resources. We will return to this later.

Supplier risk management

Supplier and supply chain risk demands intervention with certain suppliers and for that reason it is part of the VIPER relationship requirements.

Supplier risk is also an integral component within the supply base segmentation and in Chapter 4 we explored the process of assessing the degree of risk for a specific supplier. Here, as part of SM, we now turn our attention to how we develop and deploy actions in response to risk.

Supply side risk management

Risk is something we each deal with in our daily lives and we will develop our own responses to deal with risk. When my children were small my parental instinct initially compelled me to worry about, and do something to deal with, all sorts of risk. When they were old enough to be mobile, stair gates were fitted, dangerous products placed out of reach and doors were kept locked. We also found ourselves stocking medicines to be prepared for sickness and reading up on medical conditions and procedures to be followed in case of accident or incident. I'm sure most parents will recognize this as entirely normal behaviour in order to protect those we love so dearly who are yet unequipped to take care of themselves. What I did here was to attempt to prevent risks that were significant and could hurt my children but also to recognize that things may happen that I can't prevent and to be ready for these.

A similar approach is used for supply side risk and indeed any risk. Where supply side risk exists, and is of significant concern to us, we need to take action in response to the risk.

Remember there are five supply side risk types and Figure 9.3 shows ways these might relate to an immediate supplier relationship. We can use this to aid the process of risk identification.

We use the supplier risk assessment process (Figure 9.4) for each important supplier we are managing, building on work done as part of segmentation. Supplier risk assessment is an ongoing activity and the process of conducting an assessment should be repeated regularly for all-important suppliers. It is best conducted in a cross-functional group with representation from across the business, reviewing all or as many important suppliers as possible each time. Risk assessment should also look across the entire supply base to see if any new risks have emerged with suppliers who have previously been deemed unimportant. The outputs from a risk assessment therefore shape how to best direct supplier interventions.

Once we have brainstormed potential risks, assessing them (step 2) requires us to consider the degree of risk we are exposed to for a single supplier relationship using a product of the likelihood of any given risk occurring and severity of impact of that risk should it occur.

Likelihood – it is possible to contemplate the likelihood of certain risks occurring. For example, if we know a supplier has financial issues and is the sole supplier responsible for supply of a critical component then there is a likelihood of supply failure. If our business is claiming to be a responsible brand yet we don't understand what happens at the factories in the

FIGURE 9.3 The five supply side risks applied to immediate suppliers

Failure or delay risk	Brand reputation risk	Competitive advantage risk	Price and cost risk	Quality risks
Risk of complete and possibly permanent supply or service failure or risk of delays in supplying goods or providing a specific service.	Risks that, should they occur, can be disastrous for our brand either due to failure or practices in conflict with our principles and expectations of customers and stakeholders.	Risks of competitive advantage being undermined and include theft of intellectual property, counterfeiting and goods sold on the grey market.	The risk of outturn costs being higher than anticipated or planned for (with or without contractual protection).	Risk associated with quality failures, poor product or service quality and latent defects.

Examples for the immediate supplier

Failure or delay risk	Brand reputation risk	Competitive advantage risk	Price and cost risk	Quality risks
• Supplier delays. • Logistic delays. • Disruptions. • Warehouse issues. • Lack of capacity.	• Product recalls. • Practices in conflict with our values. • Affiliations, eg to criminal activity.	• Forward integration by supplier (they do what we do).	• Budget, estimated or 'non firm' price exceeded. • Total cost of ownership cost hike. • Commodity price hikes.	• Product failure. • Poor service. • Quality failure. • Latent defects.

FIGURE 9.4   Supply side risk assessment process

The supply side risk assessment process

1 Identify	Brainstorm potential risks for this supplier and what they provide. Use outputs from segmentation, portfolio analysis, supplier preferencing. Brainstorm using the five supply side risk headings.
2 Assess	For each risk assess the likelihood of the risk being realized and the severity of impact. Use either simple H/M/L assessment or any of the mathematical models available.
3 Prioritize	Identify priority risks for action according to the assessment in step 2 (ie those scoring high likelihood and/or severity). Use group discussion and debate to ensure the right priorities are identified.
4 Plan	Identify either mitigation action or contingency planning in response to the priority risks. Develop a plan for this intervention and assign actions.
5 Manage	Ensure actions and interventions are realized and manage risk assessment ongoing. Regularly review progress and repeat the process of supply side risk assessment.

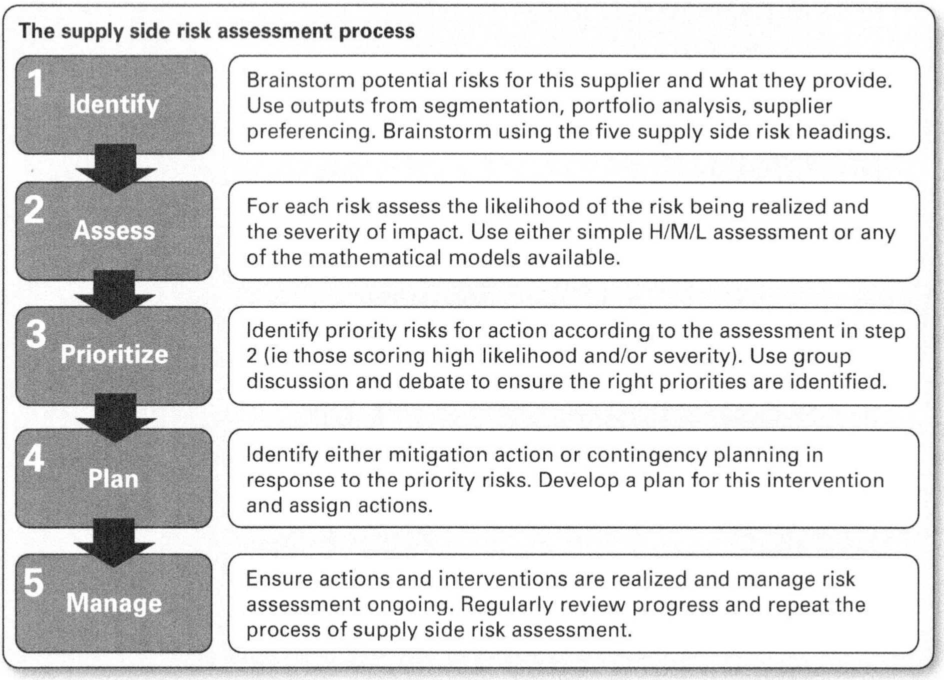

developing countries that make our products, or back at the plantations, then there is potential risk of brand damage if poor practices are exposed as well as risk of loss of competitive advantage if our intellectual property gets stolen. It is harder to contemplate the likelihood of a natural disaster; it is possible to expend great energy trying to predict the unpredictable. Whilst we would want to mitigate any risks we can anticipate, good risk management is also about accepting that some risks cannot be predicted so instead energy needs to be directed at having good contingency plans for those risks that hold the potential to hurt us the most, otherwise know as *severity of impact*.

Severity of impact – the extent of loss that will be realized should a given risk occur. If what happens, or fails to happen with a specific supplier, has the ability to dramatically hurt our business then we need to understand this and develop actions to mitigate or reduce potential impact or at least develop contingency plans just in case. Severity of impact is determined by considering the different types of risk and different scenarios within which such risks could be realized and therefore what that would mean for us. The severity of impact from a supply delay that causes a minor production problem is very different to having to do widespread product recall due to horsemeat being found in beef-based food products.

The priority risks where action is required will clearly be those with a high likelihood and high severity, but some action may also be appropriate for a risk with a medium likelihood and high severity, or high likelihood but low severity. Here group discussion is essential to consider what the priorities for action might be. It may also be appropriate to use a more complex system of assessment – a prioritization and further research on risk management will yield a wealth of mathematical models that can be used here if desired.

Once we understand the priorities for action there are two types of action we can take – we can *mitigate* the risk or develop *contingencies*.

Risk mitigation – actions to remove the risk or reduce it (eg fit a stair gate). Actions here might include:

- contract planning and provision;
- supplier audit and assessment;
- maintaining a close relationship with a supplier;
- invoking certain policies, procedures, processes or systems;
- communication; and
- training and ensuring capability of those involved.

Contingency planning – Accept that certain risks cannot be mitigated and to plan for and prepare what we will do should this risk. This might include:

- disaster recovery planning;
- maintaining readiness of alternatives;
- switching supplier;
- switching to a substitute product or service;
- working with the supplier to recover the situation;
- ceasing or pausing operations or supply; and
- simply thinking about what we might do should something happen.

Both risk mitigation and contingency planning are part of supplier risk management. There are many risks we could consider, and there is a risk that risk assessment becomes all consuming and we get lost worrying about every eventuality. We therefore need to identify and act upon those risks that are of most concern to us. Figure 9.5 gives an example of a completed supplier risk assessment.

It is easy to assume that risk is the supplier's concern, like a problem we will instruct them to fix. This is not the case. Risk is the concern of all parties. Whilst there will be risks the supplier can address, other risks may be outside the supplier's control, they may lack the capability or may need help to address them. Furthermore we may be contributing to the risk. For example, imagine if we had engaged a supplier to develop a critical precision component with us for a high-volume requirement. At the outset we leveraged hard on price and locked them in with a tight long-term contract.

FIGURE 9.5 Example supply side risk assessment

Supplier risk assessment – For *The Data Management Company Ltd*						
Supply side risk	Likelihood of occurrence	Severity of impact	Priority for action	Mitigation or contingency action in response to risk	Owner	By when
Supplier fails and goes bankrupt	L	H	Low	Ongoing monitoring of supplier and maintain close relationship	JH	Ongoing
Our data gets compromised	M	H	2	Audit supplier arrangements to ensure compliance to standards	MH	24 Mar
Major data corruption	M	H	3	Programme of ongoing mirrored back-up verification	MH	Ongoing
Catastrophe takes out data center	L	H	4	Maintain second mirrored back-up in different location/country	MH	Ongoing
Catastrophe prevents access to data or ability to switch to mirrored back-up	L	H	1	Develop full disaster recovery plan with multiple access methods	MH	31 Mar
Supplier sells data operations to bigger company	H	M	5	Maintain close relationship with supplier to understand plans	JH	Ongoing
Supplier hosts data for other customers who are at odds with our ethics and values	M	L	Low	Audit of supplier, contract for disclosure	JH	31 Mar
Our data is accessed by US government for 'security purposes'	L	M	Low	Maintain 'safe harbour' rating	MH	Ongoing

If the supplier then found it hard to maintain good yields and this meant they struggled to make good margin on these products, the result is a supplier who is locked into a contract and price point that is now working against them. This gives rise to risk that they might breach or fail to give us the attention and focus we want from them. This is a risk we are contributing to due to the nature of the contract in place. Therefore as part of the process of assessing risk we need to consider if we are contributing to the risk, and so it is essential that we really get to know our important suppliers.

Really getting to know them

How well do you know your suppliers? What are their plans for the future? Do these fit with what we need from them? How would you know if they are having problems that might present risk to us? In practice it is difficult to really know a supplier and typically we see what the supplier wants us to see; the veneer portrayed by the account manager or those in the organization who have been briefed about what can be shared. We see the performance the supplier wants us to see, just as an audience sees the actors on stage but does not see what really happens behind the scenes. So if a supplier is important to us, and presents risk to us around assurance of supply, it is essential we get to know the supplier and look beyond the stage in front of us.

If a critical supplier was experiencing financial difficulties the supplier is unlikely to want to tell us about it. They are unlikely to tell those whom they employ about it either. Often when companies go bankrupt or transition into being managed by a bank or receiver it comes as a complete shock to most of those within the business, let alone customers. We could pay to secure a report into the financial standing of the supplier such as those offered by companies such as Dunn and Bradstreet. However, such reports are only as good as the latest set of publicly available published financial information, which could lag behind significantly. We could see an apparently strong financial summary of our supplier as of 19 months ago only to find they are actually on the verge of collapse today. Access to supplier's recent financial management information can help here, but this is not information companies like to release and asking for it can stir up concern.

In practice it is difficult to truly know a supplier, but we can work to find out as much as we can and so this is an important part of SM and an ongoing part of the role of the Supplier Relationship Manager.

Supplier auditing and assessment

Supplier auditing is the systematic assessment of a supplier's management systems to a specific standard, either first hand or by a third party empowered to award accreditation to that standard. It involves visiting the supplier and spending perhaps one or more days examining the management controls in place across all the organization and sampling how things work in practice to verify the organization is actually working in the way it claims to be working.

Assessment of a supplier helps to gain a deep understanding of the organization and therefore better understand risk. Assessment can take a number of forms:

- third party assessment to a recognized standard such as ISO9001 by a certified body authorized to award a formal accreditation to the standard;

- an assessment we conduct to a recognized standard such as ISO9001;

- an assessment we conduct to our own standard; and

- industrial tourism – less structured tour of a supplier, perhaps with a degree of assessment or at least questions about processes and controls.

Being assessed is no small affair for a supplier; it requires them to dedicate resources to accommodating the assessment, they may need to protect certain secret or confidential aspects of their business, they will need to ensure the safety of the assessor and that the process of assessing will not impact negatively on their business. A supplier may well need good reason to accommodate a customer assessment. If undergoing an assessment is necessary to win or retain a large contract then this will most likely be good reason, but a less significant customer may find the supplier less willing to accommodate being assessed.

Effective audit and assessment is a special skill. Professional assessors train and need to become certified before they can practice on behalf of an awarding body and need to demonstrate ongoing that they are maintaining the currency of their skill. Good assessors understand the expected processes and practices, they know where to look and what to test or examine in order to gauge how effective management controls are. They also know what questions to ask, and how to probe to get behind the veneer of polished answers that the sales representative might be adept at providing.

Assessment of an important supplier can help give a true feeling for the firm and see how things really work but this is perhaps not a skill set that a purchasing person would typically possess. It would not be unreasonable for a supplier to ask that if they are to undergo an assessment, that an experienced individual conducts the assessment; perhaps qualified or even is registered with an assessment body. Quality functions often have a supplier quality team with remit and skills to assess suppliers. Therefore alignment and collaboration between quality and purchasing can work well with a joint team where quality 'audit' and purchasing 'observe'.

By being a passenger on a quality audit it is possible to gain an understanding of risk but also to look for areas where the supplier could be of further use or benefit or where collaboration might be of mutual benefit. However, such a visit also facilitates the collection of vital information to help get behind the supplier's price. Visiting and touring a factory allows information around likely costs, processing times, degrees of investment, utilization of overheads to be collected and this can help to construct a Purchase Price Cost Analysis (PPCA), ie to figure out what something *should cost* to produce or provide. Not every organization is equipped with a supplier quality function so professional auditing may not be an option. Accepting third party accreditations can help here; however, for an important supplier willing to win and secure ongoing business from us there is still great benefit from *industrial tourism* visits. These could simply be a tour of the supplier's facility, but could equally be a 'mini-assessment', positioned as the customer wanting to understand as much of the supplier as possible but without it becoming a full assessment. As such these 'mini-assessments' can appear much less of a threat to a supplier opening up the prospect of assessment by non-experts. Such visits can also be very useful to get to know the supplier better and gather intelligence. A basic auditing course is recommended and can help here.

Ten top tips for an 'industrial tourism' level mini-supplier assessment

1 Check any safety arrangements in advance – health and safety can often be a good reason to prevent you from seeing part of an organization. Clearly this reason may be genuine, but it can also be an excuse to keep you away sometimes. Check in advance if there are any safety considerations you need to know in advance. Should you wear protective footwear? Do you need to tell them if you have a communicable disease?

2 Take two – safety in numbers! Two pairs of eyes are better than one so if it is possible for two people to visit this can help – whilst one asks the questions the other can observe.

3 Control the agenda – the last thing the supplier wants is you wandering around their facility more than needed, so if you let them they may want to seize the opportunity to give you a nice (and long) presentation, take you for lunch (perhaps some way away at a restaurant with slow service), and have you meet lots of important people. It is easy to visit a supplier and not end up doing the thing you went there to do, which is to get a feel for who they really are. Take control of the agenda in advance and agree with them before you arrive how the day will run. Perhaps ask for a working lunch and limit presentations to no more than half an hour.

4 Avoid the Disney tour – companies may have a 'Disney style tour' for visitors to a factory or facility. This will be designed to guide you through all the bits that they want to show you and nothing else. Instead use a checklist and plan. Agree in advance all the areas you want to see.

5 Talk to those who do the job – with permission, ask those who are doing the job to tell you about it... you will often learn more from what they say or don't say than what the sales person tells you.

6 Visit the stores and the toilets – a restaurateur friend of mine once told me 'if you want to know whether or not to eat in a particular restaurant, visit the toilet first. If it is clean, then the kitchen will be clean too; if it is not, go eat elsewhere.' This has turned out to be good advice. The same is true when visiting a supplier. Once again their toilets can tell a lot about how the supplier manages its facility and takes care of its employees. If the supplier is a manufacturing facility then in my experience a visit to the stores will tell all that is needed to know about how well organized the business is. Good, well laid out stock, with proper stock management controls in place, generally means the company will be well managed too. If the stores are disorganized and chaotic so will the rest of the business.

7 How does it feel? Think what it would be like if you worked there, how does it feel, how much does the company seem to value its people, how motivated are they?

8 Is the company investing? Decide if the company is investing in the organization. Growth, new equipment, new people all show the company is serious about its future, but also might suggest new areas of risk.

9 Get to know the people. Take an interest in the people doing the front-line jobs. Find out about them, how long they have worked there? What training they receive and how often? Does the company promote its own? Establish if there is a sense of contentment and longevity. Staff churn suggests unhappy people and risk through loss of knowledge.

10 Processes and procedures – how do things get done and how do people know what is expected of them? Ask them to explain the processes and procedures for key activities then look to see how those doing the work would know this. If everything is controlled and systematic then chances are the company is well managed, if it seems a bit ad hoc and ill structured then there could be risk and it is worth looking further.

ISO9001 and other standards

The concept of a standard for how the firm operates and the controls it has in place, not just the products or services being supplied, originated from the defence sector where the entire companies operation was seen as critical to ensuring the safety, security and correct long-term functioning of defence components. In the early 1980s military AQAP standards became replaced by mainstream British Standards such as BS5750 in the United Kingdom, with equivalents in other parts of the world and then superseded by international standards starting with the ISO9000 family of standards including ISO9001; the standard for quality management systems designed to ensure organizations meet the needs of customers and stakeholders. We saw an upsurge in companies, mostly large companies, embarking on quality transformation programmes to achieve accreditation to ISO9001 during the late 1980s and 1990s. Whilst some embraced the benefits working to such a standard could bring, for most embarking on achieving accreditation was viewed largely as a necessary step in order to retain or win new business. Purchasing functions were beginning to make some differentiation between those suppliers who had ISO9001 accreditation, or were working towards it, and those who did not within supplier selection and qualification processes.

An entire audit and assessment industry sprang up and at this time there were many advocates of the new quality methodology, but there were also many who opposed it, claiming it failed to improve business (Sneddon, 2000). Others claimed it was bureaucratic, burdensome, made little difference to winning new business and was more about being systematic than helping drive improvement.

During this time in my career I spent around 10 years as a certified quality auditor, auditing many hundreds of companies so I got first-hand experience of how such standards work in practice and how they can both help and hinder an organization. In the early days there is no question that implementing a new ISO9001 compliant management system for a company that previously did not have such a thing was a big leap, and one that would have brought hitherto unseen levels of review, action and bureaucracy. For some this was a step too far. Add to this poor interpretation and application of the standard in the early days, some over zealous assessors, more concerned with the tick in the box than enabling a business for success, and achieving ISO9001 was indeed a burden not a benefit in some cases. Despite the hype at the time that if a company didn't have accreditation they would not be considered as a potential supplier, companies without the standard continued to be considered and selected as potential suppliers. Yet for others it transformed their business. However, it is not the *standard* that did this but the way the organization adopted the standard that drove this positive transformation. Across the hundreds of companies I audited who had implemented ISO9001 effectively there were a number of common factors behind the success:

- It drove cross-functional engagement and working.
- It bred a culture of quality and focus on end customer needs – everyone knew what to do about a non-conformance.
- It demanded that management teams take time to focus on its operations and review effectiveness.
- It established defined ways of working, often where none had existed previously, and provided a platform for the business to grow in other areas such as environmental management.

Some of these success factors may sound familiar, as they underpin how improvement methodologies such as *Lean* and *Six Sigma* work. They also underpin category management, SRM and good governance. ISO9001 is, in fact, another roadmap to provide specific business improvement, providing the organization embraces it.

Today there are over a million organizations worldwide holding ISO9001 accreditation (**www.iso.org**). The standard has been revised and there is much more wisdom around effective application. It is no longer an aspirational standard for the few, but the ticket to the ballpark for the many; it is what is expected of a modern, effective organization operating in the global marketplace. The controls and practices it advocates are more *standard practice* than *nice to have* today.

How a supplier functions, its management systems and overall effectiveness is of interest to us as part of supplier management, particularly in terms of risk mitigation and understanding the supplier. ISO9001 is just one standard widely adopted out there, however there are in fact a number of standards that are of interest here and the following families of standards are particularly relevant to help inform us and have a degree of confidence in how a supplier operates. These are:

- ISO9000 – quality management system standard;
- ISO14000 – environmental management system standard;
- ISO18001 – occupational health and safety management system standard;
- ISO 26000 – social responsibility; and
- ISO11000 – standard for collaborative business relationships.

We can better understand a supplier, and gain a measure of risk exposure, or more specifically arrangements that mitigate certain risks, through the accreditations to one or more of these standards that they hold. Therefore it is appropriate to be interested in such accreditations, or indeed in supplier's efforts to work towards these, as it tells a story of how serious the supplier is about mastering full and effective control over what they do. Mandating that a supplier hold accreditation, or indeed deselecting those that do not, may be appropriate in certain industry sectors or situations. For example, if our business is providing safety critical components or service then it may be essential to know our important suppliers have certain controls in place, regularly checked and verified by an independent awarding body. If our brand values are founded upon sustainability then it may be important to insist that our suppliers meet the requirements of ISO14000 and maybe even ISO26000. Furthermore, we may need to respond to demands of our customers to ensure our suppliers are selected on the basis of certain accreditations.

Suppliers accreditations to these standards help us understand them, and potentially negate the need for us to make interventions to know them more or assess them as, in theory, this has already been done. However, there are some things to watch out for here:

- Accreditations may not apply to all operations or parts of a supplier's operation – it is important to check the scope of the accreditation.

- Accreditations are based upon periodic audit and assessment, therefore years can pass between audits and things can change in that time – check when the company was accredited.

- Companies can be over-keen to show they hold the necessary accreditations – secure sight of, or a copy of their certificate.

It is important to be clear about the degree to which we might wish our supply base to hold certain accreditations and why, as in insisting on accreditations could limit our choice, make the market more difficult, reduce our leverage and exclude innovation. ISO9001 is widely adopted, the others less so, and it would be rare to find an organization with a 'full house' of standards. Adoption tends to skew towards larger companies; small businesses often lack the headroom to embark upon the programme to achieve accreditation or resource maintaining the standard going forwards. A decision to stipulating accreditation to a standard should not be made by purchasing alone, but it should be part of organizational risk management overall and needs to align with wider, agreed corporate policies and principles on quality and risk.

Maintaining a supply side risk register

'What are the top five supply side risks facing the organization today?' Not an unreasonable question for a senior executive to ask, but one that can be difficult to answer. Organizations that adopt a proactive attitude to risk consider all the key risks they face, including supply side risk, and take action in response to them as appropriate, directing resource and attention to the risk areas deemed the highest priority.

So far we have considered risk in terms of a specific supplier, later we will consider risk in the supply chain also; however, there is another macro-level view here and that is the combined effect of all the supply side risk for the entire business. This is simply a view that is formed from all the individual supply and supply chain risk assessments together (Figure 9.6). The risk register is therefore the collection of individual outputs from the supplier and supply chain risk assessments, but it should also include a summary

FIGURE 9.6 The use of a supply side risk register

Supply side risk register

Supplier or supply chain risk area	Likelihood of occurrence	Severity of Impact	Controls in place	Additional control measures required	Owner
Risk of brand damage through supply chain concerns for palm oil	M	H	Controlled sources and local audits	Find alternative	SM
Assurance of supply risk for A H Holdings Ltd – critical single source	L	H	Contingency inventory and duplicate tooling held	Develop a second source	CC
Boker Contract Manufacturing – risk of increased pricing due to bad contract	M	M	None at present	Find alternative source and/or renegotiate contract	CC
Supplier bribery at African facility	H	M	Procedures for interaction with suppliers	Audit and 'recorded meeting' equipment in meeting rooms	PC
Risk of IP theft for China supply base	M	H	Limit exposure and access to IP	As current	CC
Possible financial difficulties at Klanex could cause loss of supply	M	M	Increased inventory	Verify position, find alternative source	JH

Supplier risk assessment

Supplier chain assessment

analysis; one based upon reoccurring themes across individual assessments, the combined effect of individual risks and any single risks identified as more critical than others.

Understanding the combined supply side risk helps inform corporate strategy and in turn creates the business case for the resources needed to mitigate or plan contingencies for the risk areas deemed to warrant them. A *Risk Register* is a system of keeping a dynamic and regularly reviewed summary of the key risks at any one time. It helps inform overall purchasing strategy and where resources should get directed. If the organization operates a risk register system, then our supply side risks should form part of it, otherwise maintaining a supply side risk register would form part of an overall SRM governance approach and this is explored in Chapter 15.

Ongoing supply side risk management

Things can change and so risk management is not a once only activity, it is something we need to do on an ongoing basis; it is a continual process. In practice, this means doing a number of things continuously, and having a systematic approach to do this in order to understand and assess changing risk and to be organized to respond to them. These include:

- *Changing circumstances* – keeping a watchful eye on any changes in the supplier's behaviour and circumstances that might signal a problem, eg chasing payment, downsizing, key individuals leaving etc. Such things might warrant investigation to try to establish what lies behind the change, for example if a key individual leaves they may be bound to give you the agreed message, but during the course of a discussion to thank them for their help, by asking the right questions you may be able to read between the lines.

- *Keeping close* – keeping close to the supplier and making it our business to really understand their organization and the key individuals that drive it.

- *Supplier reviews* – specific agenda items during supplier reviews to share and discuss developments or changes in direction.

- *External changes* – keeping a watchful eye on external environmental changes that might impact this supplier or our relationship with them so that we are equipped to associate any events in the world with the potential impact they might bring and identify a new risk. Watch press, media and social media reports – announcements of new contracts won, expansions, changes in ownership, acquisitions, mergers, product recalls or safety concerns, all have implications for our supplier. These may be good or bad but when a development occurs it is important to then work to understand these implications.

- *Supplier assessment* – periodic audit or assessment of the supplier's management system, processes and activities.

These ongoing actions are part of the role of the supplier relationship manager. Not all of them can be planned for but rely upon the interest and attentiveness of the individual in this role. Some of these actions can be planned and need to form part of an ongoing programme of supplier management and therefore need to be scheduled within the supplier management calendar.

Supplier reviews

Supplier review is the planned and systematic review of all relevant aspects of performance and the relationship with an important or strategic supplier. Reviews can be planned or reactive to an issue and are conducted together with the supplier; they may take place regularly, infrequently or on an ad hoc basis. There is no one single format or approach for a supplier review but rather the nature of the review needed to support a specific supplier relationship depends upon how important that supplier is, what makes the supplier important and what is happening with the supplier and what they are supplying at any given moment in time. Supplier reviews are therefore unique to any supplier and the nature and format is dynamic according to prevailing circumstances. Suppliers who are deemed important, perhaps because they present risk might be required to participate in regular reviews so we can ensure we continue to understand and manage the risk. Whereas reviews with suppliers of strategic importance to us, who are keen to work and grow with us, with whom we have agreed joint objectives, might be much more collaborative and structured to support pursuit of these goals. Figure 9.7 shows the different types of supplier review and how the nature of these changes according to supplier importance.

The supplier review process

There are five steps to running a supplier review (Figure 9.8). A supplier review is more than the actual meeting; it is a journey that supports a bigger relationship journey. As such, good internal review pre-planning is essential. This is about data collection and fact finding to ensure that we have all the information necessary to support the discussions with the supplier. This activity might be part of more widespread arrangements, for example if we have an established system for supplier performance measurement then we may simply be able to run a report. Otherwise we may need to go and gather data ahead of the review. No matter how well organized our firm may be here it is still important to engage with key internal stakeholders ahead of the meeting, or perhaps even invite them along. Not only does this secure internal alignment so everyone involved in a particular supplier relationship knows about the meeting and can contribute, but it shows the alignment to the supplier and that prevents 'divide and conquer' tactics by them.

FIGURE 9.7 Types of supplier review by importance

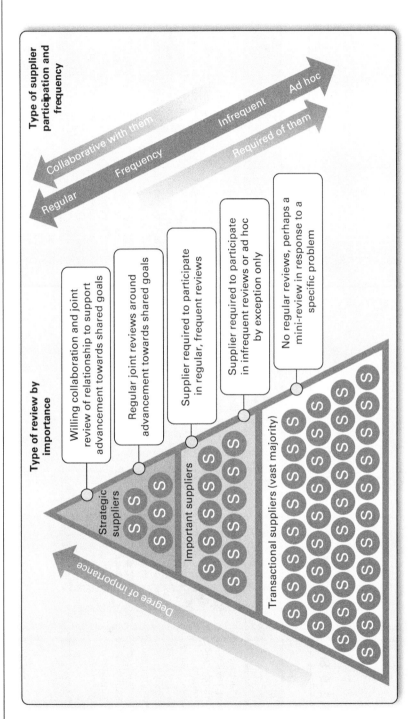

Type of supplier participation and frequency

Collaborative with them

Regular Frequency Infrequent

Required of them Ad hoc

Type of review by importance

Willing collaboration and joint review of relationship to support advancement towards shared goals

Regular joint reviews around advancement towards shared goals

Supplier required to participate in regular, frequent reviews

Supplier required to participate in infrequent reviews or ad hoc by exception only

No regular reviews, perhaps a mini-review in response to a specific problem

Strategic suppliers

Important suppliers

Transactional suppliers (vast majority)

Degree of importance

FIGURE 9.8 The supplier review process

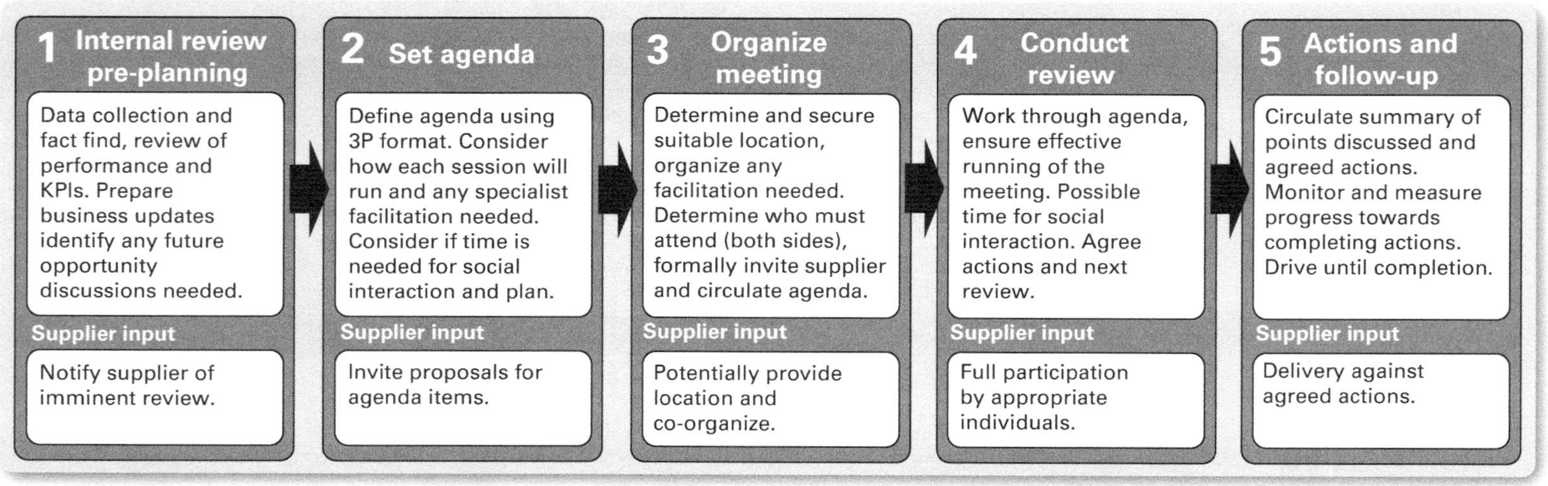

1 Internal review pre-planning

Data collection and fact find, review of performance and KPIs. Prepare business updates identify any future opportunity discussions needed.

Supplier input

Notify supplier of imminent review.

2 Set agenda

Define agenda using 3P format. Consider how each session will run and any specialist facilitation needed. Consider if time is needed for social interaction and plan.

Supplier input

Invite proposals for agenda items.

3 Organize meeting

Determine and secure suitable location, organize any facilitation needed. Determine who must attend (both sides), formally invite supplier and circulate agenda.

Supplier input

Potentially provide location and co-organize.

4 Conduct review

Work through agenda, ensure effective running of the meeting. Possible time for social interaction. Agree actions and next review.

Supplier input

Full participation by appropriate individuals.

5 Actions and follow-up

Circulate summary of points discussed and agreed actions. Monitor and measure progress towards completing actions. Drive until completion.

Supplier input

Delivery against agreed actions.

Putting the supplier in the dentist's chair

Ideally a visit to a dentist is preventative and together with good hygiene is something we do to avoid having to find ourselves sat in the dentist's chair for anything other than a check-up.

Supplier reviews are similarly preventative, like regular relationship check-ups to ensure everything is working as we need; to detect any risks or issues before they become a problem and to deal with anything that needs treatment. The frequency of when a check-up is needed depends upon how effective the relationship is to start with, how well we are managing the supplier relationship day-to-day and an assessment of the current status and any problems that need to be attended to. Supplier review frequency therefore varies but might fall into the following ranges:

- *Interim 'check-ups'* – quarterly/six monthly.
- *Full reviews* – annually or at contract renewal.

Setting the right agenda

Supplier review agendas should be set well in advance of a supplier review meeting, in consultation with the supplier, and provide the basis for how discussions will be managed. The agenda is unique to the supplier and prevailing circumstances. The supplier review provides a forum and focal point for many different aspects of SRM including performance reviews, progress towards improvements, getting to know them, exchanging information and so on. It supports the ongoing management of risk and is a means by which the overall relationship can be managed; ensuring individual relationships and point of interface across the business are understood and aligned. Supplier reviews also provide the forum to create alignment to a future direction. The agenda for a supplier review, be it an interim or full review therefore needs to provide for all of these. Table 9.1 gives a potential framework and possible agenda items for both an interim and full supplier reviews – select from these as needed.

Agenda format is important too. Most will be familiar with agendas as a simple list and sequence of topics for discussions. However, this has limitations as such a list can often be interpreted in different ways by the reader. If we seek a particular discussion, for which we expect the supplier to have prepared, then the agenda must communicate the intention for that discussion. An agenda item called *review of performance* might suggest to the supplier that they will be presented with some performance information for discussion and need to do nothing other than turn up. However, if we are expecting them to come ready to explain certain anomalies then this simple agenda item fails to communicate this.

Effective agendas make for effective meetings and do much more than provide a list of prompts for the originator. Instead, effective agendas serve as a route map for the meeting; they set overall and session-by-session

TABLE 9.1   Possible agenda items for supplier review meetings

Agenda item	Interim review	Full review
Updates	Business updates from both parties; recent or imminent changes, developments, anything that might have a material impact on performance, the other or the relationship in the near term. Use as an opportunity to condition the supplier. ***Watch for*** • Conditioning by the supplier, eg to an imminent price rise or change in their favour.	Business updates from both parties plus longer-term direction, intentions and aspirations. Use as an opportunity to condition the supplier. ***Watch for*** • Anything that suggests a future risk or misalignment. • New opportunities where their future direction might resonate with our future goals.
Review of performance	Review of past performance for the recent period and performance towards goals against leading KPIs. Review of any specific issues or concerns. Review of performance against contract. ***Watch for*** • Reviews that only look backwards at what has happened.	Review of overall progress over the last term. Review of on-going appropriateness of KPIs and measurement regime to support progress. Agreement of any changes and new KPIs. ***Watch for*** • Measurement for measurement sake or measuring the wrong things. Focus on what will make a difference.
Review of improvement initiatives and progress against agreed objectives	Review of progress and actions previously agreed against individual improvement initiatives. Agreeing new improvement initiatives in response to any performance concerns. ***Watch for*** • Signs that the supplier is unable or unwilling to really drive the improvement and is merely 'talking the talk, not walking the walk'.	Review of overall progress across all improvement initiatives. Agree new goals and targets for the next period and define the improvement initiatives that will support these. ***Watch for*** • Setting goals and targets that the supplier doesn't fully support (and so is unlikely to be motivated to achieve). • Signs that the supplier is not aligned with us here.

TABLE 9.1 *continued*

Agenda item	Interim review	Full review
Relationship review	Review of how the relationship is working, sharing details of recent and planned interactions and engagements across the business. Any personnel updates. ***Watch for*** ● Personnel changes that suggest there are hidden issues with the supplier – push for the full story. ● Signs of 'divide and conquer' through other points of engagement. ● The supplier resisting sharing any concerns they might have – be sure to encourage them to be open.	Review of how the relationship is working overall, perhaps using a two-way and business-wide survey. Review of relationship charter, interface map and rules of engagement. ***Watch for*** ● Making judgements about how the relationship is working without really understanding it. Ideally conduct a survey with internal stakeholders and with the supplier to gain insight.
Forecast and looking forward	Forecast, likely or anticipated activity, volumes or needs for the short term. Any new requirements. ***Watch for*** Inadvertently making an oral contract and giving commitment to something that is not definite.	Longer term forecast, likely or anticipated activity, volumes or needs moving forward. ***Watch for*** Inadvertently making an oral contract and giving commitment to something that is not definite.
Innovation, growth and future opportunity	Each party is encouraged to share any developments, ideas or potential opportunities that could be of benefit to either or both parties and what is needed of the other to take it forward. A course of action may or may not then be agreed to embark on further work to take things forward. ***Watch for*** ● Nice discussions but no actions. ● Raising expectations unfairly. ● Risk of theft of idea.	Working session to consider how the supplier can contribute more fully to our longer term goals and objectives. Identification of new objectives, KPIs and improvement initiatives to move forward with. ***Watch for*** ● Agreeing objectives that are unrealistic. ● Objectives for the sake of them. ● Failing to create the right environment for the supplier to contribute and feel safe when sharing innovation ideas.
Agreed actions	Action planning, with owners and timings agreed.	Action planning, with owners and timings agreed. Updated relationship charter, interface map and rules of engagement circulated.

expectations in terms of required outcomes and they provide a basis to manage to a time constraint. To develop effective agendas for supplier review meetings we can use the 3P agenda format where, for each session we plan to run, we define the *Purpose*, *Process* and *Pay-off*. Figure 9.9 gives an example of a 3P agenda for a supplier review meeting:

- *Purpose* – the purpose of this session, why it is here and what it is aiming to do. Purpose defines the outcomes needed for each session.
- *Process* – how this agenda item will run, what specific things will take place within the meeting to achieve the purpose.
- *Pay-off* – the benefits that will be achieved if this session achieves its outcomes. Note, avoid restating outcomes here – that serves only to duplicate the *Purpose*. Instead, consider the benefits parties will have secured by achieving the outcomes and how this helps us move forward. See Figure 9.9 for an example.

In addition to the agenda items, the overall objectives of the meeting should be defined so as to clearly set out the purpose of the meeting. If there is specific preparatory work required then this should be included also and the agenda sent to all invitees well in advance. The complete document then provides absolute clarity to all about the purpose of the meeting, how it will run and what is expected of all who attend and so means the meeting stands the best chance of achieving required outcomes.

Our turf or theirs?

Green (2002) suggests that making someone come to you, for example for a meeting, is a sign of power. Indeed powerful people will often invite others to their office, just like getting summoned to go to see the boss in his office, on his turf. Making others come to us gives us a small psychological advantage; putting them in unfamiliar territory, isolated from peers and that which normally provides comfort and security. When negotiating with a supplier, having them come to us can really help. Therefore surely it must follow that when conducting a supplier review we should make the supplier come to us? Perhaps, but this is not necessary beneficial to the overall relationship. A common misconception is that suppliers have some sort of inherent duty to attend meetings with us, like part of the cost of sales, a necessity for the supplier to bear, or even just a bit more discount of the purchase price because they pick up the tab. Indeed large companies will have considered and planned for this cost within what they do, which means we are indirectly actually paying for them to attend.

What is appropriate here depends upon the nature of the relationship we are seeking to have. Once again we refer back to portfolio analysis and supplier preferencing (Figure 9.10) as well as our segmentation. If we believe the supplier sees us as *Core* and we are sourcing *Leverage* categories then it may be entirely appropriate to make the supplier come to us, on our terms. However, for a relationship in *Exploitable* for *Critical* categories where we

FIGURE 9.9 A 3P agenda for a supplier review meeting

Time	Topic	Purpose	Process	Pay-off
0900	Business updates	Parties to share updates, changes and developments	• Presentation by buyer • Presentation by supplier • Action planning	Increased confidence and transparency
0915	Performance review	To review performance against KPIs	• Scorecard review • Action planning	Confidence in progress towards key goals
0945	Improvement initiatives	Progress check against agreed initiatives	• Supplier presentation: progress to project plan • Discussion and action planning	Securing value delivery and reduced risk
1000	Relationship review	Check how the relationship is working	• Recent interactions and contacts • Share results from stakeholder survey	Increased confidence in the relationship
1015	Future forecast and opportunity	Share future anticipated volumes and plans	• Forecast for next quarter	Basis to reduce lead times in place

FIGURE 9.10 Using portfolio analysis and supplier preferencing to guide how we approach a supplier review meeting

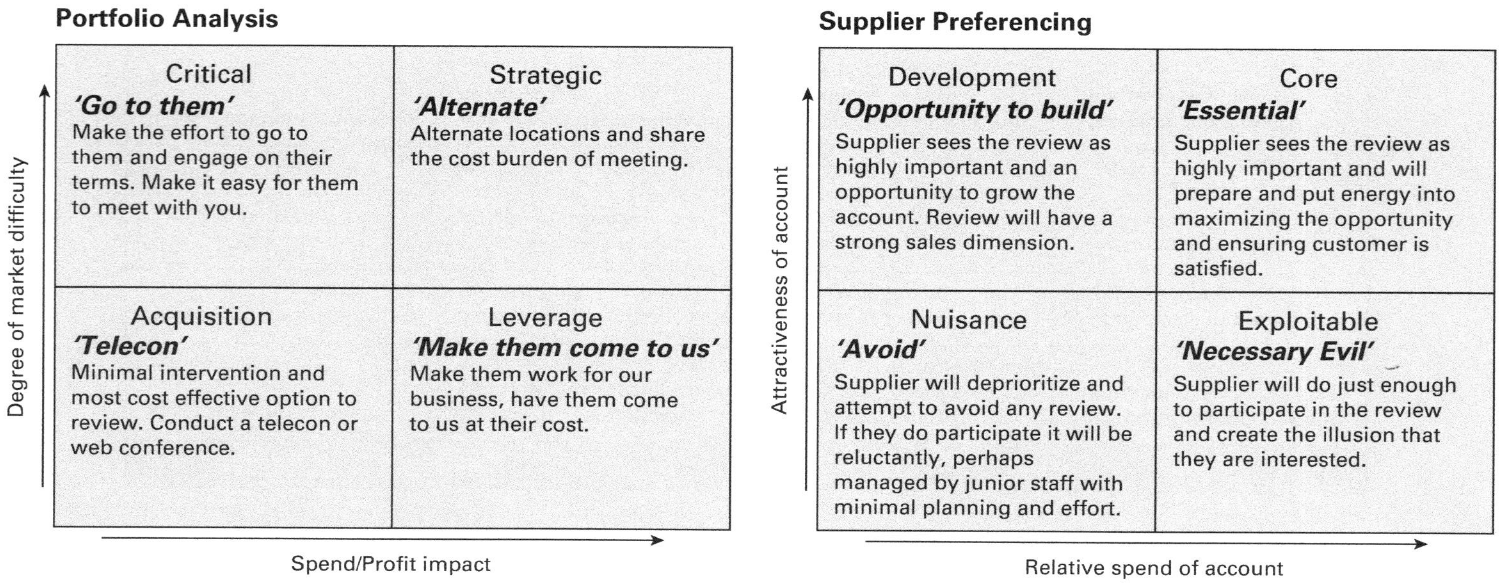

Portfolio Analysis

Critical *'Go to them'* Make the effort to go to them and engage on their terms. Make it easy for them to meet with you.	**Strategic** *'Alternate'* Alternate locations and share the cost burden of meeting.	
Acquisition *'Telecon'* Minimal intervention and most cost effective option to review. Conduct a telecon or web conference.	**Leverage** *'Make them come to us'* Make them work for our business, have them come to us at their cost.	

Degree of market difficulty ↑

Spend/Profit impact →

Supplier Preferencing

Development *'Opportunity to build'* Supplier sees the review as highly important and an opportunity to grow the account. Review will have a strong sales dimension.	**Core** *'Essential'* Supplier sees the review as highly important and will prepare and put energy into maximizing the opportunity and ensuring customer is satisfied.	
Nuisance *'Avoid'* Supplier will deprioritize and attempt to avoid any review. If they do participate it will be reluctantly, perhaps managed by junior staff with minimal planning and effort.	**Exploitable** *'Necessary Evil'* Supplier will do just enough to participate in the review and create the illusion that they are interested.	

Attractiveness of account ↑

Relative spend of account →

have identified significant risk we may need to go to them – apart from the fact that the supplier may have little interest in coming to us, but visiting them shows effort on our part and creates a degree of obligation to the relationship from them. It also provides a basis to get to know them more and better understand our risk exposure.

Where the supplier relationship is important or critical and we need and want supplier collaboration (eg *Core or Development* with *Strategic*) then our reviews should be similarly collaborative. In practice this means sharing or alternating locations or perhaps using neutral locations. It might also mean considering the cost of conducting reviews as attending any supplier review presents a cost to both in terms of preparation, effort, time, travel and cost of following up on actions. In a large organization this cost gets absorbed as part of the cost of doing business but consider an important or critical relationship with a small innovative supplier with whom we see great future potential and want to develop the relationship. Requiring that this supplier travels to meet with us for a supplier review could be a big deal, perhaps demanding a day out and the associated cost of travel. Small, developing companies typically fail to appreciate the demands large clients might place on them beyond the provision of the actual goods or services. As such they fail to plan for the cost of such demands, moreover in their enthusiasm to please the client they can simply not know how to raise a concern about the burden attending supplier review meetings can bring. As a consequence, and what might seem a normal request by a large company for regular meetings, could inadvertently drive destructive responses from a struggling supplier, perhaps causing them to feel aggrieved, cheated and driving behaviour so they seek to claw back something from us at the next opportunity. They are likely to resist attending, make excuses or resist bringing the right people. If we are seeking a collaborative relationship with mutual willingness where the supplier is helping us work towards mutual goals then requiring them to attend at their cost could undermine this. This is no time for leverage behaviour on the part of the buyer. Instead, it is essential to consider, and be sympathetic to, the supplier's position, and to take positive steps, as appropriate, to ensure the process of reviews reflects the nature of the relationship we are seeking. This might include:

- *Paying the supplier to attend* – if we see the value of supplier reviews then why should we expect this for free. Consider agreeing a 'relationship management' fee within the overall engagement with fees to cover the supplier's time here. Such an arrangement allows expectations to be clearly defined in advance including who you expect the supplier to bring for reviews.

- *Sharing the cost* – quantify the cost of parties attending for a review meeting other than time (eg travel, subsistence etc), and agree to share it equally.

- *Going to them* – travel to them, especially if they are a small supplier or we want to use the opportunity to visit their facility and assess risk.

- *Alternate locations* – share the burden by alternating locations.
- *Web or video conferencing* – web and video conferencing is now a viable alternative to face-to-face reviews, either for all reviews or just some. Consider a full review in person with interim reviews carried out remotely.

Finally, consider the nature of the location for a meeting and ensure it is conducive to what you need to achieve. If you want to host a joint collaborative meeting and stimulate creative thinking from those attending, shoehorning a bunch of people into a tiny meeting room will most likely be unproductive. Here a more pleasant environment that puts people at ease and with space to run working sessions would be more suitable.

Using portfolio analysis and supplier preferencing to guide us

The supplier's attitude towards the review meeting they are being invited to attend will vary according to how they see us. If we are unimportant to them then the meeting could simply be a necessary evil, in other words something they participate in for the sake of maintaining business and so something they will do just enough to support, perhaps sending only the sales person to represent the business. However, if we are important or hold future potential importance to the supplier then review meetings present a fantastic opportunity to grow the account and shore up and protect what is already in place. It also provides a forum to help the supplier achieve one of its ongoing objectives; to build stronger relationships and in turn generate future business. Supplier preferencing can help us understand the supplier's perspective and potential attitude towards a review meeting (Figure 9.10).

When a supplier is sufficiently interested in us (*Core* or *Development* quadrants), we can also use portfolio analysis to help guide how we should approach the review, and the degree of effort that is appropriate on our part, also given in Figure 9.10.

Every review is a mini negotiation!

Every time we meet with a supplier it is an opportunity to condition them around our future expectations and where boundaries might lie. Supplier review meetings may seem like just meetings to review progress and performance, however they are in fact also mini negotiations. Whilst we may not position them as such, the interaction may well demand agreement on particular points of our courses of action. These may have cost implications, either now or in the future and both parties will be seeking to maximize their position, either by claiming as much value as they can or creating value for both parties to share. The supplier will almost certainly view and approach a review meeting in the same way they might approach a negotiation. This is why the suppliers account manager is often keen to be involved in all discussions.

If we approach a supplier review in the same way we might approach a negotiation then we increase our chances of achieving the outcomes we want. This demands more than simply running a meeting to an agenda, but that we plan carefully how we will run the meeting, are alert to body language, use of spoken language, consider the inclusion of some negotiation tactics to help and regard any giving of ground as a concession.

The power of good facilitation

A supplier review meeting, like any other meeting, will be ineffective if not managed. It is all too easy for a meeting with a supplier to become just another thing in an already busy day where there is insufficient time to prepare. If the session ends up being little more than a nice chat about things with the supplier's sales or account manager, then this serves little purpose. Good meeting management is essential. Ahead of the meeting this should include:

- *Objective setting* – define and agree the purpose of the meeting and what needs to be achieved by the end.
- *Agenda* – define an agenda using 3P format, invite those attending to contribute to defining the agenda and circulate well in advance.
- *Time planning* – set aside enough time to achieve meeting outcomes.
- *Location* – secure a suitable and appropriate location, match the location to the type of meeting and outcomes needed.

Good facilitation can help. This is about using approaches and techniques to ensure the meeting realizes its objectives, follows the agenda as appropriate and that any interactions are effective. Good facilitation helps make joint review meetings with strategic suppliers work. It is common for parties to fail to see things from the perspective of the other, so carefully facilitated sessions designed to get all the issues into the open in a non-threatening way, can help change the mindset so then each side then figures out how to build from the new starting point in a positive way.

If facilitation support is available it should be secured. Sometimes, for critical meetings or where joint working is needed, there can be benefit in using an external professional facilitator. If this is not feasible then self-facilitation can still be effective.

The role of the facilitator is to keep the meeting on track, ensure that the objectives of the meeting are achieved and solicit the right degree of contribution from those involved. Whilst many facilitators chair the meeting also, this is not a requirement and the facilitator could be independent to the chairperson, brought in to provide process support for the chair. Facilitation is a whole topic all of its own and so further reading is recommended but here are some tips to help.

Ten tips for good supplier review meeting facilitation

1 *Lead* – have a chair or meeting leader and agree roles for all attending. Supplier meetings would typically be led by the buyer side, perhaps by the supplier relationship manager.

2 *Manage to the agenda* – stick to the agenda, manage timings. If new topics arise 'park them'. Consider placing a piece of flip-chart paper on the wall headed 'car park/parking lot' and record any points of discussion that are off agenda but need to be returned to. At the end of the meeting decide how to handle these points by agreeing actions or perhaps a follow-up meeting, if needed.

3 *Use open questions* – open questions help solicit better information. Ask things like 'tell me about...' or 'could you explain...'. Avoid closed questions like 'have you resolved the quality issues we discussed last time?'

4 *Really listen* – we all think we listen, but actually few listen well, usually we are too busy interpreting what is being said based upon our own experiences or planning what we will say when there is a break in the conversation. By concentrating on listening it is possible to hear what might be being said behind the words. Consider having someone else be part of your meeting just to observe and listen.

5 *Make everything visible to all* – don't work off individual notes but share everything so everyone can see it. Project slides or information, circulate handouts and record everything using flip charts.

6 *Make action plans* – as actions arise, note them down. Again a piece of flip-chart paper on the wall with three columns – 'what', 'who' and 'when' ensures all have full visibility of the action list as it grows. Avoid loose timeframes such as 'by next meeting' and multiple owners for actions.

7 *Provide output notes* – summarize key points as you go and record. Use simple bulleted lists not detailed minutes. Circulate afterwards and ask anyone to highlight any discrepancies.

8 *Use the boomerang* – if a problem is thrown at you, throw it back and get them talking – 'What should we do about X?', 'I have some ideas but first, tell me what you think we should do about X?'

9   *Check progress and process regularly* – check timings and progress to the agenda and also if the process being used is working towards required outcomes. Don't be afraid to change things if they are not working.

10 *Name the problem* – if things get stuck or there is a tension, name the problem and try to work past it: 'It feels like there is some sort of reluctance for this course of action?'

Contract management

10

This chapter explores contract management and how the way we use contracts can help support an overall SRM programme. We explore contract planning, managing to a contract and the process of contract creation. Finally we consider how to exit a contract where a relationship is failing.

PATHWAY QUESTIONS ADDRESSED IN THIS CHAPTER

8 Are suppliers meeting their contractual obligations?

9 What contracts are due to expire or need to be reviewed in the near term and how are we planning for this?

Introducing contract management

If we engage a supplier to work for us we have a contract with them, whether formalized or not. Contracts can take many forms and are not necessarily lengthy legal documents. The contract we have with a supplier is a key component of SRM to ensure we get what we need and want from a supplier and to protect us from the unexpected. How a contract is planned, how we manage a supplier to an agreed contract and how we exit a contract are all integral parts of supplier management.

Basic principles of contracts

A contract is an agreement between parties, and this agreement may be defined in a number of different ways. A common view of a contract is that of a document written in 'legalese', produced by a lawyer separate to the purchasing function and the direct engagement with the supplier; purchasing do the deal and then hand off to the legal team to do the contract. In fact companies are often structured to only operate in this way. I have been involved with negotiations with large US companies where, following several rounds of negotiation, we have concluded our discussions and agreed all aspects of a new supply arrangement. But then it was passed to the respective legal functions who then began another round of negotiation around specific terms and aspects of contract that had not previously been discussed. These points were more about specific legal points of principle or language than how we were going to ensure the right arrangements and relationship were in place. A necessary step? Perhaps, but in more than one instance the entire deal nearly crumbled due to intransigent positions between battling lawyers. Had these points of disagreement been understood by the purchasing function earlier in the process, it would have changed how negotiations were conducted or even how the suppliers shortlisted in the first place. Post-deal negotiations by legal teams is a common negotiation tactic; just when you think you are safely home there is a further hurdle to overcome. It can be a tactic we can use to our advantage, but it can also be a product of poor internal relationships.

Contracts, in their various forms, serve many purposes and these include, to one degree or another:

- A formal definition of what was agreed by each party; what will be supplied or provided, by when, how and to what requirements.
- A definition of what happens when things change or go wrong.
- A definition of obligations of parties as part of the contract, eg confidentiality or maintaining insurance provisions.
- A definition of how the relationship between the parties is to work.
- The level of performance or service that is to be achieved.

The Latin *pacta sun servanda* translates as 'agreements must be kept' and is the basic principle behind contracts within civil and international law. It means that what is contained within a contract is law between the parties and nonfulfilment becomes a breach of the pact. Agreeing some sort of contract with a supplier therefore makes an agreement, enforceable by law between parties for what parties are to do, or abstain from doing. Breach of this contract is recognized by law around the world with remedies available to deal with breach.

The role of purchasing and legal functions to support contract planning varies from organization to organization. Some companies, especially those in the United States, place this role firmly within a separate legal function, others have purchasing develop contracts with no support or intervention from a legal team other than to perhaps provide model or 'boiler plate' contract frameworks to work from. Some combine both with purchasing developing the definition of what has been agreed and a legal team incorporating it into a suitable legal framework. Whatever the arrangement, effective contract planning requires a combination of legal and purchasing input with parties working together from the outset. This may well be at odds with established legal department ways of working, but it is necessary if we are to put in place contracts that work for us and help us maximize the outcomes from our suppliers.

One final note is that purchasing professionals are not usually lawyers. We might have learnt our way around a contract but there is difference between our level of training and the reason why lawyers study for five or more years before they practice. This means that irrespective of how the organization is set up we can only ever go so far in the process of establishing a contract with a supplier; how far we go needs careful consideration balanced against capability, training and experience.

Why we need a contract?

So if a supplier fails to perform we can simply take them to court? This is correct, in principle, however here we are faced with the often vast difference between the legalities of a contract and the practicalities of enforcing a contract. Ending up in litigation with a supplier is a situation to be avoided at all costs. It is a process that typically ends up being hugely expensive, consumes vast amounts of time to prepare for, can be deeply damaging to those involved and, despite this, may still fail to secure the required outcome. Perhaps a judge will rule against us because we cannot demonstrate what was actually agreed, perhaps we will win but then we are no further forward as we can't work with the supplier who has wronged us or perhaps at the point where it looks like the supplier will lose the court case and have to make good they decide to wind up the business to escape the penalty. That said, there are times when litigation remains the only remaining course of action. However, with good contract planning it is possible to lay the groundwork that prevents getting to a dispute or disagreement position in the first place and provides a means to resolve any issues should they arise. Good contract management ensures that everything that has been agreed happens as agreed and where it doesn't we deal with it before it escalates.

Legal teams are stakeholders just like other stakeholders who have needs and wants from a supplier engagement. Therefore if legal are not working with purchasing early enough within the contracting process, then there will be a disconnect in terms of ensuring needs and wants are met. If we wait until we are on the verge of making an agreement with a supplier we have left it too late. In fact the contract we make with a supplier should be based upon and resonate with our business requirements and relationship requirements. It provides a place for KPIs and service levels to be defined. It provides a means to articulate obligations parties have to the relationship, as well as defining the specifics of what must be supplied. Crucially, however, the contract translates our aspirational business and relationship requirements into an agreed, legally enforceable form.

Types of contract

There are many ways a contract can be created. In its simplest form we could make an oral contract with a supplier to do a piece of work. Oral contracts are typical in small businesses or where business is done based upon the strength of a relationship between parties. A small building company may engage a tradesman to do a job with no more than a discussion and a handshake. Parties involved may even be able to successfully discuss and resolve any subsequent issues or disputes that arise. Indeed in Eastern and Middle East countries formal contracts carry little standing but rather it is the relationship between individuals that matters and the sense of personal obligation to the other that ensures the right outcomes. In the West, however, our cultures work differently and formalizing what is agreed is expected by all is vital in order to provide legal protection, but even more vital is the investment of time to clearly agree what parties will and will not do. The process of contracting with a supplier fulfils this.

At the other extreme a contract could be a lengthy written document, defining all aspects of the arrangement and how parties will work together to achieve a mutual goal and share benefits. The nature of the contractual mechanism we need with a supplier changes according to how important a supplier is (Figure 10.1). If we are simply buying what a supplier is proposing, say online, from a catalogue or in a shop then the contract usually becomes binding at the point the supplier takes our money. We have certain statutory rights here; these vary around the world according to which law applies, however in this situation suppliers typically will seek to supplement your statutory rights with additional terms and conditions designed to protect them. These might include limits of liabilities should something go wrong, how the supplier may use your personal or company data or certain rights they might assume as part of the relationship. We can see this in action as consumers every day when we buy something online; just before we complete the purchase, we are required to accept the supplier's terms and conditions, which are of course available in full to read but are generally accepted blindly; few consumers would know how to interpret such things. Furthermore, as consumers we rarely have any power to challenge suppliers' terms – it is a 'take it or leave it' scenario.

Buying on the suppliers' terms is probably OK if we are downloading something from iTunes or buying office supplies for a small business as the risk is low, but it doesn't take much for risk here to become too great for a company. There is a whole industry of salespeople who target the admin functions of small businesses offering solutions such as office shredding services, copier maintenance or franking machine rentals. The deal appears very attractive but hidden in the small print on the form signed by the admin person are terms that permit various hidden extras to be charged and establishes a rolling contract, that continues to roll on year on year and can only be terminated on one specific date of the year by giving a long notice period, making it virtually impossible to get out of the contract.

FIGURE 10.1 Typical types of contractual approach according to supplier importance

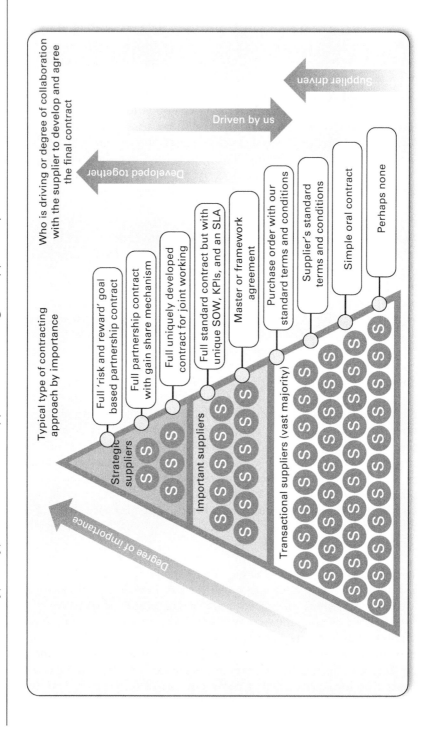

Where suppliers hold a degree of importance we need to control, or at least influence, the terms and conditions that govern the contractual relationship. We can do this by ensuring that any commitment with suppliers is supported by a purchase order defining what is to be provided together with a standard set of terms and conditions designed to protect us and define certain expectations for any supplier working with us. This is a typical approach and is useful for general purchases; however, when we are engaging a supplier to deliver something more complex or where there is significant risk this approach can fall short as the standard terms and conditions may fail to provide for what is being purchased. For example, if we are buying some bespoke software we might need to make provision to license certain code or provide for termination so we assume rights over the code. Such things would not typically be covered within a standard set of terms and conditions. Furthermore, suppliers receiving our purchase order with our terms may be keen to have the contract covered by their terms and so might acknowledge our order with their terms and conditions and an assertion that these now take precedence. It is easy to get into a 'battle of the forms', which serves little purpose.

Therefore, for our important suppliers, a more sophisticated method of contracting is appropriate; one that provides for the unique needs of the relationship and what we are seeking to source from the supplier. This might be a master or framework agreement that defines at a high level how the relationship works for every purchase order that is placed against this supplier or a full written contract developed for the relationship, perhaps incorporating standard sections but with new sections that define how the contractual relationship is to work. The different type of contract are outlined in Table 10.1.

Contract planning

Contract planning is concerned with identifying and executing the structure, format and content of the contracting mechanism we need with our supplier. Good contract planning formalizes relations between parties within a robust legal framework, but is much more besides; it is an opportunity to define the arrangements that encompass every aspect of what outcomes we want from the supplier and how we want the relationship to work. This means that we need to take an active role in the development of the contractual mechanism early on; it should not be left as a supplementary activity post negotiation.

There are three primary inputs to contract planning – the business requirements, the relationship requirements and the proven standard legal framework or terms relevant to what we are trying to contract for (Figure 10.2).

TABLE 10.1 Types of contractual approach for important suppliers

Type of contract	Definition	How terms are defined	How performance is measured
General buying (online, in-store or to a catalogue)	General everyday buying process. Typically represents the majority of corporate transactional spend. Supplier is offering goods or service for sale (invitation to treat); contract established when customer offers to buy (eg by taking goods to a till or completing an online order and check-out process) and the offer is accepted when the store or company processes the order and takes payment (consideration). Assumes both parties are capable of and intended to enter into such a legal arrangement and be bound by it.	It is common to find terms undefined other than statutory provision, for example small shop owners rarely require customers to accept their terms before agreeing a sale. Where terms are defined they are usually defined by the seller, are blanket terms covering all transactions, not readily negotiable, and agreement may be implied or require explicit acceptance (eg online checkouts requiring 'I accept terms box to be checked').	We can measure compliance to supplier stated commitments, eg stated specification and delivery promises etc. Beyond that such contracts do not usually make any specific provision to measure performance for our needs.
Purchase order	Customer places an order, either written or verbal, for the supply of specific good or services to specific requirements or terms and perhaps stating an agreed price. Purchase Order (PO) constitutes an offer, which is accepted upon the supplier processing the order for the agreed consideration.	Terms either defined in the PO, or separate terms referred to and invoked. Where terms are undefined or if the supplier acknowledges the PO but then asserts different terms, risk of uncertainty as to whose terms prevail.	We can measure compliance to PO requirements such as delivery or compliance to specification. If we require the supplier to meet specific additional performance requirements these must be made part of the PO.

TABLE 10.1 *continued*

Type of contract	Definition	How terms are defined	How performance is measured
Master or framework agreement	An overarching document that defines how the relationship and an area of supply will work. Not usually contractual (but can become so if it makes minimum commitments or resembles a contract too closely) and defines the agreed terms and arrangements that will apply for each PO placed. Contract is established when a PO in accordance with the agreement is offered and accepted.	Terms defined within the agreement and written so as to take primacy over any individual PO terms. Requires PO to specifically be in accordance with the agreed terms of the master or framework agreement.	Specific performance measurement arrangements agreed and stipulated within the agreement. We can still measure compliance for delivery and to specification as usual.
Full written contract	Supply arrangement is defined in a single written contract, or multiple written contracts, that define all aspects of what will be provided, the terms, key deliverables, what will happen should things change, agreed price or fees and timing. Acceptance when executed and signed by both parties. Typically used for high risk, high spend, high complexity areas of purchase.	Terms defined within the body of the contract. May define specific aspects of the supply arrangement in a schedule or statement of work.	Performance requirements typically stated within the contract, perhaps as SLAs, or agreed KPIs together with any obligations to measure or report against performance. We can still measure compliance for delivery and to specification as usual.

FIGURE 10.2 How business and relationship requirements drive contract planning

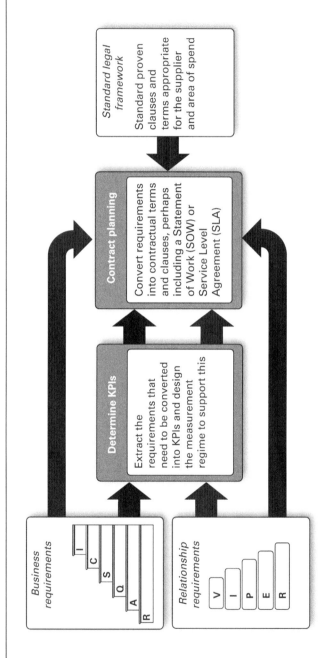

If well developed, the business and relationship requirements should embody all the needs and wants for our business, for what we are buying and how we want the relationship with the supplier to operate. They should, in theory, reflect the consolidated view of all key stakeholders, challenged and refined to define the business needs and wants (rather than individual preferences), and therefore should be the definitive statement of how we are going to source something. They are also the starting point for contract planning. Here we review the various requirements and determine those that need to be incorporated within a contract. Remember the business and relationship requirements serve many purposes and not all will be relevant for incorporation. For example, we might have an *Assurance of Supply* business requirement or a *Risk* relationship requirement centred around ensuring a supplier is sufficiently financially stable or has the necessary capacity for our needs. There would be little point in incorporating this into a contract as we cannot contract with a supplier for such things, instead we would assess the risk here as part of qualifying the supplier before we engage them. That said, we could choose to incorporate something into the contract that obliges the supplier to disclose any material changes in their operation that might impact us. Whereas if we have a *Service* business requirement that defines the need for a four-hour emergency response, this requirement can be ported straight into the contract.

Contractualizing KPIs

The process of 'contractualizing KPIs' involves the extraction of KPIs from business and relationship requirements and converting those that are relevant into contractual obligations. If this is done together with the supplier then the process of doing this can often reveal how committed a supplier actually is to delivering against the KPIs and may even cause discussions to be reopened here once a supplier realizes they will be more accountable through a contractual provision.

KPIs might typically be incorporated into a contract within a Service Level Agreement (SLA) that may be separate to, but invoked by, the main contractual framework, so as to make future updates easier.

Relationship vs contract

In some cultures it is the strength of relationships that form binding agreements and create firm obligations of parties to each other. However, doing business without some sort of formalized contractual arrangement is not recommended. It is possible to have both a contract and a relationship; a relationship where parties have a sense of commitment to each other and want to work in the best interests of the other with the contract reflecting and defining how this works in practice. If the starting point is the contract and the supplier is engaged to meet the contract they will do just that and only that. However, if the starting point is the relationship and the contract is developed to reflect the relationship both parties have agreed then it is this that will drive how things work. In practice, this might mean making specific arrangements to define how parties agree the relationship shall work in practice. There are limitations to the degree to which a contract can define aspects of a relationship, but it can set a requirement for parties to do certain things such as agree and maintain a current relationship charter (covered in the next chapter), meet a certain intervals and exchange certain information.

Multiple contracts

For less important suppliers the contracting mechanism tends to be based around *what* is being supplied (eg we decide to place a purchase order for something and select a supplier to provide it), but as suppliers get more important then the contracting mechanism shifts to *who* is supplying. Any given supplier could supply many different things to us and, depending upon how the firm is organized, be supplying many different business units in different ways. It is not uncommon for a single supplier to hold multiple contracts with an organization, perhaps even agreed with multiple points across the organization. Such an arrangement gives 'divide and conquer' power to the supplier and can make it difficult to exert any central leverage from a purchasing function. Effective contract management and indeed SRM as a whole must look beyond any single contract but to all the contracts with a supplier. Here the ideal contracting approach to establish an overarching arrangement that defines the relationship for the entirety of the supplier's activity and interface with our organization. Ideally this would be some form of 'umbrella contract' to which all other contracts are subservient (Figure 10.3). It is possible to establish such an arrangement retrospectively but sometimes the effort required to do this adds little value. An alternative approach, where a supplier is important enough and sufficiently willing, is to agree a relationship charter and make management of all contracts part of this.

Contract durations

Suppliers love long-term contracts; it means their sales team don't need to worry about us – they can go and spend time winning new business with other clients. It is easy to get seduced into believing that there are benefits in a long-term contract. Sometimes there are, but sometimes making a long-term contract can work against us. If we are attempting to develop a collaborative relationship where the supplier will work with us to achieve key goals, then a long-term contract that gives certainty of future business to the supplier and allows them to invest is beneficial to us. Whereas a supplier deemed important due to the high spend with them but are supplying *leverage* categories and products does not normally warrant a long-term agreement, unless there is clear advantage to us to do so.

FIGURE 10.3 Overarching agreement for multiple contracts

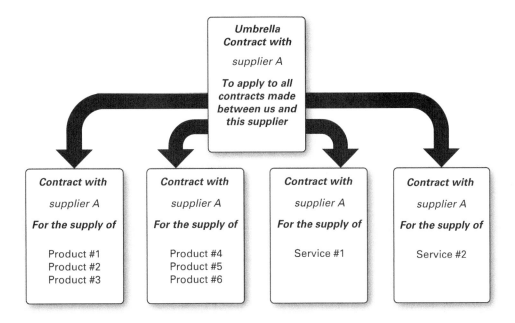

Figure 10.4 gives typical different contract durations according to impor-tance. Here portfolio analysis for what we buy from a supplier helps to determine the length of contract that is appropriate. Where there is a con-tract that is for more than just a single transaction then a short-term contract would typically be 12–18 months, medium term 2–3 years and long term could be anything above this. Note there are no hard and fast rules here, it all depends upon the circumstances but the point is careful consideration should be given to agreeing the appropriate contract duration balancing certainty with risk and commercial factors.

Contract management

Contract management is supplier specific and is about being able to answer five key questions:

1 What contracts do we have with this supplier?
2 When do they expire?
3 Do they do everything we need them to do?
4 Are there other contracts, if so what is our strategy to deal with these?
5 Is the supplier operating to the contract(s)?

FIGURE 10.4 Portfolio analysis and typical contract durations

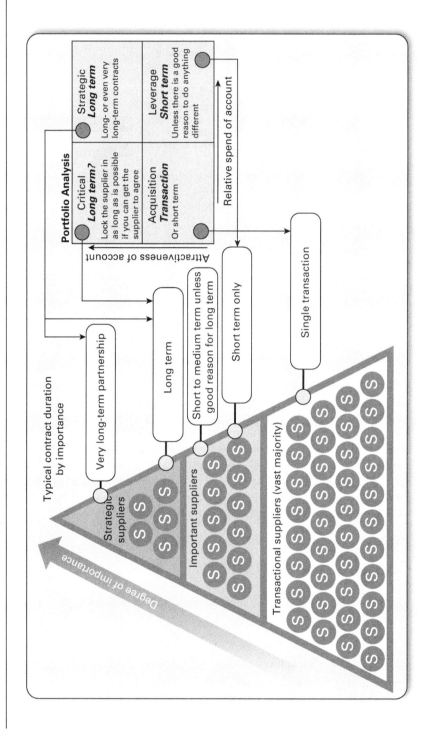

When parties sign the contract (or signal agreement by other means), if the contract is simply to be filed away, perhaps by purchasing or legal, or perhaps filed locally by an individual, ready to be retrieved should we end up in some sort of dispute, then we could be missing an opportunity. A lot of effort, energy and dialogue get spent getting to the point where both parties formally agree the contract and that contract has been designed to provide for all dimensions of the relationship and what parties are trying to achieve. The contract ideally encompasses and reflects our business and relationship requirements. So if it is consigned to a filing system we are putting away a vital roadmap that can help manage our relationship. When we sign the contract our work is not finished, in fact our work here has only just begun.

Contract management is part of supplier management within SRM and is concerned with taking a systematic approach to ensure that the supplier, and indeed all important suppliers, are working in accordance with the contract or contracts and meeting agreed targets or goals. This includes:

- ensuring any agreed performance targets or KPIs, say within a SLA, are being met;
- ensuring the supplier is meeting any ongoing obligations, eg to maintain certain insurance provisions, to notify of personal changes etc.
- ensuring the relationship proactively supports the fulfilment of the contract, irrespective of whether the arrangements here are formally defined within the contract itself. In practice this might include regular reviews to keep close to the supplier etc;
- identifying any potential risk or issue that might impede the supplier from meeting contractual obligations; and
- taking action with the supplier where there is a problem or potential problem.

Contract management is also concerned with managing the time dimension of a contract or collection of contracts. This could include activities or events that must happen at certain times and the contract expiry.

Open-ended contracts with suppliers are rare; instead it is typical and good practice for a contract to exist for a set period of time. This limits risk to parties; however, within that most contracts provide mechanisms for extension if both parties agree. However, in order for us to be in full control of our suppliers, and maximize our leverage, we need to be in control of the process of managing contract expiry. If we are taken by surprise or wait until a contract has expired or is about to expire before considering our position then we are giving power to the supplier as we may be left with no alternative but to renew and then it will be on their terms. Power in negotiation and in the process of supplier selection comes from alternatives. That means that when a contract is due to expire, and we wish to reappraise our situation and consider what the market could provide, we need to leave sufficient time in order to run a sourcing exercise. Such an exercise can take time, many months in fact to do it well and so if we are to maximize our choice and stand the chance of securing the greatest benefit, we need to plan to do this early.

Contract management is about planning for contract expiry and directing our resources, in a prioritized way, to the sourcing activities that determine in advance what will happen at expiry. This could be a number of things:

- we simply renew the contract 'as is';
- we negotiate a renewal but with new terms and requirements;
- we extend the contract (perhaps to buy time to complete a sourcing review); and
- we terminate, or let the contract terminate, in favour of some new arrangements.

Any of these routes forward at contract renewal could be entirely appropriate depending upon the circumstances. The point here is that we avoid doing nothing but rather we take a decision in good time so we are in control of the process and therefore the decision is the most appropriate. A further dimension here is managing multiple contracts, eg multiple contacts with a single supplier each with a different expiry date. This is not an uncommon scenario, especially if we have inherited legacy arrangements. However, we can often gain a stronger position as we can bring expiries into line as far as possible, which serves to give us more potential leverage. Where this is the case we need to identify strategies for managing expiry, eg:

- manage contracts individually;
- move towards all contracts being synchronized, eg through a process of extensions and renegotiations; and
- a mixed approach.

Contract management is also about making sure a contract continues to work as needed. Things change and what we might need or want can change, so too could the marketplace or the world around us. Part of the role of those in purchasing who look after key supplier relationships and categories of spend is to keep a watchful eye on the changing needs of the business, stakeholders and the changing market or environment within which we operate. Where things change around us we may need to act and agree a change to what we source or the relationship we have with a supplier. This might even necessitate a change to a contract. For example, imagine if a change in legislation meant that one of our contract terms was inadequate. We would need to agree a change to this contract with the supplier. Clearly changing a contract, and what was previously agreed, is by mutual agreement and could instigate a whole new negotiation.

Systems for contract management

Contract management should not be left to chance, instead a systematic approach for contract filing and to manage expiration is needed. There are many ways this could be accomplished. The *Supplier Calendar* can be used and may be enough to track when individual contracts expire. There are more sophisticated systems out there for contract management, some on-line, some in-house. Most modern ERM systems include a contracts module, many of the e-sourcing platforms also offer this functionality, perhaps linked to a management information dashboard, and there are some standalone software systems also. Some of these systems also track the detail of the contractual clauses that are applied. Whichever approach is preferred, it should form part of a broader system where the information generated by any system gets acted upon with individuals having agreed roles and responsibilities to support this. Success factors here include:

- a single company approach for contract retention – perhaps within purchasing or legal, on a shared server, online using a contract data base;
- contracts are available to those who are entitled to view them when needed;
- there is a forward view of contract expiry across all contracts; and
- the system provides advanced warning and prompts for forthcoming expiries.

Exiting a contract

We may need to exit a contract because it has simply come to an end and either the need has ceased or we are going to make alternative provision. However, there are circumstances where we might need to exit a contract for other reasons. These include:

- when we have ended up in dispute with a supplier;
- the supplier is failing to perform;
- things have changed;
- our requirement has reduced or disappeared; or
- we identify we are at risk with the current arrangements.

Furthermore, it is not just we who may decide we want to exit a contract, but instead the supplier could decide to exit. If this is unexpected, and the supplier is critical to us in some way, the consequences can be catastrophic.

By its very nature a contract is something where both parties have signed up to the notion that 'agreements must be kept' and have agreed to this within a legally binding framework. Parties cannot just decide they don't want to be part of it any more and walk away without consequence. That said, there are in fact a number of ways that parties can attempt to exit a contractual arrangement. These include:

- *Genuine breach* – a genuine breach has occurred and the contract can be terminated under the provisions made within it for a party to terminate in such situations.

- *Finding something* – a tactic commonly used when one party wishes to exit a contract is to search for something that allows the party to create a dispute and allege some sort of breach or failure of the other. This is an underhand tactic but nevertheless one that is often used. Typically the alleged breach will be a small technicality having not been met or finding an area that is subjective in some way. Good contracts prevent this by including a dispute resolution process and a good lawyer can help defend a supplier attempting to use this approach.

- *Terminating anyway* – just walking away from the contract, refusing to participate and breaching obligations under the contract in the full knowledge that the other party would then have legal recourse. This tactic is a high-risk approach but is one that works as the practicalities and cost of pursuing litigation mean few actually follow through here but end up cutting losses and walking away.

- *Negotiating an exit* – this is the most common approach to exit a contract early. During the global downturn between 2006 and 2013 many suppliers found themselves in negotiations with customers who were faced with no option but to scale back their operations and therefore were seeking to reduce forward commitments to their suppliers. Clearly not ideal for the supplier but when faced with the trade of some future business from a customer still trading as opposed to no future business from one that went bankrupt many suppliers were left no option but to agree.

Exiting a contract may not be possible, or may have repercussions. However, if we find ourselves needing to exit a contract, then negotiating a way out presents the least risk; reaching an agreement means both parties walk away accepting the exit. There may be a cost to this or a trade might be required as part of the negotiation. If we need to exit on less favourable terms then it is essential to be certain of our position and fully understand any risks associated with termination. Risks here might include:

- *Litigation risk* – cost and effort to defend litigation should supplier take legal action against us if they feel termination was unfair.

- *Supply risk* – risk to assurance of supply, quality and service for any remaining work the supplier has been engaged to provide.

- *Continuity risk* – any know-how the supplier has, tooling, data or equipment relating to our work may not be forthcoming or available, irrespective of any contractual obligations.

● *Competitive advantage risk* – the supplier could use know-how about their work for us to help give a competitor an advantage irrespective of any contractual obligations around confidentiality that survive termination. It can be hard to prove such a thing has occurred and if the supplier feels aggrieved they may be less willing to preserve loyalty. Furthermore, we need to consider the risk of forward integration by the supplier, ie they start doing what we do and compete with us. This might involve theft of intellectual property by the supplier to help here. Again this can often be hard to prove.

● *Negative repercussions* – damage from negative publicity, risk of sabotage or any other actions an aggrieved supplier could take to hurt us.

In addition to these risks we must also consider how any action we might seek to take fits with our personal and organization's morals, values, goals and ethics. Deliberately seeking to exit a contract with a small supplier whom we no longer need because something has changed, with the full knowledge they lack the resources to pursue any litigation against us, is morally questionable and whilst unacceptable for some, is fair game for others. Whatever the chosen approach to exit it must be one those involved are personally comfortable with but must also be reconciled with corporate value here. If a UK public sector company is embracing UK governmental expectations for its suppliers and providers to positively engage and develop small businesses, and has set out targets here within its corporate aims, sub-sequently attempting to screw over a small business by forcing an exit of a contract would be way out of line.

Exiting a contract therefore requires much more consideration than find-ing a way out in the clauses. It is in fact a major change programme that requires planning and thorough risk assessment. It is also an exercise that should be supported by good legal expertise from the outset. In my experi-ence lawyers can tend to be risk adverse in these circumstances and will advise the path of least repercussions. Often this is good advice, however, and notwithstanding the above notes on moral considerations, there are circumstances where it is appropriate to take the risk, eg to terminate a contract and accept the potential repercussions. In this case the risk must be fully quantified and understood and the decision to take the risk made in consultation with key stakeholders, just as a decision for expenditure might be made using a business case; for risk we need a similar business case for why this is the most appropriate way forward.

When we are faced with the need to exit, we need a contract exit. There are five steps to developing a contract exit strategy (Figure 10.5) as follows:

1 *Contract fact find* – the starting point is the contract and here fact find is about reviewing what was agreed and what provision the contract makes for termination or exit and any stated consequences or obligations. We also need to fully understand any other relevant or driving factors such as any performance issues or why things have

FIGURE 10.5 Steps to develop a contract exit strategy

1 Contract fact find

Gather data about the current contract provision, reason for needing to exit and any supporting evidence, eg around performance or breach if such exists.

2 Determine exit options

Determine potential options for exit:
- Run out to end.
- Negotiate exit.
- Terminate with reason.
- Terminate anyway.

3 Assess exit options

Assess the potential options according to:
1. Risk – determine the likelihood of occurrence and severity for each.
2. Likelihood of success.
3. Moral acceptability.

4 Select exit option

From assessment, rank options in priority order according to the three assessment criteria and any other relevant factors.

5 Exit strategy and plan

Determine the contract exit strategy and identify a plan for exit. Agree plan with stakeholders, assign roles and responsibilities. Commence exit project.

gone wrong. Here hearsay and vague information are not enough, instead we need facts and data about exactly what the issue is or was so if a dispute develops we are well armed. The depth here is equivalent to that outlined within the *Study* phase for the SI&D process.

2 *Determine exit options* – determine, from the results of fact find what options exist for exit.

3 *Assess exit options* – for each option conduct an assessment of:

- the likelihood this exit option could be successful;
- the risk of each option, assessing likelihood of occurrence against the five risks outlined above and the severity of impact should any or all of the risks be realized; and
- the moral acceptability of the option, personally and against any corporate values or ethics.

4 *Select exit option* – rank the options according to the output of the assessment. Consider any other relevant factors and select the preferred option and the fall back options.

5 *Exit strategy and plan* – define the exit strategy. By this point of the process it should be possible to articulate this within one simple paragraph. Agree with key stakeholders and then, once there is complete alignment for this course of action, develop a detailed plan to move forward. Assign roles and responsibility and set the plan in motion. This plan should include:

- actions to ensure continuity of supply/transition to new arrangements;
- communication of change internally;
- how we will engage with the supplier;
- actions to manage change including process, policy, procedure changes and any training or retraining required;
- provision for any post contract obligations; and
- provision to monitor for any negative repercussions.

Figure 10.6 provides a simple table for exit option assessment where each option can be scored out of 10 against these criteria, including an assessment of each type of risk. The total risk scores together with the likelihood of success, severity of impact and moral acceptability can, using a weighting system, generate a single score to help guide thinking as to the best way to exit a contract.

FIGURE 10.6 Assessing contract exit options.

Exit option	A	B	C	D	E	F	G	H	I	J	K
For each determine score and weighted score	Likelihood of success	Risk of litigation	Risk to supply	Risk to continuity	Risk to competitive advantage	Risk of negative repercussion	Summary risk (B+C+D+E+F/5)	Severity of impact (all risks)	Total Risk Assessment (GxH)	Moral acceptability	Totals (A+J-I)
Weightings	30%								40%	30%	
1 – Do nothing	1	1	1	1	1	1	1	1	2	10	
	30								80	300	250
2 – Run out	1	1	1	1	1	1	1	1	2	10	
	30								80	300	250
3 – Terminate with reason	5	5	8	5	4	4	5.2	6	31.2	6	
	150								1248	180	–918
4 – Terminate without reason	10	8	9	9	9	7	8.4	9	75.6	1	
	300								3024	30	–2694
5 – Negotiate an exit	6	1	2	3	3	2	2.2	2	4.4	8	
	180								176	240	244

Relationship management

This chapter explores how to manage relationships with suppliers across an entire business as part of a supplier management approach. It considers how to determine what the right relationship should be for an important supplier and how to realize it. Finally approaches to deal with conflict, dispute, bribery and corruption are given.

PATHWAY QUESTIONS ADDRESSED IN THIS CHAPTER

11 Do we have the right relationships with the right suppliers and are we in control of these?

12 Do we understand and are we in control of all other relationships and interfaces people have with suppliers across our business?

The right relationship

Companies don't have relationships with companies; it is the individuals within these companies that have relationships with individuals in the other company. The nature of the relationship is characterized by the nature of the relationship between individuals. Even within a business relationship there is inevitably a degree of social interaction between these individuals and this interaction defines the relationship; this is essential and helps create good relations.

In a small building company contracting with an artisan tradesman where parties are happy to work together the relationship is between just two individuals, perhaps characterized by the reliability, integrity, commitment and loyalty each has for the other. This is a typical personal business relationship with parties seeking to do what they can to look after the other as best as possible. This type of relationship based business approach can be found in the Western world to varying degrees but is even more relevant in the East and Middle East where it is the only way business is done in many cases.

In larger companies similar personal relationships between individuals exist, except here there are usually many more individuals involved on both sides and so many more relationships. Ideally, and if we were effective at managing our supplier, then all of our individual relationships with the supplier would be completely aligned to a single cause. However, in practice this is not an easy goal to reach.

For a large account or supply arrangement, depending upon the nature of what is being supplied there are usually many interface points right across the various functions in each party. Figure 11.1 shows a typical relationship interface map between buyer and supplier for a manufacturing business. Relationships exist between different functions to facilitate operations, communication or enable the right working relationships. However, these will also be relationships, most likely supplier driven, that support the purpose of growing and developing the account. This may take the form of a sales or account manager holding multiple relationships with individuals at different levels. Table 11.1 gives the factors that drive these individual relationships.

FIGURE 11.1   A typical relationship interface map between buyer and supplier for a manufacturing business

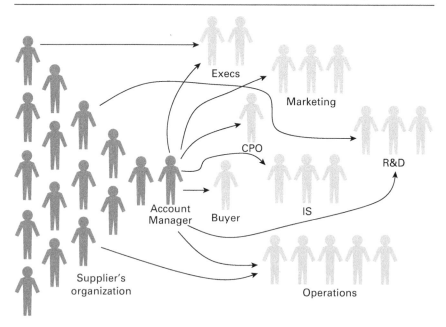

TABLE 11.1 Factors that drive personal relationships between buyer and supplier

Factor	Supplier side	Buyer side
Operations	To ensure smooth running of operations between parties.	To ensure smooth running of operations between parties.
Communication	To ensure alignment of what is being provided to the buyer's needs. To ensure future attractiveness. To create personal relationships and obligations with key buyer-side individuals.	To ensure alignment of supplier's activities with our needs. To ensure we fully know them and what is happening within their organization and between the two organizations. To gain access to information about them.
Risk management	To minimize risks associated with loss of business or later problems around what is provided.	To understand and minimize risks associated with assurance of supply, price hikes, loss of leverage or loss of competitive advantage.
Innovation and growth	To retain and grow the account and secure future business. To secure collaboration to help grow together.	To access new ideas, products, services, processes or technologies that will help growth or to develop a competitive advantage. To access their information.
Personal	To broaden experience and personal knowledge and make the process of doing business enjoyable through social interaction.	To learn from the supplier and take advantage of how a supplier can help the individual excel at his/her job and 'look good' to superiors. To enjoy the social interaction and personal networking.

Surely relationships with suppliers just happen, and naturally develop? Indeed, and this is exactly what will happen with our important suppliers if we do nothing. The problem is this relationship may not be exactly what we need and may not work entirely in our favour. Even with the closest of partnerships between buyer and supplier, it is still a commercial relationship that creates obligations for both parties and has scope for imbalance or parties following differing agendas to that they may appear to have. To prevent this we need to manage the relationship and there are two dimensions to this: the nature of the relationship and stage-managing all interfaces.

- *Nature of the relationship* – how the relationship exists and is defined, what parties do, how they do it, what is acceptable and what is not and all the factors that constitute a given relationship. In a close friendship or a more intimate relationship there are usually boundaries. How we treat the other, what we do or will avoid doing is given by social norms, respect, thinking how they might feel, wanting to please the other or by the expectations the other may have set in terms of expected behaviour. Such things may remain unsaid but those in the relationship simply know how they need to behave within the relationship. The same applies for a relationship with a supplier but here we should stage manage this.

- *Stage managing interfaces* – understanding and managing all the points of interface between the two businesses. Managing relationships with suppliers is about ensuring that the nature and extent of all relationships operate with a common purpose and that all on our side understand their role to support this.

One final note here is that, as we have seen, not every account is of interest to a supplier, and the supplier has only so much resource to put into growing and maintaining their accounts, so this will be directed at the accounts that are seen as priorities. Therefore there is little point in us identifying that we need a strategic collaborative relationship with a supplier if they are not interested in us. It is essential that we use the *Supplier Preferencing* tool to help determine how to approach the relationship with a supplier.

Determining principles for a relationship

Within close relationships with suppliers an alignment of actions towards shared goals is needed, but parties must also have mutually compatible shared principles and beliefs in order to exist together successfully.

Emmett and Crocker (2009) suggest that direction within a supplier management initiative requires clarity of vision principles and clarity of beliefs. Beliefs could extend to religious beliefs, for example Muslim-owned companies seek to trade with other Muslim-owned companies. Beliefs can also be an articulation of what is or is not acceptable, for example a company, or those leading a company, may hold the belief that forced labour in the supply chain is wrong and the belief may be sufficient to compel the organization to proactively seek to prevent being associated with such practices. Beliefs are therefore important and need to be considered as we develop a relationship with a supplier, but they become critical if there is a fundamental mismatch.

It is probably not the place of a purchasing function to define the beliefs for organizations, but rather it should attempt to understand what the organizational beliefs are and then be able to translate these into practical actions with the supply base. Ideally the organization has already defined its beliefs, perhaps as a set of principles or policies, communicated in a way that all understand them; however, in some organizations they may be less clear. The beliefs of the firm can be understood through:

- stated brand values, ethics and principles;
- organizational codes of conduct or ways of working;
- corporate CSR policies;
- environmental policies;
- anti-bribery policies; and
- stated beliefs of the owners or those leading the organization.

Beliefs that impact specific categories of spend or the supply base should be articulated within the business and relationship requirements, if this is not the case then these need to be updated to include new requirements here. Generally beliefs of one organization cannot be imposed on another; they are either compatible or they are not. What we can do is work to understand the degree of alignment or otherwise, and if there is a blatant mismatch determine if this is something that we can accept of if we need to look to move away from the supplier. For example, if our brand is built upon and promotes personal health we may see a supplier that is actively involved in the tobacco industry as one we do not wish to trade with. This may be so important to us that a system to vet and qualify suppliers prior to engaging with us is required. Ways to judge if any mismatch of beliefs here is acceptable or not include:

- the degree to which the beliefs and values of our organization are absolute, universal or things that cannot be compromised on;
- the risk of doing business with a supplier where there is a mismatch;
- the practicalities of realizing our organizational beliefs and values in the supply chain; and
- the degree of importance of a supplier and specifically whether or not we could move away from them.

There is no easy route through here. In practice an organization can set out a series of beliefs and values that are admirable, and may be realizable internally but realizing these across each and every supplier and supply chain may be impossible. This is always the biggest challenge facing any organization embarking upon a CSR programme. Therefore there must be a judgement about how far, and how fast it is possible and practical to go here. This judgement is not something that the purchasing function should make alone, but should be agreed at organizational leadership level. Organizations that recognize the limitations here and identify the priorities for where resources will be directed, tend to make progress in difficult areas such as CSR in the supply chain. It follows that alignment of beliefs and values is most critical for strategic suppliers, especially those with whom we are seeking a more collaborative relationship.

Relationship mindsets

People in organizations engage with suppliers in different ways and for different reasons. People see 'who' the supplier is differently according to their position and individual needs and wants, as well as their overall experience. This, in turn, drives different sorts of interaction. Technical or operational staff may well have close relationships because it helps them achieve their goals and no one has ever explained why another approach might be more helpful whilst purchasing might keep suppliers at arm's length to maintain competitive tensions.

There are five mindsets of supplier engagement (Figure 11.2) and people choose one or more of these, or switch between them, often without conscious thought or intention. People in organizations who have relationships with suppliers simply approach these relationships in the way they feel is right. In other words the choice of relationship is left to personal choice. For small companies with simple one-on-one relationships this may be enough,

FIGURE 11.2 The five mindsets of supplier engagement

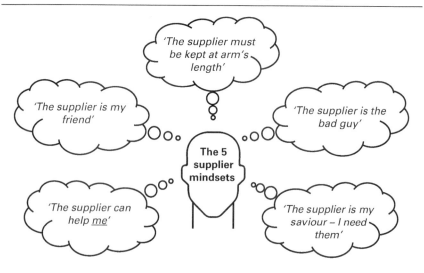

but for larger concerns, where there are multiple touch points leaving the nature of the relationship to be determined by those involved can undermine an entire SRM approach. Technical functions that view the supplier 'as a friend' may believe this to be the right approach but this closeness could compromise the commercial tensions that the purchasing function are trying to create. Similarly if the supplier is always 'the bad guy' then they will adopt a defensive stance that could be counterproductive.

Instead, a company-wide SRM approach means we need to stage-manage the entire relationship, and that includes first understanding how those in the organization view important suppliers and then educating and aligning everyone to view and approach specific suppliers in the same way, presenting a united front externally. In practice, this means gauging the different mindsets our stakeholders are adopting and attempting to understand why and then working with these people to drive in a unified and aligned approach. This requires mapping all the interfaces, education as to how suppliers operate, putting a relationship charter in to action and agreeing a code of conduct with suppliers; we will explore how to do this through the rest of this chapter.

Relationships vs degree of purchasing control

Relationships with suppliers vary according to the degree of overall control a purchasing function in any organization has with suppliers. The influencing factor is how purchasing is organized; whether it is centralized, decentralized or a mixed approach (Figure 11.3).

As you might imagine for centralized purchasing, this single function controls and manages the spend and buys on behalf of the organization and would tend to own, in their entirety, the relationships with suppliers. Furthermore, centralized purchasing naturally restricts the influence internal functions can have over supplier selection and relationships.

Where purchasing is decentralized, business users control and manage their buying. In a mixed approach a central purchasing function may be tasked with managing some or all of the spend on behalf of the business that may still retain budgetary control and may also take responsibility for some buying. Each has its advantages and disadvantages and what is appropriate depends upon what the organization does, how it is organized, what systems are in place and the history and culture of the organization.

Each approach drives different types of relationships with suppliers. In a mixed approach, which is perhaps the most typical, suppliers have relationships with purchasing, but if the supplier can have close relationships with other functions, say technical, operations, practitioners, service delivery, point of use etc, and can instil preferences for their product or service within these people, then their work is done. All the supplier then needs to do is maintain a cursory relationship with purchasing, one where they appear to be attentive and responsive, because the advocates in the business will do the rest and campaign for their supplier of choice to be used. This is in fact how many suppliers sell; they do not need to sell to the purchasing function,

FIGURE 11.3 Different ways purchasing can be organized within an organization

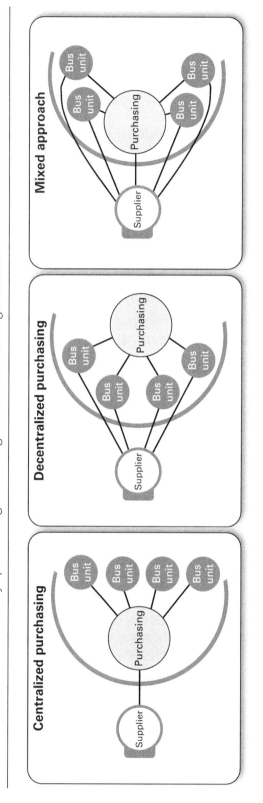

they sell to the users. For example, in both the UK and US healthcare sectors this practice has for many years hampered efforts to drive in effective purchasing. Suppliers of healthcare products and services typically carry huge sales forces and maintain close relationships at ward, nurse, doctor or consultant level with one goal: to get these individuals to specify their product. So long as end users in an organization have choice over what they buy and can exercise that choice then the supplier will seek to influence that choice as directly as they can.

Suppliers are quick to figure out how best to invest their time and resource, and one of the fundamental questions they will seek to answer is who actually makes the decision about how money is spent; who holds the budget; who is the 'economic buyer'? Armed with this understanding they can target these individuals.

In a decentralized or mixed model then purchasing functions don't typically hold budgets for organizational spend and so effective purchasing comes through working cross-functionally with those who do; any power depends upon how the purchasing function can get the wider business working in concert with them and the degree to which the function can be aware of and involved in all engagements and interactions with suppliers.

Some organizations go as far as mandating the need for purchasing to be part of every meeting with a supplier, with no exceptions. This may be impractical, unwelcome and unnecessary in many cases but unless there is at least an awareness of who is talking to whom, and those having the conversations with suppliers are equipped and know what to say and not to say, then the supplier may well be successful in dividing and conquering. When I ask purchasing people about this, I often hear them say something like 'the technical people have separate meetings with suppliers and we are excluded as there is nothing commercial being discussed'. Sounds logical enough, and these discussions may well avoid discussions around price or commercial terms; the technical staff may be clear this is something for purchasing later; however, if these discussions agree technical solutions that begin to allow the supplier to offer a differentiated solution or shape specification in their favour, then purchasing will have little room for leverage later. The reality here is in fact that every interaction with a supplier is important; there is no such thing as a meeting where there are no commercial interactions. Crucially though, those in the technical or operational functions may not fully appreciate the risk certain actions or discussions might have on subsequent leverage or commercial terms.

Staying in control of the relationship

How suppliers love to divide and conquer

'Divide and conquer', or 'divide and rule' is a strategy to gain and maintain power by breaking up larger concentrations of power into smaller groups or individuals that have less power than the whole. It was a maxim used by

Caesar and the French emperor Napoleon. It is an approach that suppliers will use in big organizations unless someone intervenes; it is also what happens by default. As we have seen, purchasing often holds little power over relationships with suppliers in a large organization. Any power here at all comes from how the organization views and accepts our role here and, more crucially, understand their role to support the management of suppliers.

There are only two ways to prevent suppliers dividing and conquering, and that is either to centralize the purchasing function and give it complete control over all organizational spend or to work together with the wider business to bring complete alignment in the way everyone is engaging and interacting with suppliers. Centralized purchasing functions can work well but create new challenges to ensure that the needs, wants and aspirations of the business are being met and, unless the organization is already set up in this way, moving from decentralized to centralized is a major organizational change demanding new systems, processes, procedures, capabilities and cultural shifts.

Working together with the wider organization is more achievable but to be effective this needs to be more than just meeting with stakeholders. Instead there must be universal recognition of the role of purchasing as integral to any business activities where suppliers need to be involved. This may be a culture shift, especially if those in other functions view it as their call to decide how they will engage with suppliers. If purchasing involvement is regarded by the wider business as a necessary interference then stakeholders will only ever be reluctantly accommodating this involvement. However, if purchasing involvement is seen as an essential enabler of overall business success then stakeholders become much more receptive and tend to positively engage with purchasing rather than reluctantly accommodate. This is not just about good relations, but purchasing functions also need some 'teeth', in other words a certain degree of power to act, prevent or stop things that might be at odds with effective supplier management. This is also about rejecting the mindset that suppliers cannot be controlled or have carte blanche to do what they want; this is not the case and boundaries can be set. When these things are in place then suppliers who previously could divide and conquer lose their power as they are presented with a united front across the entire organization. This shift does not happen easily but requires:

- executive agreement and alignment regarding the role of purchasing;
- active executive sponsorship, promotion and reinforcement of the role of purchasing;
- business-wide education across the business for anyone who interfaces with suppliers, how buyer/seller relations work, how suppliers seek to gain advantage and what to do/not to do to ensure alignment and advantage over the supplier;
- building strong inter-functional relationships between purchasing and key stakeholders; selling the benefits and reinforcing how to proceed with suppliers; and
- share success – show how purchasing adds value.

In Chapter 15 we will explore how to achieve some of these things more fully, but for now there are a number of things that we can do or put in place to take control of the supplier relationship and then stay in control of it (Figure 11.4). These are as follows and are explored over the next sections:

- Build and maintain a *supplier interface map*.
- Implement a *supplier code of conduct* for all suppliers

FIGURE 11.4   The key enabling components for managing a supplier relationship

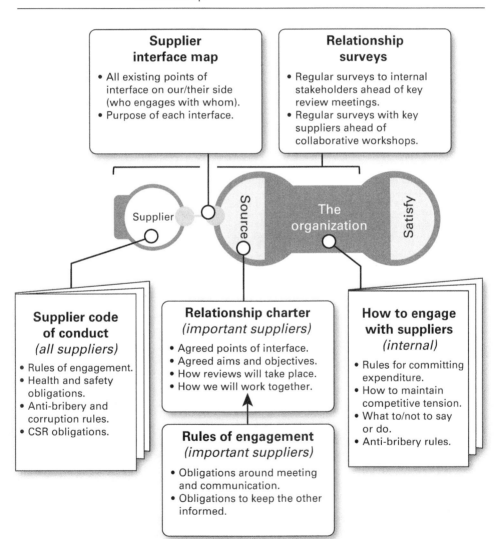

Supplier interface map
- All existing points of interface on our/their side (who engages with whom).
- Purpose of each interface.

Relationship surveys
- Regular surveys to internal stakeholders ahead of key review meetings.
- Regular surveys with key suppliers ahead of collaborative workshops.

Supplier

Source

The organization

Satisfy

Supplier code of conduct
(all suppliers)
- Rules of engagement.
- Health and safety obligations.
- Anti-bribery and corruption rules.
- CSR obligations.

Relationship charter
(important suppliers)
- Agreed points of interface.
- Agreed aims and objectives.
- How reviews will take place.
- How we will work together.

How to engage with suppliers
(internal)
- Rules for committing expenditure.
- How to maintain competitive tension.
- What to/not to say or do.
- Anti-bribery rules.

Rules of engagement
(important suppliers)
- Obligations around meeting and communication.
- Obligations to keep the other informed.

- Agree *rules of engagement* with important suppliers.
- Summarize how strategic and very important relationships will work within a *relationship charter.*
- Educate the wider business and establish principles around *How to engage with suppliers.*
- *Relationship surveys* – both internally and with the supplier.

Supplier interface mapping

A supplier interface map defines who in our organization interfaces with whom within the supplier's organization (Figure 11.5). Developing a map is the first step to bringing some order to how a company-wide relationship with a supplier gets managed, how parties interact and to gain a degree of control and visibility over the overall relationship. Interface mapping does require some effort and time so it is only something that is relevant for those suppliers who are important. There are three steps in developing a map and whilst a map is specific to a single supplier relationship, the process is such that information can be collected to develop multiple maps across different suppliers at the same time. To develop a map we need to identify who in our

FIGURE 11.5   An example supplier interface map

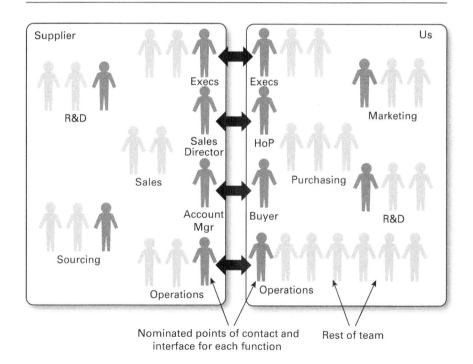

organization talks to whom in the supplier's organization, for what purpose and when or how often. We may know this already otherwise we need to ask both stakeholders and suppliers to help us construct the map. We could encounter a reluctance to cooperate here. Those internally may take issue with a purchasing function questioning or attempting to bring some control over how they engage with suppliers and suppliers may seek to resist any action that could impede their ability to establish relationships. It is important for all to support and buy into the reason behind interface mapping and this means we need to sell *why* it is important and how it helps for all involved.

Internally, supplier interface maps help ensure we can provide a united front within our business and we are fully aligned in what is and is not communicated to a supplier. It provides a basis for a purchasing function to ensure the supplier is fully supporting all parts of the business. Externally, having a relationship map suggests the supplier holds a degree of current and potentially future importance, especially if positioned as something reserved for only the critical few within discussions with the supplier, and so the supplier is likely to be more willing to share details of everyone they engage with.

With an interface map in place then it is possible to begin to secure alignment internally so that everyone knows what is happening with a supplier relationship and can play their part in presenting a unified, aligned front outwards to the supplier. Therefore those involved need to have an appreciation of why this is important and this may require education of how buyer/ supplier relationships work, how suppliers can seek advantage and the balance between maintaining competitive tension and building a relationship. The supplier interface map also forms the basis to define rules of engagement with the supplier.

Supplier code of conduct

A supplier code of conduct is a document that defines what is expected and ideally sought from suppliers; the requirements suppliers need to meet in order to be a supplier. It is also provides the facility to secure a degree of alignment to our values and goals. What is specified could be mandatory, desirable or both according to how important a requirement is, the ease or likelihood to which suppliers will be able to comply and the extent of suppliers we wish to comply. An important supplier eager to win, retain and build our account will be keen to comply whilst asking Microsoft to signal their agreement could be a waste of time. Supplier codes of conduct are therefore most relevant for important or strategic suppliers; the ones where we need to have some sort of relationship but can also apply to less important suppliers to a degree where they are likely to be interested in complying with the document.

A supplier code of conduct should be more than just another purchasing document hand-out, but rather a core reference manual, readily available to all online and perhaps as a corporate branded brochure. It might include:

- our mission aims and how we want our suppliers to contribute to this;
- our values and what we expect of our suppliers;
- health and safety obligations – eg specific rules for suppliers working on our sites;
- bribery and corruption – the specific rules and obligations suppliers must observe;
- CSR aims and specific requirements;
- how to register an interest in becoming a supplier to us;
- how those who are suppliers must engage with us – who they can and cannot approach, perhaps some basic rules of engagement;
- nominated points of contact; and
- permitted ways we will contract and commit expenditure with suppliers.

Agreement by a supplier to a code of conduct does not necessarily guarantee they can or will actually do this. It is however a first line of defence and one that begins to define our expectations. Beyond that we can then work to secure greater confidence where needed, for example compliance to our health and safety requirements or specific CSR needs might be so important to us that we need to verify this, perhaps via an audit or assessment or other risk management activity.

Codes of conduct are made effective by requiring those suppliers who need to comply to positively signal their acceptance and compliance with the code of conduct. This could be a simple voluntary agreement, but can be made contractual if referenced within contractual agreements. Agreement could also be within the process of qualifying a supplier or applied retrospectively.

Suppliers must be reasonably able to accept a code of conduct or it will fail to be effective yet it must cover the aspects of a relationship that are absolutely necessary for us. For example, consider a code of conduct that specifies *the supplier must guarantee that all their supply chains shall be free from child labour, forced labour or poor working conditions*. Whilst this is a worthy aim, and one most suppliers would support, it is however unlikely many would be able to agree to provide such a guarantee.

Rules of engagement

If the supplier is permitted to engage freely across our organization then that is what they will do. However if, as part of formalizing our relationship with them, we ask for certain rules of engagement then it can be difficult to resist agreeing, especially if they believe doing otherwise would jeopardize future revenues.

The rules of engagement are the specific set of rules and obligations for how a given supplier shall engage with us. They define what is permissible and what is not, specific actions the supplier shall carry out and things they will refrain from doing. They are relevant for strategic and the most important suppliers and could be developed collaboratively or imposed.

Rules of engagement can help bring increased levels of control over a supplier relationship and might include obliging the supplier to:

- recognize that whilst they might have many different points of interface with us, there is a single nominated point of coordination for the entire relationship who must be kept informed on all matters;
- maintain updated 'points of interface' information with us so we know who is talking to whom;
- meet at specific intervals and proactively share information; and
- comply with any specific policies or codes of conduct in engaging with us.

Rules of engagement can be informally established, but have more power if they form part of wider agreement between parties. They could even be made contractual, perhaps with a schedule or specific clauses defining specific arrangements for the expected relationship between parties. However, this is not always readily achievable. Perhaps contracts are already in place or perhaps it is difficult to precisely define in legalese how we really want things to work in practice. Therefore it is often more achievable to define rules of engagement between parties separately to any contractual mechanism, perhaps as part of ongoing discussions around developing the relationship. Supplier rules of engagement could stand alone as a agreed approach with a supplier, but they are more commonly incorporated together with other points of agreement within a relationship charter.

The relationship charter

A relationship charter (Figure 11.6) is a document built and agreed by both parties that encapsulates and defines key aspects of how the relationship will work; typically a voluntary agreement entered into by parties, but could also be referenced within a contract. It is appropriate for strategic and the most important of suppliers.

A relationship charter should include all the things that would enable an individual on either side to know what is expected of him or her in any dealings with the other and might typically include:

- definition of the scope of the relationship;
- agreed vision for the relationship;
- specific contracts the charter relates to;
- agreed points of contact and interface, and roles for various matters;

FIGURE 11.6 Example of a supplier relationship charter

Supplier Relationship Charter Template

Supplier name

Agreed contacts and interface map

Level	Us	Supplier
Executive Owner		
Relationship Lead		
Dispute resolution		
Nominated contacts		

Governance

Area	Arrangements
Quarterly review meetings	
Annual assessment	
Dispute resolution	

Scope and definition of the relationship

Agreed principles and rules of engagement

No	Principle
1	
2	
3	
4	
5	
6	
7	
8	
9	
10	

Vision for the relationship

Objectives and performance

Target	KPI

Agreed joint improvement initiatives

No	Initiative	Due by
1		
2		
3		
4		
5		

- agreed principles for the relationship and rules of engagement;
- agreed objectives for the relationship;
- agreed targets and KPIs;
- agreed improvement initiatives;
- dispute resolution arrangements; and
- governance arrangements for the relationship – schedule of reviews and other regular activities or engagements.

Relationship charters are most appropriate where we have identified the need for a collaborative relationship. They require joint agreement and for it to be effective both parties need to be willing to adopt it and work to it, therefore a charter is only appropriate where the supplier is interested in a collaborative relationship (supplier preferencing *Development* or *Core* quadrants).

Ideally charters should be developed together with the supplier's key representatives and key stakeholders from our organization during a joint working session. Here good facilitation can help. It is a good idea to have in mind an idea of how we might want the charter to end up; however, it is not a good idea to provide a pre-worked version for the group to simply agree or sign off. It is the discussion and debate amongst those involved that is most important here, which leads to alignment, agreement and most importantly buy-in from all. The relationship charter is then no more than a record or output of this discussion, but one that reflects a powerful point of group agreement.

The final charter should then be drawn up and published to all concerned. It can help cement the agreement by all individuals actually signing copies of the final version as a gesture to show commitment. Once completed it becomes a dynamic document and should be regularly reviewed together with the supplier and updated as appropriate.

Educating the business

An experienced purchasing professional knows how to understand and maximize their position in a given marketplace, and how to manage the relationship to ensure the right competitive tension is in place, perhaps following years of studying or practical experience. Yet others in the business may not be so experienced, will not have had any formal training in purchasing and yet could end up facing, interacting with and making certain agreements with suppliers. Purchasing is one of a few professions where non-purchasing people get involved and where a little knowledge or naivety can be dangerous and jeopardize the overall position. HR and Legal are others.

The only practical route through this is to educate the business and those involved as to the fundamentals of how purchasing and the buyer/seller relationship works and to equip people with some basic principles or 'dos and dont's' when engaging with suppliers. A small amount of education of key stakeholders can in fact make a dramatic difference to the overall purchasing power of the organization. The biggest win is typically a shift in understanding and therefore mindset of those who hold relationships with suppliers so they appreciate the implications of such things such as sharing budgetary information or specifying proprietary products.

In practical terms educating the business can be achieved relatively easily and things that can help here include:

- conducting short internal training, perhaps 2–3 hours or half a day around how the buyer/seller relationship works, how suppliers can gain advantage and winning ways to engage with key suppliers;
- promoting the 'central message', ie what things we want suppliers to be hearing from all they have in the contract with us. Central messages will need to change over time according to our current needs;
- publishing a simple list of 'dos and don'ts' for all who engage with suppliers. In Chapter 15 we will introduce the concept of a *Stakeholder Brochure* and this list would then form part of this. An example dos and don'ts list is given below.

Top 10 dos and don'ts for engaging with suppliers

Do...

1 *Keep it arm's length* – suppliers seek to build relationships which creates a sense of obligation. Keep it arm's length and build a relationship on your terms.

2 *Have alternatives* – if a supplier believes you have no alternative you give them the power. Make sure they believe you always have an alternative.

3 *Avoid proprietary* – differentiation, added value items or service, brand or bundled offerings give suppliers power so they become the only provider.

4 *Reveal with caution* – suppliers seek intelligence to determine their strength. Be careful what you reveal, especially about competitors, timings or future plans.

5 *Check them out* – find out their position; how busy are they, where are they heading, is there any risk, what is their overall position? All vital intelligence that can help you understand if you have power.

6 *Condition them* – set expectations about boundaries, limitations, constraints, challenges, or what you expect of them so as to apply a bit of pressure and keep things where you want them.

Don't...

1 *Tell them your budget* – if you reveal your budget you are handing over power and control unless you have a way to verify subsequent price proposals. Get them to give a number first.

2 *Make an oral contract* – be careful what you say, if you make any sort of verbal commitment you could be entering into an oral contract.

3 *Let them condition you* – watch out for suppliers 'warming you up' for something they want such as an impending price risk or bad news. Challenge it and counter it early on.

4 *Take the first offer* – unless you are building a close relationship, always negotiate, challenge and push back and seek 'something in return for something' if you need to concede.

Relationship surveys

We touched briefly on the use of surveys as a data collection mechanism in Chapter 6. For a key supplier relationship a survey is a great way to help to understand how the supplier relationship is actually working in practice for all involved, including perhaps the supplier.

Relationships can easily be misjudged, especially if our involvement extends little further than the supplier's key sales representative. But where there are multiple interface points we need to check that all aspects of the relationship are working in the way we expect them to.

A relationship survey requires a means to solicit feedback from those involved in the relationship. A simple questionnaire is usually the most effective means of opinion collection, however interviews may be useful here also. Surveys should be designed to be simple, quick and easy to complete. Questions should be considered carefully so as to providing meaningful results. For example, asking 'how do you think the relationship is working' will solicit answers as words and sentences that are subjective and require interpretation. Instead, asking 'please rate how well the relationship is working overall' and using a simple scale allows quantitative data to be collected that can then be analysed across multiple responses more easily. That said, there is always a place for comments within any quantitative data collection survey in case someone has something they want to add or wish to provide context.

Online surveys tools such as surveymonkey.com can help here and allow simple surveys to be created and participants invited to complete a survey. Some eSourcing RFI tools have this functionality also. Surveys should be run regularly, perhaps annually, internally in advance of a key review meeting and externally with the supplier in advance of a joint working session.

Surveys require management. Just because you send someone a survey doesn't mean they will complete it, but rather might need some encouragement. Key success factors here are:

- *Keep it simple* – a survey should take no more than five minutes, ideally two minutes to complete and accessing it should be just a click away. If people have to log on to a system, enter a password, they may give up.

- *Right questions* – use quantitative questions and a simple scoring or rating system. Avoid rating systems that have middle ground but rather compel people to say it is either good or bad.

- *Tell them and sell it* – avoid just sending an e-mail asking someone to complete a survey, call them up, explain what you are doing, tell them how it helps and why it is important and ask for their help. People are more likely to do something if they believe in it and less likely to respond to a cold request.

- *Share the results* – if someone has taken the time to complete something they should get to see the results.

Bribes, lunches and chai pani

Avoiding bribery and corruption

Dealing with suppliers provides increased scope for bribery and corruption. In much of Northern Europe, North America, Australia and Japan, such practices are rare and regarded as unacceptable (Global Corruption Barometer, 2013). They may also be illegal. Elsewhere it can be how business is done, and may not even be considered as bribery but nothing more than building good business relationships. Bribery is the offering, promising, giving, accepting or soliciting of an advantage as an inducement for action which is illegal or a breach of trust. A bribe is an inducement or reward offered, promised or provided in order to gain any commercial, contractual, regulatory or personal advantage.

In the UK the Bribery Act (2010) places a liability on organizations that fail to prevent people in the organization from bribing and is a significant anti-corruption standard alongside the US Foreign Corrupt Practices Act. Both the OECD (Organisation for Economic Cooperation) and the UN (United Nations) are working to ratify international conventions against bribery and corruption. Anti-corruption efforts are gaining momentum around the world (Greenaway, 2011). Anti-bribery policies, procedures and training have therefore become essential and the management of a company now needs to be convinced that the company under its watch has the right arrangements in place. This is particularly important for those in purchasing and must therefore be integral to how we work with suppliers. This starts with a company policy translated into specific practice around supplier relationships, instilling the right culture and training for those involved. Supplier codes of conduct and internal stakeholder 'how to engage with supplier' documents should include a definition of anti-bribery and corruption obligations. Anti-bribery policies should be professionally developed so as to be fully in line with legal and organizational requirements. As such they might include specific rules that prohibit the giving or accepting of the following.

- anything that could be regarded as illegal or improper or violates our or their policy;
- cash;
- gifts, either entirely or over a specified value (companies may chose to specify a value here, if so this is usually low to only allow gifts of low intrinsic value to be permitted);
- hospitality, either entirely or above a certain specified value individually or in aggregate;
- anything where there is a suggestion that a return favour will be expected or implied; and
- anything where a public or governmental official is involved or a politician or political party.

There are always exceptions and so any arrangements here should provide for these, perhaps with senior manager agreement where deviation is appropriate. There are instances where it is not appropriate to decline a gift, say when negotiating with a Chinese supplier who has travelled to meet with us. Furthermore, where we are doing business across cultural boundaries our norms around bribery could be very different to the supplier's and there could be good reasons to accommodate different approaches. It is impossible to give guidance here but whatever approach is taken should not be based upon an individual's judgement and decision but should be open and transparent and agreed in advance within the business. For example, I came across a company that worked closely with a number of Middle Eastern companies, each who had been awarded large contracts. Good relationships were essential yet the company was keen to operate in an appropriate and transparent way. Suppliers provided gifts of significant value to those in a buying roles; Rolex watches, Mont Blanc fountain pens and so on. Instead of declining the gifts, which would have been damaging to the relationship, they were accepted, declared and formally acknowledged via a letter of thanks to the supplier. A label would then be placed on the gift with the name of the supplier and it would be placed in the gift cabinet; a treasure trove of watches, pens, cufflinks and other accessories. Whenever a buyer met with a supplier they would 'check out' the relevant gems from the cabinet, wear them during the engagement with the supplier, and return them afterwards. Suppliers were not offended and believed their gifts were well received and the buyer was not placed in a difficult position. Such systems, however, are fraught with risk and difficulty; they may be appropriate in certain situations but careful thought and legal advice are needed before introducing such an approach to ensure the company and individuals are not put at risk. That said, it is easy to wind up justifying something for the sake of a cultural difference – sometimes this is necessary but not always and bridging cultural differences is two-way, meaning we can place expectations on the other party to understand our culture, what is or is not appropriate to us. In essence, companies need robust arrangements to prevent bribery and corruption and shouldn't rush to create exceptions.

Increasingly bribery is being taken seriously the world over. Training in anti-bribery is now commonplace for those who hold office and interventions have become more preventative than punitive. In parts of Africa, for example, meetings and negotiations between suppliers to officials representing public bodies now take place in special meeting rooms where all proceedings are video recorded. It would therefore be easy to assume that with this global strengthening of bribery legislation and arrangements that bribery is becoming less prevalent. However this is not the case; in fact, according to the 2013 Global Corruption Barometer, corruption on a global scale is on the increase. On average one in four people paid a bribe to a public body during 2013. Countries including Denmark, Finland, Japan and Australia have the lowest rate of bribery (less than 1 per cent); in the United Kingdom the figure is 5 per cent and 7 per cent in the United States. Kenya, Yemen, Liberia and Sierra Leone have bribery rates above 70 per cent. In India, a current destination for major outsourcing, the rate is 54 per cent. Bribery and corruption is a growing problem and anyone who interfaces with suppliers is at risk (Global Corruption Barometer, 2013).

If a supplier pushes a Rolex across the table or slips a fat, cash-stuffed envelope into our hand then clearly we are being offered a bribe. Most buyers are typically unprepared for such things and this ill-preparedness can easily lead to an individual making the wrong decision, one that is regretted later, and one that then puts them in an impossible position. However, in my experience, such open bribes are rare; instead inducements are typically made in a much more subtle way. Often those involved may feel they are not doing anything wrong. Perhaps attending a golf day or a sporting event at the invitation of a supplier is acceptable under the company's policy, but what if that event then takes place at a very expensive venue, with the chance to meet celebrity players, and prizes of value are won, apparently for playing well? What if this is one of many events? The hospitality is now much more than a simple golf day.

It's not just golf days that can cause a buyer to wind up in a position where they accept high-value hospitality. Having lunch or dinner with a supplier may be necessary or appropriate to our relationship, and essential to developing social interaction. However, lunch at high-end restaurants entirely at the supplier's expense on a regular basis is perhaps more of an inducement than building good relations. If both parties believe that social interaction is necessary to the relationship then it follows that both parties should recognize this and share the cost or perhaps take turns picking up the tab. It seems there is a, somewhat outdated, commonplace culture of 'getting whatever you can from a supplier', and viewing it as good practice for suppliers to buy lunch as if another small concession is being secured. In my experience of purchasing people having dinner with a supplier, more often than not the bill/check is left untouched on the table for the supplier to pick it up. It is rare for the buyer to intervene and say something like 'No, please can we split this?' or 'only if I can get it next time'. It remains, even in the most important of relationships, something the supplier is still expected to do. However, if we are serious about building the right relationship with important suppliers then even policies around lunch and how this can be fair and transparent are important.

It is difficult to define where giving or receiving something for the sake of good business relationships stops and something that is an inducement begins. This point will be different from organization to organization and country to country. For this reason clear company-wide policy within the context of the prevailing culture, is essential. If this is not present then it should be developed. Furthermore, if the company-level arrangements permit some gifts or hospitability, it may be appropriate for the purchasing function to deliberately adopt a stricter policy.

With a few exceptions, it is not typically bad people who end up taking a bribe; often it is good people who end up in a situation they hadn't planned to be in. After all, it may be in a supplier's interests to put you in that position and they may have a range of approaches and tactics designed to take an inexperienced buyer by surprise. It is therefore essential for any buyer dealing with a supplier that they anticipate what could happen and are ready with a response and course of action to deal with it. This means clearly understanding any company policy on what is and is not acceptable as well as having in mind a clear set of personal boundaries and being ready to stop proceedings whenever things drift outside these. It helps to have some pre-prepared lines and courses of action in mind. These might include:

- Where a supplier appears to be suggesting something inappropriate, say 'Could you please clarify for me precisely what you are proposing here?'

- Where a supplier makes an offer of something that might be marginally appropriate, 'I'm sorry but I'm not able or willing to accept this as it might fall outside our policy on such matters and it is imperative that there is nothing within our dealings that would not bear scrutiny.'

- Where a supplier clearly offers a bribe – clearly decline what is being offered, stop proceedings, end the meeting, report what happened as quickly as possible internally to a line manager or a nominated individual for such matters and seek advise on how to proceed. The question to then be answered here is how appropriate it is to proceed with a company who has attempted to bribe us.

Bribes from suppliers are rarely as obvious as them producing envelopes of cash. Such things only happen if the bribe has been previously agreed. Instead, a corrupt supplier attempting to offer an inducement will work up to the offer of a bribe. This is a bit like courtship where they need to gauge interest, gauge personality (those who are naive or inexperienced can be more susceptible to a bribe), establish personal circumstances of potential need and establish what the other party might want or be tempted to accept. This could be money but could also be sex, power or fear driven (the promise of safety against the suggestion of unfavourable consequences). It is therefore important to watch for any signs that a supplier might be working up to some sort of bribe and cut it off before it gets anywhere. Things to watch out for might be a supplier using phrases such as:

- We see this as more of a give and take situation.
- If you scratch my back I'll scratch yours/
- OK, so that's the deal, but what can we do to help *you*?
- What would it take to make this easier for you?
- There is nothing wrong here, it is part of what is expected.
- Everyone does this, now it's your turn.

Watch out too for euphemisms used to suggest something extra is called for. For example, in India a supplier might offer 'chai pani', literally meaning tea and water, but actually suggesting a bribe.

There's no such thing as a free lunch

'There's no such thing as a free lunch' is a phrase that first seems to have appeared during the 1930s referring to the practice in American bars of offering an apparent 'free lunch' in order to entice customers in to drink (Safire, 1993). It communicates the idea that it is impossible to get something for nothing. It is a concept that is core to economics (Gwartney *et al*, 2005) and even became the title of the economist Milton Friedman's 1975 book.

Whether a supplier is buying us lunch, or indeed providing something more that is outside what we have contracted for, they are giving a gift. It is a simple human fact that if someone gives you something then you become obliged to that individual and it may instil a feeling of needing to reciprocate.

In his classic work 'The Gift', Marcel Mauss (1925) suggested that when a gift is given it is never free but rather gives rise to reciprocity. Mauss proposed that the giver does not just give an object or something of value but also gives part of himself, for the object is indissolubly tied to the giver. There is a bond between giver and gift that then creates a social bond within the process of exchange and thus creates an obligation to reciprocate on the part of the recipient. Failure to reciprocate could mean one loses honour or status. In some parts of the world beliefs frameworks suggest such failure could be damaging to the individual's spiritual wealth. Mauss

(1925) suggested there are three dimensions within a gift: *giving, receiving* and *reciprocating*:

- *Giving* – the first step required in order to create and maintain a social relationship.
- *Receiving* – the acceptance of the social bond (for to refuse is to reject the social bond)
- *Reciprocating* – necessary to demonstrate one's own freedom, liberality, honour, status and wealth.

Gregory (1982) also supported the concept of reciprocity but suggested too that when we give gifts to another, be they a friend or potential enemy, it is in order to establish a relationship with them by placing them in debt. For the relationship to persist there must be a time lag between the gift and the other party making a later counter gift to repay the debt; one partner must always remain in debt for a relationship to exist. Gregory called this *inalienability of possessions*; in other words it is as if the gift is loaned rather than sold. When we sell something the rights of ownership of that thing transfer fully to the other party; it has been a fair exchange. However, in the case of a gift, it is an unfair exchange because there is no exchange, just a gift. This, combined with the fact that the gift is tied to the giver (Mauss, 1925), creates a power that compels the recipient to reciprocate and creates the debt.

Sahlins (1972) suggests three types of reciprocity: *generalized, symmetrical* or *negative* reciprocity:

- *Generalized* – a gift or exchange of value is given without tracking the exact value but with the belief and expectation that things will balance out over time.
- *Symmetrical* – a gift or exchange of value is given expecting a similar value in return.
- *Negative* – a party intends to profit from the exchange, often at the expense of the other.

The nature of gift giving varies with culture and society and depends upon the attitude to ownership of property that exists. Sider (1980) suggests that property is not a thing but a relationship amongst people about things. Hann (1998) suggests that property is therefore a social relationship that governs the conduct of people with respect to the use and disposition of things. A gift in a Western, individualistic society therefore carries a very different implication to a gift in an Eastern, collective society where it would be viewed less as the transfer of value from one individual to another but more symbolizing the invitation and welcome into the collective group. This subtle fact is crucially important when considering what may or may not be acceptable and appropriate when interacting with suppliers from collective societies.

In purchasing, whilst we may not need to worry about a supplier pushing a new Rolex across the table, some hospitality may be unavoidable and we need to appreciate that any gift from a supplier carries with it a debt and the obligation of reciprocity. This is a key mindset within supplier relationships and in fact goes beyond gifts and hospitality but must also be considered in how we exchange other forms of value. For example, if we offer the services of someone from our business to go and work with the supplier for a while to help develop them we are providing a gift here too. Yet to restrict this would be counterproductive to both parties. The way through this is simply to discuss what each party will bring to the relationship beyond what is contracted for and to work with a common aim of maintaining a fair exchange at all times. For example, we agree to provide help and support to improve the supplier, they share with us half of the efficiency gains. Therefore it is imperative that parties discuss improvement and development arrangements and how benefits will be shared in advance.

Conflict and dispute

Voice of the supplier

No matter how hard we try, there will always be situations where we end up in conflict or dispute with a supplier. When a dispute arises it can cause conflict, a breakdown in relations and a failure of communication between individuals. Despite the fact that we are talking of a professional commercial relationship between two organizations, if those involved come to feel devalued, cheated or threatened then our natural human emotional responses can drive behaviour to the detriment of the overall relationship; the supplier's account manager may say exactly what is expected of him, but if this is through gritted teeth with a hidden desire to get us back then we may not get what we need or worse the supplier could become problematic. How parties behave when a dispute arises can reveal true feelings and intent for the relationship. Ping (1997) suggests that if two businesses are dissatisfied with each other it is the degree to which a party will voice the issue that indicates the overall attitude to the relationship. He suggests that parties choose one of three responses:

- Loyalty – remaining silent.
- Voice – changing objectionable conditions.
- Neglect – allowing the relationship to deteriorate.

The first and third don't work and fail to address the issue. However, with a voice, and airing of concerns and discussion it is possible to overcome disputes. This means that having a voice, and raising concerns is an important part of relationship management and is also a sign of a healthy relationship. If the supplier doesn't voice a concern then it is easy to assume everything is OK; in fact it may be the complete opposite and the supplier is simply avoiding voicing the issue. Therefore hearing the voice, or listening for the

FIGURE 11.7 The relationship between the supplier's 'voice' and supplier preferencing

	Development	Core
	Reserved voice	*Healthy voice*
	Supplier is reserved about *voice* and treads carefully so as not to jeopardize future business or relationships.	Supplier has *voice* and is prepared to use it within the relationship to call out anything that is not right and help find solutions.
	Nuisance	**Exploitable**
	Saving voice	*All or nothing voice*
	Supplier is deliberately neglecting the relationship and will simply not bother to use *voice*.	Supplier either holds back on using *voice* to maintain status quo but could, if pushed, then use *voice* in a destructive way.

Attractiveness of account (vertical axis)

Relative spend of account (horizontal axis)

absence of a voice, is equally important, especially if the supplier is important to us. Hearing the voice in a neglect or even loyalty scenario is more difficult than it might seem. If we ask the supplier 'tell me... is there a problem' or send them a relationship health check and satisfaction questionnaire then any answers here are likely to be unreliable. Suppliers tend to avoid being open and candid about issues for risk of jeopardizing future business unless they (and specific individuals) are certain they can do so. In practice this means to establish voice we need to do some detective work and attempt to gauge the relationship in different ways. A well-designed *Supplier Relationship Survey* can help here. It also means attempting to create a climate and environment where parties will use voice. In practice, voice comes when parties begin to work together and then the relationship becomes more important or attractive to the supplier. Here we can use the *Supplier Preferencing* tool to both validate which quadrant we believe a supplier might see our relationship in and to help determine how a supplier might typically use *voice* in each quadrant (Figure 11.7).

Disputes and conflict are more likely to arise where there is no voice. A healthy voice helps keep a relationship stable, but even then there may be scenarios where dispute arises and if it does we need to have a means to deal with it.

Dealing with conflict

The first thing to appreciate is that dispute causes conflict and at the heart of all conflict is fear! Conflict is a natural part of buyer/seller relationships from time to time, and especially when negotiating so purchasing professionals need to be able to manage conflict effectively. Conflict is triggered when something threatens us. This threat may be real or perceived but it is enough to trigger some sort of emotional response. Possibly the most widely known model to understand this emotional response is the Thomas-Kilmann conflict Mode Instrument or TKI (Kilmann and Thomas, 1977), building upon the work of Robert Blake and Jane Moulton from the 1960s. TKI considers personal assertiveness in a conflict situation against the tendency for cooperation and identifies five conflict styles, namely: competing, avoiding, accommodating, collaborating and compromising. Therefore if we get into a dispute with a supplier and we revert to competing whilst the supplier does the same then we have a fight on our hands. If we tend to avoid then chances are we will run away and hide at the first sign of trouble. In practice this means we will fail to use *voice* and articulate our concerns. Figure 11.8 is based upon the Thomas-Kilmann model and shows how we need to consider the implications of our natural tendency when faced with conflict within the context of a supplier dispute. How we handle conflict can make all the difference when in dispute with a supplier; this is especially critical in strategic collaborative relationships. Therefore individuals involved in managing relationships with suppliers not only need to understand their

FIGURE 11.8 Using the Thomas-Kilmann Instrument to determine our responses when faced with conflict with a supplier; adapted from Kilmann and Thomas (1977)

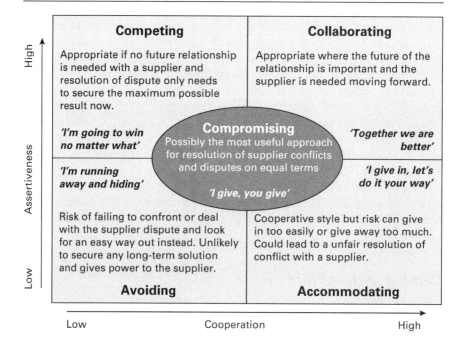

natural conflict style but also need to develop strategies to compensate if the style conflicts with that which is needed to resolve the dispute. The Kilmann Diagnostics website (**www.kilmanndiagnostics.com**) provides more on the TKI together with the means to obtain your own conflict style summary.

Ideally we would seek to avoid getting into dispute with a supplier in the first place. Many disputes often arise out of simple errors and misunderstanding, many of which can be avoided if quashed early on. There are two sources of dispute and therefore conflict:

1 *Expectations not met* – disputes caused by differences between expectations between the supplier and us. This might include disputes over:

- what, where, when, how certain goods or services were to be provided;
- who was doing what and when;
- timings;
- degree of effort that was reasonably to be expected; and
- the standard that must be achieved.

2 *Soft reasons* – these are things within a relationship that can cause conflict and therefore difficulties overall. These might include:

- poor communication – misunderstandings in things said, colouring of words or failure to communicate;
- different perspectives – how one party sees things may be seen differently by the other;
- mistakes – honest and unintended mistakes; and
- emotional triggers – actions that make the other party feel threatened in some way.

Many of these sources of dispute and conflict can be avoided. Expectations can be clearly set out and agreed and of course this is what good contracts, statements of work, clarity of purchase orders and clear points of agreement seek to do. Taking the time for clarification helps overcome communication issues, putting ourselves in their shoes helps see different perspectives and avoiding actions that contain threats is essential. However, despite doing all of these things there will be times when we do end up in some sort of dispute with a supplier that cannot be readily resolved and when this happens it is important to deal with the dispute quickly to prevent it escalating and become damaging. The process of dealing with dispute is shown in Figure 11.9.

FIGURE 11.9 The supplier dispute resolution process

The supplier dispute resolution process

1 Contain the situation

Disputes typically manifest themselves during a specific engagement or meeting. When this happens recognize a dispute has arisen and take steps to contain it. This could include:

- Taking a time out.
- Break state (momentarily changing the subject to something completely unrelated).
- Change location.
- Signal empathy to the other.
- Commit to working it out.
- De-escalate using unembellished facts at hand.

2 Determine cause

Assess how the dispute arose and how we got here. Attempt to understand what lies at the heart of the dispute. Disputes are like icebergs and the real cause will most likely be deeply personal.

3 Assess impact

Determine risk if the dispute continues, or if we concede or need to end our relationship. Engage stakeholders and assess risk and impact to supply.

4 Assess options

Determine the options open to us. Determine contractual position for exit and any escalation options. If no provision exists determine other options.

5 Invite supplier proposal

Unless communications with the supplier have broken down, invite the supplier to propose a way forward. This should be independent of any other activity by us to determine courses of action.

6 Move ahead

Determine the way forward and implement exit strategy or work towards a desirable outcome.

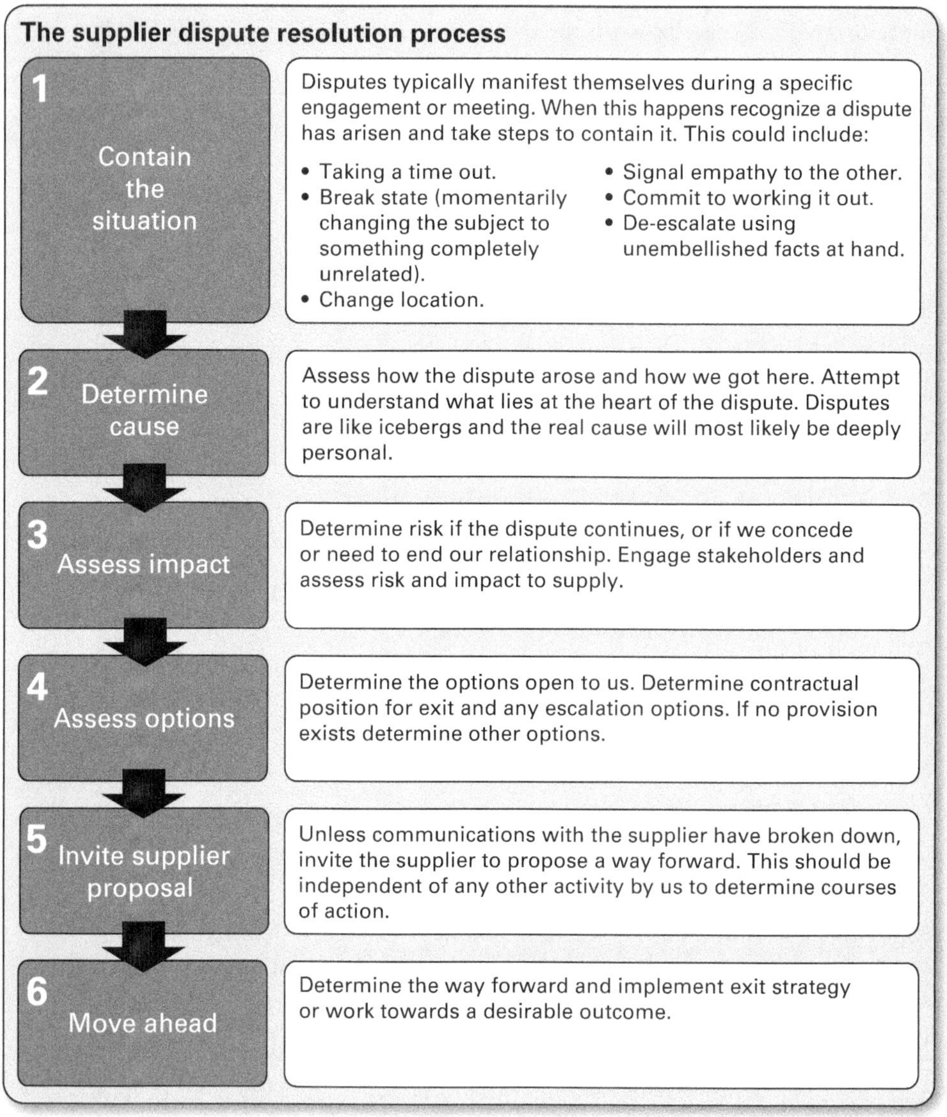

Supply chain management

12

This chapter provides an introduction to supply chain management and explores some of the key concepts. The relationship between SCM and SRM is considered and why, how and when SCM needs to form part of an overall SRM approach within a business.

PATHWAY QUESTIONS ADDRESSED IN THIS CHAPTER

7 Do we know everything we should know about our suppliers?

10 What are the risks with suppliers or back up our supply chains and how is this risk being managed?

13 Do we understand our supply chains? Are we maximizing any opportunities to make them more effective?

Introducing supply chain management

Supply chain management (SCM) and logistics is an entire topic all of its own with a wealth of publications, knowledge and education available out there so it is impossible to do justice to the topic in this book. However, we do need to explore SCM at a high level as it is a key component within an overall SRM approach, although has not traditionally been regarded as such. So far we have considered how we can have the right relationships with those immediate suppliers that are important to us but SCM looks beyond these to where there is no direct contractual relationship but to where a different type of intervention can bring competitive advantage.

Historically, the practice of SCM has been regarded as separate to the practice of strategic purchasing (where board level representation is expected and the role of chief procurement officer (CPO) is now commonplace). To the uninitiated, SCM may well be regarded as an approach to take care of transportation, logistics, warehousing; tactical, transactional and concerned with little more than the movement of goods. Today, however, effective SCM is much more than that and is also increasingly being recognized as a strategic contributor with new roles of chief supply chain officer now emerging, especially in organizations where the performance and security of the supply chain is critical. Yet, despite this, SCM and strategic purchasing remain quite different professions. The reason for this is perhaps historic – SCM has been around for millions of years and has been behind any requirement to get the right stuff to the right place in good condition exactly when needed, repeatedly and reliably. The principles surrounding ensuring an effective flow of materials and information to satisfy a customer have altered little from the building of the pyramids to the relief of hunger in Africa (Christopher, 2011). Yet strategic purchasing and SRM are the new kids on the block. Twenty-five years ago there was very little knowledge or thinking on this subject but since then purchasing has been transformed in leading edge companies; no longer the subservient function that buys things for the rest of the business, it is now the function that adds significant value and helps drive corporate strategy using approaches such as category management to help deliver the results.

A distinction also remains in the educational space in these two areas. For example, in the UK I could sign up to do an MSc in Logistics and Supply Chain Management with one of the reputable universities specializing in this area or alternatively an MSc in Strategic Procurement Management. Each has modules to introduce the other, but they are two very separate specialisms taught by different experts, using different tools and approaches, with candidates making a choice to go into one profession or the other. Furthermore, in the workplace this disparity continues with functional divides – the 'running' of supply chains is often something that sits separate from a purchasing function, perhaps being the remit of a dedicated logistics function, operations, production or even a commercial function.

So why change? Surely purchasing can look after the immediate suppliers and categories of spend and a supply chain function manage logistics and the flow of materials in order to satisfy the customer? Indeed they could but today there is now an imperative for convergence of SCM with strategic purchasing: the very thing that has increased the significance of both independently is now the very thing that now driving these two worlds to collide. That is the demands and increasing risk of our changing environment:

- The global marketplace drives global supply chains and distribution networks.
- Global distribution drives fewer 'super sized' production facilities and provides economies of scale over many regional factories.

- Global supply chains drive fewer, 'super sized' inventories.
- Corporate social responsibility means we are now interested in what happens in a global supply chain, but first-hand knowledge and understanding is more difficult to secure.
- Consumer demands for personalization are now being met through clever production technology and good logistics.
- Regional variations and localization can similarly be catered for so one product facility can produce a range of different products for different markets on the same production line in real time.

All of these factors present new challenges to an organization and levels of risk that must be taken seriously. As supply chains become bigger, more technical and more complex they become more vulnerable to environmental catastrophes and global changes. Furthermore things don't stand still and the benefits of global sourcing always demand a trade off between economies of scale and low cost production to cost of transportation. What might be beneficial today could be prohibitive tomorrow, especially as economies in third world regions develop. In fact, the trend towards offshoring and shifting production to low-cost providers has, in recent years, begun to reverse due to the cost advantage now being squeezed as the economies in developing countries develop, transportation costs have increased, true costs of low-cost country sourcing are more than anticipated and concerns are growing over carbon footprint (Christopher, 2011).

SCM is no longer just about logistics, it is a practice that can help bring significant value to a business by reducing and managing risk and bringing competitive advantage by enabling a firm to satisfy its end customers. However, the greatest impact comes when SCM is connected to, and integrated with, the wider strategic purchasing within the organization and SRM is the means by which to do this.

A world of definitions

As for many other parts of SRM, there is no universally agreed definition of SCM (Larsons and Farrington, 2006). Furthermore, it is easy to get confused by the many definitions out there, and indeed the plethora of supporting explanations, models and approaches, as they seem to focus on different things and place different emphasis on where organizations need to direct their resources in order to gain competitive advantage. Some seem to describe SCM as an inward-facing concept concerned with the interconnections within a business and how materials flow between them. Others assert SCM to be something that extends beyond the boundaries of the business to immediate suppliers and beyond. Some focus on the *supply chain*, others call it a *value chain*. Some suggest it is not a chain but a *network* and across the literature out there it can be difficult to understand exactly which bit each is focusing on, leaving the reader to fill in the gaps. Hieber (2002) states that:

> Supply Chain Management is the integration of the activities associated with the flow and transformation of goods in the respective logistics networks through improved supply chain relationships based on a common collaborative performance measurement framework for attaining close, collaborative and well coordinated network relationships to achieve a sustainable competitive advantage.

Whilst many proponents of SCM talk at length about the supply side, others suggest the chain or network continues right to the end customer.

Melzer-Ridinger (2003) suggests:

> SCM has the task to design and operate the flow of material into, through and out of the enterprise as well as the relevant administrate information and coordination processes in a way to guarantee an error-free, robust, quick and efficient servicing of the final client.

Also supported by Mentzer *et al* (2001) who suggest the philosophy of SCM must include the ability to view the entire supply chain and manage the flow of goods from supplier to ultimate customer.

There are many views on exactly what SCM does and concerns itself with; to some it is little more than the flow of materials to suit the purposes of the firm whilst to others it is about relations and interactions throughout the system, the flow of information and targeted interventions to increase end customer value. It is easy to get lost in the broad range of definitions out there, all waving the SCM banner so in this chapter I will attempt to summarize the key concepts. In terms of definitions, the one that I favour that seems to be the simplest is that of Christopher (2011) who describes SCM as:

> The management of upstream and downstream relationships with suppliers and customers in order to deliver superior customer value at less cost to the supply chain as a whole.

Benefits from SCM

There is great potential in the supply chain and here vast sources of potential value for us and other players in the chain can be found if we can figure out how to look beyond our immediate position in the overall supply chain and influence it to the advantage of all. That is the essence of SCM and if done effectively it can bring many benefits, including:

- *Reduced costs* through confidence to use new low-cost suppliers, open up the market and source globally, and reduced cost of inventory through just-in-time supply.
- *Competitive advantage* through shorter time to market and improved ability to connect supply base possibilities with end customer desires, vertical integration, linkages of activities and economies of scale.

- *Increased innovation* by better understanding and grasping supply base possibilities.
- *Reduced risk* through better understanding and risk management of the entire network.
- *Reduced asset base* through increased confidence to rely on others.
- *Greater flexibility* to respond to events and fluctuations.
- *Greater certainty* and confidence through relationships and obligations between individuals in the network.

The supply and value chain network

In order to understand and apply SCM we need to be clear what we are talking about in terms of how our suppliers are organized, how they are connected and interact and even how we are then connected to our customers and ultimately the end customer. There are fundamentally three perspectives we can adopt here and I shall explore each in turn:

- The simple supply chain.
- Looking at the end-to-end flow of value.
- Viewing the supply chain as a network.

Simple supply chains

The simplest form of supply chain is one where materials flow from the original raw material or plantation, are progressively transformed by a series of firms to create goods (or services) that are supplied to an organization. Mentzer *et al* (2001) call this the *direct supply chain*.

Simple supply chains are often represented literally as a chain, with a number of entities connected linearly (Figure 12.1). The main concern is the flow of materials and therefore how good logistics can optimize the supply chain.

The end-to-end value chain

In practice few supply chains are simple but have many players. Most definitions of 'supply chain' or 'value chain' conclude that this encompasses the flow of materials or services through a number of suppliers to us and on through to the end customer, each hopefully adding value in some way. A firm is therefore typically part of a chain rather than the end of it, and the focus is on how value is added throughout the entire chain, end-to-end rather than just the flow of materials prior to reaching us. Mentzer *el al* (2001) calls this an *extended supply chain*.

Porter (1985) defines value as 'what buyers are willing to pay' and suggests that this value exists through the entire supply chain and on to the end customer to become a 'value chain'. Porter (1985) suggests that as materials or product pass through each entity in the chain, value is added in some way to create the final product or service at the end customer. To support this he developed the famous value chain model (Figure 12.2). Here the primary activities supporting transformation (inbound logistics, operations, outbound logistics, marketing and sales and service) are supported by the firm's infrastructure, human resource management, technology development and procurement. Together these activities contribute to a firm's competitive advantage if organized effectively to do so. Porter's model includes a profit margin to recognize that buyers are willing to pay more for the combined value provided than the sum of the costs of the individual components within this transformation process.

Porter's value chain is regarded as an important concept and figures in most supply chain textbooks somewhere; however, in the 30 years since the inception of this model the world has changed and so have attitudes towards successful supply chain management. Porter's model is inwards facing, considering how value as profit is created in a single organization. Clearly the other firms in the supply chain will also have a value chain; however, the model seems to be based upon the premise that each entity in the supply chain is separate, with handoffs from one to the next. This is a traditional view of how a supply chain would typically operate without intervention, yet modern effective supply chains do not work in this way and are more integrated. It could be argued that integration extends to how the supply chain model is applied; however there are more considerations here.

Today, the value is much more than profit; as we have seen, the value organizations now need from the supply base goes way beyond profit but extends across the five strands of VIPER to a greater or lesser extent. Reducing a risk in the supply chain or improving the way it performs could be much more valuable than profit alone. The source of potential value is not confined to each firm in the chain, but rather could come from the way the chain is structured, for example the means of handoff between entities could be a source of value in itself.

Furthermore, Hines (1993) suggests that Porter's model is founded upon the premise of profit margin, rather than customer satisfaction, being the primary objective. Customer satisfaction of the immediate client in a value chain is essential, but satisfaction of the end customer, perhaps many contractual steps downstream, is even more essential as this drives everything that happens in the chain. If we have no direct relationship with this end customer it is easy to simply assume our role is passive in this respect; however, modern SCM theory suggests that it is not and that we can develop competitive advantage by understanding and having a relationship with the end customer, even if they don't buy from us directly.

Therefore by looking beyond the flow of materials to how VIPER value is added throughout the entire chain, from grower and producer right

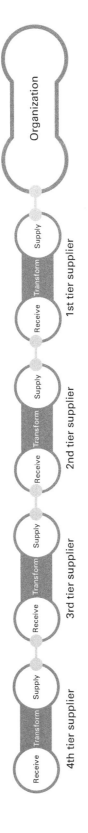

FIGURE 12.1 A simple supply chain

4th tier supplier — 3rd tier supplier — 2nd tier supplier — 1st tier supplier

Receive | Transform | Supply

Receive | Transform | Supply

Receive | Transform | Supply

Receive | Transform | Supply

Organization

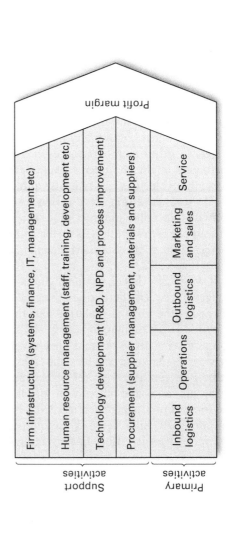

FIGURE 12.2 Porter's value chain model

Profit margin

Support activities

Firm infrastructure (systems, finance, IT, management etc)

Human resource management (staff, training, development etc)

Technology development (R&D, NPD and process improvement)

Procurement (supplier management, materials and suppliers)

Primary activities

Inbound logistics | Operations | Outbound logistics | Marketing and sales | Service through to the end customer we gain a new 'end-to-end value' perspective that opens up new opportunities for us. In the same way we used VIPER to help segment immediate suppliers, we can also use VIPER to identify the supply chains, and the points within these, where risk or opportunity can be found and where interventions can be beneficial. Building on Porter's work and using the concept of *sourcing* and *satisfying* explored earlier, a new model to define the end-to-end value chain can be created. This is given in Figure 12.3.

Supply chains as networks

The traditional view of supply or value chains as a linear or near linear series of links helps understanding but actually bears little relationship to how most are actually structured. There are in fact only a handful of scenarios where the linear chain might exist, in practice our suppliers might also be linked to other suppliers, or even directly with our customers and our customers might be linked to suppliers further back upstream and so on. In fact the value chain is typically quite a complex affair.

Christopher (2011) suggests that the word 'chain' should be replaced with 'network' to reflect the fact that there will normally be multiple suppliers and suppliers to suppliers as well as multiple customers and customers' customers in the total system. Mentzer *et al* (2001) call this the *ultimate supply chain* (Figure 12.4).

If we accept that the value chain is in fact a value network then it is the linkages between the entities that define the nature of the network. One linkage is the flow of materials but the story doesn't stop there. In fact a network can take many linkages, and today, like never before, social media connects us in networks that open up all sorts connections and information sharing. A network can be defined as a specific type of relationship that exists between a defined set of persons, objects or events involved in different processes and activities to produce value to the ultimate customer in the form of products or services (Mitchell, 1969; Christopher, 1992). Therefore, crucially, value networks are not simply networks of organizations that contract with each other but instead are complex networks of connections and linkages between individuals and firms who have some sort of common interest in the overall system. There are many different types of linkage and it is these linkages and potential linkages that present the opportunity to optimize a value network. Linkages in a value network include:

Firm to firm

- Flow of material – direct logistics between firms.
- Flow of demand – how requirements flow through the network, either by direct purchase orders or forecast.
- Flow of information – how information about what is happening elsewhere gets shared.

FIGURE 12.3 The end-to-end value chain concept

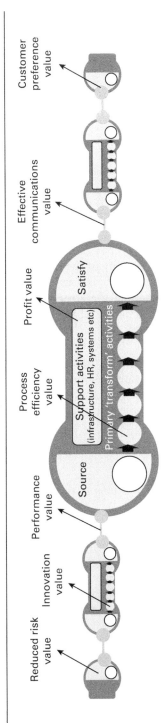

Reduced risk value

Innovation value

Performance value

Process efficiency value

Profit value

Effective communications value

Customer preference value

Source

Satisfy

Support activities (infrastructure, HR, systems etc)

Primary 'transform' activities

FIGURE 12.4 The supply chain network

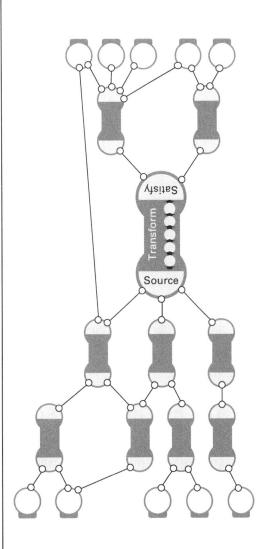

Source

Transform

Satisfy

Individual to individual

- Relationships – personal and professional relationships between individuals who interact in some way, either directly or via forums or social media.
- Knowledge sharing – sharing best practice, perhaps through an industry forum or engagement of specialist consultants who also support others in the network.

For the relationships we have with our immediate suppliers, with whom we have a contractual arrangement, we are well placed to manage this supplier and, if they are willing, they will respond to the demands we place on them. However, an entire supply and value chain network is a collection of individual entities that share some sort of common purpose but where our ability to influence these entities (often called players, nodes or actors) is limited. Influence is possible with effort and energy and the results can be dramatic and can bring competitive advantage to many of the players in the network; furthermore, by focusing on the nature of the linkages we can begin to strengthen them. Therefore by understanding the structure and nature of the value network we are part of and the nature of the linkages between entities we can begin to optimize the network.

Before moving on, we are now at a point where different terminology could cause confusion. We have covered *supply chain, value chain, value network*; definitions that are out there at large all meaning slightly different things. So, as we now know that we are part of a network not a chain and our concern is end-to-end value not just supply, for the rest of this chapter, and with the aim of resonating with established terminology, I shall refer to the *supply and value chain network* as the system we are focusing on under the 'too established to change' title of SCM.

The five pillars of SCM

We could concern ourselves only with our immediate suppliers and immediate customers and do just fine. Within this we could have purchasing manage our immediate suppliers effectively and we could have an organization that completely responds to the needs and expectations of our immediate customers. Indeed that is how many businesses operate.

However, in this scenario the business plays a passive role within the supply chain. It can only react to demand and influence over the supply chain is as good as that first tier suppliers can exert. It is completely at the mercy of what things that might happen upstream in the supply chain or downstream on the customer side. This presents risk, and drives how the firm organizes itself, with protective responses such as carrying buffer raw material and finished goods inventory to compensate for peaks and troughs, carrying redundant capacity – just in case – and sticking with known suppliers. In this scenario a firm is constrained by the network it exists in.

The science of good SCM is concerned with more holistic interventions across the entire supply and value chain network, in other words looking and operating beyond our immediate suppliers and customers, and by doing so significant benefits are possible. In order to make the supply and value chain network more effective there are five areas we need to attend to. These are the pillars of good SCM, based upon what has been proven to be effective in terms of focus and practice (Figure 12.5). They are called 'pillars' as all need to exist together for the overall structure to be solid and I shall explore these in turn. The five pillars of good SCM are:

1 *Logistics* – managing the flow of materials downstream matched with demand.

2 *Demand* – understanding and managing demand through the entire supplier and value chain network including understanding end customer needs and aspirations that might trigger future demand.

3 *Information* – the nature of, and the way information is transmitted, throughout the supply and value chain network.

4 *Risk* – understanding and proactively managing supplier and supply chain risk.

5 *CSR* – understanding the processes, practices and original sources in the supply chain and specific interventions to ensure a compliance with a CSR policy.

Making logistics effective

SCM and *logistics* are frequently and mistakenly considered one and the same. They are not. Logistics is part of SCM and part of an overall SRM approach. For SCM to be effective, management across the other pillars happens in parallel. As for much of this chapter, logistics is therefore also an entire subject all of its own, and one I cannot do justice to in a paragraph or two so further reading is recommended here if required.

Logistics is all the activities and arrangements concerned with the flow of materials and supply of specific services downstream to the customer whilst information about customer requirements and demand flow up-stream (Figure 12.6). It is concerned with activities that support managing and handling goods and materials, transportation, distribution, warehous-ing, import and export. It is also concerned with the processing of orders and information to support this. All this needs to happen in the most effi-cient, rapid and cost-effective way. Christopher (2011) states the mission of logistics management is to plan and coordinate all those activities neces-sary to achieve the desired levels of delivered service and quality at lowest possible cost.

FIGURE 12.5 The five pillars of SCM

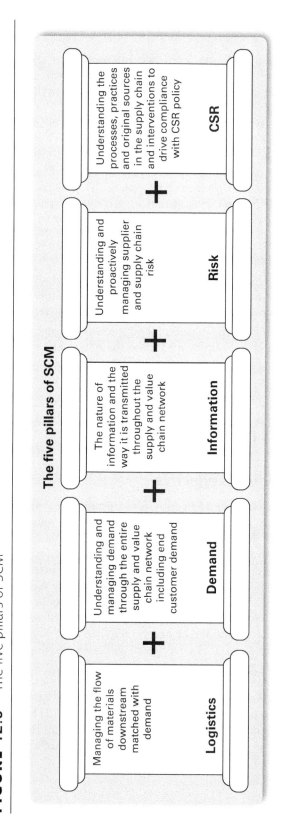

The five pillars of SCM

Logistics	+	Demand	+	Information	+	Risk	+	CSR
Managing the flow of materials downstream matched with demand		Understanding and managing demand through the entire supply and value chain network including end customer demand		The nature of information and the way it is transmitted throughout the supply and value chain network		Understanding and proactively managing supplier and supply chain risk		Understanding the processes, practices and original sources in the supply chain and interventions to drive compliance with CSR policy

FIGURE 12.6   Logistics – the flow of materials and information

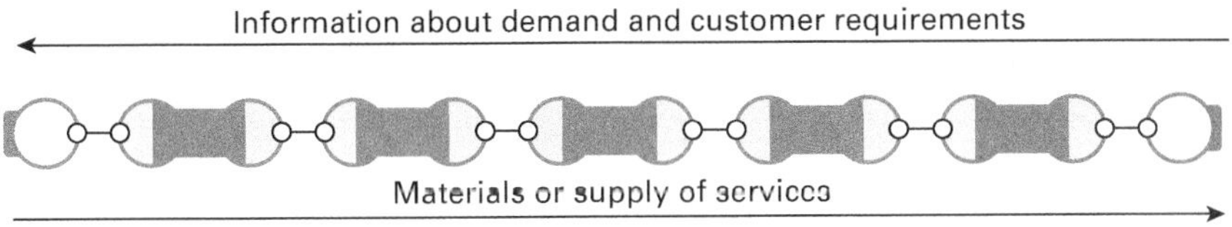

Information about demand and customer requirements

Materials or supply of services

With good logistics comes competitive advantage by being able to satisfy the customer so they get it 'faster, cheaper and better' and so on and this is the reason why giant global brands put huge energy into optimizing their logistics arrangements. Today, online shopping works because I can order something at 5.48pm and it can be on my doorstep at 7.00am the next day, having been picked, packed, loaded onto one or more forms of transport and delivered, and having had my order processed and the delivery slot coordinated with thousands of other that need to arrive somewhere near me also. Good logistics are essential for many businesses to operate but the cleverness and complexity at play passes most people by, as it is something that happens behind the scenes. When a customer walks around a super-market and all the shelves are stocked and everything they need is available nothing short of a small miracle has happened to create this convenience. It is only when there is some sort of catastrophe, strike or unforeseen event that we begin to reflect on the fragility of what we take for granted.

Logistics often involve complex systems and effective logistics happen when there is good and timely information. Behind most high-volume consumer-facing businesses are complex systems to coordinate logistics operations and even supply in response to demand and other leading indicators. If information is inaccurate, late, missing or not comprehensive then a logistics system will fail and a consumer will be disappointed and perhaps go else-where or not bother at all. Jay Wright Forrester, founder of the concept of *System Dynamics*, suggested delays and poor decision making concerning information and material flow impact the system (Forrester, 1958). This is known as the Forrester Effect and highlights the importance and value of information in any supply and value chain network.

It is easy to overlook the complexity of logistics systems, and easy to see them as little more than the interactions between one player and another. However, in practice each link where goods or materials flow is in fact a mini value chain all of its own with a series of activities and handoffs (Figure 12.7). By looking more closely at what actually happens here we can begin to open up new possibilities to make logistics work more effectively, perhaps by integration, removing unnecessary steps or the need for inven-tory. If a supplier can move what is needed from their facility direct to the point of need at precisely the time it is needed, without it having to have been inspected, stored or double handled, then we are already more effec-tive and can reduce the cost of our operation.

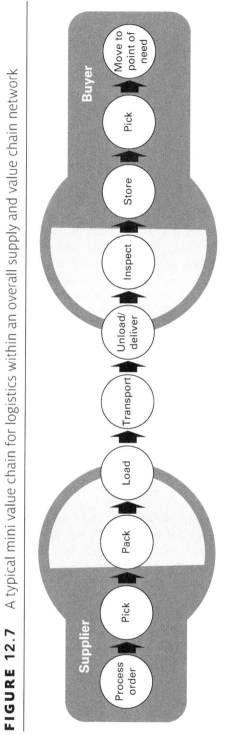

FIGURE 12.7   A typical mini value chain for logistics within an overall supply and value chain network

Managing demand

Demand management can mean different things and there are different tools and approaches out there. In essence it is concerned with balancing supply and demand and therefore requires a deep understanding of what drives demand and the nature of any volatility. For example, a company that makes sausages and burgers for supply to retail can begin to model end customer demand. Understanding when people are likely to be barbequing is a simple product of location, time of year, day of the week, the weather forecast and notable events. Volatility gets introduced when the weather is not as expected or when an issue creates concerns around certain foods such as the horse-meat scandal of 2012 in the United Kingdom. The ultimate example of demand management lies within electricity generation companies. Electricity within a supply network supply cannot be stored. Whilst we store electricity for small applications in batteries there is no such thing as a giant battery with sufficient capacity to feed a supply network. The electricity that we consume in our homes or place of work has to be generated at the point it is being consumed. The closest electricity generating companies can get to inventory is to store the means to generate, eg water upstream of a dam ready to power a hydrogenation plant. That means the electricity companies need to generate electricity to match demand in real time and maintain supply within a strict specification. Get it wrong and the supply drops in voltage or fails completely. The electricity companies cannot wait to see how much electricity people might want to use at any give point, generators take time to come online, instead they need to pre-empt demand. There is no magic formula here, but simply understanding the end customer. Demand at any given time is a product of historical average, day, time, outside temperature and what is on TV. Visit the control room in a generation companies and it might look like the controllers are sat watching TV; in fact what they are doing is anticipating demand by ramping up generation to coincide with advert breaks in peak time programming; the times when people go and make drinks or snacks and use household appliances.

The better a firm is able to understand current and future demand the better it can serve its customers. This is true for us and of course our suppliers and our supplier's suppliers. However in practice, for many, understanding demand may be little more than waiting for a purchase order to appear or at best someone in the customers purchasing function outlining what is anticipated to happen with an associated degree of unreliability. If a supplier is used to regularly being conditioned to provide keen pricing due to 'size-able future growth opportunities' then they are likely to be wary of demand forecasts. Therefore, as purchasing professionals, if we want to be effective at managing our entire supply base then we need to make a choice here; either play the short term and claim likely future volumes to incentivize a supplier to give a bit more now or be honest about future demand so we can develop a more responsive supply and value chain network for the future. We cannot have it both ways.

Furthermore, it takes time to manufacture a product or produce a service; it takes more time to procure what is necessary to support this and if there is finite capacity then waiting for capacity to be available can also take time. Most products or services therefore have some sort of lead-time before they can be available or supplied. If there is a gap between our lead-time and the customer's expectations of when they want an order fulfilled then we are failing to satisfy our customer. If we fail to have what they want then we risk losing competitive advantage or we may even lose a customer to someone else. Closing the lead-time gap gives us competitive advantage. There are two ways a firm might do this:

1 Improving the logistics between entities in the chain to make things flow faster.

2 Improving the visibility of demand, and not just the demand from our immediate customer but that of the end customer.

Making things flow faster certainly helps but there will always be a limit to how much is possible here. If we have poor information around demand then firms in the chain will carry additional inventory, additional labour and capacity and some will fail to satisfy demand (Hines and Rich, 1997). Burbridge (1984), states 'if demand is transmitted along a series of inventories using stock control ordering, then the amplification of demand variation will increase with each transfer'. This is known as *demand amplification* and is a phenomenon that stands in the way of making supply chains effective. However, if demand can be understood less inventory and capacity is required. This alone is not enough; in fact it is velocity and visibility that drive responsiveness (Christopher, 2011). We need to improve how information around demand flows down the supply chain and improve the logistics and speed of materials flows up the chain.

In practice, information about demand gets diluted the further we go from the end customer back up through the supply chain; even if there is good sharing of information amongst players, information about real demand tends to get replaced with forecasts and plans the further up-stream you go, as parties seek to protect themselves and avoid commitments without certainty. If demand could penetrate right back throughout a supply and value chain network, so that every entity is driven by real demand, there would be no need to purchase, hold or manufacture anything until a demand exists. The point in the supply and value chain network where demand pull or real demand from the end customer (eg companies responding to orders received) gives way to forecast-driven push, based upon forecasts or a plan alone is called the *demand penetration point*, decoupling or decision point in the value chain (Figure 12.8). Upstream beyond this, companies tend to hold inventories and manufacture in larger batches etc. If we can shift the demand penetration point further back up the supply chain, then we can make the chain more efficient and more demand driven. Shifting the demand penetration point can make a dramatic

FIGURE 12.8   Demand penetration point

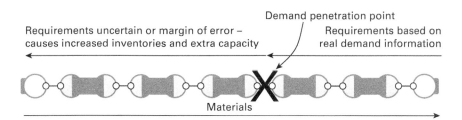

difference and achieving this is, once again, a simple matter of improving information flows within the network.

Information flow

As we have seen, the flow of information between one player and another in a supply and value chain network is essential for effective logistics, and information right up the network enables effective demand management. Information is in fact the main and core pillar of good SCM; get good information flowing across the network and we will almost certainly master it. However, this is more difficult than it might seem. Exchanging information with an immediate supplier or customer might be something we are familiar with, though even here this is not without its challenges, but getting the right information flowing between parties network wide is very difficult. There are a number of reasons for this:

- *Lack of responsiveness* – customers can be slow to act and even slower to communicate a need. This impacts the entire network but the impact is rarely understood or cared about.
- *Mistrust* – companies in the network compete with each other and respond to what is asked for, rather than offering more in case their customer will replicate what they do and they will lose competitive advantage.
- *Distorted information* – it is in the buyer's interest to be over-optimistic about demand and future opportunity so as to incentivize suppliers, however the consequence here can be distorted information that leads to mistrust.
- *Bullwhip effect* – minor frustrations with the immediate supplier due to changing forecasts or poor information get exaggerated back up the supply chain causing chaos to the ultimate suppliers.
- *Extracts only* – companies don't share the big picture, just extracts that are just enough to define what they want the supplier next step on to provide.

- *Differing interests* – it is impossible for decisions taken by one individual to fit with the entire network. Players may have different aims and agendas.

- *Lack of clarity regarding who is managing the supply chain* – any one player or individual within a network is only as strong as the contractual relationship with the immediate neighbours. Beyond this any sway or influence can only come through persuasion and getting close to other players. Inevitably other players, many steps removed, may not recognize or respond to attempts here.

- *Lack of willingness* – even with determined attempts to create network-wide flow of information it doesn't follow that all players will be willing or able to participate and play their part.

Achieving effective network-wide information flows can transform a supply and value chain network and create competitive advantage, however achieving this amongst mistrust, differing interests and levels of willingness can be incredibly difficult. These obstacles create a compelling argument for vertical integration of supply chains as it removes such obstacles. Where vertical integration is not possible or desirable then these obstacles need to be removed by an evangelical mission to build relationships, build trust and create a systematic approach to information sharing that is accepted as accurate by all involved without any contractual obligation.

Managing supply and value chain network risk

In Chapter 9 we explored managing risk specific to a supplier. However, we are also at the mercy of risks elsewhere in the supply and value chain network. Risk here, as defined by the Cranfield School of Management (2002), is 'an exposure to serious disturbance arising from risks within the supply chain as well as risks external to the supply chain'. There are in fact two sources of risk we need to concern ourselves with, risks that arise from one or more players in the network, or the way they are linked and interact, and the external risks. We have witnessed all sorts of environmental and man-made catastrophes around the world in recent years and many of these have impacted supply chains somewhere. Earthquakes, hurricanes, floods and heatwaves over the past decade have taken out whole industries or at least caused major disruption to supply chains somewhere. Whilst opinions on climate change may be divided, there seems to be agreement that extremes are here to stay, which means supply and value chain network risks need to be taken more seriously than ever before.

Our five supply side risk areas can be applied to the supply and value chain network, just as we do for an immediate supplier, except here the nature of the risks we are considering can vary. The risks might lie upstream in the network, perhaps where we have no or little visibility or direct influence and a greater emphasis on considering failure or delay risk. Figure 12.9 gives examples of risk areas under the five risk themes.

FIGURE 12.9 Types of supply and value chain network risk

Failure or delay risk	Brand reputation risk	Competitive advantage risk	Price and cost risk	Quality risks
Risk of complete and possibly permanent supply or service failure or risk of delays in supplying goods or providing a specific service.	Risks that, should they occur, can be disastrous for our brand either due to failure or practices in conflict with our principles and expectations of customers and stakeholders.	Risks of competitive advantage being undermined and include theft of intellectual property, counterfeiting and goods sold on the grey market.	The risk of outturn costs being higher than anticipated or planned for (with or without contractual protection).	Risk associated with quality failures, poor product or service quality and latent defects.

Examples within a supply chain

Failure or delay risk	Brand reputation risk	Competitive advantage risk	Price and cost risk	Quality risks
• Raw material failure or delays further up the chain. • Logistic delays. • Disruptions. • Demand fluctuations impacts capacity. • Increased likelihood of impact from environmental events due to fewer, bigger suppliers.	• Practices in conflict with our CSR policy further up the chain. • Inefficiencies in our chains give competitors advantage.	• Theft of our IP (especially in developing countries). • Upstream suppliers copy our product for black market. • Increased cost of buffer inventories. • Inability to satisfy demand fast enough.	• Cost of holding buffer inventories. • Remote country tax or export price hikes. • Transportation costs. • Commodity price hikes. • True cost of offshoring or outsourcing higher than planned.	• Heightened risk of serious product risk due to lack of local monitoring, relaxed regulations or 'back door' shortcuts.

Here we can also use the risk assessment approach outlined in Chapter 9 to identify mitigation or contingency action needed. However, the potential actions here are quite different for the supply and value chain network. These may be internal actions such as:

- Standardization and rationalization – the fewer products, SKUs (stock keeping units), parts, or offerings mean it is easier to manage.
- Build in redundancy – if one part of the operation fails, have another that can take over.
- Insurance.
- Stockpiling.

Clearly some of these actions are in conflict with that I have described previously as fundamental to making a network more efficient and effective. There is therefore a balance between how much risk we are prepared to take and overall efficiency and cost effectiveness. Yet the more we can understand specific risks, the more we can make informed decisions around what is and is not tolerable and how much mitigation is appropriate.

Responses to supply and value chain network risks may also relate to actions with immediate supplier, an entire supply base or the entire network. These might include:

- keep it close – a local supply chain that you can go and visit is easier to understand than one in a developing country;
- dual or multiple sourcing;
- understand the supplier by audit and assessment;
- make it contractual – nothing focuses a supplier like a contractual obligation; and
- effective supplier management and improvement and development initiatives.

Corporate social responsibility

On 24 April 2013, The Rana Plaza in Sevar, Bangladesh collapsed killing 1,129 people and injuring 2,515 people. The building was home to garment factories, manufacturing products destined for the racks of the leading brand name clothing outlets found on the streets and in malls in Europe and the United States. More than half the victims were women along with their children who were in nursery facilities within the building. In the weeks following the tragedy as the collapse was investigated it emerged that warnings that the building had become dangerous were ignored. The incident is considered the deadliest garment-factor accident in history (BBC, May 2013). Politicians, advocacy groups and even the Pope spoke out whilst protestors and consumers campaigned directly at retailer's outlets. The response from the fashion industry was mixed; some responded to provide help and some attempted to establish an accord on building safety in Bangladesh; in fact 38 companies had signed up to this as of May 2013 (IndustriALL, 2013). Yet 14 Major North America retailers including Walmart refused to participate claiming they had, for over two years already, been working on an agreement to improve safety in Bangladesh factories (*Huffington Post*, 2013). Later that year these and other North American companies eventually announced plans to improve factory safety in Bangladesh; however, these plans were criticized for failing to include any binding commitments to pay for improvements (Greenhouse and Clifford, 2013).

This tragedy has passed by and is no longer headline news. Pressure groups continue to campaign and consumers continue to buy garments save a few who are serious about shopping basket activism and make choices accordingly. Overcrowded garment factories in Bangladesh and other parts of the world are not uncommon, and overcrowding and poor working conditions are just the start of practices that our Western eyes would judge to be unacceptable, yet can be found all over the world in the supply chains of many of the goods we buy without question. So why is something not being done? Well it is, and corporate social responsibility (CSR) is very firmly on the boardroom agenda. Firms now consider the impact of their actions on the environment, the world and society at large in terms of what they do. CSR policies can usually be found somewhere in the annual accounts and reports to shareholders for most household name brands; some even place these centre stage, supported with resources and focus that turn policy into action within the business. The problem here comes when an organization considers how a corporate intent in this area needs to be implemented beyond the boundaries of the firm, and the supply chain presents the biggest challenge. If we believe that child labour is wrong, or farming methods that leave orangutans homeless should be stopped then we have set a standard, however being 100 per cent certain no practices upstream in our supply and value chain network contribute to these is an immense challenge. Furthermore, being certain for one supply and value chain network is difficult, but looking across all supply and value chain networks makes CSR in the supply chain one of the hardest things for any business, especially one that sources from the far corners of the world.

It could be argued there is little to compel a business to invest in CSR, after all there is no legal imperative yet to take responsibility for the actions of others in a supply chain and if customers still buy T-shirts following a factory collapse then such events are perhaps not so bad for business after all. However, the business case for CSR is now much greater than any philanthropic desire to work for the greater good and a company that ignores what is happening here does it at their peril. Consumers don't expect to have to think about the things they put in their shopping basket, they expect the brand they are buying from to have done this; they expect companies to be socially responsible (Penn *et al*, 2010).

Notwithstanding the fact that there remains a gap between expectations and consumers adjusting their buying decisions accordingly (Pelsmacker *et al*, 2005) this expectation cannot be ignored and there are packs of hungry investigative journalists out there just looking for a story that might bring a household brand to its knees. For example, in 2008 Primark found itself having to fire three Indian suppliers because they allegedly used child labour to carry out embroidery and sequin work on garments following the broadcast by the BBC of footage claimed to be from a Bangalore factory showing children at work on behalf of Primark. Primark had in fact worked to implement a strict code of practice with its suppliers that prohibit the use of child labour in its supply chain and so complained about the broadcast. Three years later their complaint was upheld on the basis that the authenticity of this footage could not be established and the BBC apologized. The problem, however, was the damage to reputation had been done. The interest in the original story appearing to show exploitation of children by a big corporate seemed to be much greater than that of the later story suggesting the footage may not be authentic.

The risk of brand damage through poor practices or even suggested poor practices in the supply chain cannot be ignored, if consumers come to lose confidence the brand is tainted. CSR action in the supply chain therefore becomes essential to reduce risk. Yet some firms have seen an opportunity to build brand values upon positive CSR initiatives, clearly setting out how their business operates and its core principles. Here CSR action is to strengthen a brand. In fact the business case for CSR is fact multi-tiered according to the starting point of the firm and its corporate aims and objectives. This is given in Figure 12.10.

FIGURE 12.10   The 'tiers' of the business case for CSR

How Innocent built a brand on good CSR

The Innocent Drinks Company holds two thirds of the UK smoothie market. Originating as the start-up company of three Cambridge University graduates the company flew in the face of the big brands and developed a new unique 'pure and healthy' brand proposition for their smoothies based around letting the ingredients speak for themselves supported by the strapline 'never ever from concentrate'. Before long Innocent 'smoothies for kids' became a feature of school lunchboxes up and down the country. Sustainability forms an integral part of the Innocent brand proposition and is apparent through the company's efforts to consider its impact on society, the environment and the world at large. Specific initiatives address nutrition, ingredients, packaging, production, and the company has set out to leave a legacy; giving 10 per cent of all its profits to help fund NGOs in the countries from which it sources its fruit. Innocent's suppliers are part of their brand and Innocent claim only to source fruit from suppliers who have to demonstrate that they look after their workers and the environment. Whilst being confident in achieving this has its challenges, Innocent is open about how its assessment approach attempts to realize this. Nevertheless Innocent's suppliers form part of its overall brand proposition and as such need to meet certain standards that align with this. The good practices at farms in third world countries help make the Innocent brand what it is.

CSR is a broad label that means all sorts of things according to what a firm feels it needs to concern itself with. This changes according to the nature of a business and what they are involved in but would typically include environmental impacts, human impacts (such as child labour, forced labour, unsafe or poor working conditions), social impacts and obligations such as being a good neighbour. There are now a number of reference points in the form of frameworks that help guide a firm as to what to look for. These exist in a number of forms ranging from documents that establish principles, guidelines and standards (CBSR, 2009). These include:

- The United Nations Global Compact;
- ISO26000;
- The Global Reporting Initiative (GRI);
- Voluntary Principles on Security and Human Rights (published by the US State Department);
- The AA1000 standard;

- The ICMM Sustainable Development Framework;
- The IFC Performance Standards on Social and Environmental Sustainability;
- FTSE4Good index; and
- Dow Jones Sustainability index.

Across the different frameworks for CSR are different areas of focus or they serve different purposes, but there is a high degree of consistency regarding the types of impacts or areas that need to be considered. A company serious about CSR could use one of these frameworks to guide its focus and action or might choose to decide for themselves the types of impact they are concerned about. Deciding on a CSR goal or standard to follow is the easy bit, making it happen in practice is more difficult and knowing where to start is even harder and here we can use supply and value chain mapping to help (see below). Tackling CSR impacts in the supply chain presents challenge because we are dealing with things we cannot easily see or understand, often in other countries, where cultural norms are very different and our Western standards or ways don't apply. Despite the difficulty here, with the right determination and resources it is possible to address CSR impacts. Wieland and Handfield (2013) suggest that companies need to audit products and suppliers and that supplier auditing needs to go beyond direct relationships with first-tier suppliers. They also state increased visibility and collaboration with local partners is crucial to successfully managing social responsibility in supply chains. The companies that have successfully addressed supply side CSR all have one thing in common and that is they have directed energy into understanding and getting close to what happens upstream. Ways to do this include:

- *Vertically integrate* – buy the supply chain. Provides control but only if you can then influence what happens locally.
- *Contractual obligations* – focuses the supplier and perhaps the supplier's supplier, but the issues of policing and compliance remain. Breaches of contractual obligation and using cheap sub-contractors can go undetected unless there is someone on the ground watching what is going on.
- *Periodic auditing* – useful to get a feel for what is happening at a factory or plantation and allows conditions to be assessed. More effective if visits are unannounced but still doesn't provide any certainty as a factory owner determined to cut corners will have any things of concern well out of sight before the auditor has got through the factory gates. Moreover if the auditor is an outsider, and does not know the local territory or how things get done they can easily be fooled or miss something.
- *Local presence with local knowledge* – someone on the ground, ideally full time, with local knowledge, ideally a local also and with

a clear role and remit to ensure standards are met. The stature, local standing and status of this individual is key to making this work and they must be incentivized so as to prevent them going native or being corrupted.

CSR is not a separate topic that can be bolted on; it has to run like veins through everything a firm does, especially the efforts of a purchasing function. CSR is not separate to SCM or SRM, it is integral, shaped only by the specific aims and goals of the organization in this respect.

Supply and value chain network mapping

Gardner and Cooper (2003) suggest that a strategic supply chain map can be quite helpful in understanding a firm's supply chain, for evaluating the current supply chain and for contemplating realignment of a supply chain.

A supply and value chain network map is a representation of the entire network specifically relating to the supply of a certain product or service, as sourced from a specific immediate supplier. The network will be different according to which immediate supplier we consider (and therefore different if we are sourcing the same thing from multiple vendors) and will be different for each product or service sourced from a single supplier. Therefore it is possible to develop a multitude of maps looking at different product and suppliers but not necessary helpful as the effort required would make it unworkable. We must therefore have a need and focus for such a mapping activity.

There are a variety of models out there that look both upstream and downstream. Perhaps one of the most commonly found is the SCOR model (Supply Chain Operations Reference) that has been endorsed by the Supply-Chain Council. Whilst this model does look end to end and considers many aspects of performance, its focus is largely around overall effectiveness of logistics and flow of materials, and the way entities communicate and interact. As such it provides a basis to drive improvements through integration and driving better collaboration. This is a good approach if the goal is to make a network more effective, but as we have seen there are more dimensions to good SCM, indeed demand management, risk and CSR may require us to study our network in a different way in order to spot things that may require different types of intervention. We therefore might need a more extensive means to analysis a supply and value chain network.

Purpose and benefits

Supply and value chain network mapping is a means to understand a network and the enabler to identify where intervention is necessary or beneficial. It can take considerable time and resources to do it effectively and what is required here increases with the size and complexity of the network as well as our perspective or the way we choose to study the network. There can in fact be many purposes for constructing a map, and the purpose influences the method we use. Purpose (and therefore benefits) of mapping is to gain an accurate understanding of:

- the players, physical structure and the nature of the network (as an enabler to search for improvement opportunities);
- risk exposure (to identify where mitigation and contingency efforts need to be targets);
- value adds – where and how value is added (to help find opportunities to add more or remove what doesn't add value);
- where cost is added (and what needs to happen to reduce cost);
- inefficiencies and wastage (and opportunities for improvement);
- demand management and information flows (and what needs to change to improve the flow of information and how demand is managed); and
- compliance with CSR policy (or where intervention is required).

Mapping the network

Supply and value chain mapping is best accomplished by a group of individuals carefully selected for their knowledge and expertise. The process begins by mapping the physical structure of the network. This is, put simply, about creating a big diagram that shows all the players in the network and who is connected to whom. A big sheet of paper is essential and unrolling some brown paper onto a large table around which the team can assemble is ideal. Once under way it is likely the team will identify a number of areas where further information and investigation is required in order to complete the map, so creating a complete network map may take several workshops to get it right.

There are five steps in the process for supply and value chain mapping (Figure 12.11). These are: map the physical structure; use lenses and search for hot spots; summarize findings concerning risk in a risk analysis; summarize and prioritize opportunities; and develop a focused improvement plan.

Step 1: Map the physical structure

Step 1 is concerned with mapping the physical structure of the network. If our supply chain is simple we may simply know what it looks like and be able to draw it out on a piece of paper. However, most networks are in fact quite complex and will need some brainpower and data gathering in order to complete one.

FIGURE 12.11   The process for supply and value chain network mapping

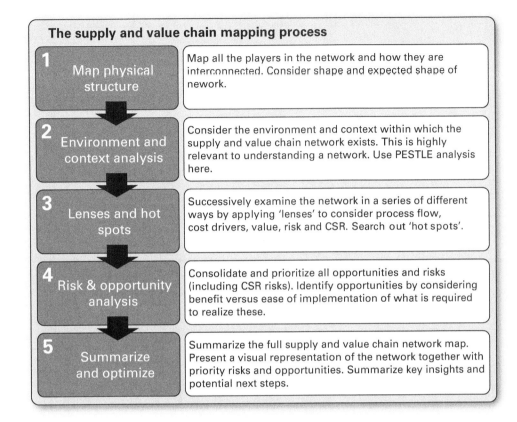

The supply and value chain mapping process

1 Map physical structure	Map all the players in the network and how they are interconnected. Consider shape and expected shape of nework.
2 Environment and context analysis	Consider the environment and context within which the supply and value chain network exists. This is highly relevant to understanding a network. Use PESTLE analysis here.
3 Lenses and hot spots	Successively examine the network in a series of different ways by applying 'lenses' to consider process flow, cost drivers, value, risk and CSR. Search out 'hot spots'.
4 Risk & opportunity analysis	Consolidate and prioritize all opportunities and risks (including CSR risks). Identify opportunities by considering benefit versus ease of implementation of what is required to realize these.
5 Summarize and optimize	Summarize the full supply and value chain network map. Present a visual representation of the network together with priority risks and opportunities. Summarize key insights and potential next steps.

Within the seven value stream mapping tools proposed by Hines and Rich (1997), a tool called the *Production Variety Funnel* is included which they describe as a tool to help understand how a firm or supply chain operates by using IVAT analysis; classifying the supply chain according to its shape and which of the four IVAT letters it most resembles. For example, where a limited number of raw materials from one or few sources are processed into a wide variety of finished products then the chain looks like a 'V'. Networks may not necessarily conform to the shapes of letters but IVAT does highlight the fact that different types of networks will naturally have different shapes. If letters help then I would add the letters O and X as these shapes are also possible; giving us OXIVAT. This is not only a good starting point, as it helps us to ensure we have a big enough sheet of paper available, but it helps clarify what we are expecting to find as we map the network and therefore ensures a greater likelihood of success. Figure 12.12 gives the different physical structure types of supply network.

FIGURE 12.12 The different OXIVAT shapes of supply and value chain network

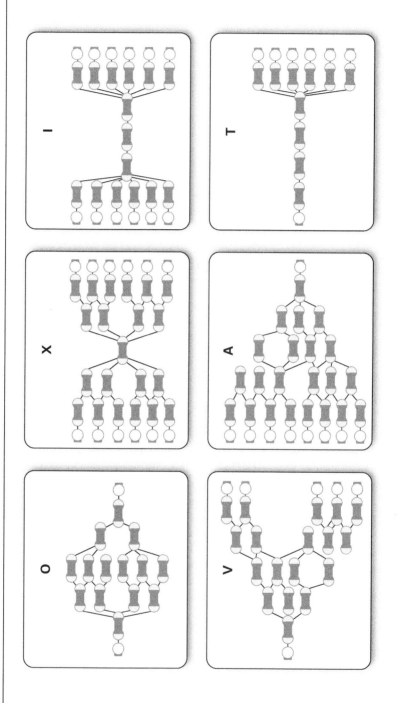

Figuring out who supplies whom can be a challenge. We understand our suppliers, but it can be hard enough to understand our suppliers' suppliers, let alone going any further upstream. The problem is this information may not be readily available and suppliers may be reluctant to share due to fear of loss of competitive advantage or a hidden agenda for backward integration, especially if the supplier is adding little value and fears the consequences of sharing such information. Here we need a bit of detective work, which will be helped if the team doing the mapping has been selected to have as much expertise as possible. Ways to help understanding the structure of a network include:

- ask the supplier;
- break down the product (or service) into its constituent parts and attempt to identify where these might be sourced from, eg by looking at any identifying markings;
- ask an industry, product or logistics expert; and
- create an obligation for the supplier to be transparent (eg batch and material traceability is often expected in defence and food industries).

Step 2: Network environment and context analysis

Step 2 is concerned with considering the environment and context within which the supply and value chain network exists. The nature of the environment and context is highly relevant to understanding a network, especially in terms of risk or to explain how certain players might behave or choose to interact. Key considerations here include:

- countries and geographies involved;
- cultural differences;
- prevailing political and economic climates;
- end customer changing needs and aspirations; and
- environmental considerations.

Environment analysis is accomplished using the *PESTLE Analysis* tool (political, economic, sociological, technological, legal and environmental). Here we consider the forces, drivers, trends or prevailing conditions under each of these headings both upstream and downstream in our supply and value chain network that could impact on the network. Work through the PESTLE analysis listing all risks and opportunities relevant to the network under each heading. Figure 12.13 shows how PESTLE analysis can be used in supply and value chain network mapping.

Understanding the context of the network is about considering all the unique factors that could individually and collectively present challenges or require specific provision and therefore compound potential risks or present opportunities. These include:

FIGURE 12.13   PESTLE analysis used in supply and value chain network mapping

- Regulation
- Regional tax regimes
- Tariff and trade barriers
- International trade policy
- Government subsidies
- Funding & grants
- Political stability
- Import/export rules

- Growth of individual markets
- Cost of labour
- Inflation
- Economic outlook
- Exchange rate fluctuations
- Interest rate fluctuations
- Seasonal factors
- Demand for raw materials

- Changes in expectations
- Special interest and pressure groups
- Cultural changes
- Media views
- Changes in ethics
- Changes in modes of work
- Social responsibility

- New technology
- Rate of change of techn'gy
- E-business, e-commerce
- Effect of internet
- Infrastructure needed
- Logistics and production technology changes
- Willingness to embrace

- Laws regulating movement of goods
- Safety and environmental regulation
- Variation in laws by country, state or region
- Monopoly legislation
- Working time/conditions

- Social pressure on pollution
- Waste disposal regulations
- Social pressure for socially responsibility
- Impact of using specific raw materials
- Carbon footprint
- Emission reduction

- complexity – of the network, processes;
- range variety or lack of standardization;
- product difficulty or complexity;
- customer requirements and uniqueness of individual requirements;
- market difficulty and inability to switch providers;
- organizational complexity and internal handoffs; and
- flow of information and how difficult it actually is in practice.

Step 3: Apply lenses and search out hot spots

Step 3 is concerned with successively examining the network in different ways and using a technique to search out areas of interest.

Supply and value chain network mapping could become an immense task in order to find anything meaningful. There are two techniques that can help to simplify the activity and enable what available resources we have to be focused more precisely. These are the use of different lenses through which we will examine the network and also by using a technique called *hot spot analysis*.

Supply and value chain network mapping is more than sketching out how the network exists and is organized. Hines and Rich (1997) suggest there is a distinction between traditional supply chain mapping and the process of developing a more detailed map, ie one that begins to reveal where intervention might be directed. They suggest looking at the supply chain in a number of different ways such as physical structure, process flow, responsiveness and how demand is or is not transmitted. However, looking at these factors is not enough as risk, CSR and information flows are missing, yet the underlying concept of looking at the network in different ways is helpful. Once we understand the physical structure of a network, if we can successively examine it from different perspectives, as if looking through a series of different lenses, then we will see the network in different ways. The different lenses we might use here include (these are expanded in Table 12.1):

- *Process flow lens* – a lens to examine the flow of materials, information and how demand is managed.
- *Cost driver lens* – a lens to help see all the cost drivers and where they are introduced into the network.
- *Value lens* – a lens through which we look for where and how value is introduced or added, where innovation might come from or how quality is created, assured or possible.
- *Risk lens* – a lens that helps us see where risk lies or is introduced.
- *CSR lens* – a lens to examine the network specifically for CSR impacts or potential risks against a corporate policy or framework.

Lenses therefore help us to see supply and value chain networks in different ways and look for different things. The output of each examination can then be merged to create a detailed map. However, even with the help of the lens philosophy we can still be overwhelmed by the complexity of one or more network and so here we can complement the lens approach by using *hot spot analysis*.

Hot spot analysis is an approach to cut through complexity and pinpoint areas to focus on without having to analyse a complex system. Instead of trying to study an entire supply and value chain network, hot spot analysis works together with our lenses by looking for areas where we are most likely to find a problem or 'hot spot', this then guides us to in these localized areas to see if there are any opportunities or areas where intervention would be beneficial.

The idea of hot spot analysis is something I learnt at an early age. As an electronics engineer, I've been trained to open up a defective piece of electronic equipment and fault find. There are many structured ways of doing this and typically I would have circuit diagrams and an array of test equipment at my disposal that would help. However, I have been opening up electronic things since childhood. As soon as I could operate a screwdriver I would have the back off as many things as I could get my hands on, but with no knowledge or training then. I learnt as I went, after connecting myself directly to the National Grid electricity network on many occasions I learnt what not to touch and where the risk areas were. I also learnt that simply looking, smelling and touching could find the majority of faults. This is less so today with miniaturization, but back then when things went wrong something often got hot. Components or circuit boards would appear burnt or hot to the touch and the familiar smell of insulation breakdown provided vital clues as to what and where something had gone wrong. This process was helped with familiarity regarding where to search first. If the unit was dead then the first place to look was the power supply and work up from there. Once the 'hot spot' was located it was simply a case of homing in on exactly what had happened and swapping out the defective component.

This same approach can help with supply and value chain network to identify where intervention is needed, except here we are not searching for a burnt component or the source of a smell, instead we are looking in the places where we might expect to find something. For example, if we are looking at a network through our CSR lens then there are known processes, industries, practices, geographies where there is, according to historical understanding, known potential issues or risks we should be concerned about and where hot spots are likely to exist.

If we are sourcing timber or lumber then we know there are issues around sustainability depending upon where it originates from. If the processing needed to create the products we buy uses harmful chemicals and this processing takes place in countries where there are few controls over discharge and pollution then this is a hot spot. If we are buying palm oil as an ingredient for food production then, depending upon where this is being sourced from, this is a hot spot as there are known impacts for this raw material.

Identifying hot spots is a matter of research and being informed about how things get made and produced. There is no magic reference point as it all depends on what is being sourced. Therefore we need knowledge and expertise and this usually resides within an organization somewhere and if not can be obtained through discussions with external stakeholders, experts and suppliers. Table 12.1 provides a starting point for what we are looking for using each lens and the sorts of hot spots that might be relevant.

Step 3 is accomplished by reviewing the physical network a number of times, each time as if looking through a different lens. Examine how the network exists and functions with this specific lens in mind. For example, if we are looking through the cost driver lens then the objective is to consider all the places and activities in the network where cost is introduced and how much each step costs. It would be fantastic if it were possible to precisely

TABLE 12.1 Lenses and hot spots

Lens	Focus and questions to answer	Areas to focus improvements
Process flow lens	The flow of materials, information and how **Hot spots to look for** • Wastage and inefficiency • Unnecessary steps • Relationships demand is managed.	• Build network-wide relationships • Improve network-wide forecasting • Share resources • Remove redundancy • Change locations • Linearly integrate • Vertically integrate • Measure performance • Reduce variability and uncertainty • Collaborate to improve
Cost driver lens	A lens to help see all the cost drivers and where they are introduced into the network **Hot spots to look for** • Inventories • Transportation • Processing • Distance • Leakage • Uniqueness • Overheads and administration • Regulation or costs that cannot be influenced Adapted from Porter (1985)	• Economies of scale • Increase capacity utilization • Reduce inventory (eg through better forecasting) • Reduce transportation (eg by changing product, packaging, processing points) • Reduce distances/change locations • Cross-industry learning and knowledge sharing (eg of best practice)

continues

TABLE 12.1   *continued*

Lens	Focus and questions to answer	Areas to focus improvements
Value lens	A lens through which we look for where and how value is introduced or added, where innovation might come from or how quality is created, assured or possible. ***Hot spots to look for*** • Points of greatest transformation or processing • Patented or unique value adds (that others cannot copy)	• Innovation • Improve upstream knowledge of our business and needs • Drive out inefficiencies (eg using Lean or Six Sigma type approaches) • Review linkages between firms and activities
Risk lens	A lens that helps us see where risk lies or is introduced ***Hot spots to look for*** • Geographies • Industries • Processes	• Switch suppliers • Develop the relationship • Manage the relationship • Reduce access to IP (eg by spitting processing activities) • Supplier and supply chain auditing • Contingency planning
CSR lens	A lens to examine the network specifically for CSR impacts or potential risks against a corporate policy or framework ***Hot spots to look for*** • Geographies • Industries • Processes	• Supplier, supply chain and factory/plantation auditing • Local knowledge and representation • Invest in original producers • Build direct relationship with original producers

FIGURE 12.14 The supply and value chain network activity and linkage table

(Lens)	Risks	Opportunities
Process flow		
Cost drivers		
Value lens		
Risk lens		
CSR lens		

quantify how cost is added right back up the supply chain. Such intelligence would enable effective decision making around what value or steps in the supply chain we want to pay for, however this understanding is hard to come by. Therefore once again we need some detective work and this is helped by looking for cost *hot spots*. Porter (1985) identified 10 major cost drivers and these can help direct us and therefore can become our *hot spots* to search for when using this lens. An adapted list is given in Table 12.2.

As we apply each lens and identify *hot spots* the findings should be recorded on the map at each point. If we can quantify something, eg what cost is added then we should do this, but where this is not possible a simple rating system can help and the more visual we can make it the easier our map will be to interpret. Figure 12.14 shows a supply and value chain network table that can be applied to each activity and linkage and considers the risk and opportunities for each lens.

Step 4: Network risk and opportunity analysis

Step 4 is concerned with consolidating and prioritizing all risks (including CSR risks) and opportunities identified in the supply and value chain network.

For risks, use the supply side risk assessment process and tool outlined in Chapter 9 and list, assess and prioritize all the risks identified within the network.

FIGURE 12.15   Supply and value chain network opportunity analysis

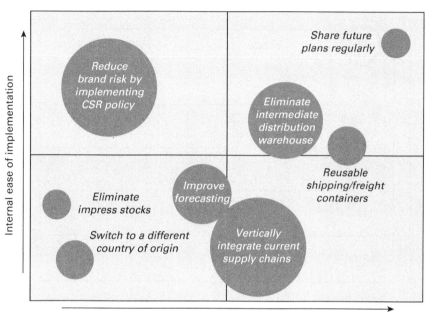

Similarly, by reviewing the entire supply and value chain network map, extract a list of the opportunities that have been identified using each lens. Quantify the scale of the opportunity, either in direct financial benefits if known or by attributing a scale according to the value that is possible relative to all the other opportunities. Then use the opportunity analysis matrix shown in Figure 12.15. Each opportunity should be plotted according to the internal ease of implementation (ie the degree to which both have control and influence over this opportunity and the ease by which we can realize it) and external ease of implementation (the anticipated degree to which it will be possible and likely to realize this opportunity easily and quickly working with other players in the network). The scale of the benefits should be represented by the size of the bubbles that are plotted, relative to one another. The result is a visual representation of the potential opportunities that enable effective decision making regarding which ones should be pursued.

Step 5: Summarize and optimize

Step 5 is concerned with summarizing the full supply and value chain network map, both in terms of a visual representation and the priority risks and opportunities identified. As for many strategic tools used within purchasing the key question we need to ask here is 'so what?' In other words, *so what* is this map telling us and what should we focus on moving forward. This summary can then inform a unique supply and value chain network strategy and approach to optimize it.

Optimizing supply and value chain networks

As we have seen for SRM, each supply scenario is different and requires unique solution, matched against available resources. The same is true for supply and value chain networks. A firm will be part of many different networks and the vast majority will not warrant spending time understanding them let alone creating interventions. Yet, for the few networks that we identify as important where intervention can be beneficial we need to be clear exactly what we are going to do, with whom and why. Mentzer *et al* (2001) suggest that one of the key philosophies within SCM is that it is approached as a strategic initiative supported by cooperative efforts to synchronize and converge intra and inter firm operation and strategic capabilities into a unified whole. Crucially we need to have an approach to direct what resources we have to develop a supply and value chain network in the most productive way. We therefore need a strategy for supply and value chain network management overall, and a strategy for the individual networks we have deemed require intervention.

A strategic perspective and therefore direction comes by linking the various areas of risk and opportunity across multiple networks with the overall direction of the firm and then determining how best to manage one or more networks. From here we can develop individual improvement plans for the supply chains where we deem intervention to be the most beneficial.

Driving supply and value chain network improvements

There are five main areas of focus for driving improvements and optimizing one or more supply and value chain networks. These are the areas where interventions have been proven to be highly effective in supporting network-wide improvements and by focusing on these areas it is possible to drive great benefit. These are as follows (and each will be expanded in turn):

1 Contracting for network performance.
2 Improving effectiveness – optimizing flow and effectiveness, performance improvement, differentiation of the network so as to adapt for specific requirements of suppliers, applying lean, agile or performance improvement as appropriate.
3 Integration within the network.
4 Collaboration and relationships amongst players – driving better information and demand management.
5 Voice of the customer and end-to-end perspective.

Contracting to drive improvement

At the simplest level improvements can be driven through the contracting process; nothing focuses a supplier like a contract! Or does it? With thought we could develop the perfect contract and impose strict contractual terms on our immediate supplier as to our expectations for what happens down the supply chain. If the supplier is obliged contractually to us then they will be motivated to place similar obligations on their suppliers and so on. Sounds like an easy solution but it is not that effective.

A UK energy company attempted to do this to help roll out a CSR initiative with one problematic supplier. They included the contractual term 'the supplier shall use its best endeavours to ensure that no child labour or forced labour exists in any of its supply chains' within its contracts with suppliers. This was not a clause that was optional but as written it left no room for manoeuvre and meant that the supplier would be in breach of contract, risking termination for breach, if they could not demonstrate that they had done absolutely everything possible and reasonable in the circumstances, no matter how costly or difficult. The supplier rejected this clause as unworkable, the energy company asked them if they really wanted to be seen to not sign up to such a clause and in the end a compromise was reached with some diluted contractual wording. The supplier argued that much of what happened upstream in the supply chain was outside its control. The energy company argued they were responsible for what happens in the supply chain.

Using contractual terms to drive immediate suppliers to take responsibility for what happens upstream in a supply chain is an approach that can have only superficial impact. At best it may serve to focus the mind of an immediate supplier and drive them to review its practices. There are a number of reasons why there are problems with using a purely contractual approach. These are:

- The difference between legalities and practicalities – even if we agree a watertight contract the process of litigation to enforce it could be onerous.
- We don't usually have any direct contractual relationship beyond those we immediately interface.
- Supply chains span jurisdictions.
- Contracts are less recognized or valued in some geographies and cultures.

Having said this, it doesn't mean contractual obligations for supply and value chain network practices are not worthwhile, quite the contrary in fact, but such contractual terms should not be the thing that drives new action as this will have little impact, but rather a reflection of what is already agreed and being worked towards by parties. The contract is in fact the output of a collaborative process.

Improving effectiveness

How a supply chain might be optimized depends upon the nature of the supply chain and what passes through it, precisely what risks and opportunities were identified during the mapping process and what the priorities for improvement might be. From here it is possible to determine specific improvement initiatives to tackle specific opportunities or areas of inefficiency. For example, where demand is predicable and lead times are long it is possible to scrutinize the chain and optimize it using Lean approaches and principles. However, where lead times are short and demand unpredictable then the supply chain needs to be more agile and able to respond quickly to customer demands.

Using the outputs of the mapping process the priority risks and areas for improvement identify scale and nature of intervention for a specific supply and value chain network. There are two levels at which we can drive intervention: tactical responding to specific findings identified during the mapping process and more strategic interventions linked to overall business strategy.

We can drive in improvements based upon what was determined using the opportunity analysis from step 4. Here, once again, we can use the STPDR Supplier Improvement and Development process described in Chapter 8 as the steps and principles apply here also but with some modulation to recognize that we may be attempting to drive improvements outside of our firm and therefore where we have little or no direct authority or influence. The steps that support improvement are the same, however the way we apply the process needs to be adapted. Figure 12.16 shows the STPDR process and how it should be deployed in the supply and value chain network.

Integrating supply chains

Christopher (2011) suggests there is a crucial and important distinction between logistics and SCM represented in what he suggests is the ultimate evolution of a supply chain and what he calls true supply chain integration. He states 'traditionally most organizations have viewed themselves as entities that exist independently from others and indeed need to compete with them in order to survive'. He states this philosophy can be self-defeating and one that leads to unwillingness to cooperate. As we have seen, each handoff introduces complexity and impedes the flow of materials and information. Integration in the supply and value chain network is therefore concerned with removing handoffs, merging or improving the flow between players and activities, both internal and external, and therefore great benefits are possible through integration.

There are many ways integration can happen. We saw at the start of this book how some retailers had responded to increasing risk and uncertainty in the supply base by vertically integrating their supply so they own and

FIGURE 12.16 Using the STPDR process for supply and value chain network improvements

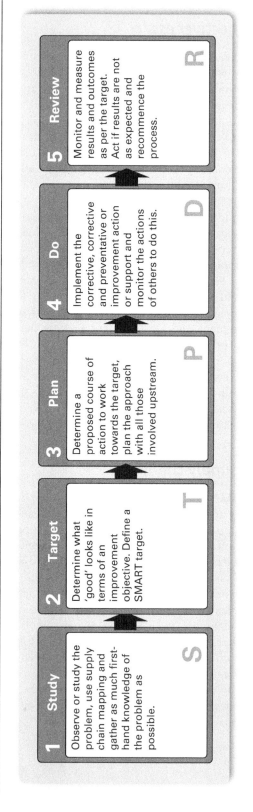

1 Study

Observe or study the problem, use supply chain mapping and gather as much first-hand knowledge of the problem as possible.

S

2 Target

Determine what 'good' looks like in terms of an improvement objective. Define a SMART target.

T

3 Plan

Determine a proposed course of action to work towards the target, plan the approach with all those involved upstream.

P

4 Do

Implement the corrective, corrective and preventative or improvement action or support and monitor the actions of others to do this.

D

5 Review

Monitor and measure results and outcomes as per the target. Act if results are not as expected and recommence the process.

R

control it. Outsourcing too helps by extending the value chain upstream of a business so an external entity operates as if part of the business to a degree. Vertical integration and outsourcing have their place and both are solutions that enable a firm to maintain direct control over aspects of the supply and value chain. However, it is impossible to acquire an entire supply base, and outsourcing only takes you upstream so far, so we still need an approach that enables intervention across the entire network, where we cannot ever have direct control.

It is generally accepted that there are different degrees of intervention for a supply and value chain network. Bechtel and Jayaram (1997) suggest there are four categories or 'schools' of intervention:

1 *Functional awareness school* – recognizes the existence of a chain that encompasses the flow of material from suppliers to final customer with members adding value. The main focus is the physical material flow, reflecting an origin from the traditional field of logistics.

2 *The linkage school* – focuses on the interfaces between entities in the supply chain and how, by managing these linkages simultaneously, these linkages can work more effectively bringing competitive advantage by smoothing the flow of material between partners and reducing inventory.

3 *The information school* – focuses on the information flow between partners both up and down the supply chain so all members have access to all relevant information in order to support their logistics planning.

4 *The integration/process school* – focuses on integrating supply chain areas into a system defined as a set of processes that adds value to the customer.

Whilst presented as separate schools, there is also a logic to these that suggest they represent degrees of intervention, ie it is almost impossible to focus on integration unless you have first considered linkages and flow of information and when integration has been achieved the issues of flow of materials, interfaces and information flow are naturally resolved. Even then there are different degrees of intervention; we can integrate internal functions and improve the process flow within our own firm and then move to look externally. Stevens (1989) suggests the process of supply and value chain network integration has four stages:

1 *Baseline* – understand the current value chain.

2 *Functional integration* – beginning to establish a limited degree of integration between adjacent functions.

3 *Internal integration* – establishing an end-to-end planning framework within an organization.

4 *External integration* – establishing linkage and coordination to upstream suppliers and downstream to customers.

Integrating every player in an entire supply network would undoubtedly be the optimum solution but can be on a par with solving third world hunger in terms of achievability. However, selective integration, where possible, practical and beneficial, can add great value. Achieving this cannot happen in isolation and requires a collaborative and relationship-based approach by players who also need to want to make it work. Such collaboration across multiple players requires a broker to make this happen and there needs to be clear benefits to all involved to participate.

Collaboration and relationships

At the heart of achieving any sort of benefit within the supply and value chain network is collaboration between players, and creating the conditions so each builds effective relationships one-to-many. Collaboration is a product and enabler for integration; an integrated supply chain is one that has evolved beyond a series of entities where there is a flow of materials between the players working in isolation to each other to one where there is cooperation and coordination between these players, and between internal functions within each player.

Across the vast literature out there proposing means to optimize supply and value chain networks, there seems to be agreement that the greatest improvement come through improved connections, relationships, collaboration and sharing, both internally and with external partners. Gradinger (2009) states a lot of leverages can be detected when improving and working on the relationships and interfaces between suppliers and clients within their value chains. Liker and Choi (2004) suggest corporations such build 'keiretsu:' close-knit networks of vendors that continuously learn, improve and prosper along with their parent companies and Christopher (2011) states the focus of SCM should be on the management of relationships in order to achieve a more profitable outcome.

Collaboration in the supply and value chain network is not something that just happens; in fact many of the players may not even know each other, are unlikely to trust each other and under normal conditions will have little motivation to build relationships beyond their immediate linkages. There are many potential obstacles that prevent supply and value chain network collaboration. These include:

- *Contractual restrictions* – any contractual obligation that might impede direct discussions upstream or downstream.
- *Lack of focus for relationship building* – without focus efforts to build relationships could be seen as little more than a nice to have discussion.
- *Unclear goal or benefits* – collaboration requires effort, commitment and resources so there needs to be a business case to justify this.
- *Lack of trust* – players are more likely to be cautious of sharing or relationship building in case it causes loss of competitive advantage.

- *Scale of effort* – getting multiple players in a supply and value chain network relationship to build relationships is no small task.
- *Commitment to information accuracy* – good relationships and the trust within them depends on good information sharing and flowing, getting truly accurate information, that those upstream can rely upon, takes away all flexibility of those providing it which could become a burden downstream.

Yet as we have seen, if collaboration and relationships can be developed throughout a supply and value chain network it can unlock value for all involved. Such collaboration and relationships need to be brokered; players need to be won over to the cause of increased collaboration and to do this, there needs to be a clear benefit, purpose and goal and a compelling reason to participate. Furthermore someone needs to take the initiative to broker such relationships and reach out to all involved. In practice, where the potential benefits are worthwhile to us, this means investing in an individual attempting to become supply and value chain network captain and assume a new role to help optimize an entire supply chain, supported by voluntary participation from other players and ideally resources to make the scheme work. Such a scheme is akin to a politician or peace envoy attempting to broker a multi-country peace deal, engaging with and negotiating with a series of country leaders for the benefit of all. Here only someone with sufficient standing will get the attention of country leaders. The same applies for the supply and value chain network so brokering participation needs to be championed by someone senior or with standing. Other key success factors here include:

- create a clear business case to get involved, quantifying the benefits where possible;
- work to secure resources and commitment from each player to work on specific projects, within or out, with their firms;
- create a focus for collaboration and improvement initiatives, eg an bi-annual symposium to review progress;
- create a programme of supply and value chain network improvements, involving all in the design;
- develop and manage a supply and value chain network-wide communications plan to improve the flow of information;
- manage the activity as if a project, using good project management, reporting and maintaining a current programme of activity;
- have players sign up to a project charter defining who is involved, the roles each has and how the project team will work together;
- use supply and value chain mapping, risk and opportunity analysis tools and the supply chain improvement process tools as appropriate; and
- give the scheme needs an identity and promote it, and the benefits for all, with good marketing communications support.

Hearing the voice of the customer

As the world around us changes the buyer ultimately has more power because they have increased choice. Christopher (2011) states 'now, instead of designing supply chains from the "factory outwards" the challenge is to design them from the "customer backwards"'. This means we are not so much managing supply chains but demand chains. Baker (2003) described the concept of a demand chain and states 'it requires turning the supply chain on its head, and taking the end user as the organization's point of departure not its final destination'. In other words the philosophical difference is we start with what the customer needs and wants, instead of end with it.

As we saw earlier in this book a major 'customer value' focus for driving any sort of improvement is that of understanding customer requirements through the Voice of the Customer (VOC). For an immediate customer this is about getting close to that customer and simply finding out what they want and need. However, our immediate customer may not be the end customer who may in fact be many steps removed from us downstream in the supply and value chain network.

If we can understand the end customer, gain insight into what they value, what would benefit them and their needs and aspirations both now and into the future, then we can begin to shape what we do in response to this and how the upstream suppliers can help fulfil this, thus building competitive advantage. Moreover, it may be the upstream suppliers that are better connected to what the end customer wants than we are. This can be seen in action within the competitive world of retail; whilst retailers are very good at modelling what their customer base will buy, this is typically based upon what has been before. Spotting the next new thing often takes giving a small supplier a way in because this small supplier might just have hit on something everyone else hasn't seen, perhaps some new trend, solution or taste that will resonate with the end customer. Retailers therefore gain an advantage by capturing ideas and trends in the market and getting them on the shelves before the competition. Hearing the VOC doesn't mean we need to do all the listening but rather we need to tune into all those with a similar interest in satisfying what the customer wants; our entire supply and value chain network.

In practice this means two things:

- *Gain end customer insight* – get as close to the end customer as possible. Understand the clusters of customers who share the same value preferences, the trends, the needs and so on. It may involve research or making direct contact with end customers, subject of course to not breaching any contractual restrictions with our immediate customer.

- *Invite network players to contribute* – working with the assumption that every player in the network would like to focus their resources to be more successful in the future, they are likely to have ideas and be working on new developments where they see a future need; for them to add value they will need to understand the value that others downstream seek and they will be listening to the VOC also. This means they will have a wealth of suggestions they can contribute.

The approach we use here is once again our RAQSCI business requirements and VIPER relationship requirements frameworks, except we are now developing these in a different context – the context of what the end customer needs and wants. End customer business and relationship requirements don't necessarily inform or merge into our high-level or individual category and supplier relationship requirements, but any differences between the two could highlight an opportunity for breakthrough. For example, if we are responding to requirements from our immediate customer for red shirts, whilst our intelligence suggests and end customer insight suggests blue might be more popular, then we can begin to push blue even if our immediate customer hasn't asked for blue yet. Here we have switched from waiting for requirements to flow down to proactively managing requirements. We can do the same for demand if we are connected to what the end customer might want and when.

Hearing the VOC helps us to be one step ahead, but if we can couple this with taking a more holistic end-to-end view so that the impact of any decision can be considered in terms of the entire supply chain, and sharing our VOC intelligence as well as using it as a basis to drive collaboration with players, then it is possible to create an agile, responsive network that is aligned with end customer needs and desires. It is also possible to work in a united and integrated way, with diminished need for inventories, buffers, long lead times created through the confidence given by ongoing sharing of information, forecasts and by all hearing the VOC.

Strategic collaborative relationships

13

This chapter defines strategic collaborative relationships with suppliers and outlines when they are appropriate and the nature of benefits possible within an overall SRM approach. Practical help to develop and build these relationships is given along with approaches to facilitate obtaining innovation from these suppliers.

PATHWAY QUESTIONS ADDRESSED IN THIS CHAPTER

15 Which of our important suppliers hold the potential to make a dramatic difference to our business and why?

16 Are we working collaboratively with those critical suppliers towards jointly agreed goals that will make a dramatic difference?

Introducing strategic collaborative relationships

A strategic collaborative relationship (SCR) is the ultimate level of relationship and one appropriate only for the critical few suppliers who are of strategic importance to us and who hold the potential to dramatically benefit our business, and most likely theirs in the process or with whom there is a critical imperative to maintain a very close relationship. Here we are right at the top of our segmentation pyramid (Figure 13.1) and even within this

FIGURE 13.1   How SCR is relevant for strategic suppliers

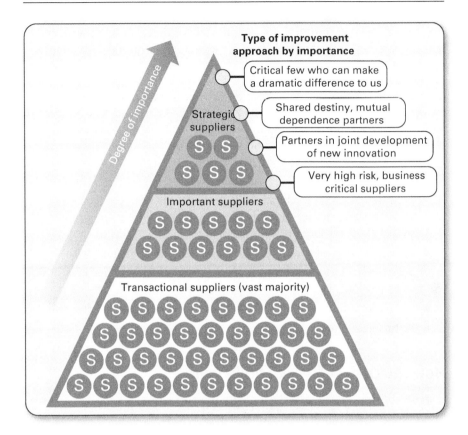

small number of suppliers our segmentation process has identified as *Strategic* there may be some suppliers that are more important or strategic than other and therefore different levels of relationship intensity.

The term SCR seems to be appropriate to differentiate what we mean here, but there are many other terms out there: SRM (perhaps meaning *strategic relationship management* rather than supplier relationship management) is frequently used to refer just to this type of approach with the most important of suppliers rather than an umbrella term for all supplier relationship approaches as outlined in this book. Suppliers here may be called *strategic suppliers*, but they may also be called *partners* or *critical suppliers*.

Characteristics of SCRs

It is easy to 'talk a supplier into strategic', or worse for the supplier to talk themself into strategic. Those managing suppliers of any importance will naturally want to think of their supplier as more important than the others as anything less than this begins to suggest their job is not that important. However, generally the number of suppliers that are truly strategic, and warrant the level of intervention that this chapter will outline, is usually very small. It is normal for the first cut of supplier segmentation to have an unusually high number of strategic suppliers. After discussion, and revisiting segmentation, there is usually consensus that most of these are in fact very important, and need strong supplier management, but not necessarily strategic.

The segmentation process outlined in Chapter 4 describes how to identify strategic suppliers and assuming this is done effectively what we end up with is a handful of suppliers that warrant a significant and unique form of intervention, either because we want to or need to. Typically these suppliers might:

- hold the potential to change something in our business that makes the share price go up (or adds great value to end users in a public or not for profit organization);
- have some sort of shared destiny and mutual dependency with us;
- be actively working jointly with us on new developments, innovation, improvements etc;
- have a long-term agreement in place with us from both sides; and
- be business critical to us.

How the critical few can build value

It seems the importance of strategic relationships with key suppliers is something that has only begun to be recognized in recent times, especially post the global downturn. In 1994 research by the US General Accounting Office suggested that effective relationships with supply chain partners may be of strategic importance (USGAO, 1994). Sheth and Sharma (2007) suggest that relationship management is becoming a strategic function and the next generation of competitive advantage may come from an effective relationship with supply chain partners.

Relationships with strategic suppliers is no longer a nice to have but rather understanding who these might be and building highly effective relationships with them is now essential for any firm wishing to survive and compete in an ever-changing, fast moving and volatile global environment. As we have seen competitive advantage can come by connecting end customer needs and aspirations with supply base possibilities and so it is the suppliers who hold the potential to help innovate or make a dramatic difference here, that we need to work with if we really want the best competitive advantage. The companies that are creating new marketplaces for things that didn't previously exist or delivering innovative products are not doing it alone, they are working with a few select partners who have the ability to help and want to be on the journey with them.

Building strategic collaborative relationships

Granovetter (1985) suggests we get partners who will work with us by having effective relationships. We don't make personal relationships work by doing a regular review of performance or agreeing a development plan. All of these have their place otherwise I've just wasted my time writing this book, but they are all mechanical means to manage a relationship; the real power in developing effective supplier relationships comes from social interaction, carefully selected with the right suppliers, just as we select who we will build a relationship with in real life, to help us achieve our outcomes.

If we create strategic collaborative relationships with our most important suppliers then we can unlock great value, so surely we should just get on and do it? Indeed we should but *just doing it* is not a matter of flicking a switch. Across much of the literature on SRM or related topics there is general consensus that joint working and collaborative relationships with shared goals is what is needed, but there is precious little on how you actually do this in practice.

As with any relationship, it cannot just be turned on, it needs to be courted, pursued, built and reinforced with consistency and persistence. Both sides need to want it and need to invest in making it happen.

Remember that companies do not hold relationships with companies, but rather individuals in companies hold relationships with individuals in those other companies. This is a crucial point as it means that strategic collaborative relationships are founded upon the relationships between individuals but supported and coordinated by companies and all with the right motivation to build such a relationship. Trumpfheller and Hofmann (2004) suggest effective relationships, and the performance possible through them, requires commitment and trust from the individual, communication and transparency from the organization together with coordination and technology; all interdependent and necessary for performance. This is a useful model; however, commitment is much more than a single factor and is needed not just at an individual level but also by the organization, and parties need to be willing and motivated to want to build a relationship. Commitment is a product of other factors, for example if we build trust we build commitment (Chao *el al*, 2013). Motivation drives commitment also.

Commitment is therefore central to strategic collaborative relationships, but this alone is not enough. Parties also need to cooperate and collaborate and by doing so motivated individuals and organizations turn the intent that commitment represents into results. Where parties have the choice as to whether or not to attempt to build strategic collaborative relationships then the non-coercive power of parties entering into a voluntary arrangement naturally promotes cooperation between them whereas an arrangement where parties are forced to work together breeds conflict (Skinner *et al*, 1992).

FIGURE 13.2   The interlocking components of strategic supplier relationships

Eliciting cooperation and collaboration as well requires a degree of stage management, but if the conditions are right this will naturally happen.

To bring this together, strategic collaborative relationships are enabled through the interdependency of individual, organizational and motivational factors; these are: trust, consistency, transparency, coordination, communication, the potential benefit to parties and alignment of goals. Together these factors converge to create real *commitment* and from that *collaboration* that leads to performance, achievement and longevity, or whatever parties seek, is realized. This entire framework is enabled through careful selection of the individuals involved in the relationship, so they have the right characteristics and personality, and through appropriate organizational structure and resourcing. This model is given in Figure 13.2 and is expanded in the following sections.

Individual: trust, consistency and sharing

Hausman and Johnston (2010) define trust as 'confidence in the integrity and reliability of another party, rather than confidence in the partner's ability to perform a specific action'. They also state that trust between partners constitutes one of the key factors for becoming long-term partners. Chao *et al* (2013) describe trust as an important factor in relationship exchange and Kwon and Suh (2004) suggest trust is a central feature of a strategic partnership. Nyaga *et al* (2010) suggest 'trust refers to the subjective belief that partners in a relationship will fulfill their obligations and thus positively influence both parties in a relationship'. Trust exists where one party has confidence in the other's reliability and integrity (Morgan and Hunt, 1994) and Tangpong and Ro (2009) suggest trust is the major differential component in facilitating relationship continuance.

Chao *et al* (2013) suggest a number of factors that lead to trust include:

- communication and information sharing;
- the perceived benefits by parties;
- relationship tenure – the more long term a relationship is the more likely that trust will exist; and
- asset specificity – the transferability of assets that support a given transaction, in other words if a relationship involves the transfer of assets or investment in assets in a partner to support a piece of work then this is a visible and demonstrable level of commitment that builds trust.

Chao *et al* (2013) also suggest that behavioural uncertainty kills trust, but rather if we are consistent, at both an individual and organization level, we can build trust. Poor information sharing leads to behavioural uncertainty, but also consistency is about being predicable and always acting in the same way, in line with some definition of good practice, an organizational code of conduct or personal beliefs. Consistency is a source of personal power; if someone is consistent you know where you stand with them and know what is or is not appropriate. In my career, the people I have respected the most are the ones who were always consistent and fair. The same is true of relationships with suppliers, if we are consistent in our dealings with them they will trust us more, even if they don't get the result they seek. Here our egos can get in the way. Imagine a supplier who flatters us and builds a strong rapport, then the supplier becomes a bit closer than they were previously and gets into a position to help us determine what we need so they are lined up. Here we have in fact given the supplier the power. Instead, being consistent here, perhaps by never faltering from a predictable set of behaviour that would rebuff this attempt or always following a prescribed code of conduct, then we retain the power of the relationship. The supplier may fail to get what they want, but the process will build trust. Furthermore, consistency is compromised by individualism. Individualism is culture specific, but is the degree to which we act for the benefit of ourselves (as opposed to society or a collective group). In all relationships people make irrational decisions (King, 2012) and individualistic behaviour fuels this, but if we are visibly acting on behalf of a company and all our actions are always aligned with a more collective objective and behaviour then this demonstrates consistency which also builds trust.

So trust is pretty fundamental to strategic relationships. Trust tends to operate between individuals but shapes the overall culture of a firm – we may feel entirely comfortable with an informal arrangement between our firm and another, yet this comfort will be based upon degree of trust with one or more key individuals. If trust exists then this in turn has a positive impact on a relationship. Trust builds commitment (Chao *et al*, 2013) and helps relationship tenure and continuity by positively reducing the likelihood of the relationship being dissolved (Tangpong and Ro, 2009).

Finally, *sharing* by individuals is key to building effective strategic relationships. *Communication* is called out as an enabling factor for the organization, but at an individual level we need more than communication, we need sharing where individuals proactively and freely exchange information that is both relevant and appropriate to the relationship. This might seem obvious yet actually remembering to do this day-to-day can in practice be difficult and so requires us to adopt a 'sharing mindset'. This only happens if we believe in the relationship and make a clear and conscious effort to share what is important.

Personality and behaviours in SCRs

If the means to build relationships between companies is through individuals (Granovetter, 1985), then the personality and characteristics of these individuals is of crucial importance. There are two dimensions here:

- *Personality* – our personality, pretty much set and defined from birth but influenced to a degree by our environment, especially in early formative years.
- *Behaviour* – how we behave. We can choose our behaviours, even those that are heavy influenced by our personalities and we can develop competencies that enable us to interact with others and secure the outcomes we need.

This means we ideally either need to select and recruit those who will manage strategic relationships based upon the required personality profile (as well as the right fit and experience) or those in such roles should understand who they are and be able to adapt behaviours for the situation. Ensuring the right match of individuals to strategic relationship management roles is of great importance. If we fail to do this the relationship would be sub-optimum. For example, an individual who is not *outgoing* and introverted might struggle to use *voice* with a supplier to discuss issues. An individual who is not *agreeable* might fail to build the rapport needed to ensure a relationship prospers. Ensuring that those who are entrusted to manage very important supplier relationships have the right personality traits or can demonstrate adaptability where there are differences is crucial.

COW SOAP ACE can help

The COW SOAP ACE framework (Figure 13.3) represents the personality types that are given (COW SOAP) and traits we can influence (ACE) that are relevant to a greater or lesser degree for any supplier interaction. It was developed specifically to match personality and behaviours to specific supplier negotiations using portfolio analysis as the determinant (the model is expanded in full in my second book *Negotiation for Purchasing Professionals*). The COW SOAP ACE traits most appropriate for a strategic supplier relationship are given in Figure 13.3.

For the ACE traits, both *assertiveness* and *conflict style* need some further explanation in the context of strategic supplier relationships. *Assertiveness* is a core skill and highly necessary for supplier interactions, especially if we are conducting a *leverage* (portfolio analysis) negotiation. In a strategic collaborative relationship assertiveness is also necessary but in excess can work against the relationship. Tangpong and Ro (2009) suggest that assertiveness leads to opportunistic 'concern for self' behaviour to the detriment of relationship continuance but instead cooperativeness leads to a fall in opportunism and therefore a rise in trust and the right conditions for relationship continuance. Therefore individuals must be able to moderate their assertiveness and choose when to be assertive but must also be able to collaborate first and foremost.

This leads us nicely into *conflict style* where we return to the Thomas-Kilmann (TKI) conflict mode instrument that we first explored in Chapter 11 when we explored conflicts with suppliers. Kilmann and Thomas (1977) identify five conflict styles according to the degree to which an individual is assertive versus cooperative when faced with a conflict situation. In a strategic collaborative relationship there is much scope for conflict to arise. New combined teams are forming and will therefore go through storming (necessary for group norms get established), together teams are trying to move towards new goals, with important payoffs for both so there is a lot at stake. All of this happens against a backdrop of parties choosing to work together rather than having to, which creates an imperative to make it work and keep it working so both remain interested. The way individuals handle conflict in such a relationship is important. Skinner *et al* (1992) state that conflict has a negative impact on cooperation – conflict reduces satisfaction of parties in a relationship whilst cooperation leads to more satisfaction in the relationship. A *collaborating* conflict style is the most helpful in a strategic collaborative relationship in terms of resolving disputes, reaching mutual goals and ensuring relationship continuance. However, this is more than an ideal personal style, it is actually essential for a highly important supplier relationship as other styles could be acutely damaging to the relationship. Similarly if an individual is not good at cooperating then the ability of parties to work together to achieve mutual goals is compromised, furthermore cooperation reduces opportunistic behaviour (Tangpong and Ro, 2009). It could be argued that the TKI style *Compromising* would be more useful for a key strategic

FIGURE 13.3 The COW SOAP ACE traits most appropriate for a strategic supplier relationship

The COW SOAP ACE model and traits most appropriate for a strategic supplier relationship
Required

The COW SOAP model of traits that are part of personality

C **Conscientiousness** — Hardworking, organized and self-disciplined with attention to detail. High scoring individuals are typically very reliable and will persevere to get thing right. ✓✓✓

O **Outgoing** — Socially confident and easily met in conversation, comfortable speaking about their ideas and making new social connections quickly. ✓✓✓

W **Will to win** — Competitive and highly ambitious. The need to achieving goals is more important to the individual than personal relationships. ✓

S **Solution focused** — Can assimilate new information accurately and rapidly and identify effective solutions. Collects and analyses data and makes data-based decisions. ✓✓

O **Open-minded** — Ability to work well in the absence of structure. Creative, imaginative and often curious. Is comfortable working in vague, fluid or rapidly changing environment. ✓✓✓

A **Agreeable** — Good natured and helpful. Places the needs of others in front of one's own needs. Acts selflessly and tries to meets the emotional needs of, and nurture, others. ✓✓✓

P **Personal calm** — Relaxed, at ease and secure. Controls own emotions and individuals scoring high are often patient and even tempered. ✓✓✓

The ACE model of negotiation traits where there is choice

A **Assertiveness** — Comfortable in asserting one's own ideas, views or needs and to remain insistent about these in the face of disagreement, criticism or adversity in order to satisfy one's own concerns. *'Can choose'*

C **Conflict style** — How one naturally behaves in conflict situations. Assessed using a conflict style instrument, eg Thomas Kilmann model (competes, collaborates, compromises, avoids or accommodates). *'Collaborative'*

E **Emotional Competence** — The ability to identify, evaluate and manage the emotions of oneself and of others and of groups. ✓✓✓

relationship. This indeed would be appropriate for many important supplier relationships and indeed is typically where negotiations with suppliers end up. However, for strategic collaborative relationships *compromising* is a compromise in itself. Results come from determined collaboration in the face of challenging relationship building and this calls for high levels of co-operative assertiveness as opposed to parties compromising for the sake of the other.

Finally, the last ACE trait is *Emotional Competence (EC)*. This is the ability to understand and manage our emotions and those of others, and to express emotion. Emotional competence of an individual is increasingly considered alongside IQ as a measure of personal capability, and can now be found being used by employers within some recruitment processes. EC is a core skill of sales people; empathy and specifically the ability to understand other's emotions and adapt like a chameleon enables the seller to build rapport and therefore aid the sales process. Emotional competence comes more naturally to some than others but is a capability we can develop with continuous practice and social experience. Strategic relationship with suppliers involve building relationships characterized by trust and consistency with key individuals. In practice this requires adaptability, compromise, understanding their position and the things that trigger certain emotions. Therefore purchasing people building strategic collaborative relationships should ideally posses a strong level of EC. If we are looking to appoint an individual into a role here the EC should be a consideration.

The ideal individual for strategic relationships

There is a further dimension beyond personality that is relevant and that is how an individual believes business interactions should take place and therefore how he or she is motivated and behaves. Granovetter (1985) suggests that business decisions are influenced by both sociological and economic concerns and that how we approach a business decision exists somewhere on a continuum between these two (Figure 13.4). At one extreme the sociological concerns such as fairness, honesty, equality, trust, altruism and common interest drive business decisions. Here progress might be thwarted by the fear of upsetting anyone. This can be seen in action in collective societies where decisions are avoided for fear of losing face or causing disrespect for the group. At the other extreme are business decisions made by an individual (and therefore how he/she acts in the relationship) that are totally influenced by economic concerns. As such this drives self-interest behaviour that is cut-throat, dishonest, opportunistic or involves wrongdoing. Again individuals at this extreme will fail, whilst they might be driven to maximize profits and returns, they will struggle to win or retain support. Most likely they will have no or few friends. Granovetter (1985) suggests that the optimum approach lies somewhere in the middle. He calls this 'embeddedness' and suggests it is characterized by networks of interpersonal relations. Personal

FIGURE 13.4   Granovetter's continuum between sociological and economic concerns

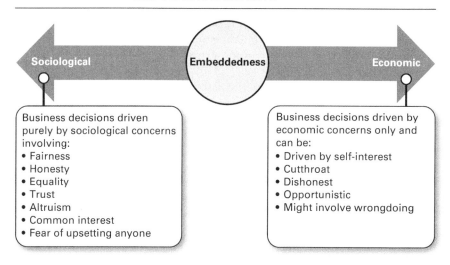

networks of individuals are highly important to strategic relationships, not because it means the individual has lots of LinkedIn connections but because of what that represents and the untapped power it offers. I will return to this later in Chapter 14 when we explore innovation.

Therefore the ideal individual to manage strategic supplier relationships has a personality that promotes relationship building, is collaboratively assertive, has strong emotional competence and is naturally good at networking. In addition there are many skills and capabilities that are needed but these are things that can be learnt and I will cover these in Chapter 15.

So far we've talked about personality and characteristics on our side but before we leave this section it is worth considering that of the seller, which is equally as important to foster commitment and collaboration and we may have more influence than we realize here. Whether a new or existing supplier, a strategic relationship is a significant thing so discussions around which individuals are to be involved is not unreasonable. Here we are seeking the same individual, organizational and motivational components that we saw in Figure 13.2 above. In particular there are two factors that are particularly relevant to look for (adapted from Tangpong and Ro, 2009):

1 *Staff turnover* – staff turnover in itself impacts relationship building, clearly because it reduces tenure and therefore reduces scope for building trust at an individual level. Moreover it can be the symptoms of deeper issues within the business.

2 *Cooperativeness vs assertiveness* – the demonstrable ability for assertive cooperation rather than competitive assertiveness.

Organizational: transparency, coordination and communication

At a company level the factors that enable strategic collaborative relationships are transparency, coordination and communication. Together these provide the conditions for the relationship to exist and thrive, whilst enabling the other party to gain confidence in the relationship, which then leads to commitment.

Transparency is about being open and honest with the other party around direction, intent and any factors that could help or threaten the relationship, and it is about positive actions to share anything that is relevant with the other. Transparency builds trust in the individuals involved, yet transparency is something that must happen at an organizational level because it concerns how a firm organizes itself to become more transparent. In an arm's length buyer/supplier relationship, with a supplier that is not particularly important, it would be normal to share only what information is necessary for the transaction. It might even be normal to mislead the other party for opportunistic or self-preservation reasons, eg to make the other believe there was a future opportunity in order to elicit more favourable pricing now. This is the opposite of transparency and is typical of a transactional relationship whereas when parties manage to open up and share more it breaks down the barriers of self-preservation and opportunism. Openness breeds honesty and therefore trust, as nothing is hidden and if parties begin to proactively share information that will help the other be more effective then transparency will positively drive commitment and therefore results.

Transparency is the aim, and this happens through good communication and information sharing and through the coordination of these activities. Achieving this in practice means instigating certain routine practices and these might include:

- exchanging 'real' company information around performance, current situation, strategy and future plans;
- ensuring accuracy of forecasts and non-contracted intentions;
- 'open book' approaches to sharing detailed cost information;
- sharing details about who is talking to whom in each other's organization; and
- using 'voice' – ensuring issues or concerns are vocalized.

All this said there is a health warning here, and that is to be careful not to completely believe the dream. The dream is a strategic collaborative relationship where parties are completely open, transparent and actively share and communicate with each other for the good of both and the relationship. If we were going to marry the supplier then the dream is good, but suppliers are different and here we are still part of a commercial relationship, no matter how close it might feel. It is essential to court closeness with caution and openness with vigilance if we are to remain objective and fully in control of our position.

Organizational readiness

The organization can only enable a strategic relationship if it organizes itself to do so. In practice this means assigning clear roles and responsibilities for those tasked here, a structure and ways of working that promote relationships and sufficient resources and investment to support a programme of ongoing relationship building with enough time and money to allow this to happen. Relationships will not happen unless the firm is serious about doing so and backs this up with real investment. Many of the attempts to develop strategic relationship that I see simply fail because an organization has attempted to just tag it onto someone's already busy job and then imposes travel constraints that prevent face-to-face meetings. Instead, if organizations want the benefits from strategic supplier relationships then they must invest in making them happen and free up the necessary resources to do so.

Motivational: willingness, benefits and alignment

Behaviour in buyer/seller exchanges can be either opportunistic, ie where one or both party acts selfishly or unilaterally for their own benefit, or can be to build and support relationship continuance (Tangpong and Po, 2009). Each party, and more specifically individuals within in each party, choose their behaviour. Strategic collaborative relationships need willing and motivated parties, who both want to act to build and support the relationship. At a simple level willingness is a product of the potential benefits available and the degree to which these align with our overall goals and direction. However, there is more here and it doesn't follow that a willing partner has the ability to convert this into positive action in the relationship. In fact, looking from our perspective, the degree to which a relationship can be built, developed and maintained with a supplier ongoing depends upon:

- *The degree to which they want to* – their interest or willingness to develop a relationship with us.
- *The degree to which we are able to* – the scope for influence of the relationship.
- *The way we attempt to* – the personality, characteristics and behaviours of the individuals involved.

Interest or willingness for the relationship can be assessed using the *Supplier Preferencing* tool; we can assess how we believe the supplier would view our relationship based upon how attractive the account is to them and the relative value of business we represent.

Determining scope for influence within the relationship is less simple because of the fact that relationships are held by individuals. Tangpong and Ro (2009) suggest that the degree to which one person can influence a relationship depends upon the boundaries of that which can be controlled. These are:

- *Relational norms* – the values shared amongst exchange partners, for example how partners determine what is or is not acceptable behaviour in the relationship. If no boundaries are set here then partners might be free to develop all sorts of relationships. *Supplier Codes of Conduct* or a *Relationship Charter* help define expected behaviour with suppliers together with boundaries that determine the degree to which the relationship can be influenced.

- *Dependency* – how dependent one firm is on the other. If one firm has the power and the other is completely dependent, then attempts to influence the relationship by the other, for example to secure supply, could be completely ignored. Put simply, the powerful party does not need to engage in the relationship.

Dependency not only affects the scope we have to influence a relationship, it also helps gauge willingness on their part. If we consider dependency alongside *Supplier Preferencing* we gain a more accurate insight into willingness. Attempting to build a relationship with a supplier who sees us as a *Nuisance* or in the *Exploitable* quadrant seems logical in order to reduce risk, especially if we are completely dependent upon that supplier, and have little choice or ability to switch. Yet there is no imperative for them to respond to our efforts to build a relationship. Dependency can be factored into our assessment by using both the *Supplier Preferencing* tool together with the *Portfolio Analysis* tool (where we consider how individual categories of spend should be managed). Figure 13.5 shows the two matrices combined and the likely degree of supplier willingness for a relationship according to each combination. With this information we are able to determine if efforts to develop a relationship are worthwhile and what we might need to work on to influence the relationship.

Are they capable of having a relationship?

The supplier may be willing but what if they are not capable of having such a relationship? This is not uncommon and many organizations are simply not organized or structured in a way that enables this to happen, and despite all the best will, attempts to establish a relationship will fail. Things that need to be in place for this to happen, and so provide indicators of the likelihood of success, are:

- clear and visible executive support within the supplier;
- supplier has organized itself so as to free up resources for the relationship; and
- visible cross-functional working and communication.

FIGURE 13.5 Supplier preferencing and portfolio analysis combined to show supplier willingness for a relationship

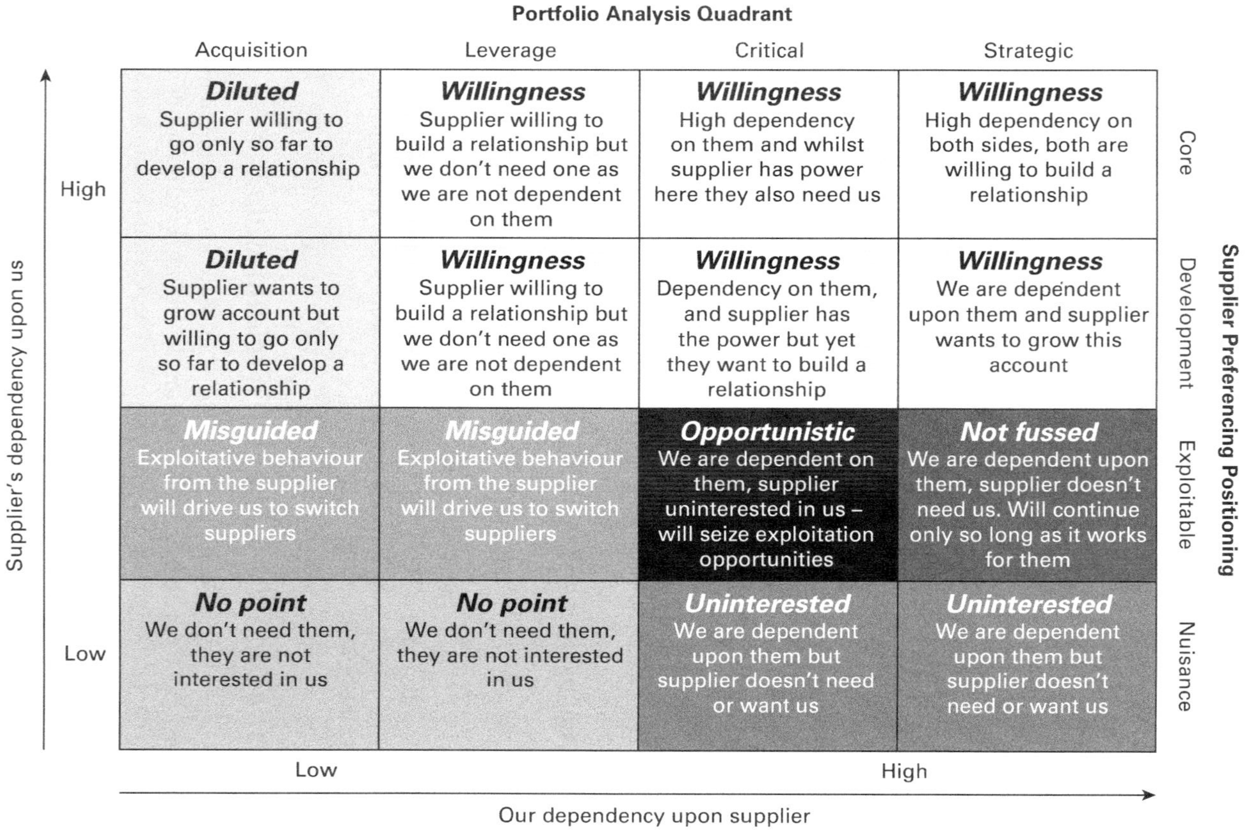

Supplier Preferencing Positioning

Portfolio Analysis Quadrant

Supplier Preferencing Positioning	Acquisition	Leverage	Critical	Strategic
Core	**Diluted** Supplier willing to go only so far to develop a relationship	**Willingness** Supplier willing to build a relationship but we don't need one as we are not dependent on them	**Willingness** High dependency on them and whilst supplier has power here they also need us	**Willingness** High dependency on both sides, both are willing to build a relationship
Development	**Diluted** Supplier wants to grow account but willing to go only so far to develop a relationship	**Willingness** Supplier willing to build a relationship but we don't need one as we are not dependent on them	**Willingness** Dependency on them, and supplier has the power but yet they want to build a relationship	**Willingness** We are dependent upon them and supplier wants to grow this account
Exploitable	**Misguided** Exploitative behaviour from the supplier will drive us to switch suppliers	**Misguided** Exploitative behaviour from the supplier will drive us to switch suppliers	**Opportunistic** We are dependent on them, supplier uninterested in us – will seize exploitation opportunities	**Not fussed** We are dependent upon them, supplier doesn't need us. Will continue only so long as it works for them
Nuisance	**No point** We don't need them, they are not interested in us	**No point** We don't need them, they are not interested in us	**Uninterested** We are dependent upon them but supplier doesn't need or want us	**Uninterested** We are dependent upon them but supplier doesn't need or want us

Supplier's dependency upon us — High / Low

Our dependency upon supplier — Low / High

If the supplier appears incapable of building a strategic relationship (despite what the key account manager might tell you), then there are just three options here:

- Work with them to get them to change and develop.
- Manage them instead of building a relationship.
- Find another supplier (if practical).

Commitment, cooperation and collaboration

So, to bring this to a summary, effective strategic relationships are born out of commitment, cooperation and collaboration. Commitment flows from the individual, organizational and motivational factors, if these things are present then there will be a natural commitment by parties to build and maintain a high performing joint relationship. Commitment is an output, but it is an activity also and one that operates at both an individual and company level. It is about decisions and action clearly being made in support of a long-term joint relationship. The visible or tangible signs of commitment are important as it is these that parties seek in the other in order to commit back. For example, if we say we are working together with a supplier but our behaviour is opportunistic and we seek to avoid committing to anything that will build joint relationships then we are just paying lip service to a stated intention; this will soon become obvious to the supplier who will fail to respond. However, if we back up our stated desire for joint working with real action then we are demonstrating commitment. In practice this can take many forms but might include, from our perspective:

- making our resources available to them to help them, perhaps with no immediate benefit to us and perhaps even without charge;
- investing time and energy in the relationship, helping them and joint working;
- making long-term investments in assets or facilities that support joint working;
- providing long-term contractual commitment to minimum volumes or spend levels;
- visibly promoting the joint relationship including, for example, co-branding or publishing marketing collateral about the relationship.

If we show commitment but reciprocation is lacking then it could indicate a lack of willingness on their part, in which case we might need to rethink our aims for the relationship here. However, it could also mean a willing supplier is holding back or individuals haven't figured out how to enable things such as communication and transparency in practice. It could also mean the individuals leading the relationship are not the right people. The reality here is that strategic collaborative relationships are hard to create in practice and often there is little experience of doing this so efforts can fail just because parties don't know what to do. If we are certain there is willingness then such issues can usually be overcome by working together to secure the necessary commitment.

It could be argued that cooperation and collaboration are one and the same, and to a degree this is true, but both are needed; cooperation involves agreeing to accommodate the other and work together with them and collaboration is then the process of actually doing this to secure results. Both are summarized by the concept of joint working, which I shall explore more fully shortly.

Go drink beer with them, but go Dutch!

When I've trained and worked with senior purchasing teams, I often suggested something like 'If you want to build a strategic collaborative relationship with your supplier you need to go out and drink beer with them.' My suggestion is typically not received well, people become visibly uncomfortable and those in charge feel compelled to issue some sort of countering or balancing remark. However, whilst I am being deliberately provocative, I am also attempting to get companies to think differently about how they approach such relationships. As we touched on earlier, as buyers we are brought up to follow the 'keep suppliers at arm's length' philosophy, and, in most Western cultures, we also tend to follow strict ethical principles that are not set up to permit anything that gets too close to a supplier. For a strategic collaborative relationship we need to behave differently, and even change the policy, if we want it to really work well, and the secret to this is social interaction.

In the vast majority of interactions with suppliers the degree of social interaction is limited to casual conversations at the start of meetings about sport, vacations and family. These moments of sharing 'personal puff', often initiated by the seller, are there to build rapport and culturally it is often expected, especially by the Italians. However, this is in fact pseudo social interaction.

If we really want supplier relationships to work then we need the individuals to be compelled to work to build the relationship, and this has to happen at an individual level, in the same way it has to within any team. This usually only comes after a good degree of social interaction; the point when people get to know each other and who they are not the title they hold. Therefore we need to create the opportunity for individuals to do just this. Suppliers have long since understood the power of social interaction in building a relationship, which is why they love to invite customers to sporting events or functions they host. However, this sort of corporate hospitality is increasingly unacceptable from the perspective of accepting gifts from suppliers, but crucially it is not appropriate because it is social interaction on their terms and creates obligation through the gift. Instead we need a form of social interaction that does not create obligation but remains entirely neutral and transparent. This is as simple as going out for dinner, going out to a bar or even an event where key individuals can get to know each other, discuss work topics as well as personal topics but where both 'go Dutch', ie they share the cost and pay their way equally, and both are investing in the process of doing so.

The '5A' SCR process

We are now halfway through this chapter and so far not a single process diagram or methodology has appeared, and for good reason! Strategic relationships don't happen by following a process, they happen through individuals.

Joint working is what happens in practice day-to-day to foster commitment, cooperation and collaboration and is about creating the right conditions to enable this. Characteristics of joint working include:

- individuals have clear roles and remit to embark on joint working activities;
- parties will have shared goals;
- parties will regularly meet to share, exchange ideas, work towards an agreed outcome and innovate;
- parties will use the 'voice' (see Chapter 11) and will raise concerns openly and candidly with the intent of changing objectionable conditions;
- parties will readily invest time and money in the relationship, often without counting the cost; and
- there will be clear benefits, shared by both that emerge on an ongoing basis.

The mechanics of joint working are actually very simple, however these mechanics will only function if all the other components needed for a strategic relationship are in place. In the orchestra of SRM joint working is possible when the various other sections of the orchestra play together, and then we can instigate a joint working programme.

Making joint working happen

Just when you thought it was safe, there is in fact a sequence of steps to achieve joint working and build a strategic collaborative relationship and this is the 5A process (given in Figure 13.6), named after the five stages of *Activate, Analyse, Ambition, Accomplish, Advance*. 5A is however much more than a simple series of steps, it is itself a comprehensive methodology

FIGURE 13.6 The 5A Strategic Collaborative Relationship process

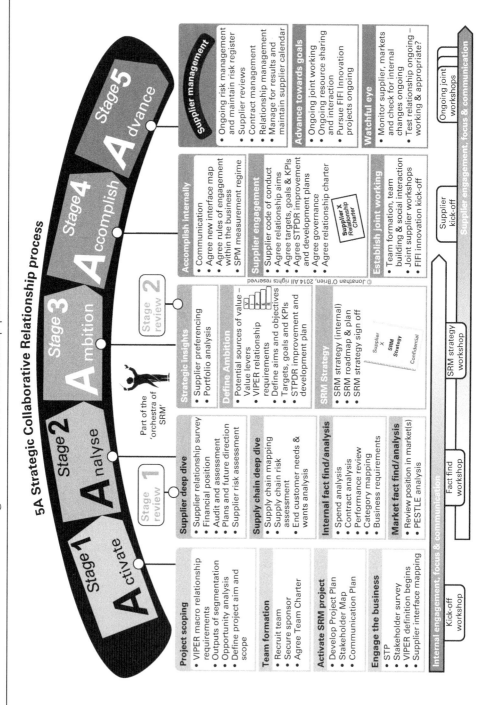

5A Strategic Collaborative Relationship process

Stage 1 A ctivate
Stage 2 A nalyse
Stage 3 A mbition
Stage 4 A ccomplish
Stage 5 A dvance

Part of the 'orchestra of SRM'

Stage 1 review

Stage 2 review

Project scoping
• VIPER macro relationship requirements
• Outputs of segmentation
• Opportunity analysis
• Define project aim and scope

Team formation
• Recruit team
• Secure sponsor
• Agree Team Charter

Activate SRM project
• Develop Project Plan
• Stakeholder Map
• Communication Plan

Engage the business
• STP
• Stakeholder survey
• VIPER definition begins
• Supplier interface mapping

Supplier deep dive
• Supplier relationship survey
• Financial position
• Audit and assessment
• Plans and future direction
• Supplier risk assessment

Supply chain deep dive
• Supply chain mapping
• Supply chain risk assessment
• End customer needs & wants analysis

Internal fact find/analysis
• Spend analysis
• Contract analysis
• Performance review
• Category mapping
• Business requirements

Market fact find/analysis
• Review position in market(s)
• PESTLE analysis

Strategic insights
• Supplier preferencing
• Portfolio analysis

Define Ambition
• Potential sources of value – Value levers
• VIPER relationship requirements
• Define aims and objectives
• Targets, goals and KPIs
• STPDR improvement and development plan

SRM Strategy
• SRM strategy (internal)
• SRM roadmap & plan
• SRM strategy sign off

Supplier X SRM Strategy Confidential

Accomplish internally
• Communication
• Agree new interface map
• Agree rules of engagement within the business
• SPM measurement regime

Supplier engagement
• Supplier code of conduct
• Agree relationship aims
• Agree targets, goals & KPIs
• Agree STPDR improvement and development plans
• Agree governance
• Agree relationship charter

Supplier X Relationship Charter

Establish joint working
• Team formation, team building & social interaction
• Joint supplier workshops
• FIFI innovation kick-off

Supplier management
• Ongoing risk management and maintain risk register
• Supplier reviews
• Contract management
• Relationship management
• Manage for results and maintain supplier calendar

Advance towards goals
• Ongoing joint working
• Ongoing resource sharing and interaction
• Pursue FIFI innovation projects ongoing

Watchful eye
• Monitor supplier, markets and check for internal changes ongoing
• Test relationship ongoing – working & appropriate?

Kick-off workshop

Fact find workshop

SRM strategy workshop

Supplier kick-off

Ongoing joint workshops

Internal engagement, focus & communication

Supplier engagement, focus & communication

through which we can secure the benefit we seek from our strategic suppliers. So why have I left it until Chapter 13 to reveal this? Quite simply because the 5A process, and indeed any meaningful sort of strategic supplier relationship, cannot realistically exist or function to any degree without all the other components of SRM. In the orchestra of SRM, the music of the strategic supplier calls for all sections to play, for some parts at least. We cannot begin to focus on achieving joint strategic goals if we don't have SPM or SI&D arrangements in place, and we still need SM.

The 5A process is akin in complexity to the 5i Category Management process (outlined in my first book *Category Management in Purchasing*). The two processes have been specifically designed to work together and share many common tools, some used differently for SRM, which have been covered as we have moved through the various sections of this book. There are also a number of generic tools and steps called out here such as communication planning, stakeholder mapping and value levers. These, and others, are standard strategic purchasing tools, and are also found within *Category Management in Purchasing* and so have not been repeated here.

The 5A Strategic Collaborative Relationship process is a five-stage process that is applied to a single supplier, identified as strategic and with whom we wish to collaborate to achieve certain goals. Stage 1 *Activate* is concerned with kicking off the project, stage 2 *Analyse* is concerned with data gathering and internal goal setting. Stages 1 and 2 are largely internal to prepare for a joint engagement. Then stage 3 *Ambition* is about defining the SRM strategy and engaging with the supplier and stage 4 *Accomplish* is about realizing the strategy and putting in place joint working as needed. Finally stage 5 *Advance* is about working towards new goals as well as ongoing relationship management. The first three stages have a mostly internal focus and our focus and the main engagement with the supplier begins in stage 4. Along the way there are a series of internal and external workshops that help move through the 5A SCR process as well as two stage reviews; key points in the process where a review and challenge of the project can help ensure the right degree of process rigour.

Stage 1: Activate

SCR begins by checking the macro relationship requirements; what the company needs from its supply base. This, together with the outputs from the segmentation process that show why the supplier in question is considered strategic, then enable us to develop an opportunity analysis and define the aims and scope of our project.

SCR projects usually require cross-functional teams as well as the involvement and support from across the business. Therefore in this stage we pull together a small team (typically five to seven individuals), selected because of their involvement, interest or how they can contribute, and an overall executive sponsor to help galvanize the project. The *Team Charter* tool can be used to define the project, aims and various roles and commitments. The first tasks for the team are to develop a *Project Plan* for the SCR project so as to provides the basis to manage the project towards an outcome, work up a *Stakeholder Map* of all in the business who have some sort of interest in this supplier and a *Communications Plan* for internal and external communications to help secure support and participation. Once developed the activities within communications plan need to be realized, perhaps requiring a dedicated role within the team to manage this.

The *STP* tool (Situation, Target Proposal) provides the means for the team to pool information, knowledge, facts and beliefs about the current relationship with this supplier and then to begin to consider possible early aims, objectives and targets for the relationship, for further refinement as well as initial steps to begin to move towards this. An internal *Stakeholder Survey* is the first piece of data collection and provides a means to begin to engage the business to understand the business-wide needs and wants for a supplier relationship as well as current and historical performance. From here we can begin the process of developing the VIPER relationship requirements. Finally in this stage a *Supplier Interface Map* helps us identify who is talking to whom, which should align with our stakeholder and communication maps and is the first step towards being able to present a united front to a supplier.

Stage 2: Analyse

In stage 2 we are gathering data and information that will enable us to determine our SRM strategy. This begins with a 'deep dive' supplier-specific fact find looking at as many areas appropriate for the supplier. This might include checking their financial position, understanding how they are structured, organized and operate, understanding their management systems and their plans for the future or where we believe they are heading. This information can come from many sources; perhaps from stakeholders, a visit to the supplier, research or by asking the supplier. A *Supplier Relationship Survey* can be a useful early engagement with the supplier to gain their perspective and a supplier risk assessment is also essential and this will form the basis for ongoing risk management for this supplier.

Depending upon what we are sourcing it may also be appropriate to conduct a 'deep dive' fact find for the supply and value chain network. Here we can use the *Supply Chain Mapping* tool and conduct a supply chain risk assessment. We can also attempt to try and understand what the end customer needs and wants are which could be valuable insight to help us determine a plan for innovation or improvement.

Internal fact find includes understanding the total spend with the supplier, necessary so we can understand our overall leverage position, the contracts we have in place, what they cover and when they expire as well as a review of supplier performance using whatever data is available. *Category mapping* is quite simply mapping categories against suppliers and not only allows us to establish all the things a supplier is providing, but also enables us to see the other suppliers that are providing similar categories, again helping us understand risk and opportunity for a specific supplier relationship. A category map together with the *business requirements* for each category allow us to extract any requirements for the relationship that need to be provided for.

Finally market fact find is concerned with identifying which marketplaces this supplier exists in and what their position in those markets are; for example whether they are a dominant player with good market share or one of many and the factors that drive this such as how generic or proprietary their offering is. *PESTLE* analysis helps also and provides insight into the external environment the supplier is operating in and what opportunities or threats they face.

Stage 2 involves many different tools and analyses, individually they are useful, but together they begin to form a picture of how we should move forward with a supplier, as if each is an individual piece of a bigger jigsaw puzzle. It is therefore crucial that we consider what each individual step is telling us; achieved by asking 'so what' does this tell us and capturing these insights. Our 'so what's' will then help us move through stage 3.

Stage 3: Ambition

Armed with the facts, data and analyses gathered during stage 2, stage 3 is about defining our ambition for the relationship. This starts by synthesizing all we have learnt and understood about the supplier and using these outputs to determine positioning in the *Supplier Preferencing* tool and *Portfolio Analysis* tool. The output from both of these begin to suggest what our strategic direction might be and specifically if collaboration is feasible and if it is even necessary.

From here we define the ambition for the relationship and the specific things we want and need the relationship to accomplish: 'the mountain we want to climb'. The *Value Levers* tool provides a means to consider the different potential sources of value for individual categories, but is also useful to consider the value we need from the overall relationship. It is helpful here as it seeks to validate our assumptions about why a supplier is strategic and the outputs of segmentation, but using it may also identify new potential sources of value to pursue. We should now be in a position to complete our VIPER relationship requirements, combining all the insights, outputs, aspirations, needs, wants and obligations that have emerged from the work so far.

In this stage, and drawing on our new relationship requirements, we can now crystallize the aims and objectives we have for the relationship overall. The SPM process connects here as we define the specific time bound targets and goals we want to realize and identify the KPIs needed to support these, ready for subsequent agreement with the supplier. Here we also turn to the

SI&D process as we define the improvements and development roadmap for this supplier.

Finally we bring all of the outputs so far together in final internal SRM strategy, with a roadmap and plan for realizing the strategy ready for the sponsor and key stakeholders to formally agree to proceed with, and actively support the realization of the strategy with the supplier. The SRM strategy is a key document and step within the SCR process and is expanded more fully below.

Stage 4: Accomplish

Stage 4 is about accomplishing the SRM strategy internally and with the supplier and so realizing our ambition for the relationship. This process starts with internal communication by ensuring all involved or who have contact with the supplier are aware of, and aligned with, the agreed plans for this supplier relationship. The interface map of 'who engages with whom' is updated to reflect the 'to be' relationship and new rules of engagement are defined and agreed with the business. It is essential that these two steps are not imposed but rather seek to involve those concerned so they understand and appreciate the plans for the supplier relationship and hopefully pledge support here. The other internal activity supports SPM and is to put in place the necessary measurement regime for our KPIs, including any ongoing data collection, analysis and output arrangements needed.

It is at this point where the full engagement with the supplier begins. So far what we need and want from the relationship has been determined internally, with any supplier involvement deliberately limited. However, now we can offer our proposed plans to the supplier for discussion, debate, adjustment, enhancement and hopefully agreement. It could be argued that it might be better to involve the supplier earlier in the SCR process; however, by taking the time to analyse, consider and plan what we believe we need and want internally first we ensure our ambition for the relationship is clear and unbiased. It is however essential not to attempt to impose our plans on the supplier, especially if we seek a collaborative relationship, but rather to use these as the basis from which to build and be prepared to change and adapt as appropriate. Supplier engagement starts by agreeing our code of conduct for the engagement and then specific relationship aims, our KPIs and scorecard and the STPDR improvement and development plans. We need to agree governance for the relationship; how we will work and interact together including how we will review the relationship, how often, what we will discuss, key roles and responsibilities and so on. Our relationship and the way we will engage and work together is then embodied in a *Relationship Charter* that becomes a key component of the overall document once parties sign up to it.

It is now that joint working with the supplier begins, requiring investment and time by parties to make this happen. This step should be regarded in the same way as the formation of any new team where a high-performance output is needed. Team building and time for social interaction are essential enablers here. In addition, establishing a programme of joint workshops, or opportunities to interact and share resources, will enable real traction towards desired targets and goals. If these involve finding innovation then we can kick off a programme of working towards this using the FIFI approach, covered in the next chapter.

Stage 5: Advance

Stage 5 is about advancing towards targets and goals and realizing the ambition for the relationship in practice. We apply the supplier management process ongoing as we would for any important supplier to monitor, manage and maintain all aspects of risk, contracts and relationship and to manage the supplier within the governance we have agreed with them in stage 4. We also apply the *supplier review* process but specifically in line with the way we have agreed this will work with the supplier.

At this point in the evolution of our strategic relationship we have moved into a phase of ongoing engagement and progression. It should not be regarded as 'steady state' but rather, as the stage name suggests, ongoing advancement. Key to this is ensuring ongoing joint working, resource sharing and interaction and progress towards innovation projects. In any relationship these activities can easily slip or be deprioritized and so good ongoing project management and governance are essential to ensure the relationship is kept front and centre by all involved.

Finally once a strategic collaborative relationship has been established and is effective, it doesn't follow that such a relationship will continue to work this way, or indeed will continue to be needed. Things change and we need to be prepared for this and identify when it is necessary to intervene or change the relationship. In practice this is about the Supplier Relationship Manager keeping a 'watchful eye' on what is happening all around; what the supplier is doing, what is happening in the market and the changing needs of the business. It is also about ongoing testing, if the relationship continues to work and be appropriate, as it is possible we could reach a point where such a close and collaborative relationship ceases to be so necessary. For example, if we have instigated a strategic relationship because we are completely dependent upon the supplier but a shift in the market opens up new possibilities for us then the need for a strategic relationship could become diluted suggesting we can either reappraise the importance of the supplier, renegotiate our agreement or simply bring the relationship to an end.

Developing the SRM strategy

The SRM strategy is an internal document that defines our ambition for a specific supplier relationship and the means and approach by which we propose to realize this. It encapsulates all key insights and outputs from the first three stages of the SCR process and provides a key decision point at the end of stage 3 for the business to either agree to, and support implementing, the strategy. Developing an SRM strategy for a supplier relationship serves several purposes:

- A basis for agreement and therefore a basis to secure resources and support to progress to develop the relationship.
- A basis for internal communication.
- A means for internal knowledge sharing.
- A catalogue of all the work done to analyse and understand the relationship and basis for the relationship.
- A basis to demonstrate a structured, transparent and rigorous approach to a supplier relationship.

The extent and content of an SRM strategy depends upon the relationship, the supplier and the circumstances. Every situation is unique so every strategy will be unique also depending upon what is needed to fulfil the points above. The SRM strategy should therefore be designed with the purpose in mind. If securing internal resources and buy-in is of primary concern, then the strategy should sell benefits and present a clear and compelling business case. If the need is to document work done then the document might be structured so to do this. Figure 13.7 gives a typical SRM strategy structure with typical or possible sections and content.

FIGURE 13.7   Typical sections and content for an SRM strategy document

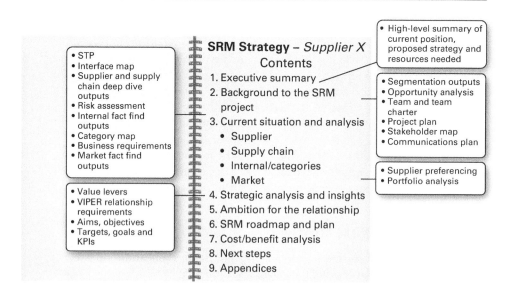

SRM strategies require time and effort to compile and are therefore most relevant where intervention is most needed, where we need clarity about how we need to manage a relationship and where we need to secure buy-in and investment to do this. SRM strategies are therefore most relevant for suppliers we have identified as strategic, but could equally be used for other important suppliers as needed or appropriate.

An SRM strategy will typically deal with commercially sensitive information as well as true intention for a relationship that we would not wish the supplier to know. SRM strategies should therefore be considered highly confidential with a very limited circulation internally and strictly not for sharing with the supplier. Whilst we may be advocating a close collaborative relationship of sharing and joint working, it still remains a commercial relationship with a degree of 'arm's length' necessary, so we should never completely reveal our position or thinking; the supplier will be doing the very same.

The strategy is a key supplier-specific document, and forms part of a number of documents we might need to create and maintain for each important relationship. We explored the other components in Chapter 11 and the degree to which these are relevant or necessary depends upon how important the supplier is. Figure 13.8 shows the different components and their applicability according to importance.

International standards for SCRs – ISO11000/BS11000

Before we leave this chapter we need to cover off international standards in this area. There is in fact a British Standard BS11000 for *collaborative business relationships*, which will become the international standard ISO11000. The standard is designed to help firms avoid the pitfalls of partnership through investing in collaborative business relationships. It provides a framework for all the things that an organization needs to put in place, defines roles and responsibilities and maps out how to make collaborative decision making a reality. Furthermore, companies wishing to adopt such a framework can also obtain certification to the standard by a recognized accreditation body.

It is perhaps curious that there should be the need for such a standard, after all success in important inter-firm engagements depends upon how good the relationship is. Having a standard for how a relationship must work feels somewhat odd and misses the point of what a relationship is and how it should be developed. Yet it could be argued that if firms were about to develop effective inter-organization collaboration then there would be a vast array of knowledge and success stories out there for us all to learn from, and there are not; these are hard to find. So perhaps an international standard can help stage manage the process.

FIGURE 13.8 Different components of a supplier relationship by importance

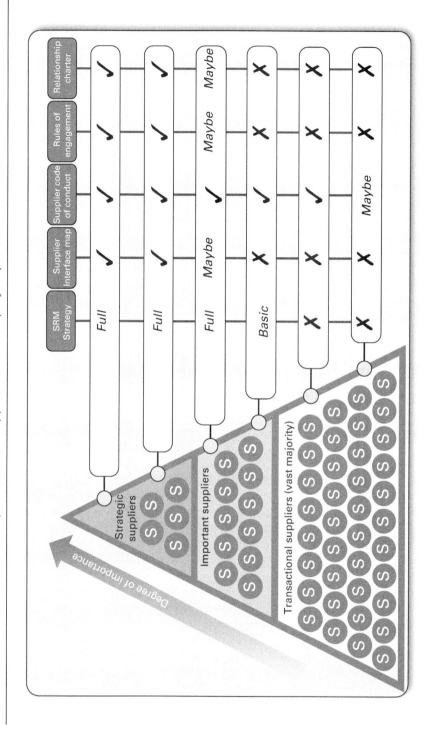

I have included a section on this standard as it is relevant and may be a consideration for any company embarking on an SRM approach. Obtaining certification to this standard will not bring about an SRM approach, that requires all of the things I have outlined in this book to be in place, but it will provide a framework that helps realize part of this and provides a badge that is visible to the outside world of the firm's commitment and ways of working here. That said there are a number of points for any firm serious about obtaining certification to ISO11000/BS11000 to consider and be cognisant of, if this is part of developing an effective overall SRM programme:

- The standard assumes you know who you need a collaborative relationship with, furthermore the segmentation approach within the standard omits factors such as importance or dependency, which are essential determinants for a key supplier relationship.
- As for any international standard, interpretation of the aspirational requirements into practical steps is required.
- The standard is framed around developing new collaborative relationships from scratch, but in practice a firm will have a mix of new and existing relationships that need to be provided for.
- It assumes a Western culture.
- The crucial linkage to category management is not included.
- The framework outlined is linear and procedural and in practice implementing collaborative relationships may not work this way.

So ISO11000/BS11000 has its place and provides a basis for establishing and improving collaborative relationships, but it is only part of a wider SRM strategy. If the goal of the organization is to achieve an internationally recognized standard for collaborative relationships with strategic suppliers then using the framework of BS11000 is entirely appropriate. The orchestra of SRM, the SCR process and other processes outlined within this book are not alternatives to ISO11000/BS11000 but an entirely complementary approach.

Innovation from suppliers

This chapter explores how innovation from suppliers and the supply chain can add value to our business. The nature of innovation and how it typically happens are explored and a structured approach to elicit specific supply base innovation is outlined.

PATHWAY QUESTIONS ADDRESSED IN THIS CHAPTER

14 What innovation do we need from our supply base and how are we going to get it?

15 Which of our important suppliers hold the potential to make a dramatic difference to our business and why?

'Let's go get innovation from those suppliers!'

Our suppliers and the wider supply base represent a powerful source of innovation that holds the potential to add great value to our business, enable business growth and can help us develop competitive advantage. We explored this at the start of this book; innovation is right up there in the VIPER hierarchy!

The opportunity here is increasingly being recognized as organizations strive to compete and make it in our ever-changing environment.

I have heard senior individuals in business say things like 'let's go get innovation from those suppliers', delivered with an expectation that the business will respond by going to make this happen somehow. It's a nice idea, and why not if the benefits are so worthwhile? However, *getting* innovation is not that easy – it is not like some magic fairy dust we can just sprinkle over our business and watch things change, in fact actually securing valuable innovation from suppliers is incredibly difficult, otherwise everyone would be doing it and everyone would be benefiting from it, so if we can figure out how to make it happen it has the potential to transform everything and gain an edge over the competition.

Supplier and supply base innovation can come from any supplier; however, it tends to be more polarized towards the top of our segmentation pyramid. Generally the more potential the innovation holds and the more collaborative the actions to secure it are, the more strategic the supplier.

Types of supplier innovation

Innovation is often billed alongside words such as 'inspiration', 'eureka', 'creative', 'game changing' and even 'magical', reflecting how some ideas for something new tend to appear. We revere the pilots of innovation as individuals who hold some sort of special ability, citing serial innovators such as Walt Disney as examples. This mindset is dangerous and risks seeing innovation as a unique and specialized process accessible only to a few. This is in fact not the case and without wishing to detract from the brilliance of the many innovators that have gone before, it is important to understand that innovation has a process behind it, no matter how naturally and instinctively certain individuals may appear to be operating when creating it. Stewart (2007) suggests 'Conceptual innovators tend to have a knack for simplifying problems, which they may solve by synthesizing old ideas in ways that no one had thought of before. They're often inspired by works from the past, sometimes borrowing from them, as Disney did in many movies and as Eliot did in citations he sprinkled through many poems, They tend to come up with bold new ideas and make plans to achieve them, which lets them delegate work to assistants, as Disney did with artists starting in the 1920s, as Warhol did with assistants in the 1960s, and as Gates has done since founding Microsoft.' Those who innovate follow different processes based upon what has been found to be successful. Disney is reputed to have used three different rooms within his 'Imagineering' process where he and his team would attempt to identify the next big thing, each room serving a different purpose and providing a different perceptual position in the creative process.

In the context of innovation from our suppliers and supply base then a process and structured approach could happen, but there is one key difference. Disney was focused and motivated by his goal to 'make people happy' and build an empire on the back of this so the process to innovation became a natural enabler and the desire to make it a success was a given. Things are different with a supplier. If their motivation is different to ours then any process for innovation becomes pointless. Therefore supply base innovation

FIGURE 14.1   The different types of supplier innovation according to how the supplier is motivated and how innovation is made available

demands the supplier to be motivated, either to provide to us or to work jointly, with a common goal. There are two dimensions to how this innovation happens in practice – how it is offered and the motivation to make it happen. A supplier could offer innovation only to us or could offer it widely to all, for example a new product being released onto a market. Furthermore the impetus for innovation could be driven solely by the supplier, motivated by their goals and ambition, or could be driven jointly if we are both motivated to achieve a mutually beneficial goal (Figure 14.1). Note that there is no mention of 'innovation driven by us' as there is, in practice, no such thing. If we instruct a supplier to innovate they may well produce something as they are being paid to do so, but *real* innovation, involving sharing the most precious of ideas and inspiration, will only flow if they believe this beneficial to them, in which case they will be jointly motivated anyway.

It also follows that a traditional 'arm's length' supplier relationship where the supplier is subordinate and required to do what they are contracted to do does not lend itself to innovation. Instead an entirely different relationship is needed and one that is more *two way* with mutual benefit. It doesn't follow that we hold the power to pick and chose who we want to innovate for or with us. Indeed history is full of small entrepreneurial niche companies who have developed a unique product, technology or service that has been quickly spotted by the big companies. In such a scenario we could find ourselves having to sell ourselves in competition with others as the right company to partner with, offering firm and attractive proposals or even having to acquire the business to secure what it is they have to offer.

Motivation is key. When motivated, parties will make the effort for joint working, which is a crucial enabler here. Furthermore, motivation requires a level of strategic commitment and intervention by both parties. Of all the companies who have mastered this, possibly the most notable is Apple who set in motion a deliberate and systematic approach to find the best suppliers and work with them to shape and develop the products we see today, which have transformed the way many on this planet live, work and interact.

Understanding the different types of innovation helps us begin to create a more structured approach to secure the innovation we need. I will explore each dimension in turn.

Supplier driven innovation

Supplier driven innovation will come from their business aims and might materialize as a new offering in the marketplace or an enhancement of a current offering. These *new on the market* offerings are often unexpected to the outside world unless there is good reason for the supplier to forward promote, eg Apple raising expectation for future generation of iPhones. Clearly this type of innovation is offered to many, but suppliers also drive innovation to help grow a specific account or open up new routes to market, perhaps identifying something that they can bring to us, that they believe will be of interest to us. Here the supplier driven innovation is uniquely aimed at us. This is how organizations typically expect to find innovation from suppliers and are then disappointed when it doesn't materialize. When suppliers get blamed for failing to innovate or not doing enough to bring new ideas, it is a bit like shouting at a capable child for getting bad grades at school in a particular subject. Yet if the child is uninterested in the particular subject where is their incentive to excel?

I was part of a meeting between a small supplier and a large global company. The supplier was effectively berated for not doing enough to innovate and was informed that they were 'not bringing new ideas'; 'tell us what the next big thing is' they were told. The supplier was somewhat surprised and explained that they would like nothing more than to have these discussions as there was much they could share but the relationship wasn't set up in a way that allowed them to do this. They said that they were kept at arm's length, meetings happened only when requested by the big company, on their terms, and then they had to travel to these and attend entirely at their own significant cost and when they did meet the only objective the procurement individuals seemed to have was to get something more without having to pay for it. There was very little opportunity or incentive for the small supplier to add any more value, in fact they were positively prevented from doing so.

Similarly a supplier needs to be interested enough in us to want to share innovation with us or specifically develop something for us, so if suppliers are not being forthcoming it doesn't necessarily follow that they are not able to innovate. Indeed supplier's livelihoods and future success depend upon them being able to not only stay in the game but find the next great thing they can develop into. Some may be better at this than others, but nevertheless innovation is out there and the supply base is typically home to incredible engines of innovation. The challenge is that this will often be hidden and will stay hidden without the right environment for innovation to flourish and flow in our direction and not that of our competitors.

Suppliers can be expected to be selective about what, how and with whom they share details of new developments. Revealing something that could change the game and provide a new competitive edge could be like revealing our hand in a game of poker too early; one minute we have something really good, the next minute we have given away our advantage to opponents who can of course use the knowledge to their advantage, leaving us out of the game. Similarly suppliers will seek to be protective about their innovations unless and until they feel confident enough to play their hand. Confidence means the supplier believes the value of their innovation will be taken seriously which is possibly one reason why suppliers will favour relationships with the technical or design staff rather than those in procurement. If the supplier shares their new innovation during a supplier review meeting and it goes no further than a note in a set of minutes then they have wasted their time. Worse if the innovation is welcomed but the supplier is told that they are expected to provide such new developments without any incremental benefit, then they are unlikely to come back a second time. Innovation costs time, money, energy and resources and these are all investments suppliers make in order to create new additional benefit. This means if we are to motivate a supplier we may need to invest in them; this may not necessarily mean an increased price but could be contract extension, increased volumes or greater margin.

Therefore, if a supplier develops something ground-breaking that could add dramatic value to our brand or give us a competitive edge, how can we be sure that supplier will bring that innovation to us and not one of our competitors? There are in fact a number of factors that can prevent a supplier from offering innovation. These are given in Table 14.1. There are also factors that can encourage and motivate a supplier to innovate, these are: *Reason* (to innovate), *Realization* (of the idea), *Reward* and *Risk*, also given in Table 14.1. Understanding these can help us begin to find and create the right conditions for innovation, shifting away from supplier driven innovation to jointly driven innovation.

TABLE 14.1 Factors that prevent and encourage supplier innovation

Factor	Prevent	Encourage
Reason	• No perceived alignment of their innovation with our business and how they understand our future direction.	• Clear alignment of their innovation with our business, wider corporate goals and future direction.
Realization	• Lack of traction – perceived inability to turn the innovation into reality. If the supplier is to share their next big thing exclusively with us they need to be confident we will do something with it. • Supplier believes we are unable to collaborate with them.	• Route to market – we hold the ability to enable the supplier to realize the potential of their idea through our route to market or distribution channels or unique ability to connect with certain customers. • Track record of implementation – we offer and can demonstrate the ability to turn ideas into action.
Reward	• Expectations to innovate for no or little incremental return. • Failure to appreciate the value of the idea.	• Willingness to create an engagement model that allows both parties to benefit.
Risk	• Risk of theft of idea or Intellectual Property. • Risk of indiscretion.	• Confidence in the value and ownership of the idea being preserved.

Jointly driven innovation

Jointly driven innovation is where we work with a supplier to help them innovate in a particular direction that we agree together, creating the incentives and providing support to do this.

If we work to help the supplier improve their capability or a particular offering then we are helping them innovate for the *greater good*. Arguably this works against us as we could be helping the supplier help our competitors;

however, unless there is a specific commercial risk, helping a supplier to develop can build a relationship, reduce risk and foster joint working in other areas that might benefit us. There are times when investing in developing a supplier will help us longer term.

The most effective type of supplier innovation is that which is driven jointly but is exclusive to us and it is through this that we can unlock great *competitive advantage*. To make this happen we use the FIFI innovation process.

FIFI can help find innovation

It is unlikely that innovation will happen by itself, and even if it does it is then more unlikely it will resonate with what is helpful to us. Therefore, if we need innovation from the supply base (as identify during segmentation), then we need to make it happen. FIFI provides a process to secure and realize innovation from suppliers and a wider supply base (Figure 14.2) and is suitable where both parties are motivated to innovate. I will explore each step in turn.

FIGURE 14.2 The FIFI innovation process

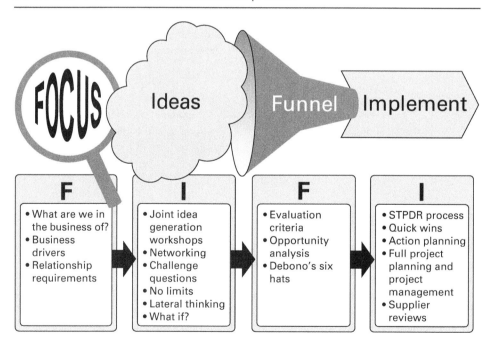

Focus *for innovation*

> The telephone is so important that, one day, every town will have one.
> Alexander Graham Bell, 1876 (quote inscribed on the inside cover of the
> first ever telephone engineer's installation and service manual.)

The first question here is *what are we trying to achieve?* Innovation without
focus, purpose or alignment will be random and somewhat 'hit and miss'.
Focus needs to be defined jointly as this is part of ensuring parties are motivated
and clear about the mountain that is to be climbed together.

Our focus for innovation should resonate with our corporate strategy;
driven by what the organization is aiming to achieve (we explored this in
Chapter 3). However, there is big health warning here, because aims flow
from corporate strategy informed by the organizational belief of what it is and
the nature of what the business will be in the future. If this belief, as shaped
by the senior team, is misaligned or limited, corporate strategy will be limited,
aims will be limited and so any focus for innovation will also be limited.

Advancements in aviation as part of World War II enabled new large passenger aircraft to be built, transforming global travel post war and bringing
the 'golden age' of the ocean liner to an end as well as heralding the decline
of the ocean liner companies. Obvious perhaps, but only with a mindset that
an ocean liner company is in the business of operating ocean liners. Perhaps
it is this very mindset that is responsible for the decline back then because if
the mindset had been 'we're in the business of moving people from one place
to another' then things may have been different. This is an important point
for focus because how we see the aim that frames our focus can make all the
difference. History is littered with many examples of how a constricted
mindset has limited potential. Bill Gates and Steve Jobs built their respective
global empires on the back of Xerox's inability to commercialize the world's
first personal computer and graphical user interface developed at its Palo
Alto Research Centre in the early 70s. Why did this happen? Johnson *et al*
(2008) suggest the problem was down to the wrong value focus – 'a disconnect
between the perceived sources of value of Xerox as an established copier
company, and Xerox as a feisty innovator of what the 1970 CEO, Peter
McColough, called the "architecture of information"'. In other words Xerox
believed the future value of its business lay elsewhere.

Focus for innovation is therefore about framing the areas where we want
something to happen and defining what we want to get from it. The components of focus are:

- *What are we in the business of doing?* Reduced to base principles:
  'we are in the business of moving people from one place to another"
  not "we are an ocean liner company".'
- *What are the business drivers?* How corporate strategy is driving our
  actions and might include new markets, new products/services, brand
  development, cost reduction or sustainability.
- *What are the relationship requirements?* Identified during the
  segmentation process using the VIPER framework.

Finding breakthrough ideas

InnovationMain.com suggest that before innovation you need creativity, then ideas and from these innovation follows. With a clear focus we can move to the creative process and generation of ideas, and the more the better so we increase the likelihood of finding amongst them the one or two game changers. This is perhaps the part of the process that appears to be cloaked in mystery, but with the right conditions, team and approach it can be more methodical than mystical.

Mark Twain once said:

> There is no such thing as a new idea. It is impossible. We simply take a lot of old ideas and put them into a sort of mental kaleidoscope. We give them a turn and they make new and curious combinations. We keep on turning and making new combinations indefinitely; but they are the same old pieces of colored glass that have been in use through all the ages.

Ideas breed ideas.

It is dangerous to view idea generation as a search for a breakthrough idea that will change the world. Very occasionally a 'eureka moment' might happen but these are in fact very rare (Johnson, 2011); instead innovation tends to happens more incrementally, fuelled by a series of ideas along the way that spark a change in direction. Whilst Thomas Edison is often credited with inventing the electric light bulb, he actually invented the first commercially practical light bulb. In fact this invention was no eureka moment, it took years. In 1870 Thomas Edison was the talk of his small New Jersey town because of his many failed experiments to invent an electric light bulb. When asked by a journalist 'Mr Edison, how does it feel to have failed 500 times? Why don't you give up?' he replied 'No, no, young lady, I haven't failed 500 times. I have just discovered 500 ways it won't work. I am so much closer now to finding a way that will work.' Therefore, in the context of supply base innovation, there may be a eureka moment waiting to happen, but most likely the innovation that could help us will be the output of a hard and resource intensive effort to find something. Creativity and ideas come from people. People who have a particular ability to see things in different ways; who can take inspiration from something they see, hear or experience and draw parallels with an unrelated problem or area and see something new; such individuals can help here if they are on the team. But what about the rest of us? It is easy to assume that innovation within organizations comes only from a small number of bright or special individuals within marketing or the R&D function, or those with responsibility for business growth. The reality is brilliant innovation grows from many sources of inspiration and then the rest is about making it a reality. Designers, architects, creators, marketers will therefore draw on the influences they encounter informed by knowledge of what is or might be possible and one of the most potent catalysts and contributors are suppliers; all working on the next thing in their respective fields of expertise. The right people to help innovate on both sides is of course those with some sort of 'creative' ability but is more about how they, and others connect and network, I'll return to this point later in this chapter.

People alone are not enough, we also need an environment that allows their ideas to flow. Organizations are generally particularly good at stifling new ideas; often the same organizations that are desperate for something new. Ideas flow when the right people come together and who are then sufficiently relaxed and eager to think of something new. We therefore need to create the right conditions that allow this. Ideally our entire organization and that of the supplier will be set up to create the right conditions for creativity; stories about such companies make exciting reading in business press. Mood rooms, bright coloured walls, meeting rooms filled with bean bags, full team holidays to exotic locations, wheel your desk where you want and so on. To the uninitiated such things in the workplace can seem silly or a waste of time that detracts from the real work, but to those who understand the creative process these crazy ideas are perfect and serve real purpose of creating the conditions for idea generation. So physical environment helps idea generation, but so too does the culture of the business and the behaviours of the senior team. If creative sessions are regarded as 'warm and fluffy' or 'the sort of thing Marketing does' as if it is not real work, then the culture is disabling idea generation. If the senior team encourage crazy practices to facilitate creativity then the right conditions emerge.

Eagerness to volunteer ideas also comes by feeling any idea will be well received and valued. Eagerness also needs permission to be given. Through the various creative brainstorming sessions I have run, I have noticed that people don't tend to contribute until they have been given permission to do so; to think the absurd. It seems, in life and work, we are very good at following rules, policies, social norms and we are conditioned to accept what has gone before. Creative sessions therefore need work up front to provide permission but their importance also needs to be embraced. There are a number of things that both stifle idea generation and help it.

Things that stifle idea generation include:

- wrong framing focus;
- closed-mindedness;
- following what has gone before;
- no permission to dream the dream;
- management behaving as if creativity is a bit silly;
- risk ideas will not be well received;
- assuming the customer knows what they want – as Henry Ford said, 'If I had asked people what they wanted they would have said faster horses.';
- Trying to change the world from behind a desk – instead ideas are sparked by networking and social interaction.

What makes ideas happen?

- Physical environment conducive to idea generation.
- Give permission to dream the dream.
- Social interaction and networking.
- Absurdity.
- Culture of 'no idea a bad idea'.

Where an organization doesn't have a 'mood room' or is not organized for creativity, this doesn't mean it can't happen, it just means we need to create the right conditions for it. This is straightforward and is about running a series of workshops that are set up in such a way to put people at ease, give permission to think differently and then use a series of techniques to get ideas flowing.

In practice, successful idea generation is about thinking the unthinkable, removing limits and boundaries and making the absurd and impossible redundant. It is through the absurd ideas that the game changers get heard. Some years ago, when having an internet presence was a new thing for companies, I worked with a company trying to improve how it responded to customer queries. Historically the company would go and visit the customer, but most of the visits were actually unnecessary. In a 'no limits' idea brainstorming session the absurd ideas were plentiful and one idea, 'teleport customer service representatives into peoples homes to help them', ruminated around the team then someone else said, 'have a virtual help assistant online to answer questions there and then'. This idea was subsequently implemented and became a great success. Online assistants are commonplace today, but back then the idea was breakthrough.

So idea generation needs the right people, a conducive environment, no-limits thinking and can be breakthrough but is more likely to be incremental. Idea generation also needs something to help elicit ideas. There are a range of techniques out there that can help here and I've included a panel in this section with some of these. Idea generation can come from individuals with the right mindset; perhaps we can all identify with those things that appear in our minds whilst in the shower or driving alone, but we can also attempt to channel idea generation with the supplier by running joint innovation workshops. The purpose of such workshops, with a willing and motivated supplier, is to get the right people together and create the right environment to try and identify innovation opportunities.

Five ways to generate new ideas

Each of these can be adopted by an individual or can be used within a group to help frame different group idea generation activities. If used in a group rules of brainstorming apply (everyone silent – ideas only, no discussion or debate, no idea a bad idea, facilitator flips charts exactly as said; continues until two minutes silence elapses).

1 *Networking* – the more you connect with others and discuss what you are trying to do, the more they will make connections about ways that might help you.

2 *Challenge questions* – why is it done that way, how do others do it, why do we need it at all?

3 *No limits* – remove the limits, start again and ask 'If we could do anything what would we do?' Works best in a group brainstorming session starting with this open question and allowing free flow idea generation.

4 *Lateral thinking* – connecting unrelated things together. Air conditioning was inspired in 1902 when Willis Carrier sat waiting for a train and watched fog roll in across the platform and that gave him the idea to cool buildings in a similar way (Johnson, 2011). It is easy to assume this is just something certain individuals can do, but lateral thinking is accessible by all by looking at the area in question, the product, service, process, what you see and so on, and asking 'what else does this' or 'where else can I see something like this'.

5 *What if?* Change something, add something, subtract something and see what you are left with then ask, 'What if it looked like this?'. Don't be constrained by what exists today, instead throw absurd ideas around, ideally in a group, as these might spark something new. For example, the question 'what if we added a fourth blue traffic light?' might seem absurd but it might also spark inspiration in someone hearing this. Works well in group brainstorming sessions.

The most valuable supply chain innovations therefore tend to arise from a well-chosen design team, aligned with corporate goals and goals that are mutually beneficial to parties involved, and one that extends beyond the organization to include all parties who have something to offer and can help change the game including certain, well-chosen suppliers. This team becomes more a *network of players* than a traditional group of individuals working together and suppliers are essential contributors within this network. It is this *network of players* concept that provides the real power to enable supplier and supply chain innovation involving key suppliers who will work together to change the game. We will come back to this concept later.

The innovation funnel – no idea a bad idea!
Well actually...

If idea generation is about being absurd and 'anything goes' in order to spark creative thinking to find that one idea that could make a difference, the problem comes in then figuring out what to go forward with. Those that hold potential and could be realized will most likely lie buried amongst the multitude of ideas. The funnel is a process of filtering out those we cannot use (eg the absurd ideas that sparked something more workable) and selecting ideas to progress.

As individuals we naturally filter ideas, subconsciously matching them against our beliefs and value. That means as individuals there is a risk we reject ideas that do not resonate with how we see the world. Perhaps this is why, following an audition in 1962, a senior executive at Decca Records famously said, 'The Beatles have no future in show business', and promptly rejected them.

The process of funnelling ideas therefore needs to be more systematic to avoid bias and prejudice from our internal filters. There are many ways to do this but typically this happens by applying a set of evaluation criteria, gauging the scale of the opportunity and the ability to realize the idea in practical terms but also by looking at the idea in different ways (Figure 14.3). Our process to evaluate ideas should ideally be developed ahead of the process of idea generation in order to completely eliminate bias. We could make a long list of factors to build into our criteria; evaluation against goals, degree to which it will help build a brand or grow market share and so on. However, we have actually done this already when we identified our business and relationship requirements (RAQSCI and VIPER) at both a high level and at a category and supplier-specific level, informed by the segmentation process. From these we can extract our evaluation criteria and we can funnel ideas based upon what we need and want from the supplier and the goods and services they provide. For example, if we need to improve effectiveness from a supplier then we filter ideas based upon the degree to which an idea might deliver this. In practice, within an idea generating workshop we might end up with many pages of flip chart ideas papering the walls and so a first pass evaluation might simply be a case of a team going through all the outputs and putting a tick by the top five ideas that would generate effectiveness. This technique can be applied multiple times using different criteria to create different shortlists.

With a shortlist of ideas the opportunity analysis tool provides a good second pass idea generation approach, allowing each idea to be assessed in terms of degree of benefit, ie the degree to which the objectives from the business and relationship requirements are met and the ease of implementation, ie internal or joint difficulty, cost, resources etc.

Finally, and also with a further shortlist of ideas, it can help to try to examine the idea in different ways or to 'stress test it' in order to be certain

FIGURE 14.3 How ideas can be filtered during the 'funnel' stage

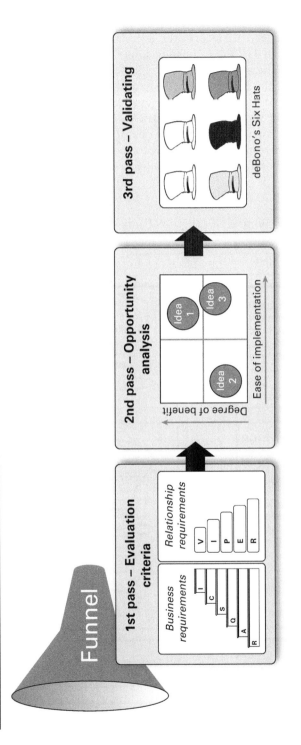

it is worth pursuing. This is an important step within a creative process as so far our funnel approach has operated entirely logically and sometimes this logic can lead us incorrectly, especially if our original requirements might be slightly lacking or missing something. There are different ways to achieve this. Edward DeBono's Six Hats (de Bono, 1985) is a tool that can be used in a group to enable the group to think more effectively by planning thinking processes and deliberately challenging the ways the brain thinks. These thinking styles can be applied to evaluating ideas and essentially involves the group putting on a series of different coloured hats in turn (either literally or metaphorically) with each representing a different thinking style the group must adopt when wearing the hat (Figure 14.4).

FIGURE 14.4   Edward de Bono's six thinking hats, adapted from de Bono (1985)

Information

White Hat

Evaluate the idea based upon only information, facts and data. This includes evaluation criteria based upon requirements and opportunity analysis

Optimistic

Yellow Hat

Consider the idea purely according to the benefits it will deliver, focus on the upsides and the harmony it will bring

Feelings

Red Hat

Use intuitive or instinctive gut reactions to consider the idea. State the emotions the idea triggers but with no need to justify them

Creativity

Green Hat

Be creative about the idea, put forward suggestions, alternatives, ideas to bring it to life. Think about growth and how the idea could build.

Caution

Black Hat

What are the risks? Think of reasons why the idea won't work

Meta or process

Blue Hat

Decide what we should do next. Consider what has been achieved and what the process steps are.

De Bono's six hats is a fascinating and very helpful approach that I've seen generate powerful results. Further reading is recommended here and there are various books on the subject and also training in applying the technique through deBono's website and franchised providers.

Implementation: bringing ideas to life

> Genius is one percent inspiration and ninety nine percent perspiration.
>
> (Thomas Eddison, c1903)

Great ideas are worthless unless we can turn them into action, and if it seemed that generating ideas was hard enough, implementing them is even harder. There are many approaches we can adopt here, ranging from simple action planning to full project management. Effective change management, stakeholder engagement and communications become essential. The STPDR improvement process provides a suitable framework to support implementation and progression should form part of supplier reviews. There may be quick wins we can realize with minimal effort or implementation may require full project planning and management.

Networking: a key enabler for innovation

Networking is a fundamental enabler for idea generation and indeed innovation as a whole yet the value of networking is easily underestimated and rarely supported. Networking can help individuals to build connections, can help companies innovate and help suppliers provide more innovation, especially when working jointly.

Six degrees of separation

The Hungarian author, playwright, poet and journalist Frigyes Karinthy suggested the concept of 'six degrees of separation' in his 1929 story *Chains*, whereby in theory we can link ourselves to any other individual on the planet through just six, or fewer, people. It is interesting to see how many steps removed we might be from the US President or a famous celebrity; however, instead if we focus on how individuals are linked or 'tied' together then this can help us figure out how to direct relationship building efforts and the benefit possible. Granovetter (1983) described what he called the strength of 'weak ties' between individuals. As the Facebook trend took hold some years ago now, I soon found myself wanting to differentiate between who I shared what with, some posts were simply too personal to share with all. Thankfully Facebook later introduced the ability to personalize settings with family, friends, acquaintances or public options for posts. The reality is we may have lots of close friends and have a number of acquaintances.

However, beyond Facebook it is these acquaintances that can offer potential, after all these each have lots of close friends and their acquaintances too. It is these 'weak ties' as Granovetter (1983) describes that are 'indispensible to individuals opportunity and integration into the community'. He states that 'strong ties breed local cohesion but lead to overall fragmentation'. So it seems we are more connected than we might realize. This can often be seen in action, especially since the birth of social media, where 'knowing someone who knows someone' can help solve a problem, open up an opportunity or has access to the precise thing we might need. Remember, companies don't have relationships with companies, it is the individuals in those companies that have relationships with other individuals, therefore, following Granovetter's idea through, if we can understand the weak ties as well as the strong ties in a relationship then we can begin to make the relationship really work for us. For example, imagine a supplier relationship founded upon the interpersonal relationship between two individuals, one on each side. This relationship may be close and ensure transactions run smoothly, there are effective day-to-day operations and any problems are dealt with quickly. However, if the extent of the relationship only ever goes this far then the relationship will be limited by what those individuals can bring to it, but if one party has a goal, and the other knows someone in the firm who knows something or someone then powerful connections are made that can be the spark for great things. Imagine the conversation between the principles of the relationship:

Buyer: 'So we think if we can find a way for customers to do this online it will make the whole process much easier, but we need to figure out how to do this.'

Seller: 'That's interesting as I was talking to one of our IT guys recently who said he was talking to an App development company who offered a customizable solution that I think does just what you need here.'

Buyer: 'Can you find out more?'

Seller: 'Why don't I get you guys connected, it is in both our interests to do this?'

Perhaps you might recognize this sort of exchange, as such exchanges are commonplace but it is easy for these to just pass us by, but they are actually very important. This type of networking, that uses connections presented by the weak ties, has unlimited possibilities; after all, if Karinthy is correct, we are just six or fewer steps away from anything, anyone, any knowledge, expertise or capability on the planet. That can really build competitive advantage if we can figure out how to access it, and that is actually not that difficult. Within our relationships with suppliers, if there is a willingness by the other party to help, and we share a need, they will make connections that might help us. Willingness comes from trust and commitment; furthermore the actual effort the other party expands here is minimal. All that is happening here is we are planting our interest in the mind of another and leaving their brain to make connections that will help us, opening up the weak ties. The reason this is virtually effortless for the other is because our brains are programmed to do this; we all naturally filter out the vast majority of information we take in apart from that we are interested in. This can be seen in action when considering buying a particular make or model of a car, suddenly we will be aware of and see lots of these very cars on the road when previously there didn't seem to be or we hadn't noticed. If we can make another interested in our interest they will make connections and may be able to access unlimited possibilities we would otherwise not see.

Social media has really opened up the power of weak ties, sites such as LinkedIn make it even easier for professional people to connect and tap into a network of possibilities. It is, in fact so powerful that this site has become the primary means for recruiters and those looking for particular skills or capabilities to search out what they are looking for.

There is no prescribed way to take advantage of weak ties through supplier relationships, but by being aware of the possibilities we can embark on active networking through the supplier relationship and beyond. In practice this involves communicating, sharing needs and aspirations, casting a wide net in asking for ideas and input. Crucially it involves following up on connections that are made. If a weak tie that might hold potential is opened up and we fail to follow it through then it is worthless.

How Starbucks is a hothouse of modern networking

Environment is important to foster innovation. Visit any Starbucks that has a seating area during a working day and most likely you will see individual and groups, sat with laptops, on phones, with papers spread across tables and of course coffee. Starbucks and other coffee houses have become modern business hubs where people who work remotely, but don't want to sit at home, can operate. JK Rowling famously wrote much of the early Harry Potter books sat in one of the coffee houses in Edinburgh, because, she claimed, it provided an opportunity to take her baby out for a walk so she would fall asleep (Rowling, 2001). One of the by-products of this modern coffee shop working is that people from different businesses begin to interact and talk and sometimes through these discussions a connection is made. Starbucks is in fact a modern hot house of idea generation, and this is not new but in the early 1700s the growth of the coffee houses provided a new forum for men to talk and swap ideas. In fact this casual gathering of like-minded coffee drinkers is credited with influencing British political and intellectual life for decades (Pelzer, 1982). Pelzer writes: 'For a penny admission charge, any man who was reasonably dressed could smoke his long, clay pipe, sip a dish of coffee, read the newsletters of the day, or enter into conversation with other patrons.'

Innovation reduces risk

There is one final point on innovation and that is the link to supplier and supply chain risk. Embedded within the process of innovation is the analysis and challenge of what has gone before to create what will be taken forward. This process naturally revisits and reviews how value is created by the supplier and throughout the supply chain and in doing so identifies and addresses risk areas. No self-respecting design team is going to deliver the final proposed innovation without the certainty that it can be realized and all the actions required to implement it have been considered and planned for. Therefore companies that continually innovate tend to have a much better understanding of supply side risk as they are continually reviewing their suppliers and supply chains and so are more connected to what is happening. Indeed the Marsh Report (2008) suggests for the supply chain that 'innovators are a whopping nine times more likely than their peers to have consistent, company-wide supply chain risk management processes'.

The orchestra of SRM is ready to play

15

This chapter describes how to make SRM a reality in an organization that is aligned with corporate objectives and delivers significant value. Arrangements for governance are outlined and we explore how SRM is likely to need to evolve in the future. Finally, all that has been covered in this book so far is brought together to complete our 'orchestra of SRM'.

PATHWAY QUESTIONS ADDRESSED IN THIS CHAPTER

17 Are all our efforts with suppliers coordinated and aligned with our corporate goals?

18 Is corporate strategy informed by supply chain possibilities?

19 Across our organization does everyone know what is expected of them when working with suppliers?

20 Do we have capability, structure and processes we need here? What innovation do we need from our supply base and how are we going to get it?

5P governance

It seems the word 'governance' does not have universal recognition; indeed in the United States the word is not commonplace, yet it is the perfect word to help describe the arrangements needed for SRM. Bevir (2013) describes governance as 'all processes of governing, whether undertaken by a government, market or network, whether over a family, tribe, formal or informal organization or territory and whether through laws, norms, power or language'. That seems to pretty much cover everything. Within SRM governance relates to how the philosophy is realized within the organization; what gets done, the processes that support it, decisions that are taken, how roles and responsibilities are agreed and arrangement to verify performance. In the orchestra of SRM governance ensures the stage is set, that all the seats are set out for all the performers, that the performers are skilled and talented musicians then it ensures there is a single conductor who will make the music happen.

There are five components within governance in, what is, I promise, the last alliterative model in this book: the 5P governance framework (Figure 15.1). These are *people*, *proficiency*, *promote*, *payoff* and *programme* and I will explore each over the next five sections. Governance is not necessarily

FIGURE 15.1 The 5P governance framework

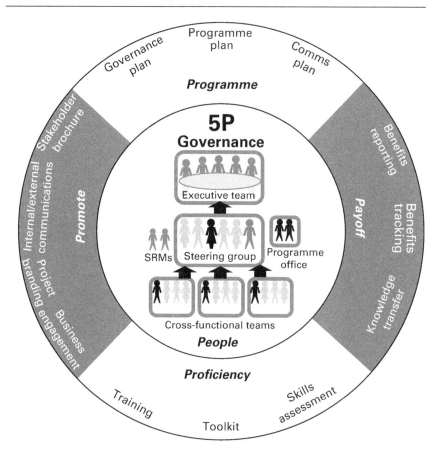

unique to SRM, but rather could support, coordinate and enable multiple strategic initiatives and projects within a purchasing function or indeed across the entire organization. Indeed it is governance that plays a key role in realizing corporate strategy by providing the means to integrate various strategic initiatives including SRM but also including other cross-functional initiatives such as category management, Lean or Six Sigma, CSR projects or any other project that helps realize corporate goals. Therefore governance should be constructed as the enabler for the function not just SRM.

Governance: people

Structure and organizational design

The first component of governance is *people* and is concerned with structure and organizational design. We need the right people, with the right capability doing the right things. SRM, and indeed other strategic purchasing initiatives, may not naturally overlay a traditional hierarchical organizational structure but rather requires a more matrix based way of working that fosters cross-functional teams and groups. This does not necessarily mean a complete organizational redesign, but rather a refocusing of roles or even parts of roles of individuals.

For SRM interventions with important suppliers any structure needs to provide for two things: individuals who need assigned roles and responsibilities to support the various aspects of SM, SCM, SPM, SI&D and cross-functional teams who will champion special projects in some of these areas but especially for SCRs. Here the cross-functional engagement becomes core to the entire project, requiring a cross-functional team to be formed, meet regularly and work towards delivering a specific outcome such as a new collaborative strategic relationship. In fact, cross-functional working lies at the heart of SRM and indeed every other strategic purchasing and business improvement project.

Creating a 'virtual structure' to foster cross-functional working

We need a functional and organizational structure that enables both individual as well as cross-functional, project driven supplier intervention. It would be impractical to structure most organizations around this but it is possible to create a new 'virtual structure' where a series of individuals can come together in a team for a set period of time, meet and work together to deliver a goal (Figure 15.2). These teams would typically be led by someone from purchasing, perhaps the Supplier Relationship Manager for SRM initiatives (described below) but could equally be led from elsewhere in the

FIGURE 15.2   A typical cross-functional team

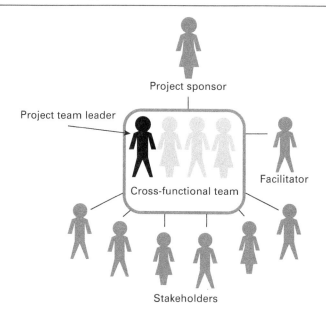

business. Each team requires a sponsor to support the team, ensure resources are available and remove obstacles, and may also demand facilitation support for key meetings. Team members may be core members but could also be extended team members or stakeholders who are involved, consulted or kept informed.

Cross-functional team working sounds an attractive and obvious pursuit for any organization, but embracing it requires commitment from the executive team and then the wider organization to make it happen. If someone from a technical function is to join an SRM team working on a SCR project, then it is likely they will need to step back from their day job but instead be seconded onto the team for a few half days each month until the project is completed. This is quite a commitment and one the business must provide for from the top down, with individual objectives and even incentives supporting this; after all if people are to contribute to a team they need to want to be there and believe there is something in it for them. Incentives could be money, but could equally be personal or career development or just the interest of something different.

At any one time a number of cross-functional teams might be needed, each working on key initiatives. How many and what they work on is a product of availability of resources and organizational priorities. Here good governance is founded on the principle that there is only so much resource and potentially many competing projects and so determines an overarching programme of priority projects and assigns these to cross-functional teams;

FIGURE 15.3   A typical governance structure

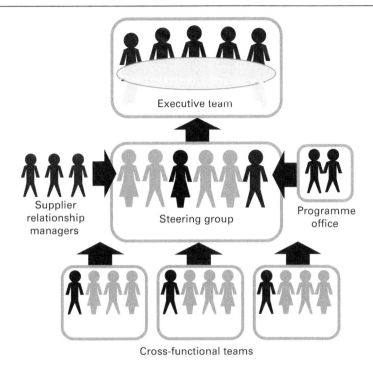

some may work on strategic SRM projects and drive in new collaborative relationships whilst others work on category management or CSR projects. This assignment of resources against opportunities is the backbone that connects corporate strategy to action and intervention and it requires a small steering group and project manager to do this.

The steering group sits at the heart of governance (Figure 15.3) and is the small group of typically senior individuals responsible for coordinating all the components of governance and therefore determining how strategic corporate objectives are met. The role of the steering group is to meet regularly to ensure:

- overall management of all initiatives;
- the required capable resources are available;
- effective communications with the executive team;
- effective and timely performance of all initiatives;
- effective managed communications to the organization and externally; and
- robust governance for SRM and all other strategic initiatives is in place.

There are a number of practical components to this including programme management, benefits tracking and reporting which I shall cover shortly but this suggests the need for some analytical or administrative support as well as a good project manager to support the steering group. This is shown in Figure 15.3 as 'programme office', as a resource separate, but connected to and supporting the steering group. Dedicated resources here may be a luxury, but if governance is to be effective it is essential that these roles are provided for, even if part time.

The supplier relationship manager role

Important suppliers need relationship managers, just like the supplier has an account manager. Great if you can have a separate army dedicated to this, but in practice we have busy jobs and the modern purchasing professional will need to cover many bases.

The supplier relationship manager is the individual who has a specific responsibility to establish and maintain one or more important or strategic supplier relationships. The role of supplier relationship manager may by a dedicated role for an individual, but is more likely to be one of many roles an individual has.

Responsibilities here might include:

- to keep a watchful eye on the market, environment and the changing needs of the business and identify when action is needed in response to any change;
- to maintain a current understanding of all supplier and supply base risk, ensuring ongoing contingency and mitigation actions as appropriate and watching for any changes that might require intervention;
- ongoing supplier management including supplier reviews and ensuring the contract continues to be robust;
- to ensure the ongoing relationship with a supplier is maintained including maintaining an up to date supplier calendar and, where appropriate, an SRM strategy and relationship charter; and
- to maintain KPIs and the measurement system.

And for strategic collaborative relationships:

- to manage a programme of joint working; and
- to lead FIFI innovation projects;.

The supplier relationship manager role requires certain skills and capabilities, and perhaps personality traits in order to be effective. In the perfect world a company implementing SRM would go and recruit a team of individuals perfectly matched to this role. In practice we are more likely to be working with the team we have and developing capability as needed. SRM, and indeed all strategic purchasing initiatives, requires a skill set that is quite a leap on from that of the traditional purchasing buyer and might include:

- Technical and process skills – SRM but also perhaps category management, CSR, Lean etc.
- Project management skills – to implement supplier improvement projects.
- Research skills – to gather and synthesize market, supplier and internal data.
- Facilitation skills – ability to successfully lead cross-functional workshops and joint workshops with suppliers.
- Communications skills – to present complex messages to many and varied stakeholders and secure buy-in.
- Conflict management skills – to deal with difficult suppliers and manage through conflict and challenge with internal stakeholders.
- Advanced negotiation skills – to negotiate deals within complex supplier relationships.
- Leadership skills – to lead and inspire cross-functional teams to work on procurement-led initiatives for the good of the business.

In addition, there are certain characteristics and traits that are particularly relevant and should be born in mind when considering individuals for such a role:

- Ability to build rapport and cultivate good working relationships.
- Confidence to voice concerns confidently (rather than staying silent or just neglecting a relationship).
- For innovation: a mindset to see things differently or challenge why things are done that way.
- Potentially experience of improvement initiatives such as Lean, Six Sigma, Kaizen, TQM etc.

Governance: proficiency

Ensuring the right capability

The second component of governance is *proficiency* and includes ensuring the right capability and supporting resources are in place to delivery SRM and any other strategic purchasing initiative. This involves selecting the right individuals to lead or participate and ensuring those selected are adequately trained and equipped for the job they are required to do. Specific actions led by the steering group might include:

- competency assessment of core team individuals;
- a rolling programme of learning and development to equip those who will lead and participate;

- coaching support along the way from an experienced practitioner; and
- education of the wider business and those who will provide a support role to key initiatives.

Establishing common language and ways of working

The toolkit is the process and supporting tools, techniques, approaches, methodologies and templates for SRM or indeed any initiative. The toolkit for SRM is pretty much laid out in this book. It exists as the third component of governance as it is essential for the organization to establish a common language and common ways of working through a single toolkit and this then needs to be available to all who are involved.

Governance: promote

The third component of governance is *promote* and is concerned with internal and external communication and engagement.

Driving business engagement

Suppliers are managed on behalf of the entire business, therefore our efforts to manager a supplier must be in concert with all the relevant stakeholders in the organization. Business-wide engagement and participation is unlikely to happen by itself but instead needs to be won. Whilst those out in the business, outside of the purchasing function, might see themselves as owning a particular dimension of a supplier relationship, it is perhaps unlikely these stakeholders would believe they have any role to coordinate supplier relationships on behalf of the business to ensure effective management of the supplier. Yet, with an appreciation of the benefits of a unified approach such stakeholders would most likely embrace and support a coordinated approach.

Governance involves purchasing, establishing and actively maintaining deep penetration into the business with ongoing engagement of key stakeholders. It is for purchasing to drive this engagement and to open channels of communication internally. Business engagement is not a once only activity, but, to be effective, purchasing, and those managing suppliers, need to have a regular and ongoing dialogue with those in the business who also have a relationship with the supplier or those interested in which supplies get selected. The purpose of purchasing-led business engagement going forwards is to:

- establish the needs and wants of users and build and maintain business and relationship requirements;

- secure cross-functional involvement to support SM;
- recruit team members to actively participate in cross-functional supplier improvement projects or to establish strategic collaborative relationships with the purpose of securing some new significant benefit;
- share what purchasing are doing to manage suppliers and the goals that are being worked towards as well as what purchasing want from the business to support this;
- share feedback about supplier performance, initiatives and engagements;
- verify and solicit input into business and relationship requirements;
- solicit feedback about specific supplier performance or issues with what they provide/do;
- to ensure complete knowledge and openness about all the points of engagement and communication with a supplier;
- to ensure that those who have relationship with the supplier are 'on message', in other words they are communicating agreed messages designed to condition the supplier and show complete alignment within our business;
- to ensure that when everyone engages with suppliers they are aligned and working towards a common purpose; and
- to educate the business on how to work with and interface with suppliers.

Managing internal communications

Internal communications are frequently forgotten but if done well can make the difference between success and failure of a business initiative. Internal communications enable business engagement, particularly for SRM if the business is to be aligned towards a single cause, prevent a unified front to a supplier and reduce the likelihood of the supplier dividing and conquering. It also helps to ensure that any supplier intervention is aligned towards the entire needs and wants of the business and ultimately corporate strategy. Communication does this by informing, inviting participation and diffusing potential resistance to change. It therefore is essential for SRM and any business initiative.

Within the 5A SCR process internal communication is part of stage 1 *Activate*. Here as the cross-functional team is formed we develop a *stakeholder map* and then a *communication plan* to engage with the business. These two tools allow us to identify *who* we need to engage with and to plan *how* we will do this. It also helps us to then assign specific communication actions and ownership for their delivery. This internal communications activity is specific to establishing a single strategic collaborative relationship.

Within governance, however, the approach is identical, except here we are attempting to communicate with the business, and to solicit their involvement and support, at a high level for all of the initiatives and the overall goals of the purchasing function. Our stakeholder map must consider the entire organization and the communications plan should feature approaches that are likely to have impact at an organization-wide level. Approaches that can help here include:

- establishing a 'mini-brand' for the purchasing function and/or key initiatives (subject to overall corporate communication rules);
- section on the purchasing intranet or internal website;
- direct internal marketing to those in business units;
- articles in internal magazines promoting success stories from key initiatives;
- internal roadshows;
- presentations at key managers meetings and briefings; and
- getting out there and selling the message.

A useful key tool to support all of these is the *stakeholder brochure*.

The stakeholder brochure

A stakeholder brochure, as touched on in Chapter 11, is an internal publication to all key stakeholders designed to help educate the business about the role of purchasing, key objectives and initiatives and what is expected of the business.

Ideally stakeholder brochures should be short, simple, professionally produced, appealing to read and typically might include:

- how purchasing adds value today and how it will need to add value in support of corporate goals in future;
- the key initiatives that support this;
- the role the wider business plays to support this;
- what to do and not to do when engaging with suppliers (see top 10 dos and don'ts in Chapter 11);
- how to report a supplier related problem;
- how to get involved or get help; and
- introduction to purchasing; who, where, how to contact.

As with any form of internal communication 'just sending it out' will only have so much impact, instead stakeholder brochures have most impact when handed out following a face-to-face engagement or presentation.

Getting the wider organization on page

Suppliers demand time. At a personal level we give our time to those who are close to us, who matter to us; who we want to help or perhaps who can help us. Most people are able to determine who is important, subconsciously applying some sort of criteria according to our feelings, beliefs, environment or needs. Most people would soon tire of devoting precious time to someone who is not important but demands time for their benefit alone. Yet organizations seem to struggle to do the same and end up spending time that adds no or little value with suppliers who simply don't warrant it. It can be hard to say no to a supplier who asks for the time. Supplier requests for review meetings, meetings to discuss performance or share developments can be hard to decline, especially if the buyer believes it is part of their role to accommodate such meetings.

A shift in mindset is required and so those who manage and interface with suppliers are clear about who they should spend time with and who they should not spend time with, no matter how keen, friendly, persistent, or enthusiastic the supplier might be. Spending time only with those suppliers it is worthwhile to do so at an organization-wide level does not simply happen by segmenting the supply base. Segmenting the supply base is just the first step and this needs to be followed by actions designed to educate and change behaviours across the entire organization so everybody that has or could have any sort of interface with the supply base understands the role they need to play (or not play). Sometimes people just need to be given permission to simply say *no* when appropriate.

Remember when doctors, nurses, engineers, marketeers, developers and other professional staff learn their profession they rarely receive any commercial awareness training and typically don't get taught how the game that suppliers play works. It is easy to believe the supplier is a friend and there to help. In practice this may in fact be impossible to change, but if our engagement and internal communications focus beyond that of extolling the purchasing function, but rather towards tackling real business issues and achieving real business goals that the wider organization can relate to, then they will stand the greatest likelihood of success.

The supplier representative who arrived in an ambulance

Healthcare is big business globally and across the profession suppliers go to great lengths to ensure their product gets specified. This typically does not happen within the bounds of a procurement function buying on behalf of a large healthcare provider but rather happens on hospital wards, in medical staff training centres and in doctors' surgeries where suppliers target teams of sales representatives with one single mission – to convince clinical staff to specify their product over other products. If a supplier can ensure a surgeon trains using their gloves then that surgeon will specify that brand of gloves for life. There are many instances where preferences are important to patient outcomes, however across healthcare providers globally immense patient care time gets diverted to interfacing with suppliers unnecessarily, often because healthcare professionals want to or feel they should do so. Suppliers know just how to take advantage of this to their favour and are resilient to any efforts to prevent them developing relationships with healthcare professionals.

One supplier's sales representative successfully managed to work his way through an entire hospital, giving medical staff samples of a new product and then spending time with them gathering opinions and feedback; all vital information for the supplier's development process. How was this possible? Surely supplier's sales staff need to check in? It was possible because the individual arrived in a fake ambulance fully loaded with samples. He parked by the accident and emergency entrance and then, dressed in a white coat with a stethoscope around his neck, he was able to come and go as he pleased and walk the wards. He approached medical staff and suggested he was working on a particular project; the busy staff were made to feel like they were remiss by not knowing about it, he gave them a gift and they felt obliged to answer his questions and to perhaps specify that product when they next placed an order.

External communications

Governance extends to the overall management of all supplier and supply base communications. That doesn't mean every external discussion must be routed via the steering group, but rather that there is a planned and systematic approach for all high-level communications. This might include:

- releasing high-level supplier briefing statements, specifically designed to communicate certain messages or changes, made available to those who interface with suppliers and, of course, containing embedded conditioning messages as appropriate; and
- publishing a Supplier Code of Conduct to all suppliers (see Chapter 11).

Governance: pay-off

The fourth component of governance is *payoff* and is concerned with the arrangements to measure, monitor, report and publish the benefits secured from specific SRM interventions or projects. It could form part of a wider purchasing benefits tracking system or it could be specific to SRM.

SRM, and indeed any strategic purchasing initiative, requires significant investment so there must be a return on that investment and we need to be able to quantify the degree to which our interventions with important suppliers are adding value to the organization overall.

The problem here is around the definition of value. If we can reduce the price we pay then there is a clear and measurable benefit that can be seen on our bottom line and will satisfy any finance team. For category management, projected benefits, often largely price or cost related, are identified at the outset via an opportunity analysis, and as we move through the process, anticipated benefits turn into actual benefits which hopefully are then realized. However, for SRM the projected benefits for a specific relationship are usually quite different, it is all the different types of value we can secure for a given supplier relationship driven by the ways we believe the relationship can improve. It is typically about reduced risk, improved operational effectiveness, better supply base performance, innovation and any other forms of value we seek; in fact the VIPER reasons for a relationship with a supplier as outlined at the start of this book from which we determine the macro and the supplier-specific VIPER relationship requirements, informed by corporate aims, the needs and wants of the business and the segmentation process.

Most of these are less quantifiable and may not necessarily point to a number, but rather some sort of improvement: 'we eliminated that risk' or 'created this innovation', 'we have improved our competitive advantage' and so on. So for SRM determining the payoff means we need a benefits tracking system that must somehow allow us to measure, monitor and report value add benefits in a way that keeps the interest of the executive team to which we are accountable and shows progression against all strategic aims and objectives.

Key to establishing any benefits tracking system is to agree the approach with the finance team, and ideally have them manage it. In practice this might mean either converting less tangible benefits into a tangible number or instead have a means to tell the story in a compelling and unforgettable way that links intervention and effort to a particular outcome. In category management benefits are classified under just three headings of price reduction, cost avoidance and efficiency improvement. These are still entirely appropriate, but for SRM there are two additional classifications, which are value improvements and brand development. Table 15.1 gives examples of benefit types and qualifying factors mapped against VIPER.

TABLE 15.1 Benefit types and qualifying factors mapped against VIPER

Benefit type	Qualifying factors/acceptable benefits	How benefits map to VIPER				
		V	I	P	E	R
Price reduction	The new price paid is less than that previously paid for a similar product/service. Price reduction can include: • A new lower price. • Rebates based on volumes. • Kickbacks or signing bonuses. • Securing additional added value at no or lower additional cost, thus lowering the overall price for the new, enhanced value-added specification. Note that this type of saving is valid only if the added-value component was actually required and identified within the business requirements. • A price lower than the normal market price (and which is demonstrable). This saving type is relevant where the product or service has not been purchased before. • A price that is lower than the original price provided (for example, within a quotation), and where the internal customer agrees that a valid price reduction has been achieved.	✓				
Cost avoidance	Avoiding costs that would otherwise have to be paid. Examples might include: • Dispensing with the area of expenditure as a result of the sourcing strategy. • Reducing spend that is contractually obligated with a supplier. • Reducing penalty payments. • In the case where budget pricing is being used, perhaps on a complex construction project, coming in under budget can count as cost avoidance. • Savings from using exchange rate fluctuations to an advantage.	✓			✓	

TABLE 15.1 *continued*

Benefit type	Qualifying factors/acceptable benefits	How benefits map to VIPER				
		V	I	P	E	R
Efficiency improvements	Improving the overall effectiveness and efficiency within a product, process or area. Efficiency savings must be quantified in terms of tangible benefits and where possible translated into financial savings through lower cost, cost avoidance or some form of increased value that is required. Efficiency savings include both those that are within the business and those within the supplier that are passed on and might include: • Improvements to a process. • Reduction in inventory.	✓		✓	✓	
Value improvements	Improvements that deliver some form of value to the business. Where possible, value improvements should be quantified in terms of tangible benefits over a given timeframe. However value improvements can be harder to quantify, where this is not easily possible, value improvements should be recognized by maintaining a 'value register'; a record listing the different forms of non-financial benefit and the way each has added value, agreed and signed off by key stakeholders in the same way as direct financial benefits. Value improvement benefits include: • Reduced cost of production, supply or acquisition • Synergy benefits from resource sharing • Benefits from collaboration or joint working • Economy of scale benefits • Benefits from outsourcing • Reduction of risk	✓	✓	✓	✓	✓

continues

TABLE 15.1   *continued*

Benefit type	Qualifying factors/acceptable benefits	How benefits map to VIPER				
		V	I	P	E	R
Brand development	Specific supplier contributions that directly create business growth or build and develop a brand. Such benefits are typically difficult to quantify, and so need to be measured in terms of linking specific initiatives to increased market share, brand awareness or brand penetration. Where benefits cannot be quantified a 'value register' approach with benefits agreed and signed off by key stakeholders should be maintained. Brand development benefits include: • Supplier innovations or ideas that create new products and or allow new markets to be reached • Supplier driven enhancements or improvements to current products • Business growth linked to supplier initiatives • Competitive advantage or differentiation from supplier initiatives • Benefits from association with supplier's brand • Benefits from exclusive access to supplier capability or product	✓	✓			

Once the arrangements for benefit determination have been agreed, then benefits tracking is simply a case of putting in place a regular reporting regime for each SRM initiative, either requiring individual supplier relationship managers to report benefits secured from time to time or a cross-functional team working on a specific initiative to report progress (eg against the 5A process) and benefits at key stages.

Governance: programme

Programme is the fifth component of governance and is the means by which all initiatives, interventions and projects are planned and managed for SRM or indeed all strategic purchasing initiatives. *Programme* is about identifying priorities and planning how these will be acted upon based upon available resource. This part of governance is managed using a dynamic programme plan identifying the key projects and activities over the short to medium term (Figure 15.4). For each project milestones linked to completion of key stages, such as the 5A SCR process, can be defined in advance, these can be linked to expected benefits delivery. Here a system of regular progress and benefits reporting is required, coordinated by good project management hence the need for a defined role here. A similar programme in the form of a 'category wave plan' is advocated within category management and so, given resources are finite for any organization, there is only room for one programme plan that manages and coordinates all the available resource, allocating it to either SRM, category management or other projects as appropriate. In addition the programme plan is most effective when used as the single planning tool for all governance activities and so should include key time bound activities such as steering group reviews, key communications and any key events on the *supplier calendar*. An example of a governance programme plan for SRM and other strategic projects is given in Figure 15.4.

The programme plan is determined, reviewed and updated by the steering group, informed by corporate strategy, aims and objectives, the outputs from segmentation (defined using supplier intervention mapping) and opportunity analysis (Figure 15.5).

Steering group reviews

The role of the steering group is to develop and maintain a current pro-gramme, meeting regularly to review progress and update the programme as appropriate. These reviews should cover:

- overall progress against delivering headline benefits;
- review of progress against benefits for individual initiatives;
- review of progress to milestones for individual initiatives;
- review of communication plan;
- ensuring availability of the required capabilities and resources; and
- review and update of the programme plan.

Where SRM sits in the organization

Integration not islands

If SRM is to be successful in an organization then it should not be considered an 'island' – a standalone initiative for a single purpose. Organizations that have recognized the significant contribution purchasing can make naturally want to respond by embarking on a journey to better resource and enable purchasing, and SRM is one enabler here. However, SRM is not the only

FIGURE 15.4 An example programme plan for SRM and other strategic initiatives

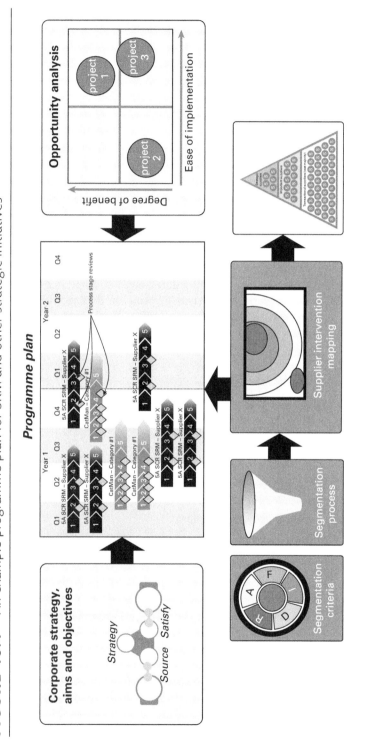

FIGURE 15.5 Factors that shape the programme plan

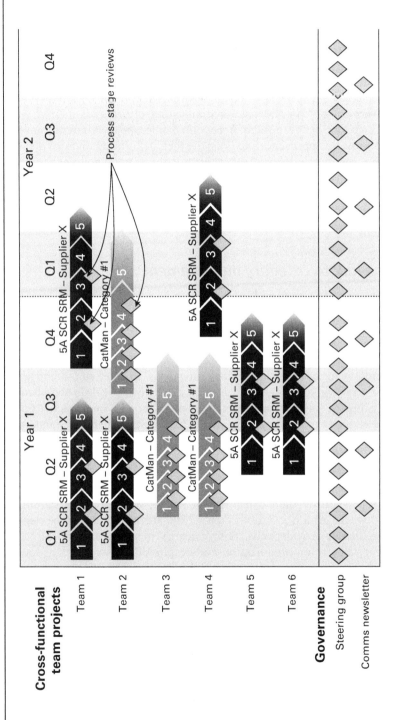

game in town, it is just one component that comprises modern best practice or world-class purchasing. A business might be working on operational initiatives such as vendor rationalization, implementing an ERP system or catalogue buying. eSourcing or Lean initiatives could be driving benefits and there may be tactical initiatives to simply negotiate or buy better. There might also be other key strategic enablers such as category management and supply side CSR and here integration of strategic initiatives is important otherwise we run the risk of duplicating effort and missing vital inter-connections between them. Across the landscape of different initiatives, it is the strategic approaches and crucially their integration that drives the greatest value. In practice, integration happens through good governance. Purchasing maturity is therefore primarily the degree to which key strategic initiatives are effective and work together to deliver dramatic benefits. Figure 15.6 shows the stages of purchasing maturity, where different approaches tend to exist within these and the typical nature and scale of value possible.

The link to category management

My first book *Category Management in Purchasing* (O'Brien, 2012) outlined the methodology that enables organizations to take a strategic approach to their entire third party spend by segmenting it into groups of products or services, or 'categories', that mirror how market places are organized (Figure 15.7). Category management is also an approach for cross-functional teams, who work on individual categories and determine and implement new strategic sourcing strategies that can deliver breakthrough benefits. It is possibly the single most vital component of modern best practice purchasing. Indeed today category management is firmly established and standard practice for large organizations all over the world and is a well-proven approach that delivers real and sustainable benefit including significant reductions in price and cost but also risk and can create additional value and new innovation.

SRM is also a strategic sourcing methodology, but of course focused on suppliers rather than categories of spend, so which one should be used and when? And if it is both then which order should they be deployed in? The answer is it depends. Both category management and SRM can add great value to an organization and despite differences in their focus, many of the supporting tools and approaches are common. Category management is spend or category centric whilst SRM is of course is supplier focused (Figure 15.8). Both have their place within a strategic purchasing function and each should be selected and deployed accordingly as part of common governance programme planning.

Category management is, more often than not, the initiative organiza-tions begin with, later putting some form of SRM initiative in place, often as category strategies get implemented and the project then reaches maturity shifting the emphasis towards ongoing supplier management in various forms and driving improvements. This makes sense but the two approaches are not necessarily sequential, in fact each could be deployed according to

FIGURE 15.6 The stages of purchasing maturity

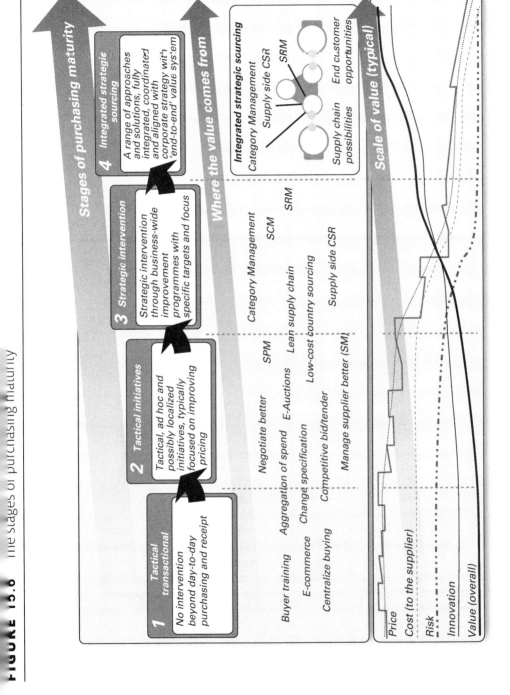

Stages of purchasing maturity

1 Tactical transactional
No intervention beyond day-to-day purchasing and receipt

2 Tactical initiatives
Tactical, ad hoc and possibly localized initiatives, typically focused on improving pricing

3 Strategic intervention
Strategic intervention through business-wide improvement programmes with specific targets and focus

4 Integrated strategic sourcing
A range of approaches and solutions, fully integrated, coordinated and aligned with corporate strategy with 'end-to-end' value system

Where the value comes from

Buyer training
Negotiate better
Aggregation of spend
E-commerce
Change specification
Centralize buying
Competitive bid/tender

SPM
E-Auctions
Low-cost country sourcing
Manage supplier better (SMI)

Category Management
Lean supply chain
SCM
Supply side CSR
SRM

Integrated strategic sourcing

Category Management
Supply side CSR
SRM
Supply chain possibilities
End customer opportunities

Scale of value (typical)

Price
Cost (to the supplier)
Risk
Innovation
Value (overall)

FIGURE 15.7   Segmentation of categories of spend

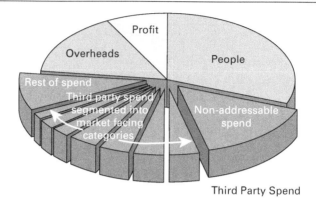

FIGURE 15.8   Categories versus suppliers

	Supplier A	Supplier B	Supplier C	Supplier D	Supplier E	Supplier F
Category 1		●		●		
Category 2	●					
Category 3		●	●		●	
Category 4		●			●	
Category 5						●
Category 6		●				

the outcomes needed and at any time it may be appropriate to transition from one to the other or even to do both.

The key to success, however, is the integration or connectivity between approaches. For example, if an individual leading a category project conducts analysis and develops insights that suggests the most appropriate way forward is to work on a key supplier relationship rather than try to leverage benefit through a competitive process it would be appropriate for that person to then switch to deploying SRM. Equally work with a supplier might suggest there are greater opportunities by looking at the wider marketplace for certain categories. Here the same individual is leading and simply selecting the most appropriate process and toolkit to use creating a natural integration of the two approaches, sanctioned through the governance arrangements. Indeed in organizations where senior practitioners manage portfolios of categories and also have responsibility to manage the suppliers associated with the categories tend to be the most effective overall – the category manager may also be the supplier relationship manager!

If category management and SRM exist separately, as if 'islands', resourced by different teams then unless there is exceptional communication between the two, the structure creates a natural disconnect that works against the organization. Furthermore many of the tools and approaches are common across both, just applied with a different lens. Category management and SRM therefore have an integral relationship.

The link to supply side corporate social responsibility (CSR)

In Chapter 12 we explored CSR and there is a similar linkage here between SRM and also category management. Supply side CSR requires the ability to understand supply chains, measure performance in key areas, drive improvements and develop relationships with suppliers who are critical. In fact, it demands all of the things SRM purports to deliver. It also connects with category management to provide a guiding requirement that helps shape future sourcing strategy. In fact there is significant crossover between supply side CSR, category management and SRM; indeed they share similar tools and approaches. Figure 15.9 shows all three key strategic initiatives and the crossover between them, but crucially the areas of commonality where similar tools or approaches are used. This illustrates the need for an integrated approach, coordinated through good governance.

SRM and public sector buying

In many parts of the world there are strict rules governing public sector buying. In Europe there are a number of directives and regulations. Any governmental or public purchasing entity is required to comply with the legislation for expenditure where the likely spend will exceed a certain, published threshold. In this case the opportunity must be advertised in the Official Journal of the European Union (OJEU). Prospective suppliers can then register their interest and potentially be invited to participate in a tender exercise according to one of four procedures.

Depending upon which approach is used, the degree for building a relationship with a supplier might appear limited and in conflict with the legislation. It would be very easy to conclude that SRM doesn't apply where EU rules apply because 'all suppliers need to treated equally so we can't do SRM'. This is not the case.

In any commercial interaction with a supplier there has to be a relationship dimension; it is unavoidable. It also follows that a supplier will need to be managed, measured and interacted with on a daily basis to ensure compliance, delivery to target and smooth running of the contact. SRM is

FIGURE 15.9 The commonality between SRM, category management and supply side CSR

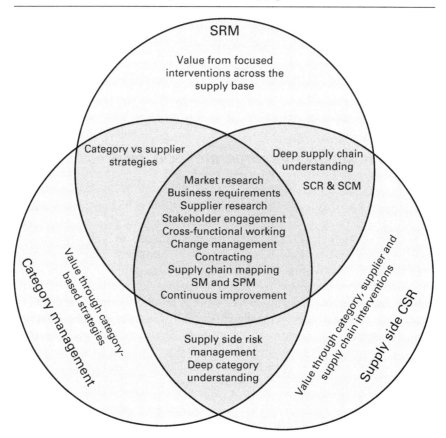

therefore very much part of a public sector supplier relationship. However, and depending upon the contracting procedure used, there are some things that need to be done slightly differently to what might happen in a pure commercial environment. These are:

- Clear definition of the requirements upfront so they include SRM elements (performance measurement, management, relationship planning, joint reviews etc). All suppliers that bidding for work are doing so in the knowledge of how the relationship will be managed before they bid. Don't add them afterwards.

- Make SRM activities part of the contract, eg with obligations to participate in review meetings, maintain a relationship charter, supply performance information, agree KPIs etc.

- Ensure that any joint goals and objectives within a continuous improvement approach is a feature of the overall contract.

What the future holds

We started this book by exploring our changing world and environment and how this is driving a dramatic change in what organizations need from the supply base. Chapter 1 closed by suggesting five future needs here: *clarity* regarding those suppliers who are most important; *confidence* like never before in our supplier's capabilities and to ensure that we are not exposed to unacceptable risk; *closeness* with those suppliers that are important; *contribution* from the important suppliers to help us achieve our goals; and *collaboration* with the critical few suppliers who can make a difference to our business.

SRM, if well executed, provides the vital framework to realize all these things and it is possibly one of the key future enablers of success for any company that seeks to claim and retain competitive edge. None of us can be certain what the future holds, but we can make sound predictions based upon what is happening today and these can help us prepare for what we need to do tomorrow.

Our future modern lives will demand innovation across technological boundaries and that will connect industries and practices that sit separate today. Companies with a core competency in one area will find themselves needing to acquire and connect with new core competencies in another and will turn to the supply base to help. The minute, electronic, wireless revolution means medicine bottles will become intelligent and message our phones to remind us to take a tablet, Intelligent refrigerators will update our shopping list as things run out. 'Things' will become the biggest users of the internet (Valéry, 2013). Today we carry computers, smartphones with many times the computing power of the space shuttle; tomorrow those computers will be many times more powerful, better connected and we will wear them like spectacles; intelligent and interacting on our behalf with the world around us in ways we have not yet considered. Our cars, pets, clothing, medical implants, toys and tools will all have their own digital intelligence and interact with us and sources of information via the internet.

Globalization; yes, but localization and personalization too. Our suppliers could exist anywhere in the world but interact with us as if they are just next door and they may not ever need to ship anything, but rather transmit a design for us to print using 3D printing technology. 3D printing will also transform the assembly line creating parts with fully integrated electronics and will equip niche providers with a never before had tool to realize whatever they dream up whenever they want. Innovation from the supply base may not be about making or shipping things but connecting ideas with where they will be turned into reality.

Advances in technology at an ever-increasing pace will keep changing the game. Cars will drive themselves, powered using technology not yet perfected and may even be created where we least expect it. Perhaps the next global car brand will be Chinese. The same revolution will transform logistics.

Medicine is set for a revolution too when smart nano particles will be available to enter our bodies, like tiny microscopic submarines travelling through the human body on the hunt for specific cells or damaged tissues ready to change state or release chemicals when they find them – precisely where needed to deliver highly precise healing. It won't just be advancements made in laboratories of global corporations that drive progress, but brilliant minds, somewhere in the world, somehow connected together to achieve common goal. In the same way that a talented teenage musician can now write, record and release a song to the global market from his bedroom and become an overnight success, small companies with the hunger and a unique and desirable offering will be better placed to become successful without the need for any significant overheads; somewhere out there may lie a brilliant contributor. The ability to find and nurture innovation externally to a business will become an important part of purchasing's role; engaging individuals and companies more as collaborators than traditional suppliers with a relationship and commercial model to suit.

There is one certainty and that is that what happens in the world will continue to be unpredictable and perhaps volatile. Unprecedented global demand will transform the way we view security of water, food and other commodities. Understanding and actively managing supplier and supply chain risk will move from something only a few alert companies do to a core role of the purchasing function. It doesn't end there but rather the future role of purchasing will be to drive strategic responses to risk and pursue new sourcing strategies that shore up future supply, building new types of relationships with key providers to do so.

As our demands and preferences, and 'better, faster and just for you' is where the game is at it is the providers who are agile and flexible enough to respond quickly and to whatever whim a customer might have that will do well. Purchasing will help create this agility with thorough effective management and incentivization of the important suppliers.

There is a certain energy and hopefulness about reflecting on how the future is shaping up, and I could fill an entire book speculating about what might happen and how purchasing might need to respond. There is no doubt there are some exciting things that will shape our future lives, but no matter which area of human progression we consider there is one common theme emerging and that is that we can't leave all this to chance. An arm's length supply base may continue to be good commercial practice for many, but not all. If we view our suppliers passively as just 'suppliers' responding to demand we determine then we could be left behind; sat on the sidelines watching as the world around us changes. Many suppliers now need to be regarded as 'enablers' or 'innovators', 'connectors' or 'assurers', operating within a new type relationship and commercial framework that encourages them to share brilliance with us. We need new skills, new mindsets, new outlooks; to shift focus to what is important; to link supply base intervention to corporate objectives; to understand where in our supply base we need to focus our effort, all according to the current and future needs of the business and the environment it sits in.

SRM has a pivotal role to play here because what we need for the future; the brilliance that will carry an organization forward may not necessarily reside within that organization, some of it might, some of it may be unobtainable in the traditional employed resource model but might exist somewhere on the planet.

The orchestra of SRM is ready to play

As we reach the end of this book we are completing a journey that considers the future role and potential of the supply base together with the ensemble of approaches that need to exist and work together to create a company-wide SRM strategy capable of unlocking this potential. SRM is an umbrella concept that enables us to determine and deploy different types of supply base intervention according to the outcomes we need and want. It can help unlock great value from the supply base that can bring us competitive advantage, business growth and brand development.

This book started with 20 pathway questions that can help gauge how ready a company is for SRM. If well executed, the approaches outlined in this book provide an all-encompassing framework that enables any organization to answer all of these with confidence.

For the orchestra of SRM to play, we start by considering the concert that needs to be staged and precisely what contribution we need from our supply base and why. VIPER provides the means here, informed by corporate aims and objectives and this then provides the basis to determine which suppliers are important and therefore where we should direct resources. Each important supplier will demand a unique mix of SRM interventions, each having its own unique piece of music, composed during the segmentation process to focus on the specific areas of value that the organization needs from that relationship.

When the music plays, the different sections of the orchestra play their bits, according to the music, coming in and out exactly when needed. The SPM part of our orchestra plays when we need to understand how our suppliers are performing and to know for sure that we are getting the most from our suppliers. SI&D plays to drive supplier improvements in areas where they will have the greatest impact. Centre stage, SM is the part of the ensemble that plays for every piece and helps better understand those suppliers that are important to us, and take a proactive approach to manage contracts and ensure contractual obligations are met. Here we will also find approaches to understand and manage risk with suppliers or those back up the supply chain. This section also plays to ensure we have the right relationships with the right suppliers whilst managing the entire business-wide supplier interface.

We spent an entire chapter looking beyond immediate suppliers and exploring how we can understand and better manage our supply chains. In our orchestra of SRM, SCM is the *cor anglais*. The Cor Anglais (literally meaning *English horn*; but is neither English and doesn't look like a horn) is part of the oboe family but with a lower, more rich and mellow sound. It is not an instrument widely known but is usually there in the background, but you wouldn't know it exists until you hear its sad melodic tones as used in film scores to depict sad, mysterious or poignant moments. Oboe players tend to avoid learning the Cor Anglais because it is a difficult instrument to play; it is longer and heavier than the oboe and playing it has been compared to trying to blow up a balloon (Meyer, 2004). As a consequence it tends to get short pieces due to issues of fatigue on your embouchure (your mouth gets tired and you run out of puff), but when it does play everyone notices, loves it and realizes how important it is. Similarly, it is easy to forget the relevance of the supply chain or to dismiss intervention here as simply too difficult, but SCM is an important component of SRM and may even need a unique composition just to allow it to flourish and skilled practitioners with an embouchure to match!

No orchestra of SRM would be complete without another group of highly skilled players, who add the most intricate and enchanting melodies but only for those suppliers that hold the greatest potential so as to secure innovation or work collaboratively to achieve joint goals.

Orchestras are more than a collection of musicians, they are organized groups, companies employing people and commercial concerns. The mission of the London Symphony Orchestra is 'to make the finest music available to the greatest number of people'. Other orchestras have similar missions. Just as everything that happens when the musicians play supports the realization of this mission, our entire SRM effort must align with and help deliver corporate goals, but also must help inform corporate strategy through supply chain possibilities. An orchestra needs a stage, a place to rehearse, talented musicians, accountants behind the scenes and someone planning and coordinating every concert and event. SRM cannot be effective without good governance; the capability, structure and processes we need and how to ensure everyone in the entire organization knows what is expected of them when working with suppliers. Governance provides the day-to-day leadership for the complete SRM ensemble just as the conductor sets the pace and provides the single point of leadership, commanding all sections but agile enough to address individual sections to have them play louder, or give more emphasis according to the what the conductor needs to hear.

We have reached the end of this book and everything we have covered comes together to complete our orchestra and the final figure is, of course, the entire orchestra of SRM (Figure 15.10). So, with the musicians assembled, the audience watching and the conductor's baton raised, the orchestra of SRM is now ready to play.

FIGURE 15.10   The orchestra of SRM

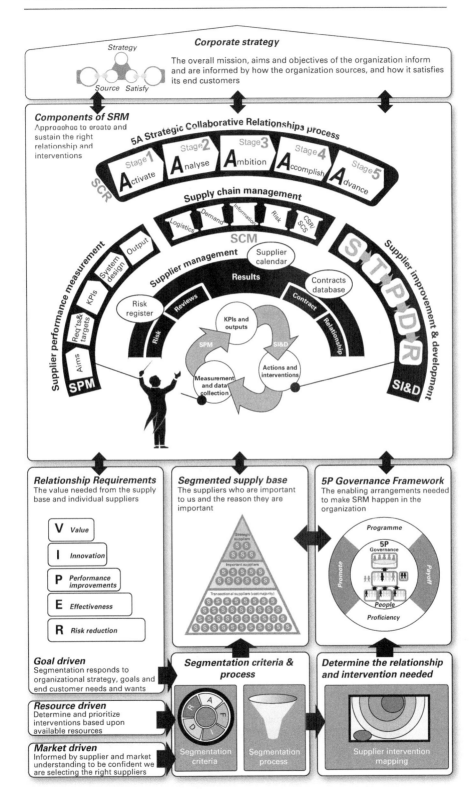

GLOSSARY

Category Management   A methodology that enables organizations to take a strategic approach to their entire third party spend by segmenting it into groups of products or services, or 'categories', that mirror how marketplaces are organized.

Continuous improvement   An approach to drive in ongoing incremental improvement in one or more aspects of performance.

CSR (corporate social responsibility)   A strategic organization-wide initiative for the firm to consider the impact of its actions on society, the environment and the world at large and to identify actions to minimize or eliminate detrimental impacts.

ERP system (Enterprise Resource Planning system)   An organization-wide system that enables an integrated, real-time view of core business processes using common databases of information and can track business resources.

First tier supplier   A supplier with whom we have a direct contractual relationship; who is immediately next to our company in the supply chain.

Grey market   An unofficial market or trade in something, especially controlled or scarce goods.

JIT   Just-In-Time is a production strategy that strives to reduce inventory and the costs of moving goods using a system of information and action to coordinate internal and supplier operations so the required materials arrive at the point they are needed when they are needed and the waste associated with storage and double carrying are removed or reduced.

NPD (New Product Development)   A process or function concerned the development of new products or services for an organization.

Project Charter   A document used at the outset of a team-based project as a basis to define and agree key aspects of the project including scope, targets, membership, roles, responsibilities and timings. May also be called a Team Charter.

R&D (Research and Development)   A process or function concerned with the research into potential new products and the development of new products or services for an organization.

RFI (Request for Information)   A solicitation tool to request various pieces of information from a supplier or many suppliers, perhaps as part of market research or data gathering. RFIs can be paper based questionnaires but these days are more commonly electronic; run online using one of the many proprietary e-sourcing platforms available.

Second tier suppliers   Suppliers who supply first tier suppliers with whom we have no direct contractual relationship with.

Team Charter   A document used at the outset of a team-based project as a basis to define and agree key aspects of the project including scope, targets, membership, roles, responsibilities and timings. May also be called a Project Charter.

Vertical integration   A style of management control (from economic theory) that describes a situation where companies in a supply chain are united through a common owner. Each member of the supply chain produces a different product and these come together to satisfy a common need.

REFERENCES

Amaratunga, D and Baldry, D (2002) Moving from performance measurement to performance management, *Facilities*, **20**, pp 217–23

Baker, S (2003) *New Consumer Marketing*, Wiley and Sons

Barnes, C, Blake, H and Pinder, D (2009) *Creating and Delivering Your Value Proposition: Managing customer experience for profit*, Kogan Page, London

BBC (2013) Bangladesh building collapse death toll passes 500, BBC News 3 May. Retrieved 3 May 2013

The Beatles (2000) *The Beatles Anthology*, Chronicle Books, San Francisco

Bevir, M (2013) *Governance: A very short introduction*, Oxford University Press, Oxford

Bechtel, C and Jayaram, J (1997) Supply chain management: a strategic perspecctive, *The International Journal of Logistics Management*, **8** (1), pp 15–34

Bicheno, J and Holweg, M (2009) *The New Lean Toolbox, The Essential Guide to Lean Transformation*, 4th Edition, PICSIE Books, Buckingham

Bovert, D and Sheffi, Y (1998) The brave new world of supply chain management, *Supply Chain Management Review*, **2** (Spring), pp 14–22

Burbidge, J (1984) Automated Production control With a Simulation Capability, Proceedings IFIP Conference Working Group 5–7, Copenhagen

Carroll, L (1865, Rev Edn 1998) *Alice's Adventures in Wonderland* and *Through The Looking Glass*, Penguin Classics, England

CBSR – Canadian Business for Social Responsibility (2009) CSR Frameworks, Review for the Extractive Industry, April 2009, downloaded from www.cbsr.ca

Chao, CM and Cheng, BW (2012) Factors influencing the future relationship of hospital procurement staff with medical device suppliers, *Social Behaviour and Personality*

Chao, CM, Yu, CT, Cheng, BW and Chuang, PC (2013) Trust and commitment in relationships among medical equipment suppliers: transaction cost and social exchange theories, *Social Behaviour and Personality*, **41** (7), pp 1057–70

Christopher, MG (1992) *Logistics and Supply Chain Management*, Pitman Publishing, London

Christopher, M (2011) *Logistics and Supply Chain Management*, Fourth Edition, FT Prentice Hall, Harlow

Cousins, R, Lamming, R, Lawson, B and Squire, B (2008) *Strategic Supply Management – Principles, Theories and Practice*, FT Prentice Hall, Harlow

Cranfield School of Management (2002) Supply Chain Vulnerability, Report on Behalf of DTLR, DTI and Home Office

Cunningham, JE and Fiume, OJ, with Adams, E (2003) *Real Numbers – Management Accounting in a Lean Organization*, Managing Times Press, Durham, NC

de Bono, Edward (1985) *Six Thinking Hats: An essential approach to business management*, Little Brown and Company

Deming, WE (1982) *Out of the Crisis*, Massachusetts Institute of Technology

Dixon, JR, Nanni, AJ and Vollmann, TE (1990) *The New Performance Challenge – Measuring Operations for World-class Competition*, Dow Jones-Irwin, Homeood, IL

DoWellDoGood Public Opinion Survey on Sustainability, Summary Report (2012) downloaded from dowelldogood.net, April 2013

Dumond, EJ (1994) Making best use of performance measures and information, *International Journal of Operations and Production Management*, **14** (9), pp 16–31

EIPM (European Institute for Purchasing Management) (2006) The EFQM Framework for Managing External Resources, EFQM, Brussels, downloaded from www.eipm.org, March 2014

Emmett, S and Crocker, B (2009) *Excellence in Supplier Management*, Cambridge Academic, Cambridge

Epstein, MJ and Manzoni, JF (1998) Implementing corporate strategy: from tableau de board to balanced scorecards, *European Measurement Journal*, **16** (2), pp 190–203

Finlow-Bates, T (1998) The Root Cause Myth, *TQM Magazine*, **10** (1)

Fitzgerald, L with Johnston, R, Brignall, TJ, Silvestro, R and Voss, C (1991) *Performance Measurement in Service Businesses*, Chartered Institute of Management Accountants (CIMA)

Forrester, J (1958) Industrial Dynamics: A major breakthrough for decision makers, *Harvard Business Review*, July–August 1958, pp 37–66

Friedman, M (1975) *There's No Such Thing as a Free Lunch*, Open Court Publishing Company

García-Arca, J, Mejías-Sacaluga, A and Prado-Prado, JC (2007) The Supply Chain Design And Its Implementation – An Analytical And Multisectorial Approach, University of Vigo (Spain), Published form the POMS 18th Annual Conference, Dallas Texas, 4–7 May

Gardner, JT and Cooper, MC (2003) Strategic supply chain mapping approaches, *Journal of Business Logistics*, **24** (2)

George, ML (2002) *Lean Six Sigma – Combining Six Sigma Quality with Lean Speed*, McGraw Hill, New York

Global Corruption Barometer (2013) Transparency International, downloaded from www.transparency.org, December 2013

Gordon, SR (2008) *Supplier Evaluation and Performance Excellence*, J Ross Publishing, Fort Lauderdale

Gradinger, G (2009) Ready for Supplier Relationship Management – A Tool for a Structured Approach, VDM Verlag Dr Müller Aktiengesellschaft and CoKG

Granovetter, MS (1973) The strength of weak ties, *American Journal of Sociology*, **78** (6), May 1973

Granovetter, M (1983) The strength of weak ties: a network theory revisited, *Sociological Theory*, **1** (1983), pp 201–33

Granovetter, M (1985) Economic action and social structure: the problem of embeddedness, *The American Journal of Sociology*, **91** (3), Nov 1985, pp 481–510

Green, R (2002) *48 Laws of Power*, Profile Books, London

Greenaway, J (2011) Deloitte – Bribery and corruption in Africa, Getting on the front foot. Downloaded from www.deloitte.com, December 2013

Gregory, C (1982) *Gifts and Commodities*, Academic Press, London, pp 6–9

Gwartney, JD, Richard, S and Dwight, RL (2005) *Common Sense Economics*, St Martin's Press, New York, pp 8–9

Hann, CM (1998) *Property Relations: Renewing the anthropological tradition*, Cambridge University Press, Cambridge, p 4

Hannabarger, G, Buchman, R and Economy, P (2007) *Balanced Scorecard Strategy for Dummies*, Wiley, Hoboken NJ

Hausman, A and Johnston, WJ (2010) The impact of coercive and non-coercive forms of influence on trust, commitment, and compliance in supply chains, *Industrial Marketing Management*, **39**, pp 519–26

Hieber, Cf R (2002) *Supply Chain Management – A Collaborative Performance Measurement Approach*, Hochschulverlag ETH, Zurich

Hines, P (1993) Integrated materials management: the value chain redefined, *International Journal of Logistics Management*, **4** (1)

Hines, P and Rich, N (1997) The seven value stream mapping tools, *International Journal of Operations and Production Management*, **17** (1), pp 46–64

Honour, D (2010) The keys to successfully managing supply chain risk, www.continuitycentral.com, feature 0823, 26 October 2010 New York

Hughes (2005) Supplier metrics that matter – CPO Agenda, Autumn 2005, downloaded from www.supplybusiness.com, May 2014

Husdal, J (2008) Supply Chain Risk – The dark side of supply chain management. Unpublished. Lecture notes, Molde University College, Molde, Norway

Imai, M (1986) *Kaizen: The Key to Japan's Competitive Success*, Random House, London

IndustriALL (2013) Global brands pull together on Bangladesh safety deal, press release, 23 May

Innocent Drinks Company (2013) Our approach to being sustainable, downloaded March 2013 from innocentdrinks.co.uk

Ishikawa, Kaoru (1968) *Guide to Quality Control*, JUSE, Tokyo

Johnson, G and Scholes, K (1993) *Exploring Corporate Strategy*, Third Edition, Prentice Hall, Hemel Hempstead

Johnson, HT and Kaplan, RS (1987) *Relevance Lost: The rise and fall of management accounting*, Harvard Business School Press, Boston

Johnson, MW, Christensen, CM and Kagermann, H (2008) Reinventing your business model, *Harvard Business Review*, **86** (12), pp 57–68

Johnson, S (2011) *Where Good Ideas Come From*, Penguin, London

Juran Institute Inc (2013) Juran's Quality Improvement Tools, Juran Institute Inc

Juran, JM and Godfrey, AB (1999) *Juran's Quality Handbook*, McGraw-Hill, US

Kaplan, RS and Norton, DP (1996) *The Balanced Scorecard*, HBS Press, US

Kaplan, RS and Norton, DP (2004) *Strategy Maps: Converting intangible assets into tangible outcomes*, Harvard Business Press

Kilmann, RH and Thomas, KW (1977) Developing a forced choice measure of conflict handling behavior: the 'MODE' instrument, *Educational and Psychological Measurement*, **37**, pp 309–25

Kim, W Chan and Mauborgne, Renée (2005) *Blue Ocean Strategy: How to create uncontested market space and make competition irrelevant*, Harvard Business Press

King, P (2012) Deep culture, *The Journal of Popular Culture*, **45** (4)

Kipling, R (1902) *Just So Stories* – The Elephant's Child, downloaded from http://en.wikisource.org, November 2013

Kotter, John P (2012) *Leading Change*, Harvard Business School Press

Kraljic, P (1983) Purchasing must become supply management, *Harvard Business Review*, **61** (5), pp 109–17

Kwon, IWG and Suh, T (2004) Factors affecting the level of trust and commitment in supply chain relationships, *Journal of Supply Chain Management*, **40**, 4–14

Lambert, DM, Cooper, MC and Pagh, JD (1998) Supply chain management: implementation, issues and research opportunities, *The International Journal of Logistics Management*, **9** (2)

Lanning, MJ (1980) *Delivering Profitable Value*, Basic Books, New York

Lardenoije, EJH, Van Raaij, EM and Van Weele, AJ (2005) Performance Management Models and Purchasing: Relevance Still Lost, Researches in Purchasing and Supplier Management, Proceedings of the 14th IPSERA Conference, Archamps, France, 20–23 March, pp 687–97

Larsons, K and Farrington, B (2006) *Purchasing and Supply Chain Management*, Seventh Edition, Pearson, Harlow

Lee, HL (2004) The Triple-A Supply Chain, *Harvard Business Review*, October 2004

Lidell, HG and Scott, R (1940) A Greek-English Lexicon, Clarendon Press, Oxford, downloaded from www.perseus.tufts.edu

Liker, JK and Choi, TY (2004) Developing deep supplier relationships, *Harvard Business Review*, December 2004. Downloaded from www.hbr.org

Lim, C, Seokhee, H and Hiroshi, I (2009) Low-cost disruptive innovation by an Indian automobile manufacturer, MMRC Discussion Paper Series

Limberakis, CG (2012) Supplier Lifecycle Management, Aberdeen Group, downloaded August 2012 from www.ismriskgroup.org

Lynch, RL and Cross, KF (1991) *Measure Up – The Essential Guide to Measuring Business Performance*, Mandarin, London

Markillie, P (2013) Manufacturing in the future, *The Economics* 'The World in 2013', 21 November 2012, downloaded from www.economist.com

Marsh Report (2008) Stemming the Rising Tide of Supply Chain Risks: How Risk Managers' Roles and Responsibilities Are Changing – Marsh Inc, 15 April

Martin, JW (2007) *Lean Six Sigma for Supply Chain Management – The 10-Step Solution Process*, McGraw Hill, US

Mauss, M (1925) Essai sur le don. Forme et raison de l'échange dans les sociétés archaïques (An essay on the gift: the form and reason of exchange in archaic societies) originally published in L'Année Sociologique in 1925. And later translated in the English in 1954 by Cunnison, downloaded from https://archive.org/details/giftformsfunctio00maus, December 2013

Melzer-Ridinger, R (2003) FAQ Supply Chain Management, Buildungserlag EINS GmbH, p 5

Mentzer, JT, De-Witt, W, Keebler, JS, Soonhong, M, NixNW, Smith, CD and A'charia, ZG (2001) Defining supply chain management, *Journal of Business Logistics*, **22** (2)

Meyer, C (2004) The English Horn: A Mournful cry of 'ahhh', *Los Angeles Times*, September 12, downloaded from www.latimes.com, May 2014

Ministry of Justice (UK), Bribery Act (2010) Quick Start Guide, downloaded from www.justice.gov.uk/guidance/bribery.htm

Mitchell, JC (1969) 'The Concept and Use of Social Networks'. In: JC Mitchell (ed), *Social Networks in Urban Situations*, pp 1–50, Manchester University Press, Manchester

Morgan, RM and Hunt, SD (1994) The Commitment-Trust theory of relationship marketing, *Journal of Marketing*, **58**, pp 20–38

Myerson, P (2012) *Lean Supply Chain and Logistics Management*, McGraw-Hill, US

Neely, AD, Gregory, MJ and Platts, KW (1995) Performance measurement system design: a literature review and research agenda, *International Journal of Operations and Production Management*, **15** (4), pp 80–116

Neely, AD and Adams, C (2000) *Perspectives on Performance: The performance prism*, Gee Publishing

Neely, AD, Adams, C and Crowe, P (2001) The performance prism in practice, *Measuring Business Excellence*, **5** (2), 6–12

Neely, A, Adams, C and Cunningham, M (2002) *The Performance Prism: The scorecard for measuring and managing business success*, FT Prentice Hall, Mainstone, Kent

Neumeier, Marty (2006) *The Brand Gap: How to bridge the distance between business strategy and design*, New Riders Publishing, Berkeley, CA

NTSB (2000) Accident Report NYC99MA17, 2000-12-12, downloaded from www.ntsb.gov

Nyaga, G, Whipple, J and Lynch, D (2010) Examining supply chain relationships: do buyer and supplier perspectives on collaborative relationships differ?, *Journal of Operational Management*, **28**, pp 101–14

O'Brien, J (2012) *Category Management in Purchasing*, Kogan Page, London

O'Brien, J (2013) *Negotiation for Purchasing Professionals*, Kogan Page, London

Page, S (2010) *The Power of Business-Process Improvement: 10 simple steps to increase effectiveness, efficiency, and adaptability*, AMACOM, New York

Pelsmacker, P, De, Driesen, L and Rayp, G (2005) Do consumers care about ethics? Willingness to pay for fair-trade coffee, *The Journal of Consumer Affairs*, **39** (2)

Pelzer, JD (1982) The Coffee Houses of Augustan London, *History Today*, **32** (10), downloaded from www.historytoday.com, Mar 2014

Penn, Schoen, Berland (2010) Corporate Social Responsibility Branding Survey, downloaded from www.brandchannel.com, April 2013

Ping, RA Jr (1997) Voice in business-to-business relationships: cost-of-exit and demographic antecedents, *Journal of Retailing*, **73** (2), pp 261–81

Porter, ME (1985) *Competitive Advantage*, Free Press, New York

Prahalad, CK and Mashelkar, RA (2010) Innovation's holy grail, *Harvard Business Review*, **88** (7–8), p 134

Pritchard, RH, Holling, H, Lammers, F and Clark, BD (2002) *Improving Organisational Performance with the Productivity and Enhancment System*, Nova Science, New York

Ross, JE (1991) *Total Quality Management*, CRC, Florida

Rudzki, R (2007) *Beat the Odds – Avoid Corporate Death and Build a Resilient Enterprise*, J Ross Publishing, Fort Lauderdale

Safire, W (1993) On language; words left out in the cold, *New York Times*, 14 February

Sahlins, M (1972) *Stone Age Economics*, Aldine-Atherton, Chicago

Sehgal, V, Kevil, D and Ganesh, P (2010) The importance of frugal engineering, *Strategy and Business*, **59**, pp 1–5

Sheth, JN and Sharma, A (2007) Relationship management, *Global Supply Chain Management*, pp 361–71, Sage, California

Shewhart, WA (1986) Statistical Method from the Viewpoint of Quality Control, Graduate School Department of Agriculture, Washington, originally published in 1939

Sider, GM (1980) The ties that bind: culture and agriculture, property and propriety in the Newfoundland village fishery, *Social History*, **5** (1), pp 2–3, 17

Skinner, ST, Gassenheimer, JB and Kelley, SW (1992) Cooperation in supplier-dealer relations, *Journal of Retailing*, **68** (2), Summer 1992, pp 174–93

Skyrms (2004) *The Stag Hunt and the Evolution of Social Structure*, Cambridge University Press, Cambridge

Sneddon, J (2000) The 'Quality' you can't feel, *The Observer*, 19 November, 2000, downloaded from www.theguardian.com, Dec 13

Sneddon, J (2000) *A Brief History of ISO9000: Where did we go wrong?*, *The case against ISO 9000* (2nd edn), Oak Tree Press

Stevens, GC (1989) Integrating the supply chains, *International Journal of Physical Distribution and Materials Management*, **19** (8)

Stewart, C (2007) Disney's Discovery: How to Avoid a Mid-Life Slump, Arts of Innovation: Walt Disney, Mid-Life Finder. May 2007. Retrieved from www.artsofinnovation.com/disney Mar 2014

SunTzu (2000BC) *The Art of War*

Tangpong, C and Ro, YK (2009) The role of agent negotiation behaviors in buyer-supplier relationships, *Journal of Managerial Issues*, **XXI** (1), Spring 2009: 58–79

Tennant, G (2001) *Six Sigma: SPC and TQM in manufacturing and services*, Gower, England

Trumpfheller, M and Hofmann, E (2004) Supply Chain Relationship Management, Netzkompetenz in Supply Chains, Gabler, p 88

US General Accounting Office (1994) Partnerships: Customer-Supplier Relationships Can Be Improved Through Partnering, Report No 94–173, Washington DC

Valéry, N (2013) Welcome to the thingternet, *The Economics* 'The World in 2013', 21 November 2012, downloaded from www.economist.com

Van Weele, AJ (1984) *Purchasing Control: Performance and evaluation of the industrial purchasing function*, Wolters Noordhof, Groningen

Viswanadham, N and Gaonkar, RS (2008) 'Risk Management in Global Supply Chain Networks'. In: Tang, CS, Teo, C-T and Wei, K-K (eds) *Supply Chain Analysis*, Springer, New York

Wieland, Andreas; Handfield, Robert B (2013) The socially responsible supply chain: an imperative for global corporations, *Supply Chain Management Review*, **17** (5)

Womack, JP, Jones, DT and Roos, D (1990) *The Machine that Changed the World* (New Edition), Simon and Schuster

Wooldridge, A (2013) Return of The Giants, The Economics 'The World in 2013', 21 November 2012, downloaded from www.economist.com

Other sources and articles

Bangladesh Factory Safety Accord: At Least 14 Major North American Retailers Decline To Sign, *The Huffington Post*, retrieved 17 May 2013

www.brandchannel.com/home/post/2010/03/30/Consumers-Want-Socially-Responsible-Brands.aspx – Article by Susanne Blecher

Co-operative sustainability plan, http://www.co-operative.coop/our-ethics/our-plan/

Corruption is getting worse, www.bbc.co.uk/news/business-23231318

Horsemeat scandal, www.bbc.co.uk/news/world-europe-21467989

ISO9001 certification top one million mark, food safety and information security continue meteoric increase, from www.iso.org/iso/news.htm?refid=Ref1363, accessed December 2013

Kellogg Company CSR policy, accessed May 2014, www.kelloggcompany.com/en_US/corporate-responsibility.html

Meat processing: Journey from abattoir to final package, www.bbc.co.uk/news/uk-21552159

Primark story, http://news.bbc.co.uk/2/hi/business/7456897.stm

Rowling, JK (2001) Harry Potter and Me, Christmas Special, 28 December 2001, Transcribed by Marvelous Marvolo and Jimmi Thøgersen. Accessed 27 February 2014 at www.accio-quote.org

Steven Greenhouse and Stephanie Clifford (10 July 2013), US Retailers Offer Plan for Safety at Factories, *The New York Times*, Retrieved 10 July 2013

Steve Jobs on Apple's resurgence: 'not a one-man show', 12 May 1998, *Business week online*, www.businessweek.com, downloaded March 2014

Tata Nano (uncredited article), www.businessteacher.org.uk/free-business-essays/supplier-involvementin-product-development-and-innovation.php

http://valuechaingroup.com/sherryblog/2012/02/17/5-aha-moments-in-supplier-
performance-management/

Walt Disney (article on) and other innovators, www.artsofinnovation.com/disney.html

Websites

asq.org/ – for example, see http://asq.org/learn-about-quality/continuous-improvement/
overview/overview.html

www.bbc.co.uk

www.efqm.org – the site of the European Foundation for Quality Management

www.ethicalcorp.com – for example, see www.ethicalcorp.com/business-strategy/
iso-26000-sustainability-standard

www.excitant.co.uk – company offering performance measurement solutions with some
useful information on their website

www.hbr.org – *Harvard Business Review*

www.innovationmain.com – site dedicated to enabling innovation in organizations and
features Apple case studies

www.lso.co.uk – website of the London Symphony Orchestra

www.tatasteel.com

www.wikipedia.com

INDEX

Note: *Italics* indicate a figure or table in the text.